New Governance and the Transformation of European Law

The development of non-binding new governance methods has challenged the traditional ideals of EU law by suggesting that soft norms and executive networks may provide a viable alternative. Rather than see law and new governance as oppositional projects, Mark Dawson argues that new governance can be seen as an example of legal 'transformation', in which soft norms and hard law institutions begin to cohabit and interact. He charts this transformation by analysing the Open Method of Coordination for Social Protection and Inclusion (OMC SPSI). While this process illustrates some of the concrete advantages for EU social policy which new governance has brought, it also illustrates their extensive legitimacy challenges. Methods like the OMC have both excluded traditional institutions, such as courts and parliaments, and altered the boundaries of domestic constitutional frameworks. The book concludes with some practical suggestions for how a political 'constitutionalisation' of new governance could look.

Mark Dawson is an assistant professor of European Law at Maastricht University. He is a member of the editorial board of the *Maastricht Journal of European & Comparative Law*, and the co-director of Maastricht University's English language LLM programmes in International Laws, Globalisation & Law and European Law School. He is also a scholar within the Maastricht Centre for European Law.

Cambridge Studies in European Law and Policy

This series aims to produce original works which contain a critical analysis of the state of the law in particular areas of European Law and set out different perspectives and suggestions for its future development. It also aims to encourage a range of work on law, legal institutions and legal phenomena in Europe, including 'law in context' approaches. The titles in the series will be of interest to academics; policymakers; policy formers who are interested in European legal, commercial, and political affairs; practising lawyers including the judiciary; and advanced law students and researchers.

Books in the series

EU Enlargement and the Constitutions of Central and Eastern Europe
Anneli Albi

Social Rights and Market Freedom in the European Constitution: A Labour Law Perspective
Stefano Giubboni

The Constitution for Europe: A Legal Analysis
Jean-Claude Piris

The European Convention on Human Rights: Achievements, Problems and Prospects
Steven Greer

European Broadcasting Law and Policy
Jackie Harrison and Lorna Woods

The Transformation of Citizenship in the European Union: Electoral Rights and the Restructuring of Political Space
Jo Shaw

Implementing EU Pollution Control: Law and Integration
Bettina Lange

The Evolving European Union: Migration Law and Policy
Dora Kostakopoulou

Ethical Dimensions of the Foreign Policy of the European Union: A Legal Appraisal
Urfan Khaliq

The European Civil Code: The Way Forward
Hugh Collins

State and Market in European Union Law
Wolf Sauter and Harm Schepel

The Ethos of Europe: Values, Law and Justice in the EU
Andrew Williams

The European Union's Fight Against Corruption: The Evolving Policy Towards Member States and Candidate Countries
Patrycja Szarek-Mason

The Lisbon Treaty: A Legal and Political Analysis
Jean-Claude Piris

New Governance and the Transformation of European Law: Coordinating EU Social Law and Policy
Mark Dawson

New Governance and the Transformation of European Law

Coordinating EU Social Law and Policy

Mark Dawson

CAMBRIDGE
UNIVERSITY PRESS

CAMBRIDGE UNIVERSITY PRESS
Cambridge, New York, Melbourne, Madrid, Cape Town,
Singapore, São Paulo, Delhi, Tokyo, Mexico City

Cambridge University Press
The Edinburgh Building, Cambridge CB2 8RU, UK

Published in the United States of America by Cambridge University Press,
New York

www.cambridge.org
Information on this title: www.cambridge.org/9781107006324

First published 2011

Printed in the United Kingdom at the University Press, Cambridge

A catalogue record for this publication is available from the British Library

ISBN 978-1-107-00632-4 Hardback

Contents

Series editors' preface

Amongst the burgeoning literature on governance in the EU, work which addresses the phenomenon of 'new governance' has begun to diversify in character. No longer does such work simply chart the emergence of new governance styles, noting in particular their utility for steering policy in areas where the member states are reluctant to cede sovereignty and to opt for the more traditional 'Community method', such as areas of social policy or even economic policy coordination. Studies are thus no longer always confined to particular sectors, or to descriptive analysis. New work now problematises the concept of 'new' governance, questioning what is 'new' about it, articulating how governance does or does not differ from the long-established term 'government' (always problematic in the EU context), and defining the parameters of an emergent legal theory of new governance. This is the central question of Mark Dawson's elegantly written new volume, where he brings the concepts of law and governance into synergy and into conversation, rather than viewing them as oppositional concepts or regulative techniques. In that sense, new governance can be studied as an integrated dimension of the composite EU legal order, in a manner which takes into account the polyvalent and multilevel character of that order, with inputs not only from the EU institutions as lawmakers, but also from the member states' constitutional frameworks and implementation apparatuses. Thus rather than being a study of a system of new governance as such, although along the way Dawson focuses on the so-called Open Method of Coordination as it is used in areas of social policy in relation to the so-called Lisbon strategy for promoting the competiveness and openness of the European economy, Dawson's work represents a confrontation with a variety of theories which seek to explain the character, scope and nature of the European legal order, which focus in particular on the reflexive and procedural character of law.

While conceptually rich, Dawson's work also has an interest for a wider audience, in a work that is fully aware of the practical implications of the EU and the member states adopting different approaches to major societal tasks, such as ensuring the sustainability of the welfare state, whilst protecting its key features such as universal coverage, as they have emerged in post second world war Europe. (Social) Law, therefore, needs to be intensely political, without losing all of its essentially normative character. Dawson's work carefully retreads that well-worn path between law and politics, and between facts and norms.

Jo Shaw
Laurence Gormley

Acknowledgments

While it has gone through some transformations since, this book began as a PhD thesis at the European University Institute. As such, I owe thanks to the many people there who made it a reality, in particular my two supervisors, Christian Joerges and John Paterson. I would also like to thank David and Louise Trubek, and the Institute for Legal Studies at the University of Wisconsin, who supported a particularly productive patch of the writing during my time as a visiting scholar in the US. Finally, I owe a debt of gratitude to my colleagues at the Faculty of Law in Maastricht for their support in the period in which revisions to the manuscript have taken place.

Through the publication process, I have been very fortunate in the support I have received from the editorial team at Cambridge University Press, and from the series editors, Jo Shaw and Laurence Gormley, for their practical advice and help after first submitting this manuscript. I would also like to thank two anonymous reviewers. I am delighted that this book is now part of this fantastic series. All errors and omissions are of course my own.

Finally, this book project has relied on a lot of personal support. My deepest thanks go to my many colleagues and friends at the EUI – particularly in its working group on legal theory – who gave me feedback on the PhD on countless occasions – never in my life have I found an environment both as socially supportive and as intellectually stimulating as Florence. Lastly, my thanks – and love – go both to my parents, and to Pierre, for their love and support over five amazing years. Without them, the experience of writing this book would not be the cherished memory that it is today.

MD

Table of cases

Case T-105/95 WWF UK v. Commission [1997] ECR II-313 263
Case C-106/96 United Kingdom of Great Britain and Northern Ireland v Commission of the European Communities [1998] ECR I-02729 170
Case C-157/96 National Farmers Union and Others [1998] ECR I-2211 260
Case T-135/96 UEAPME v. Council [1998] ECR II-2335 257–258, 273
Case 158/96 Kohll v. Union des Caisses de Maladies [1998] ECR I-1931 171
Case C-120/95 Nicolas Decker v. Caisses de Maladie de Employés Privées [1998] ECR I-1831 171
Case C-321/95 P, Stichtung Greenpeace Council v. Commission [1998] ECR I-1651 271
Case T-174/95 Svenska Journalistforbundet v. Council [1998] ECR II-2289 265
Case C-67/96 Albany International BV v. Stichting Bedriifspensioenfonds Textielindustrie [1999] ECR I-5751 40, 50, 63, 246, 250
Cases T-13/99 Pfizer Animal Health v. Council [2002] ECR II-3305 261
Case T-70/59 Alpharma v. Council [2002] ECR II-3495 261
Case C-500/00 P, Union de Pequenos Agricultores v. Council [2002] ECR 6677 270
Case T-177/01 Jégo Quèrè et Cie SA v. Commission [2002] ECR II-2365 270
Case C-76/01 P, Eurocoton and Others v. Council [2003] ECR I-0000 263
Case T-168/02 IFAW v. Commission [2004] ECR II-4135 276
EU Constitutional Treaty and the Spanish Constitutional Court [2005] 1 CMLR 981; Polish Membership of the European Union (Accession Treaty), Polish Constitutional Court, Judgment K18/04 of 11 May 2005 115
Case C-64/05 P Sweden v. Commission [2007] ECR 11389 276
Case C-341/05 Laval un Partneri Ltd v. Svenska Byggnadsarbetareförbundet and Others [2007] ECR I-11767 60, 250
Case C-438/05 The International Transport Workers' Federation & The Finnish Seamen's Union v. Viking Line ABP & Ou Viking Line Eesti [2007] ECR I-10779 61, 250
Case C-346/06 Rechtsanwalt Dr. Dirk Rüffert v. Land Niedersachsen [2008] ECR I-1989 250
Case 346/06 Commission v. Luxembourg [2008] ECR I-4323 66

Table of treaties

Table of legislation

Table of Council Decisions

Introduction

I. The rise – and relevance – of new governance in the European Union

In signalling the development of the Open Method of Coordination (OMC) through the Lisbon European Council in 2000, EU leaders were primarily interested in a particular goal – to make the EU, by 2000, the most dynamic economic area in the world.[1] Their actions, however, also triggered a deep and lasting debate regarding the development of 'new' or 'alternative' modes of governance in the EU: a debate that has found its most recent instalment in the scramble to build a new Lisbon strategy for the decade leading to 2020.[2] The very use of the term 'new governance' to describe methods like the OMC already creates the capacity to confuse. What is 'governance' anyway and what is 'new' about it? What methods of EU law and policy are included under the 'new governance' label and which are outside of it? What are the criteria against which new governance methods should be evaluated? These questions will be asked and answered in the first and second chapters of this book.[3]

A more foundational question, however, must also be addressed. Why is the new governance debate a debate fundamentally *worth* engaging in? What is it about the turn to governance in the EU that makes

[1] Presidency Conclusions, Lisbon European Council, March 2000 at 2.

[2] Commission Communication, *Europe 2020: A Strategy for Smart, Sustainable and Inclusive Growth*, COM (2010) 2020; Presidency Conclusions, European Council, March 2010, EUCO 7/10.

[3] See also, on these conceptual questions, C. Möllers, 'European Governance: Meaning and Value of a Concept' (2006) 43 *Common Market Law Review* 2; M. Jachtenfuchs, 'The Governance Approach to European Integration' (2002) 39 *Journal of Common Market Studies* 2.

analyses of these methods important, both for lawyers, and for the broader category of all those interested in EU integration? At one level we should approach this question with a healthy scepticism. As indicated by the Lisbon Council, one of the essential features of methods like the OMC is that they are non-binding. Given that new governance methods do not in most – but by no means all – cases lead to 'proper law', why should we then take their procedures and outcomes seriously? (Or, indeed, read a whole book about them!)[4]

There are three main reasons why this may be so. The first – and most central to the guiding thesis of this book – is that in examining new governance we are not just looking outside the law, but also exploring the manner in which EU law is evolving or transforming.[5] While the added value of new governance methods has often been seen in terms of their ability to provide coordination 'outside' the official constitutional structure of the EU Treaties, new governance, as we shall see, is in a relationship of continuity and interaction with traditional legal methods. The very need for a turn to governance in the EU illustrates how – as Chapter 3 of this book will argue – EU law has turned to procedural visions of law in order to cope with unique features of the EU system, such as the territorial diversity and functional complexity of regulating in a transnational context. In this sense, rather than seeing new governance as being something other than 'proper law', the development of new governance methods itself challenges what it means to make and apply law in an EU setting.

There is, however, also a second dimension to the added value of taking new governance in the EU seriously. While the overriding goal of the 2000 Lisbon Council, as already indicated, was to improve the EU's economic competitiveness, this was also to be embedded in other social goals – such as raising employment among key groups, and tackling poverty – to be delivered through new governance methods. In this sense, in examining the development of new governance in the

[4] To take an example of this, the social dialogue established under Art. 155 TFEU is often discussed under the new governance label but may lead to binding EU law where adopted by the Council. Dialogue between management and labour at EU level may also, however, remain in the form of non-binding agreements.

[5] The idea of transformation will be explained below in the context of the third wave' of governance research. It refers, however, to an idea of seeing new governance not as apart from law, but as indicative of its evolution to new 'participatory', 'experimentalist' or 'reflexive' forms. For more on this idea, see the papers of the 2009 'Transatlantic Conference on New Governance and the Transformation of European Law', Madison, Wisconsin, 20–21/11/09, (2010) *Wisconsin Law Review* 2. See also, G. de Búrca and J. Scott, 'Introduction' to *Law and New Governance in the EU and US* (Oxford: Hart, 2006).

EU context, we are also examining whether this attempt to provide a 'social dimension' to EU law, and to the EU's normal concerns, has been successful. As Chapter 1 of the book will explore, any simple reading of new governance's social potential should be understood in light of the deep ambiguity of new governance's social role – while methods such as the OMC have been used to develop social policies at the EU level, their close attachment to the Lisbon strategy have also led to accusations that the OMC may be a 'trojan horse' for the re-orientation of national welfare states along neo-liberal lines.[6] The substantive goals advanced through new governance will be explored and analysed not just at an abstract level, but through an in-depth case study of social inclusion and social protection in Chapter 4 of the book: to what extent has new governance led not just to a legal but to a social 'transformation' of EU law?

Finally, the importance of new governance also lies in the possibilities it offers for democratic transformation in the EU. Certainly, the democratic potential of OMC-like methods was a strong part of their original allure.[7] As an alternative to the type of 'direct' representation provided by the European Parliament, or through the intermediaries of national governments in the Council, the turn to governance – as heralded in the Commission's 2001 *White Paper on Governance* – was to be legitimated through principles of openness, accountability and participation, in which the direct involvement of civil society actors in forming EU rules 'from the bottom up' would substitute for traditional forms of democratic accountability. In evaluating new governance, we are also evaluating one of the original attempts by the EU to anchor the legitimacy of post-national law in a different, and more participatory, form of rule-making. The very struggle of methods like the OMC to live up to this original hope has much to tell us providing, as Chapter 5 will argue, important lessons for how new governance mechanisms could be reformed.

One should not over-state new governance's 'transformative' potential. As this book will argue, the transformations methods like the OMC have brought about in legal, social and democratic terms have often

[6] C. Joerges and F. Rödl, 'Social Market Economy as Europe's Social Model?' (2004) *EUI Working Papers (Law)* 8; M. Dawson, 'The Ambiguity of Social Europe in the Open Method of Coordination' (2009) 34 *European Law Review* 1.

[7] See J. Zeitlin, 'Social Europe and Experimentalist Governance: Towards a New Constitutional Compromise?' in G. de Búrca (ed.), *EU Law and the Welfare State: In Search of Solidarity* (Oxford University Press, 2005) at 224; S. Borras and K. Jacobsson, 'The Open Method of Coordination and New Governance Patterns in the EU' (2004) 11 *Journal of European Public Policy* 2 at 189.

under-whelmed, leaving a number of serious legitimacy concerns in their wake. The advent of new governance has not only altered the contours of EU law, but also threatened some of its most important values, such as the level of general political input and democratic oversight into its procedures. Nonetheless, the changes methods like the OMC have unleashed in their first ten years deserve attention not just for those engaged in new governance mechanisms themselves, but for all those interested in the legal and institutional evolution of the EU. New governance's evolving relationship to EU law provides important insights for sceptics and supporters of its development alike.

II. What does this book have to add? Two waves of 'new governance in the European Union'

In some senses, new governance was very much the EU's movement of choice at the beginning of the twenty-first century. Following the corruption and political failures of the Santer Commission in the late 1990s, the governance agenda seemed to offer a way forward for the Union which rejected both intergovernmental self-interest and bureaucratic centralisation. The academic debate followed this optimism, devoting countless articles to the study of political phenomena whose contours and outcomes were highly unclear. A significant academic and institutional literature on new governance thus arose.[8] What does this book have to add to that literature?

Answering that question requires a basic understanding of the existing contours of the academic debate over the relationship between new governance and law.[9] As stylised as it may be (indeed a less stylised account will be developed in the second chapter), it may be useful to consider this literature in three 'waves' of activity; waves which both embody different conceptions of the new governance project – and indeed of law itself – and carry distinct strengths and weaknesses.[10]

[8] See, for example, the hundreds of entries contained in the OMC Bibliography hosted by the EU Centre of Excellence of the University of Wisconsin (available at: http://eucenter.wisc.edu/OMC/open12.html).

[9] It should be noted that only essential references will be provided in this introduction. A more thorough review of existing literature on governance is developed at the beginning of Chapter 2, section 2.

[10] On the concept of different 'waves' of activity in the relationship between new governance and law, see M. Dawson, '3 Waves of New Governance in the European Union' (2011) 36 *European Law Review* 2.

The first 'diagnostic' wave, for example, was largely 'negative' in character. The very labelling of the term 'new governance' demanded that early literature could say both what the phenomenon of 'governance' implied in the EU context, and what was new about it. In legal literature, the simplest way of contemplating this task has been to define 'new governance' in relation to its other – the 'classical community method' of EU law (a contrast conducted by the Commission itself through its own *White Paper on Governance*).[11] Whereas the classical method – or at least the Commission's partial view of it – implied a strict division of powers between the different EU institutions, and between the EU and its member states, 'new governance' encompassed methods – like the OMC, regulatory agencies, the social dialogue, and even 'old' comitology committees – that eroded these distinctions, interweaving between different levels of governance.[12]

The threats this posed to implicit and explicit constitutional guarantees in the EU – like the 'institutional balance' and 'enumerated competences' protected under the Treaties – was justified through a unique step – the idea that, as these methods are conducted via 'soft law', they pose no direct threat to the Union's existing legal structure. This move – to simultaneously advance new governance as a significant normative project, and to downplay the significance of its pathologies through the label of 'soft law' – has been a vital focus for the academic commentary. It has led to a strong guiding idea – that in examining and developing new governance, we are somehow distancing or rejecting EU law, or the template of 'integration through law' offered by the very founders of the integration project.[13]

The significance of the label 'soft law', however, lay in its ability to encourage both proponents of the turn to governance in the EU and critics to see new governance in similar terms. For some, particularly political scientists, this softness spoke to inherent limits in the method's functional steering capacities. If the OMC was really 'soft', what incentives would states have to follow its instructions, especially when

[11] See J. Scott and D. Trubek, 'Mind the Gap: Law and New Approaches to Governance in the European Union' (2002) 8 *European Law Journal* 1. See also, later, J. Zeitlin, 'Is the Open Method of Coordination an Alternative to the Community Method?' in R. Dehousse (ed.), *The Community Method: Obstinate or Obsolete?* (Basingstoke: Palgrave Macmillan, 2009).

[12] *European Governance: A White Paper*, COM (2001) 428 final, 8–9.

[13] see M. Cappelletti, M. Seccombe and J. Weiler, *Integration Through Law* (Berlin: De Gruyter, 1986).

coupled with the 'hard' and binding sanctions of monetary union or the law of the internal market?[14] For others, this softness was precisely why methods like the OMC were attractive. Rejecting the model of 'one size fits all' regulation, soft modes of governance could allow distinct national welfare regimes to move towards shared goals without disturbing the autonomous organisational structures upon which they were based.[15] The 'rise of soft law', and its contra-distinction to the 'hard' forms of integration that had characterised the previous twenty years, was read both as the source of, and the principle barrier to, the lasting effectiveness of 'new governance' methods.

What this first wave largely ignored, however, was the paradox within. The source of the perceived 'effectiveness' of new governance methods under both readings lay in their ability to bind their participants into a common cognitive framework; one that did not require coercion. This way, a common re-orientation of national social regimes (i.e. towards ideas of 'active' and 'open' labour markets or 'sustainable' pensions) could occur without the need for the traditional legal apparatus (and the idea of 'enumerated competences' that it implied).

The more, however, the method was 'effective' in these terms (the more it was able, for example, cognitively to bind its participants, or alter their preferences), the less 'soft' it appeared. The very success of new governance in achieving concrete policy outcomes (which could then act as a trigger for domestic policy-making), would precisely undermine the argument that it could happily evade traditional guarantees of due process and parliamentary scrutiny, i.e. on the basis that it was a 'mere soft coordination procedure', parallel or complementary to 'hard law'. The need to demonstrate that the method was more than a 'paper tiger' thus could lead directly to the accusation that it was a 'Trojan horse', subverting democratic governance in the very name of a more efficient and responsive form of rule. The mere labelling of the OMC as 'soft' – as Chapter 2 will argue – does not, and should not, allow it to escape extensive legitimacy challenges.

[14] For two exponents of this 'paper tiger' thesis, see F. Scharpf, 'The European Social Model: Coping with the Challenges of Diversity' (2002) 40 *Journal of Common Market Studies* 4 at 654–656; A. Héritier, 'New Modes of Governance in Europe: Policy-Making without Legislating?', in Héritier (ed.), *Common Goods: Reinventing European and International Governance* (Lanham: Rowman and Littlefield, 2002) at 185–206.

[15] J. Zeitlin, 'Social Europe and Experimentalist Governance: Towards a New Constitutional Compromise?' in G. de Búrca (ed.), *EU Law and the Welfare State: In Search of Solidarity* (Oxford University Press, 2005).

In this way, the first diagnostic wave – while important in saying what governance was, or what was innovative about it – failed to think about what 'governance' could mean in positive terms. Its rush to define new governance in opposition to law carried the capacity to stylise both 'governance' *and* 'law', while ignoring the exchanges and interplays between them.[16] Furthermore, by viewing governance as something merely 'parallel' to 'EU law proper', first wave understandings conveniently ignored the question of whether existing EU institutions – such as committee structures, courts and even Parliaments – might need to be reconsidered in light of the regulatory environment which the dawn of OMC-like methods heralded.[17]

It was precisely to face these challenges that a 'second wave' of literature was needed. Rather than view new governance and law as compliments, second wave literature argued that methods like the OMC were indicative of law's evolution in a post-national context. While first wave literature had gone to great lengths to establish the differences between new governance mechanisms and 'traditional' forms of European law, there was nothing 'traditional' about EU law to begin with. It had to be understood – like national law – as an inherently unstable medium, capable of responding to changes in its surrounding regulatory environment.

This was both a positive and a negative thesis. Negatively, this evolution meant the evacuation of law as a universal register, in favour of more functional, or directly political, logics.[18] The dubious ideal of Majone's 'regulatory state' was central to this negative narrative – his image of a depoliticised European polity a symbol of the attempt to divorce European law from distorting forms of majoritarian politics.[19] For critics, this technocratic ideal privileged market rationality above all else – using the misnomer of 'soft law' to allow the gradual filtration

[16] See D. Trubek and L. Trubek, 'Hard and Soft Law in the Construction of Social Europe: The Role of the Open Method of Co-ordination' (2005) 11 *European Law Journal* 3; C. Kilpatrick, 'New EU Employment Governance and Constitutionalism' in de Búrca and Scott, n. 5 above.

[17] A task taken up in Chapter 5 of this book.

[18] See C. Möllers, 'European Governance: Meaning and Value of a Concept' (2006) 43 *Common Market Law Review* 2; M. Greven, 'The Informalization of Trans-national Governance: A Threat to Democratic Governance' in E. Grande and L. Pauly (eds.), *Complex Sovereignty: Re-constituting Political Authority in the 21st Century* (University of Toronto Press, 2005).

[19] G. Majone, 'The Rise of the Regulatory State in Europe' (1994) 17 *West European Politics* 3.

into national welfare states of economic imperatives that could never be agreed upon through an explicit political decision.[20]

For proponents, however, the 'transformations' being brought by new governance meant not just the removal, but the *re-invention* of concepts such as democracy and the rule of law in the EU, outwith the comfortable environs of the nation state.[21] Descriptively, a softening of legal rules, and a preference for procedural 'frameworks' over substantive prescriptions, was an increasing tendency in 'hard' forms of EU law, as well as soft. One could observe 'proceduralisation' in European law – an acceptance that, in a system made up of overlapping welfare regimes, a relatively uniform hierarchy of European norms would have to make way for the ongoing negotiation of EU rules in delicate policy fields (with law largely relegated to the role of a 'structuring device').[22]

The second wave was more, however, than a descriptive project but an attempt to defend, and indeed promote, a 'governance vision' of the very future of the EU polity. Dense theoretical models – from American 'democratic experimentalism', to Gunther Teubner's category of 'reflexive law' – were at the forefront of a claim that an EU governed by OMC-like methods provided a broader model for regional integration the world over ('EU as front-runner not outlier').[23] While new governance methods lacked the validation of a democratic sovereign, their multiplication of the number of actors involved in the formation of European rules could allow differences between national contexts to be seen as a 'democratic advantage', allowing otherwise distanced regulation to be both re-framed in a *local* context, and used to create innovative public policies potentially applicable to *all* member states. The normative vision of the second wave thus saw, in new governance, not a subversion of democratic rule, but an attempt to render it operational in

[20] C. Offe, 'The European Model of "Social" Capitalism: Can it Survive European Integration?' (2003) 11 *Journal of Political Philosophy* 4 at 464; C. Joerges and F. Rödl, 'Social Market Economy as Europe's Social Model?' (2004) *EUI Working Papers (Law)* 8.

[21] See e.g. W. Simon and C. Sabel, 'Epilogue: Accountability without Sovereignty' in de Búrca and Scott, n. 5 above.

[22] See A. Adronico and A. Lo Faro, 'Defining Problems: The OMC, Fundamental Rights and the Theory of Governance', in O. de Schutter and S. Deakin (eds.), *Social Rights and Market Force: Is the Open Coordination of Employment and Social Policies the Future of Social Europe* (Brussels: Bruylant, 2005).

[23] C. Sabel and J. Zeitlin, 'Learning from Difference: The New Architecture of Experimentalist Governance in the EU' (2008) 14 *European Law Journal* 3 at 323.

circumstances where the legitimacy of a central 'popular will' could no longer be taken for granted.[24]

Therein, however, lay the primary problem of the 'second wave'. Theories like experimentalism and reflexive law certainly had considerable success in framing the academic and institutional debate. One would find it difficult to find a major institutional document about the OMC that did not contain some reference to its 'multi-level' or 'participatory' character. The irony, however, is that these references were often made without serious or comprehensive attempts to test their guiding assumptions.[25] Owing to a number of methodological difficulties, the first two waves of literature – with some important exceptions – did not engage in significant empirical research, on the basis of the (admittedly often valid) assumption that it was 'too early to tell'.[26] Often the closest such frameworks came to empirical testing was to gauge the level of 'best fit' between the theoretical models they offered and the descriptions of the OMC given by the EU institutions.

This deductive approach carried significant limits. The first was that so much could clearly be missed out. Entering the new governance debate from particular fixed theoretical perspectives, one is tempted to claim that many theoretical accounts were quick to seize on any evidence of concurrence between their models and the 'practice' of the OMC without stopping equally to consider what failed to fit the picture. The urge on the part of the philosopher to prove that he or she is 'living in the real world' (rather than an ivory tower) is understandable, but can also potentially lead the practice to 'fit the theory' rather than the other way around. Such approaches faced the problem

[24] M. Dorf and C. Sabel, 'A Constitution of Democratic Experimentalism' (1998) 98 *Columbia Law Review* 2; C. Sabel and O. Gerstenberg, 'Directly-Deliberative Polyarchy: An Institutional Ideal for Europe?', in C. Joerges and R. Dehousse (eds.), *Good Governance in Europe's Integrated Market* (Oxford Univeristy Press, 2002).

[25] This obvious deficiency is addressed by Sabel and Zeitlin in the article cited in n. 23 above. The 'patchwork' nature of the article, however, is notable, as is the shift from seeing particular methods as 'experimental' to pointing towards a general 'experimental architecture' in the EU (where the authors can pick and choose between processes in various disparate fields in order to evidence each of their core 'experimentalist' claims).

[26] An obvious exception – albeit with limited theoretical analysis – is Jonathan Zeitlin and Phillipe Pochet's *The Open Method of Coordination in Action: The European Employment and Social Inclusion Strategies* (Bern: Peter Lang, 2005). See also, on the impact of the OMC on national reforms, J. Zeitlin and M. Heidenreich (eds.), *Changing European Employment and Welfare Regimes: the Influence of the Open Method of Coordination on National Reforms* (London: Routledge, 2009).

that – while they emphasised 'learning' and 'pragmatic experimentation' in their substantive content – they displayed little of this impulse in the framework of their own theories (with the framework deemed to be solid and complete, rather than something open to re-adjustment in light of observations emerging from experience).

The 'second wave' also, however, carried another problem. Its attempt to develop a robust account of how governance was changing law, or what 'legality' really meant in the twenty-first century, led it into a myriad of paradoxes and inconsistencies. These tensions were not only manifest in abstract theoretical models, but could also be observed in the practices of new governance and the OMC itself.

The model of 'democratic experimentalism' propounded by Sabel and Dorf is emblematic of these problems.[27] As the third chapter will argue, it faced a complex web of inner tensions. The first concerned participation. Experimentalism – as well as the other 'second wave' approaches discussed in Chapter 3 – relies on forms of direct participation to fill gaps of representation and political accountability vacated by the absence of a single or unitary popular sovereign. The normative claim that new governance could create a more responsive legal order depends on the capacity of its norms to be articulated by more than technocratic experts, but precisely those actors at the local level to whom social inclusion and employment policies are addressed.

Who though is to do the participating? It is almost impossible to conceive of an adequate threshold. Either the number of 'ideal' participants is likely to be too small – a sectional slice of the population, representing only its direct interests – or too large – so all-encompassing that any individuated, local or 'deliberative' articulation of public policy problems is impossible. While such theories relied on a participative ethic, they give few criteria over who is to take up the participatory burden, or if participants are to be selected, over who is to do the choosing. As we will see, this is no abstract difficulty, but one that is evidenced by the OMC itself, where 'the choosing' is most often conducted by the very executive actors that non-governmental participants are meant to be holding to account.

The second problem concerned the relationship of 'second wave' theories to stability. Experimentalism in particular recognises that the

[27] M. Dorf and C. Sabel, 'A Constitution of Democratic Experimentalism' (1998) 98 *Columbia Law Review* 2; J. Cohen and C. Sabel, 'Directly-Deliberative Polyarchy' (1997) 3 *European Law Journal* 4.

rapidity of modern exchange may undermine, or even render irrelevant, static legal standards. The appropriate response to this, they argue, is to make law itself 'iterative' or adaptable in light of changing environmental conditions. The very opening of law to new participants creates the possibility to adapt rules on a 'dynamic' basis, without sacrificing their inherently 'democratic' character.

What, however, if it is the very stability of the law that precisely provides it with its normative qualities, or that allows the levels of participation and deliberation upon which 'second wave' theories (and indeed *any* democratic model of law-making) equally rest?[28] The tension of such theories is that while they promote a reconciliation of values of flexibility and efficiency on the one hand, and legitimacy and legality on the other, they ignore the possibilities that these values may be mutually constraining. The danger – one that Chapter 4 will argue is all too real – is that 'flexibility' becomes a mask for an equally 'flexible' attitude towards consulting democratic institutions, or the bodies at the local level that have been vested, in the nation state, with the capacity to implement important social reforms.

Under these terms, 'second wave' literature ironically often committed the very error which it used as the basis of its contribution to the governance debate. While that contribution was predicated on the idea that we need a 'positive' situation of law in the context of legal change; that we should not stylise or essentialise legal categories; second wave theories lie accused of being engaged in their own variety of 'essentialism' – explaining away their inner tensions and paradoxes through the selective choosing of which parts of the governance project best match their account of legal evolution; discarding those elements that do not. All the while, they were all too oblivious of the possibility that legal evolution was not a process that could be modelled in uni-directional, or even gradually 'progressive' terms.[29]

[28] See e.g. W. Scheuerman, 'Democratic Experimentalism or Capitalist Synchronisation: Critical Reflections on Directly-Deliberative Polyarchy' (2004) *Canadian Journal of Law and Jurisprudence* 17.

[29] This meets a critique of reflexive law's 'evolutionary' approach offered by Erhard Blankenburg. It should be noted, however, that Teubner himself rejected Blankenburg's criticism – on the grounds that the 'evolutionist' approach of systems theory rejects the Darwinian ideal of a progressive march towards a legal–political equilibrium. See E. Blankenburg, 'The Poverty of Evolutionism: A Critique of Teubner's Case for 'Reflexive Law'; G. Teubner, 'Autopoiesis in Law and Society: A Rejoinder to Blankenburg', both in (1984) 18 *Law and Society Review* 2.

III. The need for a third wave

These failings directly lead to the 'third wave' called for by this book. What are the constitutive features of such a 'third wave'? The first feature is indicated by the choice of an in-depth case study as a central element of this book. The 'third wave' is interested and engaged in empirical work, or at least in analysing new governance methods at a 'micro' level.[30] The phrase 'new modes of governance' already lumps together too much, conflating processes that carry quite different features, and operate in different fields. While all empirical analysis (including those parts in this book), must start from certain theoretical presuppositions, attempting to analyse these processes from the perspective of democratic or legal theory without also trying to consider the specific questions and relationships such processes are directly engaged in is likely to be a futile exercise (leaving out the very concerns of participants of new governance procedures themselves). The first feature of a 'third wave' is therefore that it is inductive in its approach. Rather than deduce from theory to practice, the intention is to create a dialectical relationship between the two, in which practical examples – both successful and abject failures – can allow the theoretical models through which they have been understood to be critiqued, or re-considered.

Secondly, the aspirant third wave is critical in nature. This 'critical turn' certainly does not refer to a crudely negative view of the OMC, or of other new governance institutions. In the last few years, we have seen a wealth of literature taking this standpoint – sometimes on the basis of the (apparently contradictory) thesis that the OMC is simultaneously an irrelevance, or red herring trying to placate angry social voices, and an active neo-liberal threat to the very future of the European welfare state. This book will question this position. While the OMC may certainly be capable of instrumentalisation, it is so from a variety of policy positions, and through shifting coalitions of actors (both 'economic' and 'social', as Chapter 1 will put it). A 'critical' approach to new governance entails less a denunciation than an attempt to explore and uncover precisely the paradoxes and blind spots of the existing new governance debate.

[30] For other such studies, see in particular the 2009 special issue of the European Integration Online Papers on the OMC. S. Kröger (ed.), 'What We Have Learnt: Advances, Pitfalls and Remaining Questions in OMC Research' (2009) 13 *European Integration Online Papers* 1.

To this extent, the approach taken will be 'critical' in the sense used by one of the pioneers of the critical turn in international law – David Kennedy. In a recent piece on global governance, Kennedy argues that 'governance' as a legal and political project is fundamentally about disenchantment. While it is far easier to attribute steering power in modern societies to particular democratic institutions, or even to an all-powerful neo-liberal cabal ('the Washington consensus'), our world is far more complex. The choices we face are not between more or less regulation or more or less government, but instead lie within a complex web of instruments and mechanisms, which potentially control and check each other.

> If there are those who continue to think it is all regulation and de-regulation, public and private, who think of power as either the right to coerce, repress, punish, or as a commodity in horizontal exchange among private actors, then it is all to the good to point out the erosions and transformations these distinctions and conceptions have in fact undergone.[31]

'New governance', as a descriptive and normative project, is therefore about constructing better maps – about the ability to understand the exercise of legal and political power in societies where the power of central sovereigns is being subverted.

His critique of governance focuses on dangers inherent in this mapping exercise. The first is the problem already set out above – namely that the new 'maps', rather than reflect this lack or order and hegemony, seek to make sense of it in a coherent and totalising way, replicating precisely the old comforts of a unified 'designer' or 'man in command' that the idea of governance sets itself against. Kennedy thus worries whether the new governance literature 'continues the intellectual practice I call 'as if pragmatism' – writing and speaking *as if* things had been designed by a benign spirit responding to general needs and expressing general will'. Are we seeking to 'explain' the phenomenon of new governance or are we merely seeking to graft it onto existing paradigms and templates? In the EU order, this criticism potentially takes a form of its own – the frequent complaint that explanations of EU phenomena take as their starting point an unrealistic and idealised template of national institutions.[32] 'Critical' approaches

[31] D. Kennedy, 'Remarks on New Governance', Presentation to the Workshop on New Governance, Harvard Law School, February 2005, 3–4. See also, D. Kennedy, 'Challenging Expert Rule: the Politics of Global Governance' (2005) 27 *Sydney Law Review* 2.

[32] On this criticism, see N. Walker, 'Legal Theory and the European Union: A 25th Anniversary Essay' (2005) 25 *Oxford Journal of Legal Studies* 4.

thus entail a more reflexive awareness of the potential biases inherent in the very concepts we use to explain supposedly 'new' post-national developments.

The second danger Kennedy points to in such 'mapping' exercises is that they tend to hide, rather than reveal, the political choices and strategies that even something as diffuse as 'new governance' can entail. The choice to label a norm as 'soft', steer the course of a particular policy through an abstract 'indicator', or advance one 'procedural framework' over another, does not just represent a choice in *technique* but is also *political* in nature, opening up some policy options, and closing off others.[33] The recourse, in particular, to 'procedural' logics in second wave literature – to the suggestion that methods like the OMC merely create an abstract procedure *through which* different policy choices can be made – can easily blind us to the fact that the choice of procedures *itself* reflects directly on substantive questions – such as the type of social objectives a polity like the EU is aiming towards.

As Kennedy puts it:

> Lost [in this analysis] is the historical and cultural randomness of the regulatory system, and its porousness to instrumentalisation from without. Where, in the 'new' legal process, are the parties, the one-shotters, and repeat players – what happened to law as the dependent, rather than independent variable of political life? Where are the stakes – not constitutionally, but actually – for this round, this conflict, this rule, this standard? Who, for example, benefits from policy failure, from governance gridlock – from governance deficits, democracy deficits, from old governance or, for that matter, from 'new governance'?[34]

Who indeed? In the OMC – as we will see – examples of hidden political contestation and conflict abound.

The case of indicators is a useful example. For much governance literature, indicators are crucial in allowing processes of soft coordination to function effectively.[35] They allow European governments to exchange and adapt best practices on the basis of an abstract comparative

[33] This is an element of the critique levelled at Habermasian and Rawlsian versions of procedural justice by Frank Michelman (see Chapter 3, section 2.4). F. Michelman, 'How Can the People Ever Make the Laws? A Critique of Deliberative Democracy' in J. Bohman and W. Rehg (eds.), *Deliberative Democracy: Essays on Reason and Politics* (Cambridge: MIT Press, 1997).

[34] Kennedy, n. 31 above, at 7.

[35] See, for a prescient analysis in the social inclusion context, D. Mabbett, 'Learning by Numbers? The Use of Indicators in the Coordination of Social Inclusion Policies in Europe' (2007) 14 *Journal of European Public Policy* 1.

evaluation of what 'works' in combating social deprivation problems. They furthermore rely on experts – formed in deliberative bodies like the Social Protection Committee (the SPC), a body we will come back to in Chapter 4 – to provide them with substantive content, without resorting to crude, or easily stalled, forms of intergovernmental bargaining. In this way, even diverse welfare regimes can rely on a *common framework* within which European social policies can be evaluated and compared.

As we will see, however, the choice of 'relevant' indicators is not only technical but is seen by the actors of the OMC as a deeply political question.[36] Different groups of NGOs have been engaged in intense lobbying to secure measurements of poverty and social deprivation that adequately cover or disaggregate the groups they seek to represent. Equally, different national governments argue for the setting of indicators which either include or exclude certain benefits, e.g. for housing, care or other services, that will allow their policies to be portrayed in a positive light. Far from being questions best left solely to experts, choices of indicators reflect back upon the very question of which type of social model EU efforts to coordinate social protection policy is aiming towards. The neutral language of procedure, soft law and 'indicators', has the capacity to hide conflicts between substantive visions that can only be legitimately conducted in the open. As Kennedy wonders, does 'new governance offer a look into the practices of the technical class, into modes of regulation and styles of management, less to unravel or politicise or contest expertise, than to confirm and expand it. To my mind, by contrast, 'new governance' for the twenty-first century would mean expanding the political contestability of expert rule.'[37]

This 'expansion of political contestability' leads into the final aspect of the aspirant third wave. Kennedy's point is that the only adequate answer to the 'masking' capacity of new governance, and supposed 'traditional law' alike, is an exercise in un-masking. We must attempt to make political, and allow contestation of, procedures and values that would otherwise be taken for granted or determined only by closed or technocratic elites. We cannot assume that something like 'new governance', represents a 'natural order of things' upon which we can hold a positive or negative judgement.[38] Instead, it is a contingent series of

[36] See Chapter 4, section 6.3. [37] Kennedy, n. 31 above, at 8.

[38] The 'third wave' thus shares with the 'reflexive governance' approach of Simon Deakin and Olivier de Schutter one aspect, namely their observation that, 'the conditions under which a deliberative process may succeed can be identified, and once identified, must be affirmatively created, rather than taken for granted'. See S. Deakin and

relationships and choices; one which European citizens or policy-makers can both actively affect, and potentially rearrange.

The final feature of the third wave is therefore that it is reform-oriented in its nature. It is interested neither solely in conceptual questions – what is 'new governance' – nor in normative ones – what is desirable or undesirable about it – but also in questioning the institutions, relationships and procedures upon which methods like the OMC are based. This task should concentrate precisely on the job of unmasking procedures like the OMC – of providing European citizens, and the political bodies formed to represent them, with the opportunity to debate, negotiate and critique both the procedural rules *and* the substantive goals that animate new governance in the EU.[39]

This task will be taken up primarily in the book's final chapter. There – as explained below – it will be argued that a 'constitutionalisation' of new governance cannot be exhausted either by a documentary constitutional project, or by administrative law procedures, but should focus on expanding opportunities for political intervention in governance procedures. Three strategies – the re-integration of the European Parliament within OMC procedures, the use of the review power of the European Ombudsman, and great reliance on social impact assessment – will be explored as first steps towards meeting the constitutional challenge.

This book can only be a contribution towards a new approach to the law–governance relationship but it aims to be one that combines empirical work, political analysis and reform proposals in order both to analyse the present relationship between EU governance and law, and provide a basis for future research. To explain how, we must briefly consider the structure of the book, chapter by chapter.

IV. Methodology and structure

The structure of this book is based on an overlapping series of questions, each of them attempting to probe a different aspect of the relationship between governance and law. Chapter 1 examines the claim

O. De Schutter, 'Reflexive Governance and the Dilemmas of Social Regulation' in Deakin and de Schutter (eds.), n. 22 above.

[39] This is the inverse of a critique of new governance's critics (particularly Fritz Scharpf) offered by Adronico and Lo Faro: that their efforts to explain law's social role carry overly rigid models or blueprints (a consequence of a thick or 'heavy' conception of modernity). See A. Adronico and A. Lo Faro, 'Defining Problems: The OMC, Fundamental Rights and the Theory of Governance', in de Schutter and Deakin, n. 22 above, at 68.

that the OMC can be considered a 'new mode of governance' in the EU. The chapter's first task is to argue against this claim to innovation, on the basis that the changes introduced through the method are continuous with long-standing reforms in the field of European social law. It may be better to see the development of new governance methods not as a fundamental break with the past, but as part of a gradual 'proceduralisation' of EU law's dominant forms and categories.

The chapter also, however, carries a second task. A crucial aspect of the legitimacy and use of methods like the OMC has been seen as hinging on their contribution to solving the 'social deficits' of EU integration. In this sense, opposition to the OMC's development has been built not only on its challenge to traditional 'rule of law' virtues, but also on the view that its 'weak' norms are incapable of addressing the social imbalances the development of economic integration has brought.[40] Such criticisms have been bolstered both by recent cases of the ECJ, and by the encasement of the OMC within a 'reformed' Lisbon strategy.[41]

The chapter will conclude by arguing that the reforms to the OMC conducted through the reviews of the strategy illustrate less its 'social subordination' than the deep ambiguity of its social role.[42] While on the one hand, the OMC can be considered a 'reflexive' instrument; one capable of encouraging different functional areas, and different levels of governance, to be 'other-regarding'; on the other, it can be seen as 'colonising'; integrating welfare regimes only to hollow them out, or provide an external interpretation of their meaning. The distinction between 'reflexivity' and 'colonisation' – applied to the concrete case of the OMC SPSI in Chapter 4 – may illustrate the stark social choices for the Union the advent of new governance brings forward.

These choices have already been analysed by a rich academic literature. The analytical purpose of Chapter 2 will be to deconstruct and critique how this literature has conceptualised the relationship between governance and *law*. To begin, the book must establish a

[40] See e.g. Scharpf, n. 14 above; Joerges and Rödl, n. 20 above.

[41] See C. Joerges and F. Rödl, 'Informal Politics, Formalised Law and the Social Deficit of European Integration: Reflections After the Judgements of the ECJ in Laval and Viking' (2009) 15 *European Law Journal* 1; L. Azoulai, 'The Court of Justice and the Social Market Economy: the Emergence of an Ideal and the Conditions for its Realization' (2008) 45 *Common Market Law Review* 5; M. Dawson, 'Learning from Past Failures? New Governance in the European Union from Lisbon 2000 to Lisbon 2020' (2010) 17 *Maastricht Journal of European & Comparative Law* 2.

[42] See also, M. Dawson, 'The Ambiguity of Social Europe in the Open Method of Coordination' (2009) 34 *European Law Review* 1 at 63.

basic distinction. While – as we have seen – the first 'wave' of academic work on new governance and the OMC often assumed that it should be excluded from the discipline of law, there are numerous difficulties with such an assumption. The reality of the fields in which the OMC operates illustrates the widespread failure of hierarchical legal programmes. Both the difficulties of reaching agreement on common social standards, and reliance of European law-making on compliance by national courts and administrations, may mean that 'hard' and 'soft' law are not conceptually distinct, but often integrated within each other. The law–governance relationship, it will be argued, should be evaluated through a less stylised understanding – one that sees both categories in terms of their evolving relationship to each other.

Such a reading opens the door to what the second and third chapters will term the 'inside' view. Here the 'turn to governance' is posited not as a turn *away* from law, but instead as a transformative response of the legal system to processes of social and political change. In the EU case, significant adaptation in EU law has resulted from both the differentiation of the EU into separate national legal orders, and the need to manage rapidly changing and fragmented regulatory tasks, that require the detailed input of more than the 'usual suspects' of central political actors. Just as these pressures have mobilised evolution in national regulatory law, the 'imperative to adapt' has been greater still in the EU's post-national context.

Chapter 3 will describe, contrast and critique three such 'inside' theories. Proceduralisation, democratic experimentalism and reflexive law all provide important pieces of the governance puzzle.[43] While proceduralisation and experimentalism focus on the first spatial fracture described in Chapter 1, considering new governance as an attempt to increase law's responsiveness and democratic character, reflexive law is equally important in drawing our attention to the functional cleavages between policy-making systems (in fiscal, social and environmental policy) that see themselves in distinct and autonomous terms, yet at the same time increasingly inter-depend.[44] This reflexive view – as will be argued in Chapter 4 – not only animates the academic debate about the OMC's future (in light of the economic pressure placed on the

[43] These three schools of course encompass a gigantic literature. Simply in order to save space, this literature will not be referenced here, but in sections 2.1, 3.1 and 4.1 respectively of the third chapter.

[44] See G. Teubner, *Autopoietic Law: A New Approach to Law and Society* (Berlin: de Gruyter, 1988) at 181.

OMC via the Lisbon strategy) but sheds crucial light on the attitude and perceptions of the processes' dominant actors.

The chapter will argue that – while all three approaches must be considered together to conceptualise methods like the OMC adequately – they also share particular limits. The rush of inside approaches to reconstruct the edifice of a new 'reflexive', 'procedural' or 'experimental' form of rule has often blinded them both to specific features within practices like the OMC that fail to fit the models offered, and to the inner inconsistencies which each model itself faces. The chapter will conclude by outlining both important common features of 'inside' approaches to the law–governance relation – features to be tested in the book's empirical parts – and focusing on three 'common tensions' – of participation, hierarchy and stability – that illustrate the paradoxes of the attempt to build a legal system in the absence of the features of sovereignty and hierarchy that characterise the laws of the nation state.

As will be demonstrated in Chapter 4, these are no mere abstract challenges, but can be found in the very practice of new governance itself. These practices will be developed through the book's main case study. To what extent do 'inside approaches' adequately explain the practice of the OMC, and what can that practice tell us about the 'ambiguities' of its legal, social and democratic roles? These questions will be addressed through an extensive analysis of OMC processes in the field of social protection and social inclusion (SPSI) policy (thus policies relating to health, pensions, long-term care and poverty).

The usefulness of a case study in this field relies on the fact that both the 'social story' of the OMC's emergence, and the 'procedural' story of the gradual evolution of the dominant rationalities of EU law, can be exemplified through the social inclusion example. While the attempt to address social inclusion problems through European action represents an important commitment on the part of EU policy-makers to move beyond a purely productivist image of social policy – to imagine the Union, as Mary Daly has put it, 'as a social and political (rather than just economic) community', at the second 'procedural' level, the process also represents the closest EU governance has come to a purely 'experimental' regime.[45] While the EU still retains a number of legislative competences in the field of employment policy, in social inclusion

[45] M. Daly, 'EU Social Policy After Lisbon' (2006) 44 *Journal of Common Market Studies* 3 at 470.

no such powers are available.[46] Lacking even a 'hybrid' attachment to so-called 'hard law', the OMC SPSI has emerged as a particularly non-prescriptive process, lacking the capacity even to 'name and shame' or issue binding recommendations to its national participants.[47] Instead, as the chapter will show, it has uniquely relied on more subtle tools to encourage governments to take EU-level targets seriously. If one is intent on gauging the participatory and 'dynamic' potential of the OMC, this process is a particularly useful guide.

At the same time, some important limits remain. Created as an amalgam of separate OMC strands in social inclusion, health and pensions, the OMC SPSI encompasses a wide variety of processes, but still leaves other policy fields, such as employment, fiscal and research policy, out of its ambit.[48] The very differentiation of OMC procedures according to the functional fields in which they operate produces inherent limits in extrapolating from one field to another. The broadness of social inclusion and social protection policy – as a 'multi-dimensional' policy field, with deep links to other areas of national and EU policy-making – therefore both makes the OMC SPSI a vital showpiece for the effectiveness and legitimacy of the OMC in a larger sense, and retains the need for empirical research elsewhere.

The data upon which this evaluation will be based is taken from the Commission's 2006 investigation of the OMC SPSI. This evaluation canvassed the views (through a plethora of questions and analysis) of national governments, NGOs, social partners and local authorities towards the process in its first five years.[49] These actors suggest that significant benefits have been derived from the OMC SPSI's emergence. While, at the EU level, the initial development of the process succeeded in establishing the visibility of social inclusion on the EU agenda, at the

[46] Indeed both the Nice Treaty (through Art. 137(2) EC), and new Lisbon Treaty (through Art. 153 TFEU), rule out legislative harmonisation in these fields.

[47] See B. de Witte and M. Dawson, 'The EU Legal Framework of Social Inclusion and Social Protection: Between the Lisbon Strategy and the Lisbon Treaty' in H. Verschueren, B. Cantillon and P. Ploscar (eds.), *Social Inclusion and Social Protection: Interactions between Policy and Law* (Intersentia, *forthcoming* 2012).

[48] As a result of this procedural differentiation, there are few examples of extensive empirical work detailing the 'effectiveness' or 'legitimacy' of the OMC across all of its known policy fields. For an admirable attempt at an exception, see B. Laffan and C. Shaw, 'Classifying and Mapping OMC in Different Policy Areas' (2005) *NEW-GOV Working Paper* 2/D09.

[49] The chapter will also attempt – to use a political science term – to 'triangulate' this data with other secondary empirical sources. For more on the methodology of the case study, see Chapter 4, section 1.

national level, social NGOs identify the OMC as establishing a right of 'structural entry' and access into national discussions that often previously eluded them. These, and other, successes illustrate that the OMC – even in its less prescriptive forms – is no mere rhetorical device, or 'paper tiger', but has shaped the terrain upon which important national and EU-level social policy decisions continue to be taken.

The more this is so, however, the more it is important that vital legitimacy deficits are addressed. In terms of the first 'social' story behind new governance's emergence, the OMC SPSI displays many of the broader ambiguities of the OMC's social role pointed out in Chapter 1. While the Commission has purported to develop a 'reflexive' and cross-cutting relationship between the OMC SPSI and other processes, particularly the Integrated Guidelines for Jobs and Growth, the chapter will question whether this relationship has flourished. While the original hope for the OMC SPSI was that it could create a permanent space for social policy on the EU agenda, the era following Wim Kok's 'mid-term' review of the Lisbon strategy in 2004 has coincided with widespread anxieties among the method's participants that Lisbon's elevation of 'growth and jobs' is leaving social inclusion sidelined (a concern that remains after Lisbon's recent '2020' re-structuring).

In terms of the second 'procedural' story, similar difficulties will be evidenced. The method's 'success' in creating new constitutional participants has been accompanied by numerous failures in creating mechanisms of political scrutiny and review. Here, the paradoxes outlined in the context of 'inside' approaches come to haunt the OMC itself. In terms of participation, the 'voluntary' status of the process, while leading to new participatory opportunities, leaves the question of 'who to select' in the hands of national and European executives (either formally, through the national reporting process, or informally, through the Commission's influence over the availability of funding for transnational NGOs). The chapter will argue that this creates an obvious accountability deficit – whereas inside theories rely on harnessing the scrutiny power of a 'new public', that public is largely being brought to life by the very actors who it is meant to be holding to political account.

If this were not enough, other paradoxes may be present in the OMC SPSI too. While the OMC SPSI commits (through its third 'overarching' objective) both to a fully participatory form of rule, and to 'dynamic' reporting cycles where new issues can continually be put on the table, the very presence of rapidly iterative reporting cycles can exacerbate executive dominance of its processes, both providing conceptual justifications for the exclusion of national parliaments – whose input may be vital for securing national legitimacy for EU-level reforms – and leaving a say for social NGOs and local authorities at too late a point in the process to make a policy impact. The paradoxes of the OMC's procedural role are manifested in its continued capacity to retreat into a form of technocratic rule able neither to take advantage of the cognitive resources a European civil society can offer, nor to find legitimacy in public bodies able to debate the processes' substantive ends.

While these problems have given rise to a wealth of critical literature, this book will seek – in Chapter 5 – to consider whether we, as lawyers, can do anything about the pathologies of the present OMC.[50] What, for example, would a 'constititionalisation' of new governance, or an attempt to place methods like the OMC within particular legal parameters, look like?

Answering the question relies on engaging with a contested concept. As the chapter will argue, 'constitutionalism' as a concept not only carries dual legal and political (or 'liberal' or 'republican' meanings), but also has potentially dangerous normative side effects. The chapter will use the idea of 'juridification' to point out some of the difficulties of attempting to 'save' methods like the OMC merely by mapping them onto existing administrative law remedies. While the creation of extensive and judicially enforced participation rights, the application of the 'social rights' contained in the EU Charter of Fundamental Rights, or the development of rights to access to documents, may offer the hope of a legal 'taming' of new governance procedures, each of these remedies also contains its own limits. The limited 'openness' of the OMC is matched by a defiant lack of transparency and access within the Union's judicial system itself, such that recourse to purely administrative law solutions, or even an EU 'administrative procedures act', could reinforce rather than tackle the elite and executive dominance of new governance procedures evidenced to date.

The final substantive task of the book will be to explore whether other options may be open to us. This task must begin, of course, from

[50] For other highly critical empirical work (particularly emerging from a younger generation of political scientists), see S. Kröger, *Soft Governance in Hard Politics: European Coordination of Anti-Poverty Policies in Germany and France* (Wiesbaden: VS Verlag, 2008); M Büchs, 'How Legitimate is the Open Method of Coordination' (2008) 46 *Journal of Common Market Studies* 4; M. Lodge, 'Comparing Non-hierarchical Governance in Action: the Open Method of Coordination in Pensions and Information Society (2007) 45 *Journal of Common Market Studies* 2.

a proper understanding of the failings identified in other parts of the book. The chapter's final political solutions will focus on expanding opportunities for political and social contestation of elements of OMC-like methods that have been seen as insiders' secrets. The indicators, recommendations, committee structures, and strategic reports of the OMC, by this view, should no longer be subjected to a purely technocratic logic, or rely on 'horizontal' forms of political scrutiny; instead they should be subjected to the forms of external influence and review that existing political institutions within the EU order can offer. While the reintegration of European and national Parliaments is an obvious part of such a strategy, other options, such as the responsive forms of review and due process offered by the European Ombudsman, and the requirement to measure the social impacts of prospective reforms also offer important additional elements.

Constitutionalising the OMC is a tricky business.[51] It requires an expansive view of Europe's constitutional project, just as it demands that we see 'law' and 'new governance' not as oppositional projects, but as potentially enabling, existing in spheres that both contribute to and redefine each other. A successful constitutionalism for the OMC – just like a successful 'transformation' of EU law and governance – must result not only in an opening and broadening of EU law's dominant procedures, but in a re-evaluation of the very place and *meaning* of law in the project of Europe's ongoing social and political integration.

[51] See, on this question, the analysis of N. Walker 'EU Constitutionalism and New Governance' in de Búrca and Scott, n. 5 above; G. de Búrca and J. Zeitlin, 'Constitutionalising the Open Method of Coordination: What should the Convention propose?' (2003) *CEPS Policy Brief* 1.

1 The origins of an Open Method of Coordination

1. Introduction

The peculiar interest of lawyers in the Open Method of Coordination (OMC) has often revolved around two elements, or two supposed advantages, that the turn to governance in the EU could represent. The first has been discussed under the heading of 'directly-deliberative polyarchy' (DDP),[1] or alternatively 'democratic experimentalism'.[2] What advantages does the OMC offer for the democratic character of European law? Can it be said to provide a new basis for legitimating law in a transnational environment, or linking it to the concerns of affected parties? Or is it, alternatively, an instrument designed to centralise power above and beyond the confines of Europe's constitutional framework?

The second set of questions revolves around more social concerns. To what extent does the OMC imply not just a change in how we conceive of law's democratic pedigree, but also in its relationship to a surrounding society? Whereas experimentalism's critique aims at the static nature of the European legal order (its distance from a more dynamic 'underworld' of regulatory practice), the critique offered by those lamenting Europe's 'social deficit' is targeted at European law's obliqueness; its failure to consider the social impact of what it is doing, or engage with questions of how European integration is protecting or inhibiting the reconstruction of the welfare state.

[1] O. Gerstenberg and C. Sabel, 'Directly-Deliberative Polyarchy: An Institutional Ideal for Europe?' in C. Joerges and R. Dehousse (eds.), *Good Governance in Europe's Integrated Market* (Oxford University Press, 2002).

[2] C. Sabel and J. Zeitlin, 'Learning from Difference: The New Architecture of Experimentalist Governance in the EU' (2008) 14 *European Law Journal* 3.

In some ways, this second set of questions should not be of interest to lawyers at all. Lawyers after all, are particularly poorly placed to assess the distributive impact of legal programmes. Analysing the *effectiveness* of policies in reaching particular targets, or the worth of certain institutional arrangements over others is normally a task that we ascribe to political scientists, not to lawyers. Perhaps therefore the concern with the OMC from the perspective of a 'social deficit' is going too far; an excuse for lawyers to escape the normal (and proper!) confines of their discipline.

This chapter will dispute that conclusion. The question of the 'social deficit' in Europe does not just imply a particular vision of the European polity, but also crucially puts to the test the forms and institutions by which European integration has been forwarded. In particular though, it provides a crucial set of explanations for why something like a 'turn to governance' or a turn to methods like the OMC, took place in the EU. To understand 'the origins of the Open Method of Coordination', and its recent development, one must also see the economic, political and legal conditions which made the move to decentred forms of governance inevitable.

These conditions will be sketched out in four stages. The first concerns the place of social policy in the integration process. In its first sections (sections 2–3), the chapter will argue that while the original structure of the Treaties attempted to protect the sovereignty of the national welfare state through the territorial separation of social and economic policies, this division has been gradually eroded. While vertically, i.e. in terms of the relationship between different levels of governance, the contemporary EU can only be characterised as a system of 'multi-level governance' in which different levels of authority must coalesce around shared goals; horizontally, i.e. in the relationship between policy fields, the development of the internal market has placed constraints on the operation of the welfare state. This new legal reality – in which economic and social goals must coalesce – has fermented considerable anxiety over a 'social deficit' in the EU; a perception that EU law may increasingly serve as a vehicle for the elevation of economic programmes over important national social objectives.[3]

[3] C. Joerges and F. Rödl, 'Informal Politics, Formalised law and the Social Deficit of European integration: Reflections after the Judgments of the ECJ in Laval and Viking' (2009) 15 *European Law Journal* 1; F. Scharpf, 'The Asymmetry of European Integration or Why the EU Cannot be a "Social Market Economy"' (2009) 9 *Socio-economic Review* 1; D. J. Bailey, 'Explaining the Under-development of "Social Europe": a Critical Realization' (2008) 18 *Journal of European Social Policy* 3.

The second part of the paper (section 4) will examine the development of the OMC as a response to this deficit. The OMC was advanced as a remedy to the erosion of the Union's original 'economic constitution' on the grounds that it could utilise experimental forms of policy diffusion to build up the EU's social policy competence. In this sense, it aimed towards a strengthening of the social through an attempt to coordinate different national strategies aimed at the 'modernisation' of social welfare.[4]

On the other hand, the development of the OMC has been ambiguous. In certain respects, it stands in line with the very challenges to the 'economic constitution' of the EU it is supposed to respond to.[5] As section 4.2 of the chapter will argue, vertically, the method further challenges the compartmentalisation of national and supra-national action, encouraging a dialectic between the creation of European standards, and national reform programmes; horizontally, it throws together the social and economic aspects of its reforms; insisting, through the revised Lisbon strategy, that changes in employment and social inclusion consider their impact on both budgetary stability and economic growth. Not only is the OMC a 'response' to the social deficit, and the Treaty structure which created it, it also carries the capacity to replicate its social limits.

The final section of the paper (section 5) will illustrate this ambivalence through sketching out two possible readings of the OMC's social role (readings put to the test in the book's later empirical parts). Many negative reactions to the method can be considered under the first heading: colonisation. The integration of different levels of governance, and of social and economic policy, appears as a benevolent social strategy, yet could entail the propagation of a particular agenda by the back door.[6] As an example of this view, the response of social NGOs and other groups to the 2005–06 reforms of the Lisbon strategy highlighted numerous dangers in 'synchronising' the OMC processes in social inclusion and social protection with monetary union, and the

[4] See J. Zeitlin, 'Social Europe and Experimentalist Governance: Towards a New Constitutional Compromise?' in G. de Búrca (ed.), *EU Law and the Welfare State: In Search of Solidarity* (Oxford University Press, 2005); C. Radaelli, 'The Open Method of Coordination: A New Governance Architecture for the European Union?' (2003) *SIEPS Report* 1.

[5] See C. Joerges, 'What is Left of the European Economic Constitution? A Melancholic Euology' (2005) (2005) 35 *European Law Review* 23–30.

[6] See C. Offe, 'The European Model of "Social" Capitalism: Can it Survive European Integration?' (2003) 11 *European Journal of Political Philosophy* 4.

development of the internal market. By one view, the success of the OMC in piercing 'beneath the veil' of national policy may be a poisoned chalice, designed to subvert enduring barriers to the 'perfection' of the common market.

By another view, the very ability of the OMC to promote a reflexive and mutual consideration of social and economic goals may be its primary virtue. The synchronisation proposed through the Lisbon strategy – in both its original and '2020' variants – need not be a pathway to neo-liberal deregulation, but a means of ensuring that economic and social goals consider the functional priorities of each other. 'Reflexivity' implies a model for European law in which it chooses to locate itself neither primarily at national or at supranational levels, but instead, where EU law is designed as a mechanism to encourage the integration – within a national discourse – of the policy priorities and needs of other states.[7] Only a reflexive consideration of social goals at the national level that also considers possible impacts both on economic performance and the capacities of other governments can reconcile Europe's 'social self' to the interdependencies of a common market. Our optimism for the OMC's future may depend on the realisation and development of this 'reflexive' reading. While its contours will be outlined here, a deeper analysis of its practice – and its future – will be conducted in later parts of this book.[8]

2. The social deficit as original sin? The two axes of Europe's 'Economic Constitution'

2.1 The subordination thesis

The idea of a social deficit often begins from an assumption that the integration project lacked a social basis from the start. This belief is still common among the hard left in Europe – the project of constructing a European Union was, from its inception, a neo-liberal construct designed to usurp social advances. A brief look at the Treaties could

[7] On varying models of reflexive governance (explained further in Chapter 4, section 2.2), see the essays in S. Deakin and O. de Schutter (eds.) *Social Rights and Market Forces: Is the Open Coordination of Employment and Social Policies the Future of Social Europe?* (Brussels: Brulyant, 2005).

[8] See Chapter 4, section 5.3 'Functional integration – the colonization thesis revisited'.

confirm the suspicion. While over 100 articles lay out the conditions and rights pertaining to the development of a free market, only a few set out explicit competences in social policy.[9]

This legal exclusion has led to the development of a subordination thesis. Wolfgang Streeck has argued, in a series of influential essays, that the Community has viewed social policy primarily through an economic lens.[10] The development of the EU is synonymous with attempts observable in other international institutions to entrench orders based on free trade and commodity exchange, in the face of the redistributive efforts of the 'social state'. The 'social deficit' is not an unwanted spin-off from a process otherwise designed to protect national 'social sovereignty', but an integral part of the EU's policy design.

There may, however, be a more nuanced position. While the exclusion of social policies from the EU's original Treaty framework was no accident, it was also carried out by politicians less intent on destabilising, than on *embedding*, systems of national welfare, which had begun to act as a cornerstone for their legitimacy. The possibility of 'social subordination' was not raised only by subsequent academic commentators, but was considered carefully by the Community's founders.[11] They argued that the creation of a common market could contribute to social objectives. Firstly, free movement would lead to a more efficient job market, by encouraging workers to move from areas where labour was cheap and plentiful to areas where there was demand. As a consequence, overall wage levels would

[9] While the social *objectives* of the Union have of course been expanded via the Lisbon Treaty, the same cannot be said for the Union's *capacity* to act in the social field. Perhaps the most significant may be Art. 14 TFEU which establishes a competence for the Union to legislate on services of general economic interest. For an account of the EU's social competence post-Lisbon see D. Damjanovic and B. de Witte, 'Welfare Integration Through EU Law: The Overall Picture in Light of the Lisbon Treaty' (2008) *EUI Working Papers (Law)* 34.

[10] W. Streeck, 'From Market-Making to State Building: Reflections on the Political Economy of European Social Policy' in S. Liebfried and P. Pierson (eds.), *European Social Policy: Between Fragmentation and Integration* (Washington: Brookings Institution, 1995) and 'Neo-Voluntarism: A New European Social Policy Regime?' in G. Marks *et al.*, *Governance in the European Union* (Thousand Oaks, Sage, 1996).

[11] The issue was addressed particularly through the report of Paul Henri-Spaak, addressing the concerns of the French government that its higher comparative levels of social protections would place it at a competitive disadvantage. *Rapport des Chefs de Délégations aux Ministres des Affaires Etrangères* (Bruxelles, 1956) at 233–234.

increase.[12] Burgeoning industries could take advantage of a larger pool of workers, while those areas where wages were kept down by high unemployment would be relieved.[13]

Secondly, it was considered likely that the benefits of economic integration for trade would allow the expansion and funding of social services. The creation of a larger market for domestic goods may have had negative impacts on workers in protected or inefficient industries, but would also – provided that previous barriers to market expansion were removed – free up revenue for taxation. So long as the 'losers' of liberalisation could be compensated, the economic dividends of free trade were seen as the best route for the European economy to recover from the devastation of the war years (a logic that continues into the single market programmes of today). In this sense, the EU was created as a complementary rather than antithetical structure to the development of the welfare state.[14] It was seen as a way of expanding the reach of economic cooperation, while allowing the domestic sphere to set its own social and political priorities.

2.2 *'Embedded' liberalism*

This – what Maurizio Ferrera has described as the 'the virtuous circle' between social development and economic growth – was the noble aspiration.[15] However, it was only possible under certain conditions.[16] The ongoing freedom of a transnational market could not be assumed, but depended upon limiting the power of states to manipulate currency or trade rules in order to gain a competitive advantage. From the point of view of the welfare state, on the other hand, the autonomy of governments to develop social policies required that principles of free competition, while applicable to private cartels, did not also threaten the viability of compulsory insurance programmes, or other services

[12] The Ohlin Report, commissioned by the International Labour Organization in 1956, thus argued that a liberalised market did not require prior harmonisation of social protection systems. 'Where productivity is high because a country has rich natural resources, abundant capital, efficient entrepreneurs and well-trained workers, the general level of wages, as of other incomes, will tend also to be high': *Social Aspects of European Economic Co-operation: Report by a Group of Exports* (ILO, 1956) at 104.

[13] *Ibid.*, at 111–112.

[14] M. Ferrera, *The Boundaries of Welfare: European Integration and the New Spatial Politics of Social Protection* (Oxford University Press, 2005) at 90–95.

[15] M. Ferrera, 'National Welfare States and European Integration: in Search of a "Virtuous Nesting"' (2009) 47 *Journal of Common Market Studies* 2.

[16] Ferrera, n. 14 above, at 93.

based on practices of public monopoly. The famous observation of Karl Polanyi, that neither markets nor governments could be self-regulating, but required a surrounding normative super-structure, had to apply were the 'virtuous circle' to be maintained.[17]

This lesson was a direct consequence of the bitter experiences of the 1930s. The principle danger the post-war heads of state were responding to was the reassertion of state authority over the market characteristic of fascist Germany and Italy, and the five-year plans of the Soviet Union. Each attested to a state-led destruction of the old laissez-faire system in order to meet the rising demands of working populations for job security, healthcare and better living and working conditions.[18] The model of an unregulated international economy, prone to sudden instabilities, and underlain by extensive problems of social deprivation, was firmly rejected.

The dilemma the founders of the Community had to resolve was how to learn from these lessons. On the one hand, the defeat of economic nationalism, and the presence of an inter-locked European economy presented an obvious 'peace dividend'; on the other, it was precisely the undistorted laissez-faire order of the interwar years, unable to meet growing social aspirations, or contain class cleavages, that had led to such extensive political authoritarianism. A balance had to be sought; one able both to allow the formation of an autonomous supra-national market, and equally to foster the autonomy of the nation state to be 'socially responsive' to the socio-economic expectations of their citizens.

The answer was to be found in law – in a legally enumerated division of powers between a supra-national order committed to the depoliticised defence of the free market, and a national one, where socially redistributive policies could be determined according to the ordinary mechanisms of electoral politics. As John Ruggie famously described it:

[17] See K. Polanyi, *The Great Transformation* (Boston: Beacon Press, 1956); A. Enber, 'Polanyi's Theory of Public Policy: Embeddedness, Commodification and the Institutional Dynamism of the Welfare State', Paper Presentation, RECON Workshop on 'The Social Embeddedness of Trans-national Markets', Bremen, February 2009.

[18] See J. Ruggie, 'Embedded Liberalism and the Postwar Economic Regimes' in *Constructing the World Polity: Essays in International Institutionalization* (London: Routledge, 1998). For a similar explanation in the EU context (in light of a German ordo-liberal tradition) see P. Manow, 'Model Deutschland as an Inter-denominational Compromise' (2000) *Harvard CES Working Papers* 3.

> This was the essence of the embedded liberalism compromise: unlike the economic nationalism of the thirties, it would be multi-lateral in character; unlike the liberalism of the gold standard and free trade, its multilateralism would be predicated upon domestic interventionism.[19]

While the supra-national free market could check the temptation of states to erect trade barriers, or create 'beggar thy neighbour' fiscal policies, the presence of a robust national social state could ensure that the consequence of free trade would not be social cleavage, but a domestic order in which 'social solidarity' between economic groups, and different generations, could be preserved. The best of both worlds was still possible – a transnational space sufficiently economically integrated to make war between its members impossible, alongside a national one, sufficiently harmonious that the threat of *internal* social strife could also be managed.

Its possibility, however, relied upon law. The capacity for both 'multilateral internationalism' and 'domestic interventionism' depended on legally enumerated rules and institutions. To this end, politically the Treaties gave the power to regulate the economy to explicitly non-majoritarian institutions (the Commission and the ECJ) in order to guard against the excessive politicisation of the market.[20] Legally, they enumerated and restricted the EU's legislative powers, excluding from its ambit policies on employment, health and education still to be decided upon within the democratic confines of the nation state itself.

This new 'economic constitution' thus rested upon two vital legal divisions.[21] At the *vertical* level, the Treaties separated out the depoliticised institutions of the EU from the political organs of the state. Through the idea of 'conferred powers', i.e. that the EU could act only where explicitly provided for in the Treaties, a quasi-federal compartmentalisation of policy was carried out.[22] This vertical division of power was designed to allow supra-national institutions to forge a free market above the manipulations of short-termist national governments. The effect of this at the *horizontal* level was a further functional separation of economic from social policy. Whereas the then EC was given extensive power to strike down national barriers to trade, the ability to make

[19] See Ruggie, *ibid.*, at 72.

[20] See G. Majone, 'Independence v Accountability? Non-Majoritarian Institutions and Democratic Government in Europe' (1994) *EUI Working Papers (SPS)* 3.

[21] On the concept of the 'economic constitution', see M. Maduro, *We the Court: The European Court of Justice and the European Economic Constitution* (Oxford University Press, 1998).

[22] Art. 3b EC (see present Art. 5 TFEU).

policies for employment, health, housing and a host of other areas, was reserved to the member states.[23] A strict separation was to be observed between a supra-national economic area on the one hand, and a national space replete with the traditional steering functions of the administrative and social state on the other.

This division – legally enumerated and enforced – was the basis of the Union's original 'economic constitution'. It was the result of a delicate compromise between the bonding power of an integrated European economy, and the need for autonomy in national welfare development. The compromise was not only political, but legally defined. The 'expulsion of the social' from the Treaty framework was in this sense carried out, not as part of a social 'subordination', but as a means of embedding and institutionalising the very institutions of national social policy-making themselves. It was not to last.

3. Whither the economic constitution?

3.1 *Multi-level governance and the erosion of the vertical axis*

If the economic constitution relied upon the separation of territorial levels, and the drawing out of social from economic concerns, it faced significant problems from the very beginning. The challenges to its founding concepts are complex, yet it may be helpful to examine them as they arose along the two main divisions created by the Treaties, and outlined in the last section.

Along the first, territorial and vertical axis, the attempt to separate national from supra-national action faced a challenge that was implicit in the way European legislation was framed. While the Union was provided with relatively independent central institutions, with the power to initiate legislative proposals, the actual implementation of these rules relied extensively on the cooperation of national courts and administrations. It has been commonly remarked upon that the budget of the EU comprises little more than 1 per cent of national GDPs, while the Commission is still staffed with only a few thousand officials.[24]

[23] Art. 117 EC (see present Art. 151 TFEU) – 'Member States agree upon the need to promote improved working conditions. They believe that such a development will ensue not only from the functioning of the common market, which will favour the harmonization of social systems, but also from the procedures provided for in this Treaty.'

[24] See Majone, n. 20 above.

Given this serious deficit, it is of little surprise that the job of enforcing legislative commitments lay in the hands not of the Commission itself, but national administrations.

This gap – between the capacity of the EU to promulgate rules, and its ability to enforce them – created the initial seeds of the new governance debate. 'Comitology' – the system of implementing committees arising from the delegation to the Commission of the power to execute agricultural policy – is a first example of the need to create administrative and cognitive links between national and European officials.[25] These links were needed, not only to ensure effective 'scrutiny' of the Commission's action – the initial justification – but also to allow access to a wider pool of technical and scientific information at the national level; expertise that was needed in order for the aspirations of European programmes to be followed through.[26] In this sense, the compliance gap was not only institutional, but also cognitive, and in both cases, acted in favour of closer integration between different sites of authority.

This 'capacity deficit' in administration was replicated in the judicial sphere. While the ECJ, under what is now Article 267 of the TFEU, was given the power to censure national governments (and even courts) who failed to implement EU obligations, its ability to identify and remedy examples of non-compliance was not self-standing, but relied instead on the willingness of national judges to utilise the preliminary reference procedure. When the Court – in the decades following the Rome Treaty – began to embrace a more deeply 'constitutional' role – it owed its status not to a self-proclamation of judicial standing, but to its ability to forge alliances with national courts, who had the information needed to enforce European rules.[27]

In this sense, far from acting as a mechanism to separate different levels of authority, the legal system of the EU was increasingly built upon a series of functional and institutional compromises. These institutional, cognitive, and legal ties were the necessary ingredients to give 'teeth' to the Treaties. Yet at the same time, they undermined the separation of normative levels that the idea of the economic constitution implied.

[25] See E. Vos, 'The Rise of Committees', (1997) 3 *European Law Journal* 3 at 211–212.

[26] C. Joerges and J. Neyer, 'From Inter-Governmental Bargaining to Deliberative Political Processes: The Constitutionalisation of Comitology' (1997) 3 *European Law Journal* 3.

[27] See (from a political science perspective) K. Alter 'Who are the Masters of the Treaty? European Governments and the ECJ' (1998) 52 *International Organisation* 1; (and from a legal one) J. Weiler, 'The Transformation of Europe' (1991) *Yale Law Journal* 100 at 2419–2423.

Rather than fostering the functional independence of European and national rules, the legal system entailed *interdependence*; an ongoing negotiation and compromise over the content, scope and applicability of its norms (a negotiation that we now see as characteristic of 'new governance').

3.2 *The proceduralisation of European law*

If these were the pressures, what were the effects? Put simply, the legal structure of the EU began to change. Rather than strive towards more hierarchical power, or aim towards an 'approximation' of social or other standards, Community, and later EU, law was increasingly oriented towards a convergence of goals, preferences and ideas, in which the national political sphere was given a high degree of autonomy over how common European standards were implemented.[28] As a first example, the Union developed a directive system which began to recognise, and try to deal productively, with national diversity. While directives are now described by the governance debate as examples of 'old governance' or 'hard law', by the standards of the era, they were radical in their 'flexible' approach to legislation. Their central idea – that to give true 'effect' to EC rules, some accommodation of national legal orders was not just politically expedient, but necessary, signalled perhaps the first recognition that the segmented view of regulation espoused by the Union's original founders had failed.

Following the radical expansion in EU competence brought by the Maastricht Treaty – particularly into sensitive fields of social and industrial policy – this initial 'proceduralisation' was deepened.[29] The directives passed following the 1989 Charter on the Fundamental Social Rights of Workers, were formulated as 'framework norms', creating overall goals and principles at the EU level, but leaving more contentious (or specific) details to be elaborated later on, either by national governments

[28] As an example, the Commission's 1994 White Paper on Social Policy stressed 'the need to respect the diversity of European societies . . . This diversity means that total harmonisation of social policies is not an objective of the Union. However, the convergence of goals and policies over a period of time by fixing common objectives is vital, since it will permit the coexistence of different national systems and enable them to progress in harmony towards the fundamental objectives of the Union.' Article 18, *European Social Policy: A White Paper* (Luxembourg: Office for Official Publications of the European Communities, 1994).

[29] On the relationship between both procedural and reflexive theories and EU law (including the OMC), see J. Lenoble, 'OMC and the Theory of Reflexive Governance' in S. Deakin and O. de Schutter, n. 7 above.

or the social partners. Two directives – one on working time, and one on parental leave – exemplified this move, mixing both inflexible 'minimum' provisions (e.g. the idea of a 48-hour working week) with considerable scope for other elements to be agreed on an ongoing basis (like the timing of rest breaks, or the extent of annual leave).[30]

In the case of the Parental Leave Directive, the actors negotiating their provisions were the social partners. This legislation was part of a move, observable from the Single European Act on, of 'contracting-out' legislative functions to non-governmental actors. As a famous example, Article 118b of the Maastricht Treaty established the Social Dialogue, providing for agreements between the social partners to be either adopted at the EU level, or bypass the Council altogether through direct incorporation at the national level. Through this method, the Commission was able to push forward legislation through forging partnerships directly with powerful civil society actors (thus potentially avoiding or dissolving legislative disagreements in the Council itself).[31]

In social exclusion, this process was advanced through financial incentives. While many of the legislative proposals of its first 'Social Action Programme' in 1974 failed, the Commission succeeded in funding a series of 'Community Action Programmes' on poverty and exclusion policy, which among other things, led to the development of transnational NGOs.[32] The most active organisation in the contemporary OMC process in social protection and inclusion (SPSI)– the European Anti-Poverty Network – was a direct descendant of this effort.[33] While these networks had no legislative mandate, they were entrusted with building up the role of the European institutions as information gatherers, and even 'agenda setters', in the process of national reform. To take one example, the Poverty programmes laid the ground for two 'soft' Council resolutions that were the forerunners of the present OMC SPSI. These resolutions both defined 'common

[30] Council Directive 104/93/EC Concerning Certain Aspects of the Organization of Working Time [1993] OJ L307, Art. 4, Art. 7; Council Directive 34/96/EC On the Framework Agreement for Parental Leave [1996] OJ L145.

[31] See G. Faulkner, *EU Social Policy in the 1990s – Towards a Corporatist Policy Community* (London: Routledge, 1998) at 70–76.

[32] See Council Decision 458/75/EEC Concerning a Programme of Pilot Schemes and Studies to Combat Poverty [1975] OJ L1999/34.

[33] See C. de la Porte, 'The Emergence of the OMC in Social Inclusion', Paper Presentation, ESPANET conference 24 August 2005, 3–7.

objectives and criteria' in the fight against poverty, and entrusted the Commission with the task of monitoring and reporting upon national reforms.[34] In this sense, the gradual expansion in the scope of authoritative actors successfully granted the Commission a more robust institutional role, while laying the institutional groundwork for the more advanced coordination efforts in social inclusion and protection that we see today.

This turn to other actors also provided functional advantages. By expanding the scope of authoritative actors, 'agenda-setting' functions were given to non-governmental authorities, yet the ability of the Union to drive forward measures previously restricted by the Treaty structure, was increased. If, for example, the social partners could be persuaded to adopt agreements, their domestic political leverage could provide the EU with steering power beyond the 'veil' of national governments. The contracting out of legislative functions was not only seen as a pathway to more 'participatory' forms of European law, but also as a means of increasing central steering capacity.

Along the vertical axis, a certain trade-off was made. The hierarchical ambitions of early Community law were abandoned to make way for increasing intergovernmentalism. At the same time, the power of the Union to interfere in previously *national* discussions (and to ally with non-state actors in pursuit of particular causes) was heightened. Already by the 1980s, the tentative outlines of the 'turn to governance', and with it, the decentring of central authority indicative of the OMC, began to be put in place.

While these changes did not happen in a single revolutionary moment, they allowed the original terms of the economic constitution to be reconsidered. While that idea referred to a horizontal division between national and supra-national action, the new system required the extensive sharing of power between different levels of authority. Rather than a system which divided separate decision-making sites *from* one another, EU law was designed to facilitate the *integration* of European programmes with the administrative organs at national and regional levels that were able to implement them. The popular characterisation of political science – that the EU appeared as a system of

[34] See Council Recommendations 441/92/EEC On Common Criteria Concerning Sufficient Resources and Social Assistance in Social Protection Programmes and 442/92/EEC On the Convergence of Social Protection Objectives and Policies [1992] OJ L245/26.

'multi-level governance' – was given a legal, as well as a political, meaning.[35]

3.3 The internal market programme and the erosion of the horizontal axis

The economic constitution that was the product of the original Treaties was a child of its times. It coincided with the post-war 'economic miracle', and with it, the effort to spread the fruits of economic growth more broadly. Domestically, the Keynesian model of a mixed economy, with high overall levels of taxation to support social services, was a common inspiration. By the 1970s, however, the outlook had changed. The oil crisis had halted both the year-on-year advance of economic growth in Europe, and the 'golden age' of its welfare development.[36] Those states that attempted a national response, based on stimulating aggregate demand, faced economic ruin.[37] European states now coexisted with a more globalised economy, in which capital could easily relocate elsewhere, and the policy tools traditionally used to tackle economic uncertainty (e.g. state subsidies or currency devaluation) were failing to turn the tide.

For states unwilling to adopt the more radical programmes of reform then being tested by the 'new right' governments of the US and UK, the EC offered a solution. The Community, just as it had earlier provided a supra-national alternative to political conflict, now offered a pathway out of economic sclerosis. The route out was to be paved through an internal market programme, which used the Court – and the instrument of mutual recognition – to break down non-tariff barriers to trade. If the neo-liberal experiment could not be embraced domestically, it would have to be managed through supra-nationally steered reforms designed to increase the European economy's competitiveness.

The move to 'complete' the internal market was not only radical in its economic ambitions but carried potentially explosive political consequences. It involved expanding the Union beyond a customs union into a free economic area, in which both direct and indirect

[35] L. Hooghe and G. Marks, *Multi-level Governance and European Integration* (Lanham: Rowman and Littlefield, 2001); F. Scharpf, *Community and Autonomy: Institutions, Policies and Legitimacy in Multi-level Europe* (Frankfurt: Campus, 2010); F. Scharpf, 'Multi-level Governing in Europe' (2000) *MPIFG Discussion Papers* 5.

[36] E. Hobsbawm, *The Age of Extremes* (New York: Pantheon, 1994).

[37] The foremost example may be the reflationary efforts of the Mitterand government in France. See, Ferrera, n. 14 above, at 111–114.

forms of discrimination against foreign providers were eliminated.[38] It posed a crucial question: what if the very institutions of the welfare state – universal, compulsory and monopolistic (and designed so precisely in order to deliver *equality* in the delivery of services) – themselves presented obstacles to the realisation of economic rights (those entitlements to freedom of trade and establishment now seen as the cornerstone of a free supra-national legal order)?

The erosion of the 'firewall' around the welfare state was forwarded through the Court's ambitious reading of economic rights. Two were particularly important. In the case of free movement, a right that once meant merely opening up national labour markets to foreign and migrant workers was increasingly reread (for example, from the Court's early *Unger* decision in 1964) so as to provide these workers with access to social security in other states.[39] This was arguably a paradigmatic case of functional 'spill-over' – distortions in the labour market arising from the social risk of moving across borders led to the need for 'coordination' in an area that was previously considered a bastion of national social solidarity (and hence excluded from EU intervention under the terms of the Treaty). Eventually governments were forced to respond to the Court's boldness, passing a series of regulations codifying the new regime and, in effect, opening up social protection systems to 'outsiders'.[40] In such cases, while the formal balance of power between the EU and its member states was left unchanged, the Court indicated a willingness (evident to this day) to read policies *outwith* EU competence in light of the economic rights contained and protected by EU primary law.[41]

[38] In the words of the ECJ's judgment in *Dassonville*, any measure, 'capable of hindering, directly or indirectly, actually or potentially, intra-community trade' was subject to review. In this sense, virtually any form of market regulation was now subject to review on grounds of its compatibility with Treaty provisions. Case 8/74, *Procureur du Roi* v. *Benoit et Gustave Dassonville* [1974] ECR 837.

[39] Case 75/63, *Mrs M. K. H Hoekstra (nee Unger)* v. *Bestuur der Bedrijfsvereniging voor Detailhandel en Ambachten* [1964] ECR 379.

[40] See e.g. Council Regulation 1612/68/EEC On Freedom of Movement for Workers within the Community [1968] OJ L 257; Council Regulation 1408/71/EEC On the Application of Social Security Schemes to Employed Persons, to Self-Employed Persons and to Members of their Families Moving Within the Communities [1971] OJ L 149.

[41] Consider for example, the Court's insistence in the Laval line of judgments considered below that while the right to strike is not an EU competence, its exercise by the member states must nevertheless be in accordance with EU law.

The changes in free movement were replicated in freedom of establishment. In the case of pensions, the increasing tendency of governments to contract out supplementary provision to private or quasi-private entities made the principles of competition law more applicable.[42] An important judgment came in *COREVA*, where tax privileges granted by the French government to a supplementary pension scheme for farmers were deemed contrary to competition rules, insofar as they provided preferential treatment to (public) insurance providers.[43] The stage was set for challenges to public monopolies, which precisely in order to maintain their 'universal' and compulsory character, effectively excluded foreign providers from accessing the domestic market.

While cases such as this one led some commentators to conclude that states were now 'semi-sovereign' in the social sphere, the challenge that eventually materialised was a more subtle one.[44] On the one hand, cases like the Court's famous ruling in *Cassis de Dijon* illustrated a Court more assertive in questioning national justifications for the creation of market barriers.[45] In *Cassis*, the Court refused to accept the argument of the German government that a ban of French liquor could be justified on public health grounds. Such exceptions, the Court argued, had to be read narrowly, ensuring that 'the public interest' did not become a catch-all label, invoked by any government seeking to circumvent internal market rules.

On the other hand, the Court's dismissal of the German claim was based not on that fact that minimising the risk to public health was an illegitimate goal, but rather on the basis that a less restrictive measure (labelling the drink's alcohol content) could achieve the same purpose. In accepting the legitimacy of the state's social role, yet at the same time, urging that role to be read in a way that minimised the detrimental effects of national legislation on Treaty provisions, the Court signalled a new legal role. Rather than separate 'transnational' economic claims, and 'national' social ones, tests of 'proportionality' and 'necessity' were required precisely in order to manage the *integration* of social and economic objectives once seen as belonging to separate territorial spheres.

[42] Ferrera, n. 14 above, at 145–148.

[43] Case C-244/94 *Fédération Française des Sociétés d'Assurance* v. *Ministère de l'Agriculture et de la Pêche (COREVA)* [1995] ECR I-04013.

[44] See S. Liebfried and P. Pierson, 'Semi-sovereign Welfare States: Social Policy in a Multi-tiered Europe' in Liebfried and Pierson (eds.), n. 10 above, at 50–65.

[45] Case 120/78 *Cassis de Dijon* [1979] ECR 649.

Similar examples emerged in the field of social policy itself. In *Albany*, the Court considered the objections of a company with its own supplementary pension fund, who claimed that a requirement of compulsory affiliation to a Dutch sectoral scheme breached rules on free competition, and thus represented an 'abuse of a dominant position'.[46] In its decision, the Court rejected the view (supported in submissions by the Commission, and a number of member states) that EU competition law did not apply to social matters. In doing so, it upheld Albany's position that, irrespective of its larger social purpose, the government's pension scheme represented an 'undertaking'.[47] As with *Cassis*, the nature of the scheme as oriented towards a social purpose did not exempt it from review, but rather made a determination of its compatibility with internal market law all the more necessary.

At the same time, the Court argued for a distinction between undertakings that were 'public', and those that were 'economic' in nature.[48] While the former aimed towards monetary gain (an example would be a scheme where benefits were directly linked to contributions), the former were aimed at cross-generational solidarity; they attempted to use the affiliation of active workers to subsidise the least well off. Given that the scheme at issue played a role in spreading social risks – and given that all workers, irrespective of their medical histories, were eligible for its benefits – it was deemed to fulfil a public, 'solidarity-enhancing' role.[49]

The balance struck in *Albany* illustrated a different attitude on the part of the Court towards the relationship between EU law's social and economic dimensions.[50] In refusing to rule out core social policies from the ambit of economic law, the Court opened the door to a central reorganisation of the welfare state. Yet in stressing the relevance of

[46] Case C-67/96 *Albany International BV v Stichting Bedriifspensioenfonds Textielindustrie* [1999] ECR I-5751. See also, Case C-70/95 *Sodemare SA and others v Regione Lombardia* [1997] ECR I-3395.

[47] See the Advocate General's opinion in *Albany*, *ibid.*, at [330].

[48] *Albany*, n. 46 above, at [80]–[84]. [49] *Ibid.*, at [111].

[50] On this, and other cases invoking the 'solidarity' principle, see T. Hervey, 'Social Solidarity: A Buttress Against Internal Market Law?' in J. Shaw (ed.), *Social Law and Policy in an Evolving European Union* (Oxford: Hart, 2000); C. Barnard, 'EU Citizenship and the Principle of Solidarity' in G. de Burca (ed.), *Social Welfare and EU Law* (Oxford: Hart, 2005); C. Barnard, 'Solidarity and the Commission's Renewed Social Agenda' in M. Ross and Y. Borgmann-Prebil (eds.), *Promoting Solidarity in the European Union* (Oxford: Oxford University Press, 2010).

other social objectives, it also underlined the need to balance social and economic objectives, or see one in light of the other. While there was no prima facie exception or constitutional 'shielding' of social policy from the law of the Treaties, there was also to be an effort to ensure that economic claims, rather than being elevated into an absolutist or 'trumping' position, were read in a way that would minimise their social impacts (and vice versa).

In this way, the Court's rulings indicated a search for precisely the opposite of the promise of functional 'separation' the original Treaties held out. If neither 'primacy' – the superiority of one set of objectives over another – nor 'compartmentalisation' – their artificial separation – was possible, the job of European law was to be one of encouraging the *reflexive integration* of social and economic concerns. The 'constitutional' role of the Treaties was, under this view, reimagined not as an exercise in functional or territorial delineation, but in 'reflexivity' – the incorporation, at different levels of governance, and in different policy areas – of the ideas, priorities and rules of other fields. If the realisation of economic goals could not be achieved apart from social policy, or even relied upon certain social conditions (e.g. welfare states that included foreign providers), the role of the judiciary was to ensure that conflicts between these objectives could be resolved with minimal external disturbance.

This was not a task that could be resolved by the judiciary alone. The boundaries between the national welfare state and a supra-national market could not of course legitimately be managed by judicial fiat, but were likely to require the input and steering power of Europe's governments. They too had to become engaged in the reflexive enterprise, considering the impacts of their most important welfare programmes on the freedom of the European market (and its impact on them). It would after all be them, not Europe's courts, who would have to face up to the monetary and political consequences any significant reorganisation of the national welfare state would entail.

Whereas the erosion of the economic constitution along its vertical axis would significantly alter the legal landscape, the functional changes brought about by the internal market would be truly revolutionary, both sparking increasing claims of a 'social deficit' in the EU order, and demanding that political actors step in to actively do something about it. Their response would not only signal the final nail in the coffin of economic constitutionalism but create this book's subject – an emergent 'Open Method of Coordination'.

4. 'New governance' and the birth of the OMC

4.1 The social deficit

The erosion of the economic constitution has not only signified a changing role for European law, but also ignited an intense debate over the future of 'Social Europe'. For some, it has signified the entry and encroachment of market rationality ever further into the institutions of the welfare state. At the same time, the EU has failed – under the conditions of a restrictive Treaty structure – to build up social policies of its own.

During the 1990s, this debate intensified. Perceptions of a 'social deficit' in the EU were fortified by two factors: firstly, the drive towards monetary union, and secondly, the emergence of unemployment as a serious threat to the financial sustainability of welfare states.[51] These two factors were dangerously linked: while monetary union had imposed strict austerity measures designed to ensure the viability of the common currency, these measures did little to tackle (and arguably exacerbated) levels of unemployment which were beginning to spiral out of control.

Just as unemployment made the burden of active to passive workers, and thus the balance of payments on social security, more unfavourable, so the convergence criteria for European Monetary Union (EMU) had the effect of limiting the policy options available to governments. It was now untenable for states either to absorb the rising costs of social security through running higher budget deficits, or to cushion unemployment through providing state aid to key sectors of the economy.[52] While EMU made the need for a national response to employment problems more pressing, it also made its traditional solutions more difficult to achieve.

Levels of confidence in the EU were little higher. Coinciding with a period of growing economic instability, European voters began to associate the Union with precisely the forces of economic globalisation that they blamed for rising insecurity at work. The frustration was summed up at Maastricht – whereas the UK refused to give up further power

[51] See (on these factors) D. Trubek and J. Mosher, 'New Governance, Employment Policy and the European Social Model' in J. Zeitlin and D. Trubek (eds.), *Governing Work and Welfare in a New Economy* (Oxford University Press, 2003) at 35–38.

[52] See F. Scharpf, 'The European Social Model: Coping with the Challenges of Diversity' (2002) 40 *Journal of Common Market Studies* 4 at 648–649.

through its rejection of the Social Chapter, voters in France and Denmark gave the Union a bloody nose, citing, as France did through its constitutional referendum over ten years later, an increasing perception that the EU was out of touch with everyday social priorities.[53] The Union was effectively in a double-bind – whereas it had limited the options available to national governments, its ability to make employment and other social reforms relied on the acquiescence of states who were totally unable and unwilling to hand further powers to an unpopular European bureaucracy.[54]

It was through this impasse that the instrument we now know as the OMC was developed. If the structure of European law had made impossible any attempt to build up social policies at the EU level, the answer lay in instruments of political coordination that could operate outwith the Treaty framework. Rather than focus on a harmonisation of regulatory standards, the new European Employment Strategy, developed from the Luxembourg European Council in 1997, encouraged a convergence of goals, preferences and ideas, with member states given the tools both to pool information, and develop nation-specific reform strategies.

The OMC's principal advantage was not the explicit 'innovations' it forwarded, but rather what it kept hidden. While it represented a 'Europeanisation' of previously national competences, at the legislative level, law-making powers still resided with the nation state. Even if states agreed to cooperate on particular matters, governments remained the key decision-makers, able to claim the credit where unemployment or poverty were reduced, and shift the blame when accused of ceding further ground in the battle to maintain national 'social sovereignty'.[55] As a result, the method was made non-binding. While the European Employment Strategy (EES) – and later the OMC in social inclusion – produced particular strategic objectives, a failure by any state to follow them would result neither in financial penalty nor in judicial sanction. If objectives were to be achieved, they had to be forwarded through positive inducements – like the opportunity to

[53] See, for example, the consecutive decline in overall support for EU Membership noted in *Eurobarometer No. 40: Public Opinion in the European Union* (Office for Official Publications of the European Communities, December 1993) at 2.

[54] Zeitlin, n. 4 above, at 5–8.

[55] See A. Schäfer, 'Beyond the Community Method: Why the Open Method of Coordination was Introduced to EU Policy-making' (2004) 8 *European Integration Online Papers* 13 at 8–11.

learn from other states, or the desire to appear as a leader rather than laggard in the Commission's annual benchmarking of performance – in the absence of a judicial shadow to force actors into line.[56]

4.2 The OMC as an example of 'new governance'

The exclusion of the Court was vital in framing the academic debate over the OMC's development. Both proponents and critics quickly absorbed it into arguments about regulatory reform, which posited the OMC as part of a larger challenge to the existing structure of EU law (and even, as we will see in Chapter 3, to 'modern law' in a broader sense). Its innovation was seen as its clean break from the idea of uniform regulatory standards, or the hierarchical 'approximation' of European rules, to be projected across the EU polity as a whole.[57]

While such common standards were likely to succumb to the significant diversity of national welfare regimes, and the strictures placed on social policy by the Treaty, the method represented an acknowledgement that adequate social policies required an ongoing system of review, with priorities and objectives shifting according to the particular circumstances of the national social sphere itself. In this sense, the method was, for its proponents, more than just a temporary compromise, but part of an underlying change in the EU's governance architecture (from a law-mediated to 'experimentalist' or 'procedural' form of rule).[58]

At the same time, the association of the OMC with 'new governance', and the stampede of academic and institutional interest in its procedures, also deserves cautious treatment. This excitement relied primarily on the idea that the method could be seen as a 'law alternative'.[59] By this view, the EU required the soft, flexible and iterative norms of the OMC because its existing legal structure was so inadequate. If European law was socially oblique and hierarchical – unsuited to the diversity of European welfare states – perhaps, in the OMC, there could

[56] On mechanisms for policy change under the OMC, see D. Trubek and L. Trubek, 'Hard and Soft Law in the Construction of Social Europe: The Role of the Open Method of Co-ordination' (2005) 11 *European Law Journal* 3 at 360.

[57] See J. Scott and D. Trubek, 'Mind the Gap: Law and New Approaches to Governance in the European Union' (2002) 8 *European Law Journal* 1 at 3–6.

[58] For a summary of the former, experimentalist position, see Sabel and Zeitlin, n. 2 above; for the latter procedural position see the essays in Deakin and de Schutter, n. 7 above. Note: these positions are sketched out in far greater depth in sections 2.2 and 3.2 of Chapter 4.

[59] See Chapter 2, section 2.1 'Outside theories: governance as external to law'.

be found an instrument peculiarly adept for the political task of welfare 'modernisation'.

There was, however, a stick in the mud; the sort of objection that comes from the cranky historian, always claiming that every revolution is another case of history repeating. This objection is to argue for the importance of understanding the OMC not simply as a 'law alternative', or a way out of the Treaty structure, but as something continuous with the way that European law had begun to evolve, both in its 'vertical', or territorial, and 'horizontal', or functional, dimensions. Just as the OMC – in order to be a credible instrument – had to emphasise its multi-level or participatory character, so European law itself had come under considerable pressure to reform *its own* principle regulatory instruments, both in acknowledging the need to bring new actors on board, and in recognising that economic policies aimed at the 'completion' of the internal market were, and must remain, socially embedded. With this perspective in mind, the idea of the OMC as new mode of governance *par excellence* seems less secure.

This thesis on the 'continuity' of new governance of law – which will be the subject of the next section – may be an unexciting one for those who have heralded the OMC as a decisive breakthrough for Social Europe. At the same time, it may be the only thesis that can provide a picture of the OMC's development *in light of* (rather than in opposition to) the surrounding normative structure of the Treaties. Having considered European law in its historical context – as a framework in transition – the OMC appears continuous with it, both in integrating social and economic objectives, and in embracing 'multi-level' rhetorics.

4.3 The continuity thesis

The continuities between the OMC, and the development of EU law, can be seen in the context of both the vertical and horizontal erosions of the Union's original 'economic constitution'. In the previous section, this erosion was represented – along its vertical axis – through the necessary attenuation of European law as a mainly hierarchical structure. EU law, particularly during the 1980s and 1990s, began to appear as increasingly 'procedural', in using flexible legislation and the incorporation of 'new' constitutional actors to acknowledge, and even take advantage of, diversity among European welfare regimes. The legitimacy advantage of such an approach was that – while some central 'steering' capacity was lost – the EU was able to have a say in fields of action previously closed off under the terms of the Treaty, or under the high decision-making hurdles it set out. An 'integrated' cooperation between different levels of law-making could thus represent a way out of the difficulties inherent in the 'segmented' view envisaged in the original Treaties.

In strategies like the EES, the Union engaged in a similar trade-off. On the one hand, the EES was designed and marketed as a 'decentralising' instrument. In order to accommodate inter-state disagreement, most of its recommendations were designed at a high level of abstraction. National ministries were permitted, and even encouraged, to interpret EU-level guidelines, for example 'achieving a high level of female participation in the labour market', according to their own legal structures, and policy agendas.

This decentred approach fed optimistic claims of a 'participatory' turn in EU governance – one where the obvious affront to institutions like the European Parliament created by OMC-like mechanisms would be compensated by new participatory opportunities for non-governmental actors.[60] In this vein, both of the main early OMC processes (in employment and in social inclusion) established 'Community Action Programmes' designed to fund transnational social NGOs, and in the process, create suitable conditions for extensive local and non-governmental involvement in national reporting.[61] These features indicate a similar 'procedural' logic as the one observed in the larger sphere of EU social law – towards seeing the EU's function as one of integrating different levels of governance in pursuit of common goals.

There was, however, a deep ambiguity in what otherwise appeared as a 'decentralising' political strategy. While the 'softness' and abstraction of OMC guidelines represented a seemingly poor replacement for the central steering power of 'ordinary legislation' it also allowed the Union a greater say than ever before in discussions that had previously been seen as the prerogative of the national social sphere alone. Now national social policies would be influenced not only by domestic politics but by the comparative evaluations provided through EU-level

[60] See C. de la Porte and P. Pochet, 'Participation in the Open Method of Coordination: The Cases of Employment and Social Exclusion' in J. Zeitlin and P. Pochet (eds.), *The Open Method of Coordination in Action: The European Employment and Social Inclusion Strategies* (Bern: Peter Lang, 2005); Scott and Trubek, n. 57 above, at 5; K. Armstrong, 'Inclusive Governance? Civil Society and the OMC' in S. Smismans (ed.) *Civil Society and Legitimate European Governance* (Cheltenham: Edward Elgar, 2005).

[61] See *Final Synthesis Report of the EU Programme to Promote Member State Cooperation to Combat Social Exclusion and Poverty* (Office for Official Publications of the European Communities, 2006) at 43–46.

benchmarks and indicators. In the name of managing policy externalities, employment and social inclusion policy had become a 'common concern'; one where the relationship between national policy and other EU-level programmes, like the project of monetary union, was now a relevant subject for EU discussions. The barriers of the national welfare state were thus loosened in the very name of their entrenchment, or protection.

One can even see this paradox of 'decentring' in the case of NGOs. While the Community Action Programmes – like the Community's embrace of the Social Dialogue a decade earlier – seemed to devolve power by creating a place for new voices in the legislative process, it also created a new set of allies for the Commission, to be deployed, when needed, against recalcitrant member states. The enthusiasm of Jacques Delors for the Social Dialogue emerged from his early realisation that the social partners could be crucial allies in the domestic sphere, provided they saw more favourable negotiating conditions for themselves in Brussels than in Paris, London or Rome.[62] Equally, the networks of transnational social NGOs set up by the action programmes, with important and influential contacts among national ministries, could be vital strategic partners in encouraging member states to follow the 'soft' EU-level objectives contained in the social OMCs. A 'decentred' process could in fact significantly augment central steering power, both opening up new opportunities for EU action, and extending the functional reach of existing EU programmes.

4.4 *The ambiguous nature of 'Social Europe' in the OMC*

The congruence between what has been characterised as a shift of European law towards integrating different levels of authority, and the 'multi-level' rhetoric of the OMC is a fairly simple link to make. The most famous academic account of the OMC in its early life, for example, had already posited its development as an example of a 'constitutional compromise' between different levels of authority.[63] This 'compromise' suggests that rather than conduct an exercise in delineation between different levels of authority, EU social policy would be increasingly conducted through the ongoing inter-institutional negotiation of EU-level and national rules.

It is important, however, to go further than this. The 'continuities' of the OMC with the reforms going on to the Union's original 'economic

[62] See Faulkner, n. 31 above, at 84–95. [63] Zeitlin, n. 4 above.

constitution' also concerned the relationship between economic and social policy. The method not only represented an attempt to break down barriers between different levels of governance but also to transcend a segmented view of the social and economic dimensions of the integration process.

In 'ordinary' EU law, this was represented, as indicated above, by the realisation that a segmented approach to the construction of the internal market, and the protection of the four market freedoms, would be impossible. Giving effect to economic rights would also entail some accommodation with social policies, given the numerous cases where 'market-based' and 'social' entitlements would conflict. Rather than see social and economic policy in separate normative spheres, EU law sculpted out for itself an increasingly important role in mediating between the needs of a transnational market and the role of the national social state in providing for the welfare of the individual.

This role, however, and its considerable normative ambiguities, also became an important part of the OMC.[64] While the EES was the product of 'social democratic' governments, they were hardly administrations that saw their principle task in government as the protection of the rights of the unemployed.[65] Instead, they adopted a 'reciprocal' approach to the relationship between social and economic policy. Paradigmatic was the case of the UK, where 'New Labour' had achieved power through a strategy aimed towards the full 'modernisation' of the welfare state. This involved adapting welfare institutions from rigorous protection of those without jobs, to making the facilitation of employment, and the 'entry' of individuals into the labour market, the primary purpose of welfare provision.[66] 'Social policy' was seen as a pathway to greater economic dynamism, without which expanding health and education services could not be afforded.

The idea that social and economic reforms should be mutually reinforcing quickly became the EES' central substantive concept. When the EES was created in 1997, its original guidelines were organised around four headings: employability (focusing on increasing skills and

[64] See also, M. Dawson, 'The Ambiguity of Social Europe in the Open Method of Coordination' (2009) 34 *European Law Review* 1.

[65] J. Goetschy, 'The European Employment Strategy: Genesis and Development' (1999) 5 *European Journal of Industrial Relations* 2 at 121–124.

[66] On the influence of 'third way' thinking on the development of the EES, see J. Kenner, 'The EC Employment Title and the Third Way: Making Soft Law Work?' (1999) 15 *International Journal of Comparative Labour Law and Industrial Relations* 1.

training), adaptability (increasing the flexibility of employees), entrepreneurship, and gender equality.[67] Under these guidelines, governments were not only instructed to raise employment rates as a general target, but do so through a broader recalibration of their welfare regimes. The strategy's objectives and indicators were designed to favour those states eliminating subsidies for the inactive, encouraging the provision of opportunities for individuals to retrain in order to find work.

The 'modernising' philosophy was passed on to other OMC processes. While the open coordination of policies on development and research was a direct result of growing fears that the comparatively low R&D budgets of the EU would disadvantage Europe in relation to its main economic rivals, the OMC in social inclusion adopted, as one of its main objectives, the need to tackle exclusion primarily through breaking down barriers to work.[68] Rather than see social policy as separate from the market, or something primarily designed to 'correct' it, the method sought to integrate social and economic policies into a singular policy framework.

Nowhere was this reciprocal philosophy more clearly articulated than through the Lisbon strategy. The purpose of the OMC's expansion at Lisbon was not only to facilitate the 'coordination' of social inclusion policies, but also to encourage those policies to 'feed in' to those aimed towards competitiveness and economic growth.[69] Following a perception that Europe was falling behind its main economic competitors, the main objective of the summit was not only to consolidate the social and environmental competences established through the Amsterdam Treaty, but to tie them to Lisbon's magical 2010 target to make Europe 'the most competitive and dynamic knowledge-based economy in the world'.[70]

The discourse of the OMC was thus Janus-faced. In the case of both employment and social inclusion, Lisbon was used to integrate the OMC with the dominant processes of economic integration. In the Barcelona Spring Council in 2002, the European Heads of Government suggested

[67] Part II, Conclusions of the Luxembourg European Council on Employment.

[68] This is the third of the 'common objectives': to ensure 'effective and mutual interaction between the Lisbon objectives of greater economic growth, more and better jobs, and greater social cohesion, and with the EU's sustainable development strategy.' *Common Objectives for Social Inclusion and Social Protection* (European Council, 2006).

[69] See Presidency Conclusions, Lisbon European Council, 23–24 March 2000, at [32].

[70] *Ibid.*, at [5].

that the EES should be merged more comprehensively with the process of economic coordination.[71] The first set of 'integrated guidelines for jobs and growth' were designed both to cut down on reporting requirements and recognise the interdependency of fiscal and employment policies (e.g. that employment reforms should be tied to the sustainability of national budgets).

Similarly, a Commission Communication in 2005, suggested 'streamlining' of the OMC for social inclusion; an effort to facilitate closer integration between the reform of social protection policies and the ongoing efforts to 'implement' Lisbon's objectives. According to the Communication, 'the OMC should parallel and interact closely with revised Lisbon – "feeding in" to growth and employment objectives while Lisbon programmes "feed-out" to advance social cohesion goals'.[72] This was facilitated through a move – from 2006 – to synchronise the reporting timetables for the OMC inclusion with the Integrated Guidelines for Jobs and Growth.

These reforms created a 'social ambiguity' within the OMC akin to the ambiguities of 'decentring' discussed in the last section. On the one hand, the OMC was built as a *response* to Maastricht, to the strictures of EMU, and to the edifice of economic integration. On the other, it was designed precisely to *buttress* or feed in to those projects. The OMC was not just built to give 'balance' to an otherwise socially oblique Treaty structure, but to render the objectives of the Treaty, and attempts by states to 'recalibrate' their welfare systems, more compatible.

There is something in this logic of integration of social and economic policy objectives that takes us back to the Court's reasoning in *Albany*. There, the Court defended legitimate social objectives, but refused – in the tradition of the old 'economic constitution' idea – to do so through a segmentation of social and economic concerns. It insisted instead that social and 'market-enabling' goals necessarily coalesced. The challenge was to find a way of managing the expansion and enforcement of economic rights in a way that allowed legitimate interests being pursued in the national social sphere, to be respected.

In the context of the Lisbon strategy, a similar move to integrate social and economic policies can be observed. The Lisbon discourse is

[71] Presidency Conclusions, Barcelona European Council, Part I at [49].

[72] Commission Communication on 'Working together, Working better: a new Framework for the Open Coordination of Social Protection and Social Inclusion Policies in the EU', COM (2005) 706 final, at 4.

Janus-faced precisely *because* it plays down the existence of an inherent tension between concepts like 'social cohesion' on the one hand, and demands for economic growth on the other.[73] Instead, one is seen as implicated or reflecting back upon the other. On the one hand, the multilateral surveillance of employment policies is oriented towards the reconciliation of employment reforms with the project of monetary union; on the other, the integration of the OMC in social inclusion with the Lisbon strategy is designed not only to give Lisbon a 'social dimension', but also to ensure that considerations relating to 'making work pay', boosting competitiveness and productivity, and raising growth rates, can be fully mainstreamed within social inclusion and protection reforms.

Along its horizontal dimension, the erosion of the economic constitution referred to a shift from a segmented national social space to a view of European law as an integrator of social and economic policies. EU law was no longer separated from the social, but entered into a discourse about how the cohabitation of economic rights and the solidaristic basis of the welfare state could be achieved.[74] In so much as the OMC is not only about advancing social reform, but also tying employment and inclusion policies to the dominant projects of economic integration, it is fully consistent with this move. In this sense, the OMC cannot be seen as an independent voice for 'Social Europe' against an otherwise oblique Treaty structure, but only as part of European law's ongoing attempt to more comprehensively regulate, and define the parameters between, a larger European economy, and the institutions of the welfare state. The consequences of this move, and the way in which it should be understood, will be the subject of the next section.

5. Reflexivity or colonisation? Two readings of open coordination under a revised Lisbon strategy

5.1 *The OMC as paper tiger*

If the OMC is truly 'continuous' with the reforms that have taken place to the Union's original 'economic constitution', what does that really mean? Does it now provide the potential to overcome Europe's purported

[73] M. Daly, 'EU Social Policy After Lisbon' (2006) 44 *Journal of Common Market Studies* 3 at 468–472.

[74] See Dawson, n. 64 above, at 63–69.

'social deficit', or, as some proponents have suggested, provide a new and experimental way of conducting policy in the EU? Or alternatively, has it shattered the very edifice, and political compromises, that allowed both a successful supra-national market, and a 'golden age' of welfare expansion, to be built?

While these are complex questions, the continuity thesis has some important implications for one influential critique of the OMC's development. This criticism – associated with the work of Fritz Scharpf – has attacked the OMC on the basis of its comparative 'weakness', both in delivering policy outcomes, and in contrast to the 'hard law' advanced through the Treaties.[75] Whereas economic freedoms have been backed-up by justiciable rights, the norms proposed under the OMC are of a different character. They are intentionally 'flexible', leaving the Court unable to rely on them for the purposes of 'balancing' social with economic policy, and allowing member states to quietly offload or downplay proposals that they happen to disagree with.[76] Given these disparities, how can a mechanism like the OMC really achieve lasting political change? It is at best, a distraction from the real constitutional battles going on in the EU institutions; at worst, a cover up for the further erosion of the welfare state by internal market law.

This thesis, however, relies on particular assumptions. While the OMC may be 'weak', it is only considered so in comparison to a 'hard' legal structure seen as providing economic freedoms with a quasi-constitutional status. An example is monetary union's 'Stability and Growth Pact', which imposes strict and escalating financial penalties on states who run-up deficits placing the stability of the euro-area in jeopardy.[77] The 'weakness' of soft law is condemned largely in contrast to the hierarchical and functionally segmented structure of 'EU law proper'.

One wonders, however, if this is really a credible picture of European law as it now stands. While the EU's main legislative instruments have rarely taken the form that Scharpf imagines – of a series of universal,

[75] See Scharpf, n. 52 above.

[76] This could perhaps be characterised (somewhat ironically) as a more common concern among political scientists working on the OMC than with lawyers. For an example, compare (i) A. Héretier, 'New Modes of Governance in Europe: Policy-Making without Legislating?', in Héritier (ed.), 'Common Goods: Reinventing European and International Governance' (Lanham: Rowman and Littlefield, 2002) with (ii) Trubek and Trubek, n. 56 above.

[77] See Scharpf, n. 52 above, at 654–656.

hierarchical and coercive norms – the evidence of the last section is of a Court that has itself been forced to integrate competing social and economic objectives. Neither the 'hard' and raw power, nor the social obliqueness, of the Treaties can be taken for granted; rather 'hard law' faces the same 'weaknesses' and functional conflicts that can be observed in the OMC itself.

Monetary union is an important example in illustrating the point. In contrast to the view of a determinate and hierarchical programme, EMU's short history has revealed the continued capacity for strong states to use their political influence to evade financial penalties under the Pact's 'Excessive Deficit Procedure'. While surrounded by a penumbra of 'hard' legal penalties, the Pact has not been immune to political manipulation, particularly in circumstances (like the recent euro crisis) where the economic weather demands a more 'flexible' approach.

At the same time – and ironically for Scharpf – the only process that *has* had some success in encouraging states to avoid unwanted spending has been an OMC equivalent (the Broad Economic Policy Guidelines, or BEPG).[78] Where there have been examples of default, member governments, and the Commission, have preferred to use tools of multilateral surveillance, rather than direct penalties, to cajole defaulting states back into line. Monetary union in this sense illustrates not the 'strength' of the OMC, or its 'success', but rather that all legal and political programmes, including those protecting economic rights in the EU order, rely on forms of 'soft power'. The point of contrast for the 'soft' OMC may not be the legal leviathan that Scharpf and others have imagined but a legal structure that also has to persuade and convince in order to succeed. The continuity thesis may, in this sense, allow stylised contrasts between 'new governance' and the institutions of European law, to be avoided.

5.2 *The OMC as Trojan horse*

As some objections appear less pressing, others may arise in their place. The continuities of the OMC, and a reformed 'economic constitution' may challenge the claim that the method is 'too weak' in contrast to the laws of economic integration, but it certainly does not lead us down the

[78] See e.g. W. Schelkle, 'EU Fiscal Governance: Hard Law in the Shadow of Soft Law?' (2007) *Columbia Journal of European Law* 13. Note: these guidelines are now 'integrated' within the EES.

road of unbridled optimism. This is so because our optimism depends on what the 'integration' of different levels of governance, and different functional areas of action, really means. It can suggest two things. In its positive light, the mutual reflection of different objectives, or the ability for spheres of action that were once separate to take better account of one another, in an important achievement of open coordination methods. This 'reflexive' potential may be ever more vital as the boundaries between the project of market integration in the EU, and the 'reform' of the national welfare state, become more blurred.

In its negative light, however, the very features which provide the OMC with a reflexive potential also open the door to the accusation that it is 'colonising' – that the method's 'integration' of different objectives, and levels of governance, may be designed not as an act of reconciliation, but implicitly to elevate EU-level economic priorities over all others. Lurking within the Lisbon discourse, and in the OMC itself, may be both of these meanings.

The second reading (what I will term 'colonisation') has arisen as an important suspicion following the reforms undertaken to the Lisbon strategy in light of a mid-term report by the Dutch Premier, Wim Kok, in 2004.[79] While the original Lisbon strategy was conceived as three overlapping pillars of employment, growth and social cohesion, Kok's report identified a severe 'implementation gap' in the strategy. It was unclear, Kok argued, both who was ultimately responsible for carrying out Lisbon's main goals, and what those goals really were – the battle to accommodate various constituencies meant that Lisbon was now about 'everything and thus nothing'. Kok's answer was that the strategy had to be 'simplified', or 'refocused', in order for the political momentum behind reform to continue.[80]

The outcome of this 'refocusing' was radical. While the strategy had originally been seen as three overlapping 'pillars' of growth, employment and social cohesion, 'growth and jobs alone' were now to be the central focus. Logically, he argued, the message of Lisbon should be that the viability, both of the internal market project, and the future of European welfare states, depended on increasing the EU's

[79] *Facing the Challenge: The Lisbon Strategy for Growth and Employment*, Report of the High Level Group on the Lisbon Agenda (Office for Official Publications of the EC, 2004), see http://ec.europa.eu/growthandjobs/pdf/kok_report_en.pdf.

[80] *Ibid.*, at 16.

competitiveness. If Lisbon was to reach its targets, the Union had to, in the words of the Commission, place 'jobs and growth centre stage'.[81]

One wonders, however, what this entails. There seem to be potentially pathological consequences from this philosophy, for example, for the OMC in social inclusion and social protection, which takes as its focus not just the pursuit of growth in itself, but the equitable distribution of social resources, ensuring that gains in prosperity are translated into more cohesive societies. The move of Lisbon towards a growth priority would seem to raise the possibility either that such goals were no longer of equal worth, or worse, that interventions in social protection systems were being sought not to improve their efficacy, but to move out of the way potential obstacles to competitiveness (e.g. the burdens of taxation imposed on business to protect health and housing needs).[82]

This is described by Claus Offe as the OMC's 'hidden curriculum'. Not only are OMC processes heavily integrated within economic reforms, but they are arguably subservient to them; appearing as a mechanism for social reform, yet acting as a proxy for proposals designed to boost competitiveness (and no more). As Offe questions, what if the goal of open coordination is not 'mutual learning', i.e. the gradual reform of welfare systems to tackle common challenges, but 'unlearning', i.e. the progressive loss of memory for the achievements of the welfare state in spreading the fruits of economic growth more broadly?[83] If this is so, the OMC may not only aid and abet national social and political discourses, but act as an instrument for their *functional colonisation*. The meaning of 'colonisation' is not only that the OMC – as its proponents claim – is a 'procedure' for negotiating common norms, but also that it has particular functional objectives. Just as vertically, the OMC may have succeeded in bringing policy issues previously reserved to the nation state to the European table, horizontally, it may have brought and integrated social policies originally designed to 'correct' the market under the banner of further economic integration.

[81] Commission Communication 'Working Together for Jobs and Growth: A New Start for the Lisbon Strategy' COM (2005) 24 final, at 13.

[82] There are elements of the Kok report that lend some credence to this interpretation: 'The Lisbon Strategy aims to raise Europe's growth and employment, and to embed the European commitment to social cohesion and the environment in the heart of the growth process – to be a means of growth rather than a claim on it.' See n. 79 above, at 39.

[83] See C. Offe, n. 6 above, at 462–466. See, for an attenuated but similar interpretation, D. Chalmers and M. Lodge, 'The Open Method of Coordination and the European Welfare State' (2003) *ESCR Centre for Risk and Regulation Studies Discussion Papers* 11.

The reforms carried out in the wake of Kok's proposals may reinforce this danger. The move to 'integrate' employment and fiscal policy guidelines agreed in 2002 was partly replicated, following the Kok reforms, in the social inclusion case, with an attempt to 'synchronise' the OMC process in social inclusion, with both the new 'integrated guidelines' and national reports on implementing the Lisbon strategy. Social inclusion, rather than act as a free-standing process was encouraged to 'feed-out' to growth and employment policy, just as those processes were to 'feed-in' in order to bolster social cohesion objectives. While this was designed to further the reciprocal ideal of a mutually reinforcing Lisbon architecture, it could potentially allow the carrying over of the priority of growth targets into national plans for social reform. Even Jonathan Zeitlin, a leading proponent of the OMC, has shared this fear – the Lisbon reforms, rather than encouraging a 'mutual interaction' between different policy areas, could mean a return of the Union 'to the one-sided coordination of Member States' social policies, in pursuit of financial sustainability and employment promotion, which the OMC in Social Protection and Inclusion was developed to overcome'.[84] It could 'integrate' social and economic objectives only to subsume one within the other.

Finally, the spectre of colonisation seems pressing when considering the latest turn in the EU's governance debate – the adoption in June 2010, of the new 'Lisbon 2020' strategy.[85] Dominating the strategy's renewal was a reflection on the failure of Lisbon to achieve its main headline targets. Following the reasoning of the Kok report, much of the blame was laid by the EU institutions at the door of the OMC, and its severe 'implementation gap'.[86] Radical targets had been agreed, without carrying sufficiently robust instruments to deliver those goals at the national level. The 2020 renewal also involved a reflection on the balance between the strategy's social, economic and environmental dimensions. While the strategy post-Kok had attracted criticism for its

[84] J. Zeitlin, 'Strengthening the Social Dimension of the Lisbon Strategy' (2007) *La Follette Working Papers* 22 at 3.

[85] Commission Communication, n. 81 above; Conclusions, European Council, 17 June 2010, EUCO 13–10.

[86] See e.g. the criticisms of the OMC in the Commission's evaluation of the first ten years of the strategy: 'While the OMC can be used as a source of peer pressure and a forum for sharing good practice, evidence suggests that in fact most Member States have used OMCs as a reporting device rather than one of policy development.' Commission Staff Working Document, 'Lisbon Strategy Evaluation Document', SEC (2010) 114 final, at 21.

supposedly 'one-sided' focus on 'growth and jobs alone', the Commission indicated in its earliest proposals a willingness to return the strategy to its original 'three pillar' structure, with goals relating to growth and investment, environmental sustainability and social inclusion, seen as mutually reinforcing and equally important.[87] There was even – for the first time – an explicit anti-poverty goal to be included in the new strategy, with the EU institutions committing themselves to lifting 20 million people out of poverty by 2020 – surely a fillip to those mourning the Union's purported 'social deficit'.

At the same time, there are reasons to be sceptical over the ability of the new strategy to defuse the criticisms of 'colonisation' outlined above.[88] While there is a new anti-poverty target, it was only agreed after significant disagreement between the member states over the suitability of a target in a field controlled largely by the member states forced the issue to be decided at a later Council meeting. The 20 million goal eventually agreed to was in fact lower than the target originally proposed by the Commission, which involved cutting by 25 per cent the number of Europeans 'at risk of Poverty' by 2020 (a significantly more ambitious objective).[89] Finally, the new strategy continues to emphasise the need for 'integration' between coordination policies in social inclusion and employment, and those in fiscal policy, insisting even further on the 'synchronisation' of the integrated guidelines for jobs and growth with reporting under EMU's growth and stability pact. The continued willingness of the Union to see social policies in terms of their contribution and impact on economic growth – and lack of reflection on social failings in the first ten years of the strategy's life – seems to leave the possibility of 'colonisation' a pressing challenge.

5.3 *Laval, Viking and the possibility of 'reflexive governance'*

This, however, is only one reading. It is a reading that depends, in part, on how we see the functional spheres of action the OMC is attempting to regulate. Offe's criticisms tend to assume a particular view of social policy, in which social protection systems play a role in alleviating conditions that would normally pertain from distributing resources

[87] 2020 Communication, n. 85 above, at 3.

[88] On the promise and limits of the new strategy, see M. Dawson, 'Learning Past Failures? Governance in the European Union from Lisbon 2000 to Lisbon 2020' (2010) 17 *Maastricht Journal of European & Comparative Law* 2.

[89] See 2020 Communication, n. 85 above, at 3.

merely according to market criteria.[90] Social policy has to be shielded from this type of logic – it should not be left to the economy to determine which social programmes are 'affordable' and which are not.[91]

The larger truth, however, is that this is a view of social policy which few, but the most optimistic of social democrats, would now subscribe to. The view of social policy as a largely corrective device has been criticised in particular by 'welfare recalibrationists', who argue that the end of ever-expanding growth rates, and of favourable demographic conditions, has led to an ever-diminishing economic pot from which to fund universal social services (a pot that, in the current financial climate, is steadily depleting).[92] While the outcome of these conditions cannot be the abandonment of the modern welfare state, it has resulted in a very different view of its role (encapsulated by the 'new' centre-left discussed in the last section). Rather than see welfare provision as a check on market expansion, the future of the welfare state, according to the recalibrationists, may rely on the realisation of positive synergies between social protection goals and the economic growth required to meet them.

Given this changed view, Europe's efforts to create a social policy of its own can be seen as part of a 'dual strategy' for reform. On the one hand, the EU must assist the national effort to ensure that welfare entitlements survive economic globalisation. This includes taking a proactive approach to social inclusion challenges – ensuring that social protection and economic progress can, as much as possible, be made positive rather than limiting factors for each other. Under this view, social protection reforms should be oriented towards allowing a more active and flexible labour market, creating the economic conditions through which more expansive welfare provision can be afforded in the future (a curious descendant of the social policy arguments advanced by the Community's founders).

On the other hand, the EU must ensure that national social states can coexist in an integrated economic sphere, where the right to cross

[90] This would seem to fit with T. H. Marshall's famous definition of social policy: 'a political power to supersede, supplement or modify operations of the economic system in order to achieve results which the economic system could not achieve on its own.' T. H. Marshall, *Social Policy* (London: Hutchinson, 1975) at 15.

[91] Offe, n. 6 above, at 463.

[92] P. Pierson, 'Irresistible Forces, Immovable Objects: Post-industrial Welfare States Confront Permanent Austerity' (1998) 5 *Journal of European Public Policy* 4; See also, the essays in Zeitlin and Trubek (eds.), n. 51 above.

borders in pursuit of economic activity is respected. These rights need not be purely 'economic' in nature, but could involve crossing state lines in pursuit of better healthcare or education, creating burdens for social provision elsewhere. The notion of the social state as a 'black box' of national social solidarity thus has to take account, increasingly, of the needs and entitlements of 'denizens' and other economic outsiders.

In such circumstances – where the very effort to 'renew' the national welfare state depends as much on an embedded transnational sphere, as it does on the spending priorities of the domestic state itself – EU intervention need not be seen as a merely colonising effort to bring ever-greater spheres of life within the ambit of European rules, but rather as a legitimate attempt to mediate between competing national and supra-national objectives. This view of the EU – as a 'reflexive coordinator' of national action – envisages EU law as a mechanism designed to encourage an 'other-regarding' attitude along both the 'horizontal' and the 'vertical' axes discussed earlier in this chapter.[93]

Horizontally, while social protection reforms, including those guided under the OMC, may still have socially ameliorative priorities, this reflexive view requires a recognition that guaranteeing social inclusion is not just a matter of providing social assistance benefits, but of ensuring access to a 'multi-dimensional' response, which no one set of actors can achieve on their own. It thus requires reaching across functional boundaries, creating positive synergies between different policy fields (including to those processes of sustainable budget-setting without which much-needed funds would be unavailable).

In this context, the 'feeding-in' and 'feeding-out' which Lisbon suggested for the OMC SPSI is not only oriented towards fighting bureaucratic excess, but towards ensuring that the commitment of the EU to reducing social deprivation can be realised. The challenge of the OMC is not simply to 'coordinate' a given set of policies, but to encourage the integration of objectives, rules and priorities that were once considered autonomous. It is to encourage a discourse on growth that considers its effects on social cohesion, as well as ensure that the attempt to provide individuals with realisable social rights does not undermine

[93] On 'reflexive coordination', see S. Deakin, 'Two Types of Regulatory Competition: Competitive Federalism Versus Reflexive Harmonisation. A Law and Economics Perspective on *Centros*' (1999) *Cambridge Yearbook of European Legal Studies*; R. Rogowski, 'Flexicurity and Reflexive Coordination of European Employment and Social Policies' in H. Jorgensen and P. H. Madsen (eds.), *Flexicurity and Beyond* (Copenhagen: DJOF Publishing, 2007).

the stability of core economic programmes, like the viability of the common currency. Horizontally, the job of a reflexive OMC is to avoid 'colonisation' precisely by illustrating that the achievement of one set of policy priorities requires input and cooperation from other fields.

This 'reflexive' rationality can also be identified at the second vertical level. The evidence of the previous section has indicated that national and European law cannot be seen as segmented legal systems, but structures that must rely on each other in order to achieve normative force. The trend towards 'proceduralisation' evident in the EU's legislative instruments illustrates a recognition that neither the central institutions, nor any single member state, carry all the information necessary to conduct a meaningful programme for social reform. The reflexive alternative is to seek a more dialectical relationship between the two levels.[94] While common European norms – including the economic freedoms of the internal market – can play a 'framing' role in relation to national programmes, European regulation can only be truly responsive to its surrounding environment if it is able to take advantage of the expertise, preferences and opinions of those it is attempting to 'guide'. The method – in both steering national reforms through common guidelines and objectives, and allowing those objectives to be reformed in the localised discourse of the nation state – may also allow a vertical reflexivity (to complement Lisbon's integration of functional areas). This reflexivity is structured around the belief that European and national administrators exist in an interdependent environment; one where the success of each depends of internalising the goals and priorities of others.[95]

As a final illustration of this reflexivity, however, it may be useful to move outside the immediate context of the OMC. In two important cases from 2008 – almost instantly elevated to 'star' legal status by European legal academia – the ECJ was asked to consider the necessary boundaries between economic and social rights. In *Laval un Partneri Ltd*, the Court had to consider the legality of a strike by a Swedish Union against a Latvian company, which had employed posted workers from another member state, yet had refused to sign a collective agreement in Sweden.[96] The dispute was regulated by both the free movement provisions of the Treaty and intricate national labour laws, and the

[94] See Lenoble, n. 29 above, at 30–37. [95] *Ibid.*, at 33.

[96] Case C-341/05 *Laval un Partneri Ltd v Svenska Byggnadsarbetareförbundet and Others* [2007] ECR I-11767.

provisions of Directive 96/71/EC on Posted Workers.[97] In *Viking Lines*, the Court was asked to consider a different yet related issue – the legality of a circular, urging affiliates of a European peak organisation (the International Transport Workers Federation) not to sign a collective agreement with a shipping line which had attempted to reflag its vessels in another member state. The shipping line had done so in order to negotiate more favourable terms of employment in Estonia than it could ever receive in Finland (and so had sought to conclude, in Estonia, a collective agreement).[98]

In both cases, the Court had to weigh and balance two conflicting rights – the rights of a company (and its workers) to offer their services abroad, against the rights of trade unions to engage in strike action. The cases were emblematic of two looming sets of conflicts of which the demise of the 'economic constitution' spoke – firstly, the presence of extensive wage competition between 'new' and 'old' member states following the Union's eastern enlargement, and secondly, the increasing inability of EU law to avoid examples of conflict between national social claims and the Court's ambitious forging of a supra-national economic sphere.

Both the judgments of the Court, and the opinions of the Advocates General, indicate precisely the dual opportunities and dangers the demise of this compromise has brought.

The reflexive reading of the judgments relies on the Court's rejection, in both cases, of the segmentation of national social policies, and European rules on freedom of establishment. Even if, for example, the right to take collective action represented a 'fundamental' national social right, and was thus regulated solely at the national level, this did not, so the Court argued, exclude it from the scope of EU rules. As the Court put it in an important passage in *Viking*:

> It is sufficient to point out that, even if, in the areas which fall outside the scope of the Community's competence, the Member States are still free, in principle, to lay down the conditions governing the existence and exercise of the rights in question, the fact remains that, when exercising that competence, the Member States must nevertheless comply with Community law.[99]

[97] Directive 71/96/EC Concerning the Posting of Workers in the Framework of the Provision of Services [1996] O.J. L. 18.

[98] Case C-438/05 *The International Transport Workers' Federation & The Finnish Seamen's Union v Viking Line ABP & Ou Viking Line Eesti* [2007] ECR I-10779.

[99] *Viking*, *ibid.*, at [39]–[40].

Rather than see economic and social claims as compartmentalised, the increasing cases of conflict between them necessitated an attempt to 'balance' social and economic claims. Rather than see market-based and social policies in separate normative spheres of activity, the Court insisted that each had to be read in light of each other.

This balancing relied on a reciprocal consideration of the Union's 'social' and 'economic' objectives. Part of the emancipatory potential of the judgments lay in their argument, encapsulated by the opinion of Advocate-General Poiares Maduro in *Viking*, that the Community was founded on a 'social contract'. The basis of this contract was:

> That workers throughout Europe must accept the recurring negative consequences that are inherent in the common market's increasing prosperity, in exchange for which society must commit itself to the general improvement of their working conditions.[100]

Here we see yet another formulation of the trade-off originally articulated in Article 117 EC – increasing prosperity and ameliorative social conditions must be mutually reinforcing. In pursuit of that contract, the Court refused to establish a presumptive hierarchy between either national social rights or the economic provisions contained in the Treaty; rather it insisted that both the right to collective action, and the freedom to establish and provide services abroad, were 'fundamental principles of Community law'.[101] This elevation resulted in a very different approach to adjudicating the boundaries between national welfare provision and the European market. As Loic Azoulai has put it, the Court moved in the judgments from a 'conflictual' to a 'consensualist' approach to the relation between different categories rights. Whereas the conflictual conception saw 'social' and 'market' Treaty objectives in exclusive normative spheres:

> This consensualist conception envisages, on the contrary, demands which can be balanced, interests which may concur, voices in concert. This is the conception supported by Poiares Maduro: participation and collective action by workers are not excluded from the scheme of economic integration; on the contrary, they contribute to increasing the efficiency and proper functioning of the integrated market. Choosing this route, the Court affirms the productive ambiguity of the Community project.[102]

[100] See the Advocate General's Opinion in *Viking*, n. 98 above, at [59].
[101] *Laval*, n. 96 above, at [91].
[102] L. Azoulai, 'The Court of Justice and the Social Market Economy: The Emergence of an Ideal and the Conditions for its Realization' (2008) 45 *Common Market Law Review* 5 at 1349.

The elevation of social claims to constitutional parity required a reflexive attempt to balance and integrate competing functional and territorial objectives. The Court thus asked, in *Viking*, whether the restrictions on free establishment struck 'a fair balance between the fundamental social right to take collective action and the freedom to establish and provide services'? Furthermore, it asked whether, if there *was* a restriction, it was 'objectively justified, appropriate, proportionate, and in conformity with the principle of mutual recognition'.[103] Social objectives could be pursued, but under the condition that they reflected upon, and *minimised*, their impacts on other forms of entitlement (e.g. the legitimate interest in *Viking* of setting up a business across borders and, in *Laval*, of seeking or providing temporary work abroad). It was the failure to do this – the inability of each Trade Union to, as *Viking* put it, 'pursue other means at its disposal least restrictive to freedom of establishment' – that led to the upholding of the restriction to freedom of services protected under Article 43 of the Treaty.[104]

As with *Albany*, the job of European law is seen in the cases as encouraging the formulation of both social and economic objectives in a way that internalises or reflects upon the priorities of the other. The discourse of a 'reflexive' OMC – that effective reform requires cooperation and negotiation, both between different functional objectives, and levels of governance – is here reflected in the Court's embryonic attempts to manage accusations of social ambivalence through the direct *linking* of social and economic projects.[105]

With the very same set of moves, however, the Court placed on a 'level footing' parties and objectives that operated within a quite different set of constraints. In the first case, the seemingly emancipatory pronouncement that the right to strike is a 'fundamental principle of Community law' seems less so when one considers the historical exclusion of the Union from the field of labour law.[106] The 'elevation' of social priorities to the level of 'balancing' brings to the European (and judicial) level a set of questions that were previously determined locally, through a unique set of domestic political trade-offs (in the Nordic case,

[103] See *Viking*, n. 98 above at [27]. [104] *Ibid.*, at [87].

[105] For a developed reading of this 'reflexive' approach in the context of both *Laval* and its Posted Workers Directive, see M. Nance and D. Trubek, 'The Strange Case of the Posted Workers Directive: EU Law as Reflexive Coordination?', Paper Presentation, Workshop on Laval and Viking, Cambridge University, September 2008.

[106] See B. Bercusson, 'The Trade Union Movement and the European Union: Judgement Day' (2007) 13 *European Law Journal* 3 at 282.

between trade unions and workers on the one hand, and governments and corporations on the other). The judgments were radical in giving truly horizontal effect to the provisions of the then Article 43 EC, finding an infringement of the freedom of services, not on the basis of state, but *non-state* action, i.e. the activities of European trade unions. Instead of observing a system of private bargaining between social partners, the ECJ treated Union activities as if they were transnational substitutes for state action; thereby ignoring the origins of Swedish, and much European collective bargaining, in systems of tripartite negotiation, often directed *in opposition* to state authority.[107]

In *Laval*, a similarly ambiguous move was carried out, although this time in interpreting the Posted Workers Directive – a piece of secondary legislation designed to forge a compromise between allowing workers temporarily to provide services abroad, and ensuring that a minimum of regulatory and working standards applied to their work. The Court argued that the directive permitted collective action, but only insofar as it was designed to enforce the 'essential working conditions' enumerated in Article 3(1) of the directive.[108] As the strike in *Laval* aimed to force the company to observe standards that went beyond statutory minimums (in Sweden, a statutory minimum wage had not been established by legislation, but was itself the subject of collective bargaining), strike action could not be used to achieve this purpose.[109] Ironically – for a directive designed to establish a social 'baseline' for workers posted abroad, without precluding states wishing to *go beyond* minimum standards – the effect of the Court's ruling was to declare illegal Union activity designed to achieve precisely this purpose.[110]

[107] C. Joerges and F. Rödl, 'Informal Politics, Formalised Law and the Social Deficit of European Integration: Reflections after the Judgements of the ECJ in *Viking* and Laval' (2009) 15 *European Law Journal* 1 at 11–15.

[108] See *Laval*, n. 96 above at [99].

[109] To be more precise, two concerns were raised by the court here: firstly, that the collective agreement demanded by Swedish Unions concerned rates above minimum rates of pay, and secondly, that it was not 'universally applicable' within the terms of the directive, i.e. did not apply to the whole construction sector in Sweden. As such, it could not be used to establish the 'minimum conditions' of Art.3 of the Directive.

[110] See e.g. the commitment in Art. 3(7) of the directive that 'paragraphs 1 to 6 [i.e. the minimum conditions] shall not prevent application of terms and conditions of employment which are more favourable to workers'. On this concern, particularly in light of threats of regulatory competition triggered by Laval's reading of the Posted Workers Directive, see S. Deakin, 'Regulatory Competition in Europe After Laval' (2008) *REFGOV Working Papers* 16 at 36.

The outcome of the rulings seems likely significantly to impede Union activities that could be seen as infringing Treaty rights. The threat of 'colonisation' seems to be present on both a vertical and horizontal level – the establishment of something like a European 'right to strike' – while seemingly seeking to expand social rights – in fact has simply brought under the ambit of EU rules, areas of action that once depended on a national, not a European, 'social contract'. As Joerges and Rödl put it:

> The ECJ's argument implies that European economic freedoms, rhetorically tamed only by an unspecified 'social dimension' of the Union, trump the labour and social constitutions (*Arbeits* and *Socialverfassung*) of a Member State.[111]

Secondly, one wonders what gives the European courts the legitimacy to determine the proper 'balance' between social and economic claims (a task we normally ascribe to the political, not the judicial sphere). The aggressive reading of economic rights contained in the judgments – and the significant efforts to use market freedoms to reorganise domestic constitutional structures of collective bargaining – opens the door to the use of supposedly 'social' rhetoric to further accumulate vertical power (with the EU no closer to the legislative position of being able to build a robust 'social policy for Europe' of its own).[112] 'Colonisation' is also present in the potential use of law both to bring social questions under the ambit of the internal market, and to make the 'balance' between competing values a *European* question (one determined largely by judicial, rather than political, organs).

While the debate over *Laval* and *Viking* is almost as polarised as that over the OMC, most commentators admit that many of the enduring questions of the judgments remain unresolved.[113] In particular, it is unclear whether the fears of regulatory competition among European labour markets will be realised. The omens are not good. The approach to balancing free movement rights with the right to strike has been confirmed by later cases, two of them occurring after the EU's Charter of Fundamental Rights – with its own legally binding commitment to the right to strike – was incorporated within the

[111] Joerges and Rödl, n. 95 above, at 18.

[112] See F. Scharpf, 'The Only Solution is to Refuse to Comply with ECJ Rulings: An Interview with Fritz Scharpf' (2008) 14 *Social Europe* 1.

[113] See e.g. Joerges and Rödl, n. 95 above, at 19; Nance and Trubek, n. 105 above, at 22.

Treaties.[114] The very nature of the 'balancing' approach – which leaves the judiciary itself with a strong role in determining which restrictions on the market freedoms are justified on public policy grounds and which not – leaves the place of social rights in the EU legal order in a state of constant flux.

The purpose of this excursus is merely to illustrate some of the quandaries and opportunities the demise of the EU's 'economic constitution' presents an instrument like the OMC. One would expect the OMC to have some role in the process of mediating between social and economic claims begun by the Court's decisions. At the territorial level, its obligation upon states to consider their policies in light of the experience of other members suggests an (albeit imperfect) commitment to an integrated polity. At the functional level, the requirement, in the OMC process in social protection, to balance social reform against the demands of monetary union also belies an acknowledgement that social and economic objectives must find some way of working in tandem. Perhaps, at the political level, the method can carry on the Court's purported attempt reflexively to integrate social and economic concerns (an issue expanded upon in the epilogue of this book).[115]

At the same time, there is a difference between abstract commitment and political delivery. If the OMC is to make any kind of contribution, it cannot take its progressive potential, or its 'multi-level' rhetoric for granted. The success of the method, in making the transition from 'paper tiger' to 'reflexive tool', depends on translating its deeds into action. Here, Zeitlin's diagnosis of 'one-sided coordination', and the numerous criticisms of the method from the perspective of its legitimacy (i.e. levels of transparency and participation) and effectiveness (i.e. ability to constrain national action) once again come to the fore.[116] The question of 'colonisation' and 'reflexivity' cannot merely be posed in the abstract but must be analysed and described in the context of the concrete practice of the OMC process (a task taken up in the fourth chapter of this book).

[114] See Case C-354/06 *Dirk Rüffert v Land Niedersachen*, [2008] ECR I-1989; Case 346/06 *Commission v Luxembourg* [2008] ECR I-4323; Case C-271/08 *Commission v Germany*, judgment of 15 July 2010; Case C-515/08 *Vitor Manuel dos Santos Palhota et al.*, judgment of 7 October 2010.

[115] See also, M. Dawson, '3 Waves of New Governance in the European Union' (2011) 36 *European Law Review* 2.

[116] See e.g. Chapter 4, sections 2–6.

6. Conclusion: towards a new 'economic constitution'?

The concept with which this paper began – the idea of an 'economic constitution' for Europe – has been an important inspiration for the development of the EU. Yet its contemporary meaning is quite different from that envisaged by the Union's founders. Whereas they saw law as a mechanism to divide and demarcate economic and political power, the self-understanding of contemporary European law defies such categorisation. Along both its vertical and horizontal axes, European law has begun to integrate elements that it once kept apart.

While the OMC has been hailed as a 'new mode of governance', it is fully consistent with these moves. Vertically, the method slipped easily into the growing academic discourse about 'multi-level governance', seeing European action less as a transnational decision-making exercise than an ongoing and cooperative engagement in policy review. Horizontally, it equally stands in line with an effort by the Union, and its courts, to create economic and social objectives which can successfully cohabit. While the method has been seen as a way of 'balancing' a Treaty framework that privileges 'market-making' policies, its most consistent narrative has been that social policy in Europe, if it is to succeed, must complement, not challenge, processes of economic integration.

For those faithful to the idea of the 'economic constitution', this move can only lead to anxiety. In so much as the Treaty structure sought to separate out a transnational economy from the social politics of the member states, the OMC is truly undermining the paradigm of 'integration through law'.[117] This fear is increased if we see the method as a neoliberal policy instrument. The more open coordination succeeds in 'piercing the veil' of the nation state, the more access the economic programmes of the EU are likely to have to the solidaristic core of the national welfare state. I have characterised this reading as 'colonisation' – the belief that new governance is part of an implicit functional political programme.

Our optimism for the method (and even for new governance more generally) may depend on an inversion of this reading. While it seems clear that the OMC 'integrates' national social policy with the project of constructing an internal market, if it can also encourage the reflexive

[117] See Joerges, n. 5 above, at 5–9; M. Cappelletti, M. Seccombe and J. Weiler (eds.), *Integration Through Law* (Berlin: De Gruyter, 1986).

consideration of social and economic goals – the sovereignty of a national policy discourse that is also open to the outside – the colonising instrument of the OMC could yet be read as a benevolent structure. This book will not, of course, leave these questions unanswered, but return to them. Only in considering the distinction between 'reflexivity' and 'colonisation' in the concrete circumstances of a particular OMC process and policy field can they really begin to be answered. As a consequence, the question of the OMC social contribution will be taken up again in the empirical analysis of the OMC SPSI conducted in Chapter 4.

Either way, the continued revision of the Lisbon strategy towards 2020, and the pursuit of 'Social Europe' under conditions of economic globalisation is likely to pose further challenges to the legal framework of the Union. The question of the EU's new 'economic constitution', under conditions of social and economic interdependency, remains an open one.

2 Relating governance and law

1. Introduction

The academic debate over new governance contains one aspect that may be surprising or even counter-intuitive to those approaching it for the first time. While new governance is most often seen as a political or administrative project, it has been defined through the categories and distinctions of law.[1] This shouldn't be. The Lisbon European Council decided that the OMC should be non-binding, and therefore not subject to the normal role of courts in practising judicial supervision and review. There are few cases in which the method has been discussed, and none in which its principal recommendations have been overturned. If governance lacks jurisprudence (the lifeblood of legal practice), then of what concern is it to the categories and distinctions of law?

At the same time – for something so far away – it is remarkable how much of the governance debate has been considered and defined in legal terms. Legal academics have probed the basic design and structures of governance, to the extent that much of the debate in which it is immersed has revolved around a limited number of influential legal studies. These studies have contrasted two projects; on the one hand, the attempt to 'constitutionalise' the EU through more clearly mapping the boundaries of European and national action – a project that has now metamorphosised into the present Lisbon Treaty – and on the other, the

[1] For brief evidence of this, see the articles cited below (e.g. by Christian Joerges and Jurgen Neyer, Michelle Everson, Charles Sabel, Christophe Möllers, Gráinne de Búrca, Joanne Scott and David Trubek). Those at the forefront of the governance debate have often been – and continue to be – European, public, international or administrative lawyers.

development in Europe of a multi-level governance structure (in which competences have been divided and shared). Lawyers have in a key sense set the terms of the policy debate *in the absence of law*; or, at the very least, in the absence of what we have traditionally understood by that concept.

How can this interest be explained? Is governance outside legal categories – something peripheral to the process of 'legal integration proper'? Or is there something in the new governance project of direct relevance not only to the legal discipline, but to how its boundaries have been shifting? This chapter will argue in favour of this latter explanation. While political science has probed the functional tasks carried out through the OMC, lawyers have observed in such methods something pulling at the boundaries of legal obligation and, in many cases, taking over or displacing legal functions. They have seen – as the historical story has illustrated – that the problems the OMC respond to also implicate the status and future of European law in a wider sense.

This purpose of this chapter is to explore why this is the case. What lessons do governance and the OMC provide for the place of law in the European integration process, and what role might legal institutions play in supplementing or limiting the operations of new governance? In the most basic terms, what is the emerging relationship in the EU between governance and law?

Structurally, this task will begin (in section 2) through drawing a basic conceptual distinction. To talk about the relationship between 'governance' and 'law' at all implies an externality between the two – that we see the categories and features of each as distinguishable, either in the EU, or at the level of the nation state. This is not, however, a position that should be taken as given. There are important schools of thinking (introduced in this chapter, and developed in the next) who have urged us to see governance as something 'inside' legal categories – adapting or 'transforming' legal structures and institutions to take account of a more fractured, complex or differentiated political reality.[2] The inside/outside distinction the chapter will develop may be crude but it can allow a mapping exercise between different positions in the governance debate to be conducted. What

[2] For three schools – proceduralism, deliberative polyarchy and reflexive law – see sections 2.1, 3.1 and 4.1 of Chapter 3.

are the basic structures which draw the various branches of 'new governance' together?

In section 3, the chapter will move onto more critical terrain. While the dominant 'outside' position may be a useful way of articulating what it is, for example, about new governance that can properly said to be 'new', it displays telling weaknesses. Building on the arguments of the first chapter, the section will argue that the terms of the new governance debate have often been based on an over stylisation of the differences between concepts which should be understood in terms of their emerging relationship with each other. 'Governance' and 'law' are not distinct projects, but instead categories that have evolved from common pressures of functional specialisation and territorial differentiation in the EU order. Just as the last chapter of the book argued for a 'continuity' between the OMC and other forms of social law, so this chapter will argue that 'outside' approaches run the risk of downplaying the significant interrelations between 'hard' and 'soft' legal methods.

This argument opens the door to other readings. Section 4 will develop a critical account of both the difficulties and opportunities that a procedural or 'inside' understanding of the law/governance relationship might bring forward. This 'inside' reading – to be developed in Chapter 3 – argues that, rather than see new governance as an extra-legal development, methods like the OMC should be conceptualised as an *internal* response of the EU's legal system to processes of social and political change. In such an environment, important legal and political concepts, like accountability and the rule of law, are not only under threat, but in a process of ongoing reformulation.

Finally, the chapter will consider the limits of such an 'inside' approach. While 'governance' and 'law' cannot be seen as static categories, it is not yet clear whether 'inside' approaches can resuscitate the core normative values of the EU as a legal order, or whether instead, such accounts merely provide academic justifications for the centralisation of executive power and sidelining of democratic institutions critics of the OMC allege it has created. An adequate conceptualisation of OMC-like methods must go further, both considering the internal inconsistencies of such 'inside' approaches, and analysing the practice of new governance processes themselves. These two tasks – one conceptual; the other empirical – will be the focus of the third and fourth chapters of this book.

2. Theorising governance in law

2.1 Outside theories: governance as external to law

It would be difficult to argue with the statement that governance is a hard term to pin down. Explicitly, it sets itself against the idea of a central authoritative actor, while still suggesting steering of some kind. Beyond this vague intuition, the term is conceptually unclear.[3]

The debate over new governance has often suffered a similar fate. Deprived of any other common ground with which to link processes like comitology and the OMC, new governance has been articulated through opaque concepts (such as 'differentiated integration' or 'networked governance'). Alternatively, it has sought to define itself negatively, encouraging us to see the shared features of 'new governance' through their differences to law traditionally understood.

It is from this negative division that 'outside' theories have emerged. Their common starting point is that governance and law should be seen as external to one another, in carrying different conceptions of both the mechanisms and end points of the EU's integration process. Perhaps the most popular means of drawing the distinction has been through a contrast between 'new governance' – epitomised by the development of the European Employment Strategy from 1997 – and the project of creating an overarching Constitutional Treaty (CT) for the EU.[4] These two projects – one of developing a functional but differentiated procedure for agreeing European laws; the other creating a structure of foundational norms – are posited by outside theories as offering different views of the dynamics of the integration process.[5]

To do this argument justice requires a closer analysis of the differences between the two projects. At one level, they share important common features. The *White Paper on Governance*, which represented the official response of the Commission to the development of the

[3] For an attempt to provide clarity, see C. Möllers, 'European Governance: Meaning and Value of a Concept' (2006) 43 *Common Market Law Review* 2.

[4] G. de Búrca, 'The Constitutional Challenge of New Governance in the European Union' (2003) 28 *European Law Review* 6; G de Búrca and J. Scott, *Law and New Governance in the EU and US* (Oxford: Hart, 2006). See also the use of the legislative/non-legislative distinction in A. Héretier, 'New Modes of Governance in Europe: Policy-making without Legislating?' in Héretier (ed.), *Common Goods: Reinventing European and International Governance* (Lanham: Rowman and Littlefield, 2002).

[5] J. Scott and D. Trubek, 'Mind the Gap: Law and New Approaches to Governance in the European Union' (2002) 8 *European Law Journal* 1, 5–6.

OMC, spoke (like the CT) of a functional division of power between the European institutions.[6] Constitutionalism and governance are engaged in a similar project insofar as they both attempt to find new ways of forwarding political integration through institutional and procedural redesign (rather than – in the case of the internal market programme – through a particular functional project).

There are, however, overwhelming differences. The first and most obvious concerns the question of competence. Whereas the European Employment Strategy (EES) – as stated in the last chapter – was developed in areas where the EU's competences to act are weak – the Constitutional project explicitly set itself against this way of conducting integration. In its most famous sections, the Constitutional Treaty created a competence catalogue – now found in Articles 3 to 6 of the Treaty – attempting to set out at which level different powers should be held in the EU (and giving the ECJ the task of enforcing its division).[7]

The EES, by contrast, has sought to be multi-level. 'Policy-making' under the strategy involves a sharing of norm-making power between the European institutions (which set out overall goals and targets) and the member states (who are responsible for implementing these goals through national legislation). The question that the Constitutional Treaty sought to clarify – of who in Europe is responsible for creating European legislation and in what areas – is largely deferred, or left open.[8] In this 'law-generative' sense, constitutionalism and new governance would seem to be antithetical projects.

[6] 'To deliver better policies, the Union must revitalise the Community method. Everyone should concentrate on their core tasks: the Commission initiates and executes policy; the Council and the European Parliament decide on legislation and budgets, the European Council exerts political guidance and the European Parliament controls the execution of the budget and of the Union's policies.' *European Governance: A White Paper*, COM (2001) 428 final at 29. For a critique of this US-style 'separation of powers' aspiration, see G. Majone, 'The Future of the Union: Montesquieu versus Madison' in Majone, *Dilemmas of European Integration* (Oxford University Press, 2005). For a wider critical reading of the White Paper, see C. Joerges et al., 'Mountain or Molehill: A Critical Appraisal of the Commission White Paper on Governance' (2001) *Jean Monnet Working Papers* 6.

[7] Title III, Draft Treaty Establishing a Constitution for Europe, 2003.

[8] Indeed this is seen as the OMC's specific achievement – see Jonathan Zeitlin's argument in 'Social Europe and Experimentalist Governance: Towards a New Constitutional Compromise?' in G. de Búrca (ed.), *EU Law and the Welfare State: In Search of Solidarity* (Oxford University Press, 2005).

This difference may be belied by a second division; a difference in the respective 'objects of analysis' or methodology of the two projects.[9] The distinction between law and governance, for outside theories, goes to the heart of how integration in Europe should be analysed and evaluated. For such theories, governance – and the academic debate it has provoked – has succeeded in bringing to light realities that more abstract studies of constitutionalism have often ignored. Whereas legal academics, for example, have often seen Europe through its most 'fundamental' public law conflicts (i.e. the competing authority claims of national and European courts), analysis of governance takes us to a different level – to an 'underworld' of regulatory practice.[10]

In this world, no one actor or institution can achieve their goals alone, but have to harness the cognitive resources of different bodies in order to succeed. In comitology, for example, the need constantly to integrate technical and scientific information has necessitated a delegation of authority to committees, who reflect neither the preferences of their 'governing' institution (the Commission), nor the will of the member states (whose representatives man their committees).[11] In this messy regulatory space, the ebb and flow of 'ever closer Union', the content of the Treaties, and the jurisprudence of its guardian court, count for little. The everyday business of integration ducked beneath the headlights of the official constitutional structure, just as President D'Estaing and his colleagues ascended to the ether.

This difference is underlined when the two worlds ('constitutional' and 'functional') come into contact. This contact is undeniable. Comitology, for example, has been a long-standing part of EU law, and was partly codified through Council Decision 87/373/EEC, now Decision 2006/512/EC. 'Outside' theories seem to run counter to the reality of a regular interchange between law and the governance processes (such as comitology and regulatory agencies) that are under its supervision. While such outside theories do not deny that such interaction exists, this interaction can also easily be seen as a rejection, or misconstruction, of what the other really means.

9 On this aspect, see K. Armstrong, *Governing Social Inclusion: Europeanization through Policy Coordination* (Oxford University Press, 2010) at 229–262.

10 J. Weiler, 'Epilogue: "Comitology" as Revolution – Infranationalism, Constitutionalism and Democracy' in C. Joerges and E. Vos (eds.), *EU Committees: Social Regulation, Law and Politics* (Oxford: Hart, 1999).

11 C. Joerges and J. Neyer, 'From Inter-Governmental Bargaining to Deliberative Political Processes: The Constitutionalisation of Comitology' (1997) 3 *European Law Journal* 3.

The ECJ, for example, through its *Meroni* jurisprudence, has either drawn comitology into one of the EU institutions (i.e. seen it as simply a part of the Commission) or ignored it altogether.[12] The gap between the law of the Treaties and the practice of new governance is such that the two can only coalesce through an attitude of mutual ignorance. The principles of supremacy and institutional balance can remain because they selectively disregard those institutions which blur institutional boundaries, while the OMC can develop and expand because – as the *White Paper on Governance* we will go on to examine puts it – it operates only in areas where action under the Community method is impossible.[13] As long as the paradox is not confronted, the two may go on largely as they are.

The problem of course is when this paradox is revealed. We can observe this at three different levels. Below the level of the nation state, regional governments (like the German Lander) complain that the reporting requirements of each OMC cycle have succeeded in gradually centralising the framing of national policy towards the federal level.[14] Between the nation state and the Union, national governments have wondered whether the OMC (through creating coordination structures) contravenes Article 5 of the TFEU, and the principle that the EU does not have the right to determine its own competences.[15] At the EU level, meanwhile, the European Parliament has asked how a decade-long expansion of its influence can be squared with its almost complete exclusion from the formulation of the OMC's functional priorities.[16] These three inter-locked objections illustrate how,

[12] As Scott and Trubek argue, the courts here, 'squeeze new governance into law's existing categories in order that the woeful inadequacy of law's traditional tool-kit – for example, judicial review of decisions in conditions of complexity and uncertainty – may remain unspoken'. See n. 5 above, at 18.

[13] *White Paper on Governance*, n. 6 above, at 22.

[14] For an example in the context of social inclusion, see M. Büchs and D. Friedrich, 'Surface Integration: The National Action Plans for Employment and Social Inclusion in Germany' in J. Zeitlin and P. Pochet (eds.), *The Open Method of Coordination in Action: The European Employment and Social Inclusion Strategies* (Bern: Peter Lang, 2005). See, for a more in-depth analysis of regional and local exclusion under the OMC SPSI, Chapter 4, section 4.3.

[15] See e.g. the concerns expressed by the working groups of the constitutional convention, n. 20 below

[16] See, for an early case, the defensive response of the EP's Committee on Constitutional Affairs to the Governance White Paper at www.europarl.europa.eu/meetdocs/committees/afco/20011112/446181EN.pdf. See also, more recently, the highly sceptical Resolution of the European Parliament 'On the Institutional and Legal Implications of the Use of Soft Law Instruments' 2007/2028(INI).

at each level, subtle pressures upon the EU's constitutional structures have been brought to bear.

In spite of this pressure, the institutions of the Union have continued to promote the idea of difference. In 2001, when the Commission published its first official response to 'the governance turn' in integration through its *White Paper on Governance*, it encouraged an 'outside' view. Like previous European Councils, it recognised the potential of the OMC in achieving particular tasks, for example, by building up the coordination of social and employment policies where ordinarily forbidden under the Treaties.[17] What the OMC could not do, however, was represent a replacement. The presence of 'coordination' could only be useful where not subject to the constitutional constraints imposed by the Treaties. At the same time, the achievements of the foundational texts in creating a law-bound community would only be undermined where the method coexisted in areas where ordinary 'hard law' applied. The two ought to be kept conceptually and functionally apart.[18] The positive contribution of governance can be preserved only through difference (i.e. through its separate functional and procedural role from 'ordinary' community law-making).

Joseph Weiler, for example, has similarly argued that, in comitology, the insistence by the Court for the formal delegating responsibility of the Council has often privileged the formal actors in the process above more unrecognised participants.[19] Similarly, the Working Groups examining the open method in the context of the Constitutional Convention worried that constitutional inclusion or adjudication might come at the expense of the flexibility of OMC processes, or their capacity to take on board new constellations of actors.[20] By this argument, if we insist on viewing governance through law, or through the traditional categories of constitutionalism, we risk doing damage either to the novelty of its processes, or its own 'constitutional self', i.e. the way in which the OMC has developed its own distinct forms of

[17] *White Paper on Governance*, n. 7 above, at 21.

[18] 'The use of the open method of co-ordination must not dilute the achievement of common objectives in the Treaty or the political responsibility of the Institutions. It should not be used when legislative action under the Community method is possible.' *Ibid*. at 22.

[19] Weiler, n. 10 above, at 5.

[20] See Final Report of Working Group VI on Economic Governance, CONV 357/02 (2003), at 5. See also G. de Búrca & J. Zeitlin, 'Constitutionalising the Open Method of Co-ordination: What Should the Convention Propose?' (2003) *CEPS Policy Brief* 1.

legitimacy. Here outside theories develop a more normative argument about what the 'gap' between governance and law can achieve.

On the other hand, this normative argument cuts both ways. Whereas some see the difference between governance and law as positive, for others, it is potentially malign. As much as governance could supplement existing legal structures, it could also hollow them out, acting as a channel to which policies ordinarily agreed under established legal methods are increasingly diverted. While under the former view, methods like the OMC are improving the effectiveness and legitimacy of European law, under the latter they represent a retreat from legality; a rejection of law-mediated power in favour of a more malleable and instrumental form of rule. If there is (as Scott and Trubek term it) a 'gap' between governance and law, what is this gap really doing?

In the next section, these differences will be considered through a two-fold axis. The first is functional – what can new governance methods like the OMC offer that traditional EU law cannot. This may, of course, be either a positive or a negative contribution. Does the OMC allow greater steering power, or does it steer only at the expense of other values (e.g. legality, democratic legitimacy and so on)? The second is procedural – what are the opportunities (and dangers) which the law/governance relation might offer for the constitutional structure of the EU? The same point applies – whereas new governance could offer a beneficial 'constitutional compromise', it could also be seen as further exacerbating the Union's democratic and social deficits. 'Inside' accounts may be joined by a conceptual exclusion of governance from law – yet the implications they draw from this move illustrate a failure to agree on its meaning.

2.2. Between complementarity and agonism: what do outside theories mean?

For many theorists of the OMC, the difference between governance and law is not only important in allowing us to understand governance better, but presents particular functional advantages. The notion of a complementary gap between law and governance is based on such an argument. It relies in this sense on two things; firstly, an idea about what governance can do that 'traditional' forms of Union law cannot; and secondly, on the notion that this difference could be *mutually* beneficial.

Most commonly, the argument begins from the conceptual distinctions which the comparison between governance and constitutionalism has drawn – the dynamism of new governance, its multi-level structure, or the exclusion of methods like the OMC from the instruments of hierarchical control that constitutionalism embodies. These differences, such theorists argue, may allow functional tasks to be carried out which traditional legal mechanisms could not achieve on their own. Often these tasks cross over boundaries, either in implying the integration of complex scientific or technical advice, or in creating externalities between member states.

In environmental protection, for example, the assessment of what product or project is dangerous differs between local contexts, and is likely to require the input of officials other than judges or parliamentarians.[21] To this extent, the use of formal legislation – politically agreed, uniformly applied, and interpreted according to a static single text – is unlikely to achieve the intended results. It is in the context of these constraints – and attempts to overcome them – that many new governance processes first arose. The first – comitology – was created by a council that quickly realised its inadequacies in the face of complex regulatory decisions.[22] Just as, at the national level, calls for executive discretion, and the use of secondary legislation, grew in keeping with growth in the state's regulatory tasks, so in the EU system, the expansion in EU competences brought by successive treaties has created a demand for more specialised bodies. It is precisely because these institutions illustrate a relative independence from the static and hierarchical model of institutional accountability, that they are able to function effectively.[23] The difference between governance and law is – in this case – productive.

More sceptical accounts on the other hand see precisely these trends as illustrating why the turn to governance ought to be resisted. The gap between governance and law is agonistic in so much as the expansion of

[21] For more on this example in the context of this section, see J. Scott and J. Holder, 'Law and New Environmental Governance in the European Union', in de Búrca and Scott (eds.), n. 4 above; P. Cottrell and D. Trubek, 'The Law of Global Space: Rethinking the Legalization of World Politics' (2010) *Wisconsin Legal Studies Research Paper Series* 1124 at 26–31.

[22] E. Vos, 'The Rise of Committees' (1997) 3 *European Law Journal* 3 at 211–212.

[23] A good example in this regard may be the development of regulatory agencies, which attempt not only to provide informational and scientific input into the legislative process, but also to conduct decision-making in areas where hierarchical political control is deemed inappropriate. See M. Everson and G. Majone, 'Institutional Reform: Independent Agencies, Oversight, Coordination and Procedural Control', in O. de Schutter, N. Lebessis and J. Paterson (eds.), *Governance in the European Union* (Luxembourg: Office for Official Publications of the European Communities, 2001).

new governance (and the OMC) has gone hand in hand with a retreat of law to the periphery of the integration process. As the OMC has grown to include more and more fields (including those where the EU has 'complementary' competences) the relevance and place of Union law is increasingly being lost.[24] EU law is colonised by functional logics (about how to adapt policies to new scientific, economic and social information) that could precisely deplete law's ability to *restrain* political or economic power, subjecting it to procedural constraints.[25] The procedural guarantees which ordinary European law can offer, by this view, cannot simply be bought and sold according to whether they achieve instrumental goals, just as the right to take an institution or member state to court for its failure to meet policy obligations cannot be sacrificed in the name of flexibility. Such a right is no less than a basic requirement of due process.[26]

Such theorists have therefore wondered whether the opposition between governance and constitutionalism is in fact an invasion from the outside – a colonisation of a legal discourse – in which what counts is the authority of law's rule (or its ability to structure conduct in advance) – by a technical discourse, over what is possible or efficacious. Does the demand of legal adaptation leave law with a distinct normative character, or does governance treat legality instead merely as an instrument to reach other ends?[27] For many lawyers, this is the reality of OMC-like methods – their inability to mediate practice through rules; the effective giving up of law *by* law; makes the gap between governance and law a dangerous one.

In the *White Paper on Governance* both of these readings came to the fore. On the one hand, the capacity of governance to expand the steering power of the community was recognised; on the other, the Commission saw the governance project as posing an explicit threat to its institutional role. The OMC was thus praised 'as a way of encouraging co-operation, the exchange of best practice and agreeing common targets and guidelines for Member States'. Yet it was also cast as a threat,

[24] See V. Hatzopoulos, 'Why the Open Method of Coordination is Bad for You: A Letter to the EU' (2007) 13 *European Law Journal* 3 at 319–323.

[25] E.g. the duty to consult different institutions.

[26] For an overview of these concerns, see C. Joerges, 'Integration through De-legislation? An Irritated Heckler' (2007) *European Governance Papers* 3.

[27] This is quite concisely put by Möllers – (in governance), 'legality is not an expression of democratic self-determination and liberal respect for individual rights, it is an instrument.' See n. 3 above, at 7.

capable of 'upsetting the institutional balance' or 'diluting the political responsibility of the institutions'.[28]

In as much as the differences between governance and law provided functional advantages, they also threatened the hard won autonomy of the Commission, and with it, the Union's existing constitutional and institutional balance. Where they are to be used, the Commission argued, methods like comitology, the OMC and the social dialogue must be put to the service of the Community method (not the other way round); focusing on 'strengthening' and 'revitalising' classical community law.[29] The danger of an agonistic relation between governance and law was recognised insofar as methods like the OMC were pushed to the periphery of EU action. For functional sceptics like the Prodi Commission, it was only here that they could play a fruitful role.

The ambiguity begins, in this example at least, to take on explicit constitutional and procedural dimensions. This is another point of division within outside theories; how are the differences between governance and law reflected in the constitutional structure of the EU? Do they leave that structure untouched, or have processes like the OMC begun to subvert Europe's delicate constitutional balance?

In its attempt to answer these questions, the governance debate has (predictably) been swept up into the traditional dichotomy of integration studies – between supra-national and neo-functional theories on the one hand, and intergovernmental accounts on the other. On the other hand, for some proponents, the virtue of governance methods is that they can precisely *avoid* this dichotomy. Instruments like comitology cannot be reduced to the preferences of member states, but nor can they be viewed as a mouthpiece for powerful central actors.[30] The OMC is not merely a form of intergovernmental negotiation, but neither does it 'Europeanise' altogether the policy fields in which it operates. It is better seen as a pragmatic 'constitutional compromise'; one whose very advantage lies in its ability to move beyond the present impasse associated with competing claims of authority.[31] The OMC balances national and supra-national concerns by seeing decision-making as less a question of 'finding the ultimate arbiter of a legal conflict' than one of political negotiation (or deliberation) between different levels of

[28] *White Paper on Governance*, n. 6 above, at 21–22. [29] *Ibid.*, at 8.
[30] See Joerges and Neyer, n. 11 above, at 287–290. [31] Zeitlin, n. 8 above.

authority (deliberative supra-nationalism).[32] The constitutional structure is preserved in new governance because no particular actor is ever seen as decisive.[33]

For opponents, this is merely a language; a means of marketing a more underhand rebalancing of how integration is managed. Why, they insist, would the EU develop the OMC if it did not see potential steering opportunities, or a capacity to build alliances, and develop a policy infrastructure, in fields previously ruled out of reach? The flip side of the method's ability to allow European action in areas previously reserved to the member states is the abandonment of that settlement's most basic principle – the idea that the EU cannot itself determine the range of its powers.[34]

Avoiding the 'hard' sanctions of European law does not mean that the constitutional structure is left as it is, but simply provides new means to divert our attention from what Majone famously termed 'integration by stealth'.[35] Such a position can be held by sceptics and fans of the European project alike. While for Europhiles, the method represents a retreat to intergovernmental bargaining, for Eurosceptics, it could allow supra-national institutions to set goals and targets, and create administrative networks, in areas previously reserved to the states (even thereby paving the way for formal transfers of competence in the future).[36] The intergovernmental/supra-national dichotomy is not sidestepped; instead a new battleground is opened up.

In these terms, opponents are almost pushing on an open door. Proponents of 'complementarity' face an 'efficacy paradox'. On the

[32] C. Joerges. 'Deliberative Supra-nationalism: Two Defences' (2002) 8 *European Law Journal* 1; see also Joerges and Neyer, n. 11 above.

[33] See L. Hooghe and G. Marks , *Multi-level Governance and European Integration* (Lanham: Rowman and Littlefield, 2001).

[34] See Art. 5 TEU. See S. Smismans, 'EU Employment Policy: Decentralization or Centralization through the Open Method of Coordination?' (2004) *EUI Working Papers (Law)* 1. For the contrary position – that the OMC in fact represents a form of 'reverse competence creep' – see Hatzopolous, n. 24 above, at 318. Arguably, such a concern is reinforced by the most recent Lisbon judgment of the Bundesverfassungsgericht.

[35] See Majone, n. 6 above.

[36] For the OMC as a retreat to a more managed form of intergovernmental negotiation, see (rather unsurprisingly) A. Moravscik, 'The European Constitutional Compromise and the Neo-Functionalist Legacy' (2005) 13 *Journal of European Public Policy* 2. For an attempt to conceptualise the Europeanisation capacities of the OMC, and governance more generally, see Möllers, n. 3 above, at 12–18; D. Hodson and I. Maher, 'The Open Method of Coordination as a New Mode of Governance: the Case of Soft Economic Policy Coordination' (2001) 39 *Journal of Common Market Studies* 4.

one hand, they have to prove that the OMC can be effective in bringing about policy changes (that it can reach even into domestic political cultures); on the other, they have to prove that it is not *too effective*, i.e. that existing institutional practices and structures are not overridden. The OMC has to generate power in order to be credible, yet the more it does so, the more the question of its illegitimate use is likely to be asked.[37] Opponents can either cast the OMC as a 'paper tiger' or if the beast is truly real, a threat to law's legitimate and independent normative authority.

This undoubtedly leaves us with a rather unattractive choice. If governance and law are conceptually distinct, do we either accept a naive complementarity between the two, or do we see them in conflict? On the first reading, governance merely 'runs alongside' law (complementarity); in the second, it is in competition with it (the relation is agonistic; two fighters competing for the same prize).[38] This is the dilemma to which 'outside theories' seem to lead.

Yet is it a choice we have to make? As Charles Sabel has wondered, the distinction begins, under this scenario, increasingly to become either/or: 'either new governance with its capacity to contextualise and update rules, or the rule of law, by means of stable and constraining rules'.[39] The choice is imposed upon us, however, only where the dichotomy is retained, i.e. where governance and law are seen as antagonistic projects, not interdependent ones; where they are cast as elements of a different functional or procedural enterprise.

As the next section will explore, however, there is now a weight of empirical and theoretical evidence available to cast doubts on this claim. While processes like the OMC – when treated in isolation – may seem divorced from 'classical' EU law, and from a hierarchical constitutional structure, the practice of new governance illustrates a more complex, nuanced and area-specific reality. Governance and law may be interlinked or congruent, either in creating 'hybrid' institutions, or in carrying forward Europe's most vital regulatory tasks into a more complex post-national arena. While the distinction between

[37] For an account that tackles the question of power under both the OMC, and the framework of 'directly-deliberative polyarchy', see P. Kjaer, '3 Forms of Governance; 3 Forms of Power' in E. Erikssen, C. Joerges and F. Roedl, *Law, Democracy and Solidarity in a Post-national Union* (London: Routledge, 2008).

[38] I.e. the right to be the *modus operandi* of the integration project.

[39] C. Sabel and W. Simon, 'Epilogue: Accountability Without Sovereignty', in de Búrca and Scott (eds.), n. 4 above, at 397.

governance and constitutionalism has thus allowed the very novelty of 'new' governance to emerge; it has also concealed too much; hiding from view many of the legal and structural pre-conditions which have made the development of a 'governance architecture' for the EU credible. The task of the next section will be to reveal important limits to the 'outside' thesis; limits which may allow new readings of the law/governance relationship to emerge.

3. The problem with outside approaches

Outside theories rely on a certain 'rationality' gap between law and the practice of new governance. Whereas one is associated with formal rules – hierarchically designed and applied – the other is an explicit opt-out from this process. One of the reasons why 'new modes of governance' have aroused such intense academic and institutional interest is their perceived conceptual innovation: differences posited as offering important advantages compared to a static and inflexible model of legal rule.

The danger of course is that these distinctions are over-stylised.[40] By defining governance as 'whatever is outwith classical methods', we leave open the possibility: (a) that we conflate processes that are quite different, (b) that we celebrate as 'new' what is in fact long-established, or (c) that we ignore the interrelations between the law and governance (or between 'hard' and 'soft' law). While the differences between governance and constitutionalism may have allowed us to say 'what it is about governance that is different', they could also be taken too far, either in ignoring the continuities between governance processes and their historical precursors, or in downplaying the obvious interactions between classical Community law and supposed 'governance alternatives'.

Accounts emphasising 'hybridity' between law and new governance have developed from this argument.[41] The new, they insist, may be nested in the old, just as the processes of the OMC may illustrate a

[40] See N. Walker, 'Constitutionalism and New Governance in the European Union: Rethinking the Boundaries', in de Búrca and Scott (eds.), n. 4 above.

[41] see D. Trubek and L. Trubek, 'Hard and Soft Law in the Construction of Social Europe: The Role of the Open Method of Co-ordination' (2005) 11 *European Law Journal* 3; D. Trubek, P. Cottrell and M. Nance, 'Soft Law, Hard Law and European Integration: Toward a Theory of Hybridity' in de Búrca and Scott (eds.), n. 4 above; D. Trubek and L. Trubek, 'New Governance and Legal Regulation: Complementarity, Rivalry and Transformation' (2007) 13 *Columbia Journal of European Law* 3.

close and reciprocal relationship with traditional legal institutions. More often than not, we do not see a freestanding 'governance structure' in contra-distinction to a legal one, but significant continuities between the two; the presence of processes that combine 'hard' and 'soft' elements.

3.1 *The integration of governance and law*

Trubek, Cotterrell and Nance point out two examples of this hybridity – employment policy and macro-economic coordination.[42] In the first, hard directives on anti-discrimination and health and safety at work have combined with monitoring and review structures under the EES. In the second, soft coordination under the Broad Economic Policy Guidelines has worked in tandem with fixed rules that set out definitions and sanctions for inflationary 'excessive deficits'; rules that have been strengthened following the legislative package proposed by the Commission in 2010.[43]

The two display a particular combination – in the first instance, there is a functional division between governance and law; the directives create general principles and goals that can be 'filled out' through national coordination later on. Soft law supplements hard law because it creates an ongoing monitoring and review structure for anti-discrimination above and beyond the mere formal commitment by member states to implement a static text.[44] In the second instance, monetary union, the functional division can be seen the other way around. Governance does not serve law, allowing it to interact more closely with evolving national strategies, but law instead acts as a 'latent

[42] *Ibid.*

[43] This functional division is between the multilateral procedure set down in Art. 121 TFEU and the excessive deficit procedure specified under Art. 126 TFEU. On the most recent legislative package (which would significantly strengthen the sanctions applied under the procedure, see Proposal for a Regulation 'On the Effective Enforcement of Budgetary Surveillance in the Euro Area', COM (2010) 524 final; Proposal for a Regulation 'On Enforcement Measures to Correct Excessive Macro-economic Imbalances in the Euro Area', COM (2010) 525 final.

[44] See Directive 43/2000/EC 'Implementing the Principle of Equal Treatment Between Persons Irrespective of Racial or Ethnic Origin [2000] O.J. L 180/22; Directive 78/2000/EC 'Establishing a General Framework for Equal Treatment in Employment and Occupation' [2000] O.J. L 303/16; Directive 113/2004/EC 'Implementing the Principle of Equal Treatment Between Men and Women in the Access to and Supply of Goods and Services [2004] O.J. L 373/37. On the interaction between these directives and soft law governance, see G. de Búrca, 'EU Race Discrimination Law: a Hybrid Model?' in de Búrca, and Scott, n. 4 above.

threat', operating in the background to ensure that those failing to take their commitments seriously also face the more real threat of judicial sanction (and with it, hefty financial penalties). OMC-style procedures are thus entrusted – under the economic policy guidelines – with ensuring budgetary stability only on the basis that hard law measures – the stability and growth pact – apply in cases of default. As Fritz Scharpf has suggested, governance operates here 'in the shadow' of legal hierarchy.[45]

The relationship between the two is cast in this light as an example of functional hybridity. The EU must draw on two elements – both the need to coordinate diversity (to accommodate the specific factors which lead to budgetary problems while avoiding policies that are mutually destabilising) and the need to deter and constrain self-interested behaviour. It must require formal implications for default but equally encourage states to reform through positive incentives to do so. As Trubek, Cotterrell and Nance put it:

> Given these varied and possibly conflicting goals, it is no surprise that the Union has sought to draw on both hard and soft methods and processes, and to marry them in a single system.[46]

It is this marriage that empirical evidence of hybridity suggests. Governance and law are not external to one another, not only because they interact, but because they cohabit in a single system.

As Imelda Maher has argued, the economic policy example illustrates the empirical reality of an 'integrated' law/governance relation in most cases.[47] Soft measures link and compare different national practices, while hard ones encourage governments to commit to overall programmes. Governments (and other parties) are able to engage in a learning process because they know that their commitment to exercising fiscal discipline will not be to their disadvantage; equally, they may sign up to potentially costly legal programmes in the knowledge that they themselves will be in a position to steer the process of adapting European policies in light of their own national commitments and traditions. The open method is soft law, but it is 'operating within a legal framework', where one process potentially gains credibility by its

[45] F. Scharpf, 'Common Concerns versus the Challenges of Diversity', in Joerges *et al*, n. 6 above, at 11.

[46] Trubek, Cotterrell and Nance, n. 41 above, at 34.

[47] I. Maher, 'Law and the Open Method of Coordination: Towards a New Flexibility in European Policy-making?' (2004) 2 *Zeitschrift für Staats- und Europawissenschaften* 2.

association and grounding in the other.[48] The empirical picture of governance and law points less towards parallel structures than to a reciprocal or mutually enabling relation between the two.

In employment and social inclusion we can see a similar relationship emerging. While the open method has expanded significantly in both areas, this has not led to a quantitative decrease in the volume of traditional legislation.[49] Instead, the two have developed in tandem, and in combination with other incentives, such as the monetary rewards available through the European Social Fund (ESF) on the one hand, and Community Action Programme on Social Solidarity – 'Progress' – on the other.[50]

In one example, recent directives on race, age and disability discrimination have been matched by action points in the guidelines of the EES on how states should go about developing discrimination strategies.[51] Similarly, reform proposals for the ESF have encouraged its recalibration 'to support the European Employment Strategy and the National Action Plans for employment linked to it'.[52] The move towards integration has encouraged the use of different types of instrument in combination, constructing a policy edifice that includes both sanctioned commitments and processes of ongoing coordination. As Kilpatrick has argued, the view of the OMC as an alternative to 'hard' law may therefore 'overlook the extent to which integration of governance tools constitutes already, in a significant number of areas, actual practice'.[53]

De Bùrca and Scott have identified three models for this integration. Hard law has been used in conjunction with OMC-like methods, either as a 'baseline', setting out the most important rights and obligations, as

[48] *Ibid.*, at 6.

[49] See M. Rhodes, 'Employment Policy: Between Efficacy and Experimentation' in H. Wallace, W. Wallace and M. Pollack (eds.), *Policy Making in the European Union* (Oxford University Press, 2005).

[50] see C. Kilpatrick, 'New EU Employment Governance and Constitutionalism', in de Búrca and Scott (eds.), n. 4 above.

[51] The relevant directives are: (on race discrimination) Council Directive 43/2000/EC 'Implementing the Principle of Equal Treatment Between Persons Irrespective of Racial or Ethnic Origin' [2000] O.J. L 180; (on discrimination on grounds of age, disability and sexual orientation) Council Directive 78/2000/EC 'Establishing a General Framework for Equal Treatment in Employment and Occupation' [2000] O.J. L 303. For the relevant portion in the EES, see Council Decision 63/2001/EC 'On Guidelines for Member States' Employment Policies', Point 7.

[52] Preamble, Regulation 1784/99/EC On the European Social Fund [1999] O.J. L 336 (quoted in Kilpatrick, n. 50 above).

[53] Kilpatrick, n. 50 above, at 131.

a 'default', to be reverted to where the process breaks down, or as a 'developmental device', where governance fills out the substantive content of a legal regime.[54] The point with each is that governance and law cannot be presented as either/or: while governance is defined in contrast to hard law and constitutionalism, it is able to *maintain that difference* only because of its mutual integration within legal frameworks. Even if we see governance as a threat to law-mediated power, the extent to which this threat can be located entirely *outside* the legal medium is open to question.

3.2 *The congruence of governance and law*

In these hybrid accounts a further objection emerges (even if it is not always explicitly voiced). This objection questions whether governance and law are really as far apart as they seem.[55] It is not just that governance processes and community law 'interrelate' – such a notion maintains the original distinctions between the two by continuing to separate governance out through ideas about its adaptability or differentiation in relation to 'traditional' community law. Instead, it is that the distinction rests on differences that are often illusionary. 'Outside' approaches in this sense create a binary where the reality is that no one element sits on either extreme of the spectrum. The OMC shares things in common with 'hard', constitutionally authorised laws, just as traditional EU law may be softer and less hierarchical than it first appears.

Here, the historical story set out in the first chapter may be instructive.[56] It illustrates the origins of the OMC in the gradual proceduralisation of European social law in the 1980s and 1990s. In employment policy, 'hard' directives have both promoted heterarchy (through delegating certain decision-making functions to the social partners) and engendered flexibility (in providing broad targets that could be met by member states in different ways). By the time that the EES was created, conducting policy on a multi-level basis, with flexible implementation and few detailed provisions, was *already* standard practice in the employment and social inclusion domains.

[54] G. de Búrca and J. Scott, 'Introduction' to *Law and New Governance in the EU and US*, n. 4 above, 6–7.

[55] In the words of David and Louise Trubek, 'hard law may be softer than you think', just as soft law may sometimes take on a hierarchical and subtly coercive character. See n. 39 above, at 355–361.

[56] See Chapter 1, sections 3.1–3.3.

As Claire Kilpatrick has pointed out, here the EU has largely simply mimicked the way much of social and labour law functions at the national level. A more differentiated or 'procedural' solution to social problems has been a long-standing part of national practice, where the perils of central intervention by the national government has given way to the idea that social standards should be seen as part of an ongoing process of negotiation, contingent both upon economic conditions, and the bargaining power and demands of 'constitutionalised' social partners. As Claire Kilpatrick argues:

> Employment policies have never typically been associated with a hard law 'command and control' model. Instead, the governance tasks employment policies perform generally require, on the one hand, the spending of money, and on the other, the creation of guidelines, targets, indicators and plans in attempt to steer labour markets in directions considered desirable ... it should come as no surprise that employment policies at EU level similarly predominantly involve the same set of tools.[57]

A similar point can be made in the context of the debate over hard and soft law. The OMC is commonly described as a mere bureaucratic exercise (soft) because it does not carry the strong sanctions and incentives needed to drive through social reforms.[58] It is a transitive and weaker alternative, attempting to achieve reform through persuasion and the creation of common standards.[59] The alternative of a hierarchical, stable and centrally defined set of common rules is left out.

On the other hand, few commentators or practitioners now really see European law this way. The view of a hierarchical and self-applying legal order is widely recognised as mythical.[60] In the areas where the OMC is used, 'traditional' Union law has increasingly taken on soft colours in embracing framework directives, and delegating decision-making functions either downwards to national and sub-national authorities or sideways to European 'peak' organisations, like trade unions. In this sense, Union law – at least in the social field – has moved away from the model of a highly prescriptive regulator, towards

[57] See Kilpatrick, n. 50 above, at 124.

[58] See e.g. Fritz Scharpf's objections, n. 45 above.

[59] I.e. through the creation of common standards at an epistemic, rather than legal, level.

[60] On why, see the discussion of Sabel and Simon in section 4 below. See also, M. Dawson, 'EU Law Transformed? Evaluating Accountability and Subsidiarity in the "Streamlined" OMC for Social Inclusion and Social Protection' (2009) 13 *European Integration Online Papers* 1 at 3–6.

one where law takes responsibility primarily for the procedures by which national plans are developed. Law has relied upon the virtues of persuasion, diffusion and administrative networking which 'soft law' is also said to carry.

The issue of compliance adds a further dimension to this argument.[61] For all the controversies that this debate has produced, it has unveiled the unique dilemma the EU faces in bridging the gap between its political aspirations and the distinct legal systems of its member states. This problem arises from a specific difference. Whereas in the national context, the institutions which create legal programmes are also responsible for applying them, European institutions have to rely on national governments to implement common rules.[62] All European law in this sense faces significant gaps – in terms of how rules are interpreted and enforced, and even of possible 'cheating' on rational or normative grounds – between the rules set out in legislation, and the way law is implemented in national systems.

As Joerges and Zürn have discussed in a recent study, this does not make post-national law-making impossible.[63] Even in the absence of a statist monopoly on violence, or significant material resources, international studies have pointed to the willingness of states to implement norms in the absence of a coercive hierarchy. Yet, if laws are to be obeyed on this basis, they must operate through a different strategy. The implementation of transnational law is not achieved through the relaying of commands but involves persuading national actors of the benefits of transnational programmes, and their applicability to the structures and norms that have already been developed in the nation state.

In this context, many accounts have spoken of 'horizontalisation'; the need to apply rules through the development of a partnership between

[61] This is obviously a cursory treatment of the compliance issue for a specific purpose. For a more in-depth overview, see the essays contained in J. A. E. Vervaele (ed.), *Compliance and Enforcement of European Community Law* (Alphen aan den Rijn: Kluwer Law, 1999). See also, T. Börzel, T. Hofmann, D. Panke and C. Sprungk, 'Obstinate and Inefficient: Why Member States do not comply with European Law' (2010) 43 *Comparative Political Studies* 11.

[62] Weiler thus invokes a distinction between a normative and material hierarchy: 'community norms trump conflicting member state norms but this hierarchy is not rooted in a hierarchy of normative authority or a hierarchy of real power. Indeed, European federalism is constructed with a top-to-bottom hierarchy of norms, but with a bottom-to-top hierarchy of authority.' J. Weiler, 'Federalism and Constitutionalism: Europe's *Sonderweg*' (2000) *Jean Monnet Working Papers* 10.

[63] M. Zürn and C. Joerges (eds.), *Law and Governance in Post-national Europe: Compliance Beyond the Nation-state* (Cambridge University Press, 2005).

different levels on authority, founded on a willingness to put common policies into practice.[64] This partnership is likely to include a range of actors, including private parties and sub-national or non-governmental organisations. It is not likely to be the hierarchical application of rules, but the ability to conduct effective negotiations between different actors in a policy community, that will lead to effective compliance.

If this is the case, some of the assumptions of the hard law model are again subverted. If there is no easy congruence between the creation of European laws and their application to national discourses; if the implementation of European rules (even binding regulations and directives) involves ongoing negotiation, delegation and review; in what sense is the hard/soft law distinction really useful? It would seem that while the issue of compliance has often represented a legal 'blind spot', it has thrown into relief the way in which European law has already developed specific structures for dealing with the challenges of diversity.

A similar argument has been advanced by Francis Snyder.[65] His famous 1993 essay on 'the effectiveness of European Community law' identified some of the EU's deficiencies in achieving compliance, and explicitly linked this problem to the creation of soft law. In the absence of clear mechanisms to enforce states to comply with directives, the Commission began to make use of non-binding measures such as declarations and communications. These measures were used as a device for negotiation; allowing the European institutions and member state governments to, 'identify what is settled and what is in dispute, circumscribe the arena for debate, and define the agenda for negotiation, and if necessary, litigation'.[66] They were used in essence not to exercise a binding authority on states (a power withheld from the Commission in the first place) but to open up a possible discussion about how common European programmes should be implemented.

In this sense, softer forms of negotiation, compromise and coordination sit on a continuum with harder ones.[67] Hierarchical instruments, and even Treaty provisions, rely for their effectiveness precisely on the structures of horizontal learning that the governance debate often uses

64 Horizontalisation is thus a trend towards negotiation; 'replacing relations of command and control by relations of negotiation between supposedly "equal" partners'. R. de Lange, 'General Aspects of the Horizontalization of Law Enforcement in a European Perspective', in Vervaele (ed.), n. 61 above, at 37.

65 F. Snyder, 'The Effectiveness of European Community Law: Institutions, Processes, Tools and Techniques' (1993) 56 *Modern Law Review* 1.

66 *Ibid.*, at 33. 67 See Maher, n. 47 above.

as an explicit contrast. While outside theories thus rely on a discontinuity between governance and law – a distinction between the rationality of one and the processes of the other – these changes would seem to suggest that such theories have carried over an inaccurate picture of what post-national law-making (or even modern law in its national setting) really entails.

The problem therefore is not with the notion that governance poses normative challenges for the legal system. Evidence of linkages between governance and law certainly do not render neutral any of the arguments about the possible dilution of constitutional or due process guarantees that sceptics of governance and the OMC have offered. It is even possible that these doubts could increase – the mutual integration of the OMC and other legal processes may simply illustrate how far away from the ideal of a community of law the EU has travelled.[68]

What they may achieve, however, is to show the danger of basing our choice of governing instruments on overly stylised views of what legality – or the pursuit of the rule of law in Europe – really entails. The choice is unlikely to be between the OMC on the one hand, and a 'classical method' on the other, but made in the context of a murky space between stable and general rules, and the more differentiated or negotiated provisions that the new governance debate has sketched out. We must be careful, in short, not to essentialise legal categories, but to consider them in a process of change, that both subverts traditional assumptions, and involves an explicit interplay between different modes of rule.

It is here that other 'inside' accounts may be helpful. Some theorists have argued that if methods like the OMC cannot be meaningfully conceptualised as external to law, then they should be seen the other way round – as part of a process by which the structures and categories of modern law are in a process of change or *transformation*. It is from the arguments developed above – that the 'gap' between governance and law is not always real, but premised on a mythical account of contemporary law and administration – that theories which posit the internality of governance to law have emerged.

These accounts (and three particular schools of inside theorising) will be developed in the third chapter. There, the purpose will be to examine possible theoretical frameworks within which to consider

[68] See e.g. M. Dawson, 'Soft Law and the Rule of Law in the European Union: Revision or Redundancy?' (2009) *EUI Working Papers (RSCAS)* 24; R. Peerenboom, 'The Future of Rule of Law: Challenges and Prospects for the Field' (2009) *Hague Journal on the Rule of Law* 1.

governance as an example of legal proceduralisation. This chapter will be the basis of a case study in Chapter 4, designed to tease out both the explanatory potential and the contradictions that may emerge from inside theories. Now, however, we must both introduce this way of thinking and, with it, develop the theoretical and conceptual background from which inside accounts have emerged. How can a critique which sees governance on the 'inside' of legal obligations shed some light on the changing nature of the EU, and its legal and political structure? Do inside theories provide answers to the limits of the 'outside' view?

4. Towards an inside theory?

4.1 Remodelling the European 'rule of law'

The project of 'constitutionalisation' carried on from the late-eighteenth century is associated with an attempt to juridify political relationships. It is perhaps then a natural impulse for lawyers to see law in governance as a device of constraint. The legal challenge of processes like comitology and the OMC is to 'constitutionalise' them, i.e. to subject a messy realm of political negotiation to legal reason and order while still preserving their functional advantages.[69] Looking from a normative perspective, therefore, we are likely to see the contribution of law to governance in terms of the injection of procedural values into an otherwise arbitrary political sphere.

On the other hand, for many accounts, the contribution should be seen the other way round. It is not only that changes in the EU's governance structure can be read and evaluated from the perspective of the legal state, but that they can be seen as contributing to our understanding of law. Methods like the OMC – consigned by the *White Paper on Governance* to the periphery of integration – exemplify the evolution of European law, from a hierarchical structure mimicking the sovereignty concerns of the nation state to a new reality, in which legal steering goes on without clear red lines telling us where authority really lies. It is not, therefore, only a question of what law can do in the context of European governance, but also how governance is changing the way European law is operated upon, and conceived.

[69] See Joerges and Neyer, n. 11 above.

This move, inside theories insist, requires us to come to more radical conclusions than the current governance debate has allowed.[70] Just as it has diagnosed the essential features of new governance – policy linkage, adaptability, differentiation and so on – its mistake is to see these features as external to law rather than the outcome of pressures which the legal sphere may also face. If we look at the traditional branches of European and international law, we see many of the changes to which theorists of governance have devoted their careers. It is this possibility – that the governance debate has committed what Majone terms 'a category error' in its approach to law – that has inspired and driven forward 'inside' theories.[71]

These accounts, however, do not come from nowhere. Instead, they have extended the insights of domestic administrative and private law to a new transnational setting.

In administrative law, for example, the challenges of European governance have been depicted as relating closely to the search for new channels of administrative accountability in the face of an expansion in the state's regulatory functions. In the US for example, as the need to delegate responsibility for policy implementation to independent agencies has grown, so has the realisation that administration is not just a technocratic task, nor is it one that obviates the need for significant discretion.[72] The 'transmission' belt of institutional accountability, whereby lower-level actors are accountable to higher ones on the basis of a prior defined mandate, has been seen as out of step with the reality of delegation, which often occurs *precisely because* legislators lack the knowledge necessary to define in advance the ambit and goals of policy programmes.[73]

70 See, for example, Sabel and Simon's critique – 'new governance may or may not be an answer to the dilemmas of this situation, but distinctions between working traditions and fanciful innovations are not. Indeed the suggestion at the core of much new governance discussion that societies can and should innovate at the margins without profoundly perturbing the arrangements that enable the innovations ignores the enduring insight of nineteenth century social theory that great innovations only arise in conditions that undermine their antecedents.' See n. 39 above, at 396.

71 Majone, n. 6 above, at 21.

72 M. Shapiro, 'Implementation, Discretion and Rules' in Vervaele (ed.), n. 61 above, at 27–31.

73 R. B. Stewart, 'The Reformation of American Administrative Law' (1975) 88 *Harvard Law Review* 8 at 1675. See also Mashaw's critique, n. 74 below, at 1–11.

Instead, new models have arisen in their place.[74] If accountability, for example, cannot be forwarded as a hierarchical model of rule application, perhaps it can be undertaken on a dynamic basis, where administrators are accountable to *other* competing forms of technical and scientific information.[75] Perhaps the duty is not to answer to a political sovereign, but to those directly affected by regulatory programmes. Maybe, in effect, what is important is not to whom we are answerable, but merely the process of being *held* accountable, i.e. having to generalise our reasons in terms that transcend individual self-interest, and that are understandable to others.[76] These have been some of the models that academic studies responding to national changes have brought forward.

In spite of the common objection that the EU is somehow *sui generis* (and therefore an inappropriate object for national comparison) such models have frequently been adapted to the European case. While the EU does not command an administrative machinery akin to that of the nation state, its regulatory functions have expanded as nation states have sought to create European bodies armed with a high level of technical and scientific expertise, distanced from the direct political oversight of national governments.[77] As such, many of the methods discussed under the rubric of new governance – particularly comitology and regulatory agencies – have attested to the steady growth of administrative structures in the EU modelled on national developments.

As in the national example, the virtue that these institutions bring to the table is often their distance from a model of hierarchical political control. The legitimacy of a regulatory agency is not dependent on the extent to which it follows the will of a political master, but rests upon its ability to bring its *own* expertise and values to bear in regulatory decision-making. It may even depend – see, for example, the case of

[74] This has arguably been the central preoccupation of modern administrative law. For a particularly prescient discussion, see J. L. Mashaw, 'Structuring a "Dense Complexity"': Accountability and the Project of Administrative Law' (2005) *Issues in Legal Scholarship* 4.

[75] See, as examples of similar approaches (including their dilemmas), C. Harlow and R, Rawlings, 'Promoting Accountability in Multi-level Governance: A Network Approach' (2006) *European Governance Papers* 2; C. Scott, 'Accountability in the Regulatory State' (2000) 27 *Journal of Law and Society* 1.

[76] This Habermassian approach is exemplified by Joerges and Neyer. For a more recent re-evaluation, see Joerges, 'Deliberative Political Processes Revisited: What Have We Learnt About the Legitimacy of Supra-National Decision-Making?' (2006) 44 *Journal of Common Market Studies* 4.

[77] For a more complex discussion, see Everson and Majone, n. 23 above.

the European Central Bank – upon a level of independence from central political control.[78]

Similar pressures apply to the OMC – how can national governments be answerable to a prior-articulated statement of outcomes when the process is envisaged not as an act of law appliance, but based on goals and principles to be elaborated through the application of European objectives and targets to a highly particular national discourse?[79] The same problem – of how power can be delegated but at the same time constrained – therefore arises: how can administrative structures and officials be answerable to other actors when the goals and priorities they implement cannot be articulated in advance?[80]

Inside theories, however, have insisted that as old models have been broken down, so new ones may be emerging. The OMC clearly rejects the hierarchical model of accountability, but it may introduce others in its place – models which suggest that traditional legal values are both departed from and reformulated. In the open method, while there may be no real hierarchical accountability, e.g. to parliaments, or a similar sovereign body, there may be horizontal equivalents. Instead of seeking accountability upwards to a central sovereign, or backwards to a prior enactment, Sabel and Simon suggest that we look 'forward and sideways: forward to the ongoing efforts at implementation, sideways to the efforts and views of peer institutions'.[81]

We are thus accountable in governance in a dynamic or deliberative sense. Just as the criteria for what is acceptable or unacceptable are shifting, so our justifications must be evaluated directly by those who are implicated in either the successes or the failures of European projects. In particular, we are accountable not to a singular sovereign but instead to *other states*, who have a mutual interest in ensuring that governments take common social commitments seriously.

As Sabel and Simon put it:

[78] See M. Everson, 'Independent Agencies: Hierarchy Beaters?' (1995) 1 *European Law Journal* 2 at 182–189.

[79] I.e. a rigid distinction between rule-making and rule-application is ruled out. For a lengthier exposition, see the approach of Jacques Lenoble outlined in the next chapter, Chapter 3, section 2.2.

[80] The question may even be further problematised in the European context, where the key administrative actors are both particularly spread out and where the political 'sovereign' to which governance structures may be answerable is not only divided, but arguably absent (i.e. where 'constituent power' is held primarily at the national level).

[81] Sabel and Simon, n. 39 above, at 400.

> Accountability is strengthened not when the actions of the agent are constrained but when the agent is required to explain and justify his actions to those who have the necessary knowledge to understand and evaluate those actions.[82]

The challenge of accountability in Europe is to design mechanisms and institutions by which executive actors can both *explain* their actions in light of common objectives and indicators, and *justify* them, in relation to the preferences and needs of the policy community as a whole. The very existence of the EU as a 'flat' polity, lacking a central sovereign, in this way can be channelled into an accountability network; a community in which each actor has a stake in monitoring the conduct of others.

4.2 'Dynamic accountability' and its limits

While the view of accountability forwarded by Sabel and others is surely a vital contribution, it still carries a number of deficits. Indeed, its limits may lead us to view the 'dynamic' model as limited, or offering a partial rather than complete replacement for the practices and institutions it is designed to replace.[83] It will suffice here to mention two possible objections.

The first objection can only be understood if we consider the various meanings that could possibly be ascribed to accountability as a principle of constitutional and administrative law. The UK's leading administrative lawyer, Carol Harlow, has distinguished between two possible understandings of the concept.[84] While on the one hand, we may speak of accountability in an administrative sense, where we are accountable to agreed upon targets or objectives, accountability is also a political concept. The political meaning of accountability refers to the use of administrative law as a mechanism to connect administrative action to political institutions, and ultimately to the preferences and needs of a general public. While recent decades have seen an increasing focus on accountability in the first 'administrative' sense, the ideal of a democratic state also depends on its second meaning. Political accountability does not just refer to a group of actors answerable to each other, but to

82 P. Nicolaides, *Improving Policy Implementation in an Enlarged European Union: The Case of National Regulatory Authorities* (Maastricht: European Institute of Public Administration, 2003) at 46. Quoted in Sabel and Simon, n. 39 above, at 401.

83 For an empirical assessment of this account, see Dawson, n. 60 above, as well as the analysis contained in Chapter 4, sections 3.1–4.5.

84 C. Harlow and R. Rawlings, *Law and Administration* (London: Butterworths, 1997) at 128–151.

the ability of the executive to answer to the needs of those on whose behalf public policies are conducted.

One wonders whether the dynamic model has anything to contribute to accountability in this second political sense. Accountability to peer institutions may indeed ensure that – in the absence of fixed and knowable mandates – the administrative bodies charged with making policy are answerable for the power they wield. It may not, however, do much, if we are concerned not just with the act of being held accountable, but also the question of *to whom* accountability for decisions is directed. While there is much in the procedural rules of the OMC to ensure that national governments are answerable to other administrations for their interpretation of European indicators, there are few points at which this micro dialogue becomes an exercise involving general publics. In this sense, the critique implicit in Harlow's account of European administrative law may also apply to Sabel. At what point can dynamic accountability transcend the dialogue of sectoral or national actors, negotiating their own interests or world views, and become a link between executive action and the agency of 'us', the people of Europe?[85]

Without such outward links, the 'very real risk', as Harlow puts it, is that horizontal accountability networks will:

> De-generate into a complacent 'old boys network', their accountability function blunted by mutual interest. Mutual accountability networks tend to be more concerned with policy in-put and long-term relationships than retrospective evaluation; even external actors may then be 'captured' and sucked into the network rendering the possibility of thin accountability remote, and thick accountability even more so.[86]

In the case of soft law, this possibility is real. The operation of dense peer review structures may less lead to a more accountable form of rule than a network of mutual interest, where states refuse to rock the boat. While one of the objections to the OMC was that it insulated decision-making from the external input of national and European Parliaments, creating an 'insider's club' of executive administrators and 'invited' participants, 'dynamic' forms of accountability seemingly reinforce, rather than address, this objection. In this sense, while the OMC has

[85] See also, M. Bovens, 'Analysing and Assessing Accountability: A Conceptual Framework' (2007) 13 *European Law Journal* 4.

[86] See Harlow and Rawlings, n. 75 above, at 7.

invoked a search for new means of imagining legal values, these models are not without significant challenges of their own.

Much of course, depends on how peer review is conducted. Sabel and Zeitlin, in a recent paper, recognise that their model, as it stands, will not necessarily lead to politically or democratically legitimate outcomes.[87] A necessary foundation, they insist, for transferring horizontal accountability into a democratic form of rule is that the process of peer review is both as transparent and as participatory as possible.

> A necessary foundation for all forms of democratizing destabilisation is transparency: the citizen's right to know not just what the authorities are deciding but also the evidence and arguments motivating their decisions.[88]

Peer review is not sufficient in and of itself: it must be combined with these other values. The problem arises when we consider the possibility of conflict between these values. The experience of OMC committees in dealing with the principles of 'transparency' on the one hand, and 'deliberation' on the other may be one such example. In order to create conditions where national actors can speak freely, the OMC has built up extensive committees, which both evaluate national plans for reform, and develop key indicators. These committees are the main site in which deliberation between policy actors takes place. As Kerstin Jacobsson has argued, many of the features which are routinely ascribed to deliberative structures can be found here.[89] The committees (as Joerges and Neyer observed in the late 1990s) do not just represent fixed, prior interests, but bring forward different forms of scientific and technical information.[90] In short, their 'deliberative'

[87] 'Democracy requires not only that citizens be equally subject to the law, but also that they be jointly and equally its authors. In this regard, peer review and directly deliberative polyarchy more generally are doubly suspicious: first because the rules they make are not validated by the familiar processes of representative democracy through legislative enactment and control; second, and worse still, in deviating from norms of representative democracy and principle–agent accountability, they appear to deliver decision-making into the hands of a technocratic elite, whose potentially self-interested manipulations are cloaked in the robes of dispassionate deliberation'. C. Sabel and J. Zeitlin, 'Learning from Difference: The New Architecture of Experimentalist Governance in the European Union' (2008) *European Governance Papers* 2 at 47.

[88] *Ibid.*

[89] K. Jacobsson and A. Vifell, 'Integration by Deliberation?: On the Role of Committees in the Open Method of Coordination', Paper Presentation, Workshop on 'The Forging of Deliberative Supra-Nationalism in the EU', (Florence), February 2003, 18–21.

[90] Joerges and Neyer, n. 11 above.

and 'polyarchical' qualities (i.e. the extent to which they bring in the knowledge and concerns of diverse constituencies) are high.

At the same time, the Committees may indicate the extent to which a trade off in the EU may occur *between* deliberation and transparency. The committee structure – in order to safeguard its deliberative character – often displays a high degree of opaqueness.[91] National actors are willing both to put pressure on other governments, and admit to defects in their own approach, because they know that the transcripts of meetings will not be widely disseminated. Their deliberations are of a high quality largely because they can achieve a level of complexity that leaves their discussions unsuited to the scrutiny of ordinary citizens, or representative institutions and assemblies.[92] In short, the creation of an 'epistemic community'; providing a high level of expertise for the elaboration of political programmes; may not always go hand in hand, but may even work *against* the models of transparent and accessible regulation that Sabel and others observe. While the transition of dynamic accountability from a model of elitist citizenship, to one representing a more directly democratic form of government may require a blending of deliberation and transparency, these are also values which potentially conflict.

Beyond this discussion, a further question emerges. To what extent is accountability co-extensive with legality? Safeguarding the rule of law in Europe would seem to mean more than rendering someone answerable for how policy is conducted, but suggests that functional programmes should be mediated through rules. While models of peer review may constrain self-interested behaviour, they differ markedly from the idea that public life should be guided by basic legal standards set down in advance, and knowable to all. If dynamic accountability is all that we are looking for in Europe, what is the point of anchoring the integration process in the Treaties, and in enumerated legal texts, at all?

Re-evaluating accountability in this sense is different from re-evaluating legality. The latter would seem to imply not only a form of governance that is constrained, but one that is abstractified from particular acts of application, i.e. it does not only concern the actors *to whom* officials are answerable, but also *the manner in which public power is wielded*. In the famous words of American constitutionalism, legality

[91] See S. Smismans, 'New Modes of Governance and the Participatory Myth' (2008) 31 *West European Politics* 5.

[92] Jacobsson and Vifell, n. 89 above, at 21–23.

entails an order where government is conducted 'through laws not men'; and hence, where a portion of political conduct (including things like the protection and enforcement of fundamental rights) are ring-fenced from the ordinary boundaries of political negotiation.[93] Under the dynamic model, it is difficult to see where the boundaries between the a priori normative orderings of the law, and the ordinary contingencies of power politics, are being drawn.

This would particularly seem to apply if we consider the role of traditional legal and political institutions, like courts and parliaments. While, under the old model, courts had a central role to play in holding administrative bodies to received mandates, they are seen by Sabel and Cohen as overtly static institutions, often incapable of properly understanding or constraining the regulatory regimes they are entrusted with keeping in check. While the deficiencies in terms of expertise that courts everywhere face is widely documented, the model of dynamic accountability does little to sculpt out an alternative role for judicial institutions.[94] If judges are not seen as appliers of politically agreed rules, or as giving meaning to the purpose or letter of the law, but as one among many other actors capable of acting in a process of peer review, the centrality of courts like the ECJ to the narrative of European integration, would seem to be threatened, not by an explicit relegation of court procedures, but a conceptual failure to provide an alternative legal vision.

A similar deficit may apply to parliaments. What role does Sabel and Simon's model provide them bar that of another 'reviewing' actor, providing its input to be considered along with everyone else? The removal of parliaments from the equation deprives 'dynamic accountability' of one of its last chances to transcend an 'insider's club' of administrative actors and connect to the preferences and concerns of a wider European public (an omission that this book will come back to in its fifth chapter).[95] In a manner emblematic of 'new governance' in a broader sense, the rush on the part of dynamic models to overcome a hierarchical ideal of the democratic sovereign may have led its

[93] G. de Búrca, 'New Modes of Governance and the Protection of Human Rights', in P. Alston and O. de Schutter (eds.), *Monitoring Fundamental Rights in the EU* (Oxford: Hart, 2005) at 31.

[94] On such a role, see J. Scott and S. Sturm, 'Courts as Catalysts: Re-thinking the Judicial Role in New Governance' (2007) 13 *Columbia Journal of European Law* 3.

[95] See Chapter 5, section 7.

architects to throw the baby out with the bath water; ignoring precisely the function of critical review that parliaments the world over hold.

These objections would seem to be pressing. However, to what extent can they be accommodated? Inside theories – as the next chapter will explore – constitute a complex theoretical edifice. There are at least three significant schools of thinking that have attempted to explore methods like the OMC in the context of social and legal change. Determining whether or not an 'inside' approach to the law/governance relation is convincing requires more than the superficial engagement conducted here, but a broader analysis of each theory.

The point of the analysis above is simply to show the dilemma we face. While inside accounts may avoid undue stylisations of legal categories, they simultaneously provoke an extensive anxiety about the fate of law in the European integration process. If governance represents a 'transformation' of legal categories, one wonders whether this transformation can be reconciled with important democratic or rule of law virtues. The success and limits of such a reconciliation will be the central concern of the next chapter.

5. Conclusion

One important school of inside thinking has labelled its approach an example of 'democratic experimentalism'.[96] Yet it may be law that is in its experimental phase. In the OMC certainly, it is not just certain policy provisions, but the very procedures by which policy is formulated, which is in a process of flux. The question then becomes: what are these experiments, and do they leave enough of what we value or depend upon in legal processes and institutions in tact? If we see governance on the inside of legal obligation, what kind of law are we now dealing with?[97] The next chapter will take this question as its starting point.

As this chapter has argued, however, any answer is likely to be based on uncomfortable truths. If we see governance inside law, it is not law as we presently know it. The challenge is to find means of rescuing the values upon which legality in Europe depends *in the knowledge* that we

[96] M. Dorf and C. Sabel, 'A Constitution of Democratic Experimentalism' (1998) 98 *Columbia Law Review* 2.

[97] See also, M. Wilkinson, 'Three Conceptions of Law: Towards a Jurisprudence of Democratic Experimentalism' (2010) *Wisconsin Law Review* 2.

live in a different functional and social space than we did before. This space means that governance and law are not likely to be competing alternatives; one a hierarchical expression of political sovereignty; the other a structure of functional demands; but elements which are implicated in each other. We should see governance neither as a clean break from the past, nor as an extra-legal structure, but instead part and parcel of how the EU's legal structure is transforming.

It is for this reason that the negative definition of governance is unconvincing. It simply leaves too much out. We cannot see governance in opposition to law (in the face of so much evidence of integration between the two), but neither does this leave us with a naive complementarity. Instead, we must find more positive means of identifying the contemporary meaning of governance, and with it, look differently – not away from law to see what governance is not, but within it, to how law, both in its national context, and in a new transnational environment, is building alternative forms and structures.

This positive definition – of governance as a proceduralisation of European law-making – will be the subject of the next two chapters. Here, in Chapter 3, three approaches to seeing governance inside legal categories will be introduced and evaluated, first from a theoretical standpoint and then, in Chapter 4, from an empirical standpoint. Do inside theories capture the relationship between governance and law adequately? Do they give evidence of how our basic legal concepts are being re-evaluated? And what lessons do they provide about the way in which both law is informing European integration, and the integration process is changing our understanding of law and its associated concepts?

Having posed these questions, however, we may now be able to answer the puzzle with which this chapter began – why are lawyers so interested in the governance debate? Why, in the absence of practical legal involvement in processes like the OMC, have lawyers been so influential in conceptualising what governance in the European Union means? In answer, looking at processes like the OMC is in part looking at law itself; by examining the governance debate, we are peering into a potential legal future. The significant uncertainties over what this future holds are likely to hold the gaze of lawyers in Europe and beyond for some time to come.

3 Governance as proceduralisation

1. Introduction

The last chapter sketched out the skeleton of an 'inside' theory of the relationship between governance and law. It is not yet, however, clear what seeing governance 'inside' legal categories really means. If the OMC is law, it is unlike most of the laws we see in the EU, or its member states. This comes through in the method's characterisation as 'soft'. While the OMC carries forward legal functions, it is not law in the proper sense; it lacks the ability to sanction and enforce conduct which 'real' law-making implies. Given these facts, it is easy to see 'new governance' as a threat to law-mediated rule, or alternatively, as parallel to the Union's 'official' constitutional structure. It is simpler to adopt a 'negative' definition; to see OMC-like methods as external to law, or as elements of a more directly 'political' form of rule.

The purpose of the last two chapters has been to dispute and contest this argument. Firstly, there may be significant continuities between hard and soft legal programmes. The association of law with sanction – long an obsession of eighteenth and nineteenth century jurisprudence – is not as relevant as it once was. Indeed it may be a particularly difficult task in the EU context, where the implementation of legal rules also requires the cooperation and consent of national administrative and judicial authorities. The reality of European social law implies not only the rise of 'new governance', but the presence of framework directives, social dialogues and other soft methods, which in combination have created a loose legal infrastructure. This implies that the association of legality with hard, determining and hierarchical rules should not be taken for granted.

The more important question may be where this analysis now leaves us. On the one hand, the old, 'negative' definition of the law–governance relationship is inadequate. We have to find ways of connecting the 'fact' of new governance practices, with our ethical commitment to law-mediated rule. On the other, a more positive definition is difficult to construct. What is it that draws the various strands of the new governance debate together? And how can we conceptualise methods like the OMC adequately without either relying on external concepts, i.e. those of the social sciences, or basing our understanding of legality on a static or formalistic conception of the legal order?

The chapter's guiding argument will be that answering such questions requires us to revisit some old debates. The chapter will develop, analyse and critique three theoretical approaches that take the difficulties of regulating pluralistic and complex polities as their starting points. These three approaches – proceduralisation, deliberative polyarchy and reflexive law – have argued that the method can be seen as 'internal' to law in the sense of adapting traditional understandings of legality to a more functionally complex, or normatively divided, Union. They merit careful attention, and set up a theoretical framework which will be tested in the book's fourth empirical chapter.

They also, however, merit criticism. Firstly, each approach is developed from a particular context. One must question, rather than assume, their suitability for transportation both to the case of the EU, and to the practices of new governance. The purpose of the chapter will not only be to situate methods like the OMC in the broader scheme of procedural and experimentalist theory, but to question those aspects of the governance debate that 'inside' theories can describe, and those aspects that they cannot.

Secondly, they all leave certain questions that remain unanswered. All three register founding tensions, particularly in terms of the relationship between the softer, or more experimental norms they identify as being fundamental to contemporary legal governance, and the 'old' hierarchical structure they are said to be replacing. To take the first 'procedural' school as an example, it criticises the formal and hierarchical application of norms, but also relies upon procedural values (rights to fair access, voice, non-discrimination and so on) that effectively recreate a form of hierarchy. This poses an obvious question – if substantive norms require greater adaptability, surely some of the same pressures apply in the case of secondary values? In reading this chapter, and in the later development of a case study in social inclusion, it will be important to keep these tensions in mind.

Finally, while the chapter will attempt to apply three theoretical accounts to the OMC, there will never be a perfect fit. One of the things the chapter will criticise is precisely the assumption that new governance, or any of its constituent processes, can neatly fit into one or another of the 'experimental', 'deliberative' or 'reflexive' boxes. We are dealing with something that is too complex for exhaustive categorisation. The chapter will proceed instead on the basis that any attempt to consider the OMC as a procedural or 'experimental' regime requires both that one tests preliminary assumptions and that one maintains a critical distance. The analysis of the OMC, and comparison to the theoretical approaches on offer, is based on the OMC's design, but not necessarily its practice. The vital function of the fourth and fifth chapters that will follow is therefore to ask: to what extent are these theories operational: what does switching to a more concrete, more practical and more narrow perspective – one based on the practical experiences of actors under the OMC process in social inclusion – mean? 'Governance as proceduralisation' may provide a more 'positive' definition of 'new governance' than those currently on offer. Does it, however, also describe the experience of its most important political and social participants?

2. Governance as proceduralisation

2.1 Paradigms of law

Perhaps the most famous of all procedural accounts of modern law has been provided by the German philosopher and sociologist Jürgen Habermas. In his magnum opus, *Between Facts and Norms*, Habermas argues that proceduralism is not just a significant *form* of law in modern societies, but part of a 'paradigm shift'. Borrowing from the use of the 'paradigm' in the natural sciences, he argues that judicial and political actors operate with a certain 'implicit image of society'.

In the Weberian tradition, twentieth-century law has been dominated by two of these images: one material, the other formal. Habermas' break with Weber is his argument that while the two paradigms envisage the role of law differently their normative orientation is fundamentally the same. In both, law is oriented towards securing the conditions for 'private autonomy'; the freedom for individuals to secure their life plans without undue interference from others. The difference between the two lies in the 'perceived social context' within which this is to take place.[1] The formal model assumes that the mere protection of individual rights and agreements will lead to socially just outcomes. The person is viewed as an autonomous unit, able to operate relatively independently of larger forces of economic and social power.

Under the material paradigm, this assertion is undermined. In the face of structural inequalities (the Habermas of 'the critical school') it is inferred that individual agreements in the marketplace themselves conceal biases; they favour stronger parties over weaker.

> In such a changed social context, the universal right to equal social liberties could no longer be guaranteed through the negative status of the legal subject. Rather, it proved necessary on the one hand, to specify the context of the existing norms of private law and, on the other, to introduce a new category of basic rights granting claims to a more just distribution of social wealth.[2]

The result of this process has been law's 'materialisation'. Modern law is not only geared towards the realisation of individual rights, but also 'to achieve specific goals in concrete situations'.[3] Law is to take responsibility not only as a policeman for a minimalist or formal legal order, but as an entity that must 'constitutionalise the economy'; placing individuals in an economic context where real private autonomy – or private bargaining on an *equitable basis* – is possible (beyond the veneer of a formally 'equal' granting of individual rights).[4]

In spite of the liberalising effect of the Treaties, we see evidence of this 'materialisation' everywhere in the contemporary EU. In its more positive guise, it has succeeded in creating the social protection systems the OMC was (supposedly) designed to coordinate. It has also resulted in repeated, and often failed, legislative attempts – from the Union's first

1 J. Habermas, *Between Facts and Norms: Contributions to a Discourse Theory of Law and Democracy* (Cambridge: MIT Press, 1996) at 400.

2 *Ibid.*, at 402–403.

3 'Whereas formal law clearly viewed itself to be confined to the de-limitation of abstract spheres for private-autonomous action, material law legitimates itself by the social results it achieves by regulation.' G. Teubner, 'Juridification: Concepts, Aspects, Limits, Solutions' in Teubner (ed.), *Juridification of Social Spheres: A Comparative Analysis in the Areas of Labour, Corporate, Antitrust and Social Welfare Law* (Berlin: de Gruyter, 1987) at 15.

4 I.e. the right of each to sleep under the bridges of Paris. See (on the fourth welfarist 'thrust' of juridification – the use of law to 'constitutionalise' or democratise' the economy) J. Habermas, 'Law as Medium and Law as Institution' in G. Teubner (ed.), *Dilemmas of Law in the Welfare State* (Berlin: De Gruyter, 1986) at 208–211.

1974 'Social Action Programme' onwards – to build up a 'social dimension' to the Union's activities.

In its pathologies, however, it has also evidenced 'normalising' or 'colonising' tendencies.[5] Materialisation has encouraged what Habermas (infamously) terms 'the de-coupling of system and life-world'.[6] This de-coupling means that – whereas the purpose of political action was once understood in terms of an exchange of normative reasons or an ability to justify and negotiate political decisions inter-subjectively – the rise in the state's regulatory functions has placed increasing pressure on the ability of the state to act and communicate in these terms. Processes of inter-subjective bargaining have been displaced by abstract principles (criteria of 'efficiency', 'money' and 'power'), designed to relieve some of the burden. Talking through the medium of money for example, allows decision-making to be conducted through the mutually comprehensible language of 'profit' and 'loss' rather than through a complicated process of normative justification.

The normative outcome of this move – Weber's characterisation of 'the iron change' – has been an increasingly technocratic form of rule. In the modern welfare state, the individual is both provided with new social entitlements and locked into new relations of dependency. Habermas explains this normative ambiguity in a brilliant, yet often overlooked, article written in 1987. In the context of regulatory law:

> The situation to be regulated is embedded in the context of a life-history and a concrete way of life; it has to be subjected to violent abstraction not merely because it has to be subsumed under the law but in order that it can be handled administratively. The implementing bureaucracies must proceed very selectively and *choose* those instances of social needs which, using the means of a legally-proceeding bureaucratic rule can be brought under the legal fiction of the compensation situation.[7]

His critique is that welfarist law – in order to treat the cases before it equally – must remove the claim to welfare provision from its original social context. Individuals are increasingly treated as 'clients': rather than being seen as the authors of the laws that apply to them, individuals become the *addressees* of ameliorative programmes that are managed 'in their best interest'.[8] The price of more just social conditions is

[5] See Habermas, *ibid.*, at 216.

[6] J. Habermas, *The Theory of Communicative Action (Vol. 2)* (Boston: Beacon Press, 1987) at 153–198.

[7] Habermas, n. 4 above, at 210.

[8] Habermas, n. 1 above, at 407.

an increasingly impersonal form of rule; one in which the original normative intentions that underlie the law are displaced (or even considered irrelevant altogether).

His critique of material law thus leaves Habermas searching for new answers. Unsurprisingly, they are to be found in others parts of his theory, particularly his claim that the materialisation of the social state must at the same time be anchored in *democratic* constitutional principles.

Habermas thus insists that *both* paradigms (material and formal):

> lose sight of the internal relation between private and *political* autonomy, and thus lose sight of the democratic meaning of a community's self-organisation. The still un-resolved dispute between these two parties is focused on specifying the material conditions for the equal status of legal persons as addressees of the legal order. These persons are autonomous, however, only insofar as they can at the same time understand themselves as authors of the law to which they are subject as addressees.[9]

The failure of each paradigm lies in its predilection to lose sight of public autonomy as a factor without which private autonomy would be impossible. They lose sight of the fact that both the form of law, and its goals, cannot simply be 'given' but must be retrieved from within the practices, preferences and normative self-understandings of the citizen him- or herself.[10]

This potentially provides an answer to some of the dilemmas of the welfarist model as it stands. The welfare state centralised decision-making power in order to bring the collective resources of the population to bear in taming economic distortion; at the same time, this centralisation deprived it of a crucial resource – the knowledge that self-determining citizens themselves can bring to bear in informing legal processes. Law must thus play a role in 're-entering' the citizen; in allowing public policy access not just to the macro-resources of the administrative state, but the micro-information contained in everyday legal interactions.

Habermas thus advocates a jump akin to the one made by Wiethölter, Teubner, Lenoble, and the other theorists of the 'procedural turn' that this chapter will invoke – a jump from the substantive to the procedural. The role of law in advancing social goals ('societal guidance through law') cannot be given up on.[11] These goals, however, must be articulated *directly* by those who are subject to legal procedures (and to

[9] *Ibid.*, at 408. [10] *Ibid.*, at 408.

[11] 'The social-welfare project must neither be simply continued along the same lines nor be broken-off, but must be pursued at a higher level of reflection.' *Ibid.*, at 410.

the material programmes they are intended to deliver). It must be the *addressees* of the law – those to whom everyday legal 'rights' and 'responsibilities' apply – who define the scope and boundaries of the programmes being advanced in their name.

In practice, this implies two elements, to be explored further in the following section. Firstly, it implies the explosion of a distinction in law that was previously considered vital – the distinction between the creation of rules and their application to particular 'facts'. Whereas ideas like the 'rule of law' have often been predicated on the idea that rules should be formulated independently of the context in which they are to be applied, the 'procedural paradigm' drives us towards a reconsideration of whether the law *can* be articulated and developed in an abstract sense, or whether a more 'reflexive' or 'responsive' relationship between the legal sphere, and its surrounding social environment, is possible (or desirable).[12]

Secondly, it implies a shift in the focus of law-making; a shift from the formal insistence upon 'pedigree' (or material one upon 'function') to a procedural focus on the *democratic genesis* of law; a focus on those conditions capable of securing the participation of those affected by norms within the process of norm-elaboration. It asks us to consider law not only as a medium for implementing 'given' rules and procedures, but one whose overriding concern is the entry of individuals into a larger legal and political discourse.

2.2 The idea of proceduralisation

The famous accounts of Habermas and Weber have served as a direct inspiration for theories of law and democracy attempting directly to apply the insights of procedural theory to the problems of EU integration. For Jacques Lenoble, and others working within the broadly defined tradition of procedural theory, the question of governance is also one concerned with the failure of the dominant formal and material programmes of modern law.[13] While the twentieth century was

[12] As Wiethölter describes: 'The point is no doubt that "goals" are so interwoven i.e. "private" and "social" goals so inter-penetrate that, in consequence, framework regulations and implementation have to be justified along with each other; notably through the social sub-systems equipped with competence for this e.g. courts, firms and associations.' R. Wiethölter 'Materialization and Proceduralization in Modern Law' in Teubner, n. 3 above, at 227.

[13] See J. Lenoble and O. de Munck, 'Transformations in the Art of Governance' in O. De Schutter, N. Lebessis and J. Paterson (eds.), *Governance in the European Union* (Luxembourg: Office for Official Publications of the European Communities, 2001) at 29.

concerned with a crisis of formal legality, in which the individual and positivistic basis of the legal order was challenged, our current debates over institutional change are preoccupied with the failings of the material model which succeeded it.[14]

Procedural accounts both follow and draw lines of continuity between these two traditions. Following Habermas, they see both the material and the formal as legal paradigms associated with 'heavy modernity'.[15] This modernity implies a method which can uncover particular positive laws of reality – in the formal tradition, a general law of behaviour, which can 'self-deduct' onto particular factual circumstances; or in the material one, a teleological norm designed to achieve a pre-stated 'purpose' or goal. In both circumstances, legal reasoning and interpretation is to be based on an objective social condition, first 'captured' within the confines of a legal text, and then applied – through the rigours of judicial reasoning – to the concrete facts of a particular case.

In doing so, these two forms carry in common an important distinction. It is one thing to create a rule; another to apply it to particular circumstances and facts.[16] The creation/application distinction essentially demarcates the boundaries between legal and political action, with the political sphere given the authority legitimately to determine the *content* of the law, and the judiciary retaining the task of interpreting it in light of a longer body of jurisprudence. By virtue of this distinction, the question of 'what the law is' is not something left in the hands of legal officials, but enumerated in advance. Officials are to be constrained by rules, which also provide guidance to citizens over the nature and scope of their legal obligations. These rules are to stand as an independent and a priori yardstick through which the conduct of

[14] Wiethölter thus observes proceduralisation as a shift in how law is reconstructed – 'most recently, legal programmes – beyond both formalization and materialization – have increasingly been re-oriented towards proceduralization, or more exactly, aimed not at social guarantees (as "rights to freedom") nor at provisions (as "political administration") but at the conditions for the existence (and then organisation, procedure, implementing personnel) of such guarantees and provisions'. The relevant question is not one of 'what is permitted' or 'what is to be achieved', but 'what are the *conditions* by which social aims can find their reflection in general law'. Wiethölter, n. 12 above, at 226–227.

[15] A. Adronico and A. Lo Faro, 'Defining Problems: The OMC, Fundamental Rights and the Theory of Governance', in S. Deakin and O. de Schutter (eds.), *Social Rights and Market Forces: Is the Open Coordination of Employment and Social Policies the Future of Social Europe?* (Brussels: Bruylant, 2005) at 68.

[16] See Lenoble and de Munck, n. 13 above, at 40–41.

legal actors can be judged. Legal disputes are not therefore simply a matter of balancing individual interests, or deciding according to the judgement of the legal official; instead social conflicts are to be subject *to the governance of rules.*[17]

While this distinction may underlie a conventional understanding of legality, it has been heavily problematised in the EU context. It faces a complexity challenge presciently described by William Scheuerman as 'the problem of time-space compression'.[18] In a modern economy, in which the shape and boundaries of the state's regulatory tasks are in a state of adaptation, the legislator will often lack the necessary knowledge to create detailed rules a priori. Habermas also discussed this problem – the creation of adequate legal standards may depend on precisely the knowledge and resources of those to whom the law is 'applied'. 'Centralisation' of regulatory power is necessary in order to meet the demands of a modern citizenry (or in the EU case, those of interdependent European states); yet at the same time, it opens up a potentially fatal distance between the law and its surrounding regulatory environment.

In such circumstances, how can we maintain the creation/application distinction? The 'central' or 'hierarchical' actor (if we can even identify one in the European context) can only ever create general or provisional rules, likely to be quickly outrun by changes in the regulated field itself.[19] The temporal and functional complexity of modern societies potentially pushes together stages that were once clearly separable. The question of 'what the law means' is now contingent on social information that is not constant, but in a state of change (and held ever further away from the central legislator him or herself).

The problem Scheuerman has identified presents further challenges still at the level of the EU. On the one hand, there is a clear challenge to the notion of the EU as a 'law creator'. The shift from a national to a European context adds to the complexity of the social basis upon which the legal system must act. EU law must create rules which can overcome not only problems of temporal rapidity, but also the entrenched normative differences between different national, social and political systems. It is no easy task – particularly in the areas where methods like the OMC operate – to create standards that can be implemented by a European

[17] L. Fuller, *The Morality of Law* (New Haven: Yale University Press, 1969) at 106.

[18] W. Scheuerman, 'Reflexive Law and the Challenges of Globalization' (2001) 9 *Journal of Political Philosophy* 1 at 90.

[19] *Ibid.*, at 91–94.

community of actors that do not necessarily share a common view of the role of European law in particular fields of action.[20]

This challenge also applies, however, to the notion of seeing national legal orders primarily as 'addressees' of the law. In the present-day EU (neither seen nor desired as a federal polity), the nation state is not simply a lower level unit to whom power can be 'delegated', but a sovereign power in its own right, vested, in areas from labour law to taxation, with exclusive legislative authority. To this extent the creation/application distinction not only sits uneasily with Europe's diversity, but also with the existence of the EU as an order in which sovereignty is fundamentally 'divided'.[21]

In this story, 'proceduralisation' entails an acceptance that this central division – between the creation of the law and its application to local needs and context – is in a state of transformation. In order to apply rules adequately, i.e. to 'implement' the will of a political principle, courts must often reframe them in light of a particular social context. Law is no longer simply an exercise in delineation but an attempt to reconsider decisions precisely in light of the needs and preferences of those most affected by legal decisions or acts.

This creates possibilities for a *dialectical* approach between the 'rule' and its 'application'.[22] Not only do the peculiar circumstances of the nation state (or another 'local' context) demand a re-evaluation of the scope of European rules, but this very application of the law is itself to become a reflexive exercise. The reformulation of norms in light of a local context is also able to provide information *for future rule-making*. The case is not only a set of circumstances to be subsumed under the relevant norm, but a means to reformulate the law in light of a surrounding environment too complex, or too diverse, to be captured and regulated entirely a priori.[23]

[20] This refers clearly to an argument raised in other parts of the book, namely Scharpf's claim that the OMC arises from problems of 'welfare diversity'. For an analysis of this claim, see Chapter 4, section 5 ('Law as integrative'). See also, F. Scharpf, n. 33 below.

[21] N. MacCormick, *Questioning Sovereignty* (Oxford University Press, 1999) at 137–157.

[22] 'The proceduralization of which we ourselves speak pre-supposes a dialectic between the rule and its application. And this dialectic must be based on the concept of learning.' Lenoble and de Munck, n. 13 above, at 41.

[23] 'The judge is not there to tell the truth in the place of the executive or the legislature. But the movement towards a changed and strengthened role for the judge must be conceived in terms of monitoring the discussion process which must itself be thought of as a learning process. Whether this is in social, administrative law or family law, we are gradually seeing checks being put in place on the process of argument that puts law in context.' Lenoble and de Munck, *ibid.*, at 42.

In practical terms, this proceduralisation strategy implies not only a changed role for courts, but a decentering of decision-making power in a more general sense. This aspect of the procedural approach is particularly prominent in Wiethölter's original usage.[24] The devolutionary move refers to an idea long since abandoned by Habermas – that the law should seek the 'external constitutionalisation' of different spheres of action.[25]

To trace the origins of this idea, we have to return to Habermas' prior thesis. As we have seen, he argued that the effects of law's materialisation had not only been to provide individuals with particular social rights but also to colonise or 'juridify' those areas of action (of school, family and religion) that still purely relied upon, or were integrated by, normative justifications.[26] The problem was seen not merely as the failure of the administration to deliver social entitlements, but the exhausted capacities of *law itself* to understand the plural motivations and beliefs driving social actors.[27] Legal interventions are as likely to undermine or misread this pluralism as they are to provide individuals with effective social entitlements.

The idea of the external constitution is seen by Habermas as a means of accommodating this pluralism. Under its terms:

> Legal interventions ought not to go beyond the enforcement of principles of the rule of law; beyond the legal institutionalisation of its *external* constitution. The place of law as a medium must be replaced by procedures for settling conflicts that are appropriate to the structures of action oriented towards communication.[28]

By this view, legal institutions are no longer simply institutions that 'apply the law', but primarily structures that seek to condition or mediate deliberations between actors. These actors must themselves articulate the meaning of the law in a distinct 'life-world context'. Law is an

[24] In his reply to Wiethölter, Kennedy neatly summarises this point: 'the basic idea of proceduralization is that the court is to act as interest arbiter, but to do so by defining the broad conditions of interaction that claim a right to decide and a share in the proceeds of the decision.' D. Kennedy, 'Comment on Rudolf Wiethölter' in C. Joerges and D. Trubek, *Critical Legal Thought: An American-German Debate* (Baden Baden: Nomos, 1989) at 514.

[25] 'Modelled after self-governing bodies and arbitration boards, these forms are intended to enable involved parties to manage their own affairs and resolve conflicts by themselves. In this way, the individual's private autonomy could by supplemented or replaced by a kind of *social autonomy*.' Habermas, n. 1 above, at 412.

[26] Habermas, n. 4 above, at 212–217. [27] Wiethölter, n. 12 above, at 505.

[28] Habermas, n. 4 above, at 218.

institution *within which* forms of social bargaining and deliberation can take place, such that the outcomes of any particular legal programme are not, and cannot, be presupposed.

As we have already discussed, law remains under this model; but in a quite different form. Certainly, it is not assumed that the conditions for a free form of deliberative engagement can be taken for granted. Habermas' 'life-world' is not only a haven for free-flowing normative arguments, but also a world in which exclusionary political narratives, and real inequalities of social power, are latent. It was precisely a recognition of such conditions (e.g. in the patriarchal structures of the family, or in the unequal relation between capital and labour) that led to law's materialisation; conditions that a 'bare' form of proceduralism could easily replicate. The need for 'law', in its proper or (to use the terminology of the governance debate) 'hard' sense, is not obviated.

Instead, proceduralism involves legally engendering the conditions through which successful forms of 'local' or 'experimental' deliberation can take place. Here the mistake of what have been termed 'outside' approaches to the law–governance relation can become apparent. Law is not something external to processes of decentralised deliberation, instead it is only *through law* that the conditions for fair and equal access to the political process can be reached. As Habermas has written, 'political power should not be seen as externally juxtaposed to law, but is rather *presupposed* by law, and itself established in its form'.[29]

Hierarchy is both rejected and reintroduced. It is rejected in the sense that 'given' normative orderings are undermined; at the same time, it is reintroduced through the need to tackle distortions of power – or its 'normalising' effects – through realisable individual rights (of voice and of access); rights that can protect against the descent of deliberative law-making into a paternalistic or manipulative policy discourse.

2.3 Proceduralisation in the EU

The suitability of proceduralisation for describing the present stage of legal integration in the EU depends on going through some of the steps that Habermas and Wiethölter themselves took. At one level, the OMC is particularly unsuitable for their approach. Firstly, it involves stretching the concept of proceduralisation beyond its original national context to consider forms of supra-national, rather than domestic, law-making. Secondly, it involves comparing law's 'proceduralisation' to a method

[29] Habermas, n. 1 above, at 134.

that has commonly been characterised as invoking an 'expulsion of law'.[30] Whereas Habermas' conception implied the anchoring of deliberative procedures under an explicit constitutional framework, methods like the OMC seem to leave the idea of a constitutionally bound polity behind.[31] Most famously, the OMC has been encouraged (by the Commission itself) to operate only in those areas where the EU's official legal competences are limited.

For those who have tried to apply procedural theories to the 'new governance' debate, however, precisely this move opens the door to a reconsideration of the role and place of law in post-national settings like the EU. In such a polity, both the 'formal' and 'material' paradigms of law have little explanatory potential. In spite of the efforts of the European Court, the development of doctrines of supremacy and direct effect has failed to endow the Union with an unproblematic 'hierarchy of norms'. Recent conflicts between the ECJ and national Constitutional courts have served only to illustrate something that we already know – that claims to 'ultimate legal authority' in the EU are contested, and are likely to remain so for the foreseeable future.[32] We cannot credibly view European law as a normative structure built on principles of legal formalism alone (private autonomy, legal hierarchy, deductive legal reasoning and so on).

Against this, the material paradigm of law emerges with even less credence. In spite of the attempt of the Union – described in the first chapter – to give the EU a more robust 'social dimension', European legislation in the social sphere has in no way resembled the welfare institutions of the nation state.[33] While one would have hoped that this could leave EU law relatively immune from the legitimacy crises that have afflicted retreating European welfare regimes, it has instead focused academic discussion on the EU's 'social deficit'. Many have mourned – but few have provided concrete solutions – for the ongoing imbalance between the expansion and deepening of the internal

[30] See C. Joerges, 'Integration Through De-Legislation: An Irritated Heckler' (2007) *European Governance Papers* 3 at 12.

[31] G. de Búrca, 'The Constitutional Challenge of New Governance in the European Union' (2003) 28 *European Law Review* 6. See also, Chapter 2, section 2.1.

[32] See, as an example, the recent judgment of the Spanish and Polish Constitutional Courts: *EU Constitutional Treaty and the Spanish Constitutional Court* [2005] 1 CMLR 981; *Polish Membership of the European Union (Accession Treaty)*, Polish Constitutional Court, Judgment K18/04 of 11 May 2005.

[33] F. Scharpf, 'The European Social Model: Coping with the Challenges of Diversity' (2002) 40 *Journal of Common Market Studies* 4 at 645–649.

market, and the failure of the Court to respect the basic parameters of national welfare provision.[34] Far from attempting to secure the private autonomy of the individual through protective social entitlements, EU law may have left both the private autonomy of the individual vis-à-vis a more globalised European market, and the public autonomy of citizens still able to *choose* welfare policies through democratic election, seriously imperilled.[35]

It is only in this 'social' context that any effort to consider the OMC as a procedural regime can be conducted. The method rejects a 'materialisation' strategy in so much as it displays a refusal to specify the overall goals of European social policy (bar at a high level of abstraction). Social law is not seen in terms of a prior-defined 'blueprint' for reform, but as a *process*, open both to future elaboration, and to differentiation along territorial lines.[36] 'Materialisation' is rejected in that the ends of European law are not specified in advance, nor is an 'approximation' of social standards seen as an explicit goal.[37]

Precisely this feature, however, also underlies the method's distance from a more formal view. The constant iteration of OMC procedures – the entry of new information – and new constellations of actors – leads to a deferral of legislative decision-making. Law is never *made*; instead, targets or objectives are reformed in their very application to new circumstances and facts. In place of formal 'deduction', 'clarity' and 'stability', the method offers a law-making procedure that is itself in a state of flux.

What we may be left with instead is a fundamental erosion of the creation/application distinction, along the lines that Lenoble and others have described. In the EU context, it is impossible to separate the question of what the law 'is' from the material conditions in which it is to be

[34] For a recent restatement of these problems, see C. Joerges, 'A New Alliance of De-legalisation and Legal Formalism? Reflections on Responses to the Social Deficit of the European Integration Project' (2008) 19 *Law and Critique* 3.

[35] *Ibid.*, at 2. [36] See Adronico and Lo Faro, n. 15 above, at 73–74.

[37] This is part of Lenoble's critique of the 'actor-oriented institutionalism' shared by the sceptical Scharpf and Heretier. This states that the incorporation by actors of an institutional framework still involves a perception of their own ends that is brought to bear in influencing outcomes. Lenoble wants to emphasise though that 'the taking into account of the various possibilities opened up by the context grows by itself', i.e. an understanding and placement of a situation in its proper context *is itself* relevant for the selection of ends to be pursued, and for the relevant actors' understanding of the situation around them. J. Lenoble, 'OMC and the Theory of Reflexive Governance' in Deakin and de Schutter, n. 15 above, at 33.

applied (i.e. the distinct social welfare structures, and political culture, of the nation state). A proper response to cultural and structural diversity means a rejection of the notion that laws must be supra-nationally defined and then 'executed' through the administrative and legal systems of the member states.[38] Instead, it is within a more particular national context – the application discourse – that the question of 'what the rules are' can be meaningfully articulated.

As with the larger procedural move, this entails some devolution of legislative power. Under the method, choices over the substantive means by which social entitlements are to be delivered remain at the national level. Similarly, common European objectives are only ever stated at a sufficiently high level of generality that numerous welfare models could potentially claim to meet them. The need to generalise the EU's social policy objectives – if we return again to the issues of 'welfare diversity' discussed in the first chapter – has been precisely one of the reasons for the method's introduction.[39]

As the first chapter also argued, however, the characterisation of the method as entirely 'heterarchical' is often misleading. The removal of substantive hierarchy has also been accompanied by its reintroduction at others levels. 'Soft' legal norms continue to condition both the internal procedures by which national reforms are conducted, the policy discourse (i.e. ideas about the relationship between social and fiscal reforms) through which those reforms are evaluated, and the institutions – like 'peer review', 'social protection committees' and so on – in which interdependencies between states can be managed. The influence of 'the centre' returns, even if at a more abstract and procedural level.

It is this distinction in the method – the distinction between its substantive and procedural aspects – that has given credence to a procedural approach. On the one hand, methods like the OMC shows examples in which process, rather than particular external ends, are a

[38] S. Deakin and O. de Schutter, 'Reflexive Governance and the Dilemmas of Social Regulation', in Deakin and de Schutter, n. 15 above, at 2.

[39] This possibility for substantive renegotiation both matches the procedural insistence that policy goals must be retrieved 'from within a specific life-world context', and has led to frequent accusations that the OMC is a 'paper tiger'; too open to empty rhetoric, or so broad that virtually any programme, from an honest effort to 'recalibrate' social protection systems, to a neo-liberal attempt to 'hollow out' the welfare state, could honestly claim to meet it. See, on this latter point, C. Offe, 'The European Model of "Social" Capitalism: Can it Survive European Integration?' (2003) 11 *European Journal of Political Philosophy* 4. See also, Chapter 1, sections 5.1–5.3.

priority. To take two examples that are explored in greater depth in the following chapters, its reporting cycles ask member states not only to report on social reforms, but also scrutinise their efforts to include, consult and 'activate' non-governmental actors.[40] Its peer review procedures – if they are to achieve substantive reforms – can only do so through the dissemination and scrutiny of examples of 'best practice'. In both of these cases, potential space is sculpted out for a policy discourse to emerge, in which actors beyond 'the usual suspects' (national administrators, Commission officials and the like) have a meaningful stake.

The normative question may be over how this new 'deliberative space' is used. Its potential to bring European action closer to the concerns of its citizens is surely matched by the spectre of a more centralised *national* decision-making process. This process is likely to be overseen by a central executive no longer accountable to external legal standards, but only to the concerns of a civil society whose boundaries *the executive itself* must effectively constitute (again a problem returned to in the fourth chapter). Here the normative ambiguities of a proceduralisation – which both opens up the law, and *opens it up to potential abuse* – are readily apparent.

2.4 Problematising the procedural paradigm

It is here that the application of proceduralisation to the example of the OMC becomes dilemmatic (in a way that present accounts do not fully realise). On the one hand, the Habermasian approach that many procedural approaches to the OMC follow involves a recognition that – in Deakin and de Schutter's words – 'the conditions under which a deliberative process may succeed . . . must be affirmatively created rather than taken for granted'.[41] We cannot simply see the law as an obstacle to the creation of more effective regulatory strategies, or as a break on accelerated processes of mutual learning and norm elaboration; a more procedural form of law-making provides the background context into which any legitimate form of decentralised governance must fit.

It is difficult to imagine, however, how this context could be supplied bar the very hierarchical modes of law-making that methods like the

[40] To give an example, the third of the three overarching objectives of the OMC SPSI is: 'good governance, transparency and the involvement of stakeholders in the design, implementation and monitoring of policy'. See, for a deeper and more critical exploration of this objective, see Chapter 5, section 4, 'Law as participative'.

[41] Deakin and de Schutter, n. 38 above, at 3.

OMC are being said to supplant. Part of the means by which national democracies have achieved conditions of political deliberation – 'the right to have one's voice heard' – has been through the instruments of public law (and fundamental rights) that are said, in the context of European social law, to be lacking. Going down the road of 'hard law', however, potentially leads us to a paradox. If the procedural approach assumes the open texture of rules, and their context dependence, surely this condition also applies to these procedural standards too, i.e. to the rules *through which* more equitable conditions for political deliberation are to be established.

Frank Michelman has forwarded a version of this argument in the context of theories of deliberative democracy.[42] While the deliberative ideal (in both Rawls and Habermas) attempts to tackle moral pluralism through seeking agreement at a more abstract procedural level, what if it is *precisely at this level* that our true conflicts really lie? Does the attempt to tackle contestation through procedural solutions offer a real alternative or does it merely duck the problem?

The difficulty lies in the move from the substantive to the procedural shared in common by Habermas, Wiethölter and Lenoble. While the substantive worth of any particular policy depends on its mediation – through procedures designed to include all relevant voices – 'the question of what *is* (for this purpose) an adequate or proper process' is one that must *itself* be 'legitimised through procedure'.[43]

This invokes certain questions that are not just of a 'procedural' but also 'substantive' nature:

> Is the procedure relevantly and properly democratic only in the absence (as some would claim) or only in the presence (as others would oppositely claim) of certain controls on economic inequality or certain social and economic guarantees? In the absence (or oppositely, in the presence) of worker security, collective bargaining, or other industrial democracy rights? In the absence (or in the presence) of affirmative action, or of cumulative voting, or proportional representation? All these variables (and others) are sharply contested in our political culture, just as matters of what a democratic procedure properly is. Yet solving them seems to be quintessential grist for democracy's mill – questions for democratic resolution if any questions are.[44]

[42] F. Michelman, 'How Can the People Ever Make the Laws? A Critique of Deliberative Democracy' in J. Bohman and W. Rehg (eds.), *Deliberative Democracy: Essays on Reason and Politics* (Cambridge: MIT Press, 1997).

[43] *Ibid.*, at 162. [44] *Ibid.*, at 163–164.

In this sense, any reference to procedural values itself opens up room for substantive contestation, or for the claim that, beneath the 'objectivist' reference to procedure, and its emphasis on the 'democratic genesis' of the law, there is behind an implicit *elevation* of one type of social ordering over another.

Finally, one must note that, in the case of the OMC, a similar 'problem of hierarchy' could easily apply. Who gets to decide on the objectives, indicators, targets and metrics of the OMC, and when they are decided, are they really as beyond political contestation as the procedural approach would seem to suggest? Do they not instead precisely invoke competing conceptions of what the boundaries of a 'European social model', or adequate principles of 'good governance' in the European Union, really are?

The danger of course is that what is presented as an example of decentralisation involves a reassertion of hierarchy at a supposedly 'abstract', but instead latently politicised, level. While decision-making power is devolved to national or sub-national contexts, these discussions may still be steered by norms that either 'mask' substantive values, or are open to manipulation by the most powerful political actors (a problem that – as the fourth chapter will illustrate – shadows the practice of indicator formulation within a number of OMC processes).

This analysis brings us to two conclusions. While proceduralism may be a useful analytical framework for analysing changes in EU law – and a crucial one in order to address broader shifts in the forms of post-national law-making – it is not without significant problems. How these problems play out within the specific context of the 'new governance' debate in a general sense, and in the case of the OMC in particular, will be the subject of the following chapter, which will seek to test the procedural approach to new governance through its concrete application to the OMC processes in social inclusion and protection.

Secondly, however, this analysis leads us to a necessary evaluation of proceduralism's limits *in and of itself*. A purely procedural approach to new governance leaves certain issues unaccounted for. What is its relationship, for example, to more 'thick' readings of legality; those that emphasise 'the democratic genesis of the law', or the use of new governance mechanisms to address the EU's current legitimacy deficits? Can we complement proceduralism, and the accounts of Deakin and de Schutter of 'reflexive governance', with other models, which take as their starting point not the distinction between 'substance' and 'procedure', but the need for more experimental and deliberative forms of social organisation?

The limits of a procedural theory of governance both demand concrete answers (that at the moment can only be deferred) and have led the new governance debate in Europe to look beyond its shores; to polities at once divorced from the peculiar features of the EU and, at the same time, immersed in similar debates. The next approach - directly-deliberative polyarchy or 'experimentalism' - may, in looking to the US example, provide a vital extra starting point in unpacking the law–governance relation.

3. Governance and experimentalism

3.1 *Directly-deliberative polyarchy and the pragmatist challenge*

The name 'directly-deliberative polyarchy' (DDP) gives something away, which is that DDP is a particularly complex, and at times convoluted, theoretical framework. This complexity is associated with its attachment to a number of normative and organisational values - polyarchy, experimentalism, deliberation and direct participation - which the various accounts of DDP try to weave together. In this sense, it is a framework in transition; a lesson one can again decipher merely from its title, which has migrated over the years from 'legal pragmatism' to 'deliberative polyarchy', and finally to a new home, 'democratic experimentalism'.[45] While there may be subtle differences, and while each term may emphasise some elements over others, it is probably fair to describe these approaches as contributing to both a common yet evolving theoretical edifice.

Without question, this edifice has a different historical and theoretical trajectory to the procedural accounts developed in the last section. This is so in two senses. Firstly, it has been developed in a US context, with certain features - from a marked decline in public confidence in the federal government, to a tendency to provide public and social services outwith the state - that are not necessarily replicated in the

[45] As well as Simon below, see for the most influential essays, M. Dorf and C. Sabel, 'A Constitution of Democratic Experimentalism' (1998) 98 *Columbia Law Review* 2; J. Cohen and C. Sabel, 'Directly-Deliberative Polyarchy' (1997) 3 *European Law Journal* 4; O. Gerstenberg and C. Sabel, 'Directly-Deliberative Polyarchy: An Institutional Ideal for Europe?' in C. Joerges and R. Dehousse (eds.), *Good Governance in Europe's Integrated Market* (Oxford University Press, 2002).

European experience. Secondly, experimentalism consequently has its own theoretical obsessions. Whereas accounts in Europe have commonly taken as their starting point Weber's famous thesis about formal and anti-formal tendencies in modern law, experimentalism emerges from an equally influential pragmatist strand in American legal thought.

In an influential essay, Bill Simon has attempted to contrast this pragmatism with a dominant model to permeate the practice and education of the American lawyer – liberal legalism.[46] This legalism appears in Simon's account both as an ethical attitude towards the place of law in society, and as a sociological description of the role of the lawyer as an intermediary between the individual and larger institutions. Ethically, legalism takes the side of the functionally weaker party against larger and more powerful actors (corporations in the private sphere; states in the public one).[47] To take an example from popular culture, it echoes the image of the heroic trial lawyer (epitomised by the novels of Harper Lee and John Grisham), riding to the rescue of the victimised and voiceless.

Operationally, legalism carries this task through drawing a circle of procedural protection around the individual.[48] The legal system individuates particular claims, allowing – through an objective adjudicative procedure – redress for potential infringements of individual rights. The lawyer is the gatekeeper of this process – all channels of information relevant for the conduct of a trial must go through him or her. This function is carried out in order to protect the client from self-incrimination, manipulation by officials, and undue intrusions upon their privacy. We access the law *through lawyers* in order to reinforce the ethical commitment to giving all parties – including the weak – effective legal remedies.

The pragmatist challenge to this structure derives less from an objection to the ethical imperative to legally address inequalities of power, than from a scepticism that liberal legalism as it stands can achieve this goal. Legalism's rights discourse gives poorer or weaker individuals the legal tools to challenge negative infringements on their rights, but precisely works *against* the positive policy mechanisms that have proven most central to advancing their position. Its procedural rules, so

[46] W. Simon, 'Solving Problems vs Claiming Rights: The Pragmatist Challenge to Legal Liberalism' (2004) 46 *William and Mary Law Review* 127.

[47] *Ibid.*, at 133–135. [48] *Ibid.*, at 139–140.

Simon argues, have empowered lawyers largely to protect *their own* interests – particularly in extracting substantial fees through protracted tort proceedings – rather than the claims of the 'victim class' they are said to represent. This class would benefit less from individuated claims than from civic organisation – the exercise of social power through collectivities – either in the form of class action suits against companies externalising risks onto consumers, or social unions and agencies with the power to distribute resources, or provide services.[49] In so much as these collectivities have sought to provide solutions to problems of social and economic deprivation (access to housing and access to child services are two widely discussed examples in the literature) the legalist approach has impeded, rather than enabled, their progress.

In its place, pragmatism suggests a different attitude. The lawyer is there not to protect victims, but to *activate citizens*. These citizens do not simply passively react when existing legal programmes threaten their private 'rights', but must actively seek to organise themselves into groups capable of advancing social and public policy goals.[50] Abuses of power are to be rendered accountable not through the paternalist impulses of a lawyering class, but through political institutions and groupings within society as such, who share common goals, and who are prepared to assert their interests as a community. At least in this sense, it is of little surprise that experimentalism should have arisen in the context of an American polity, where both the ideal of associational democracy, and the responsibility for social provision of non-governmental institutions (e.g. church, family and community) are particularly strong.[51]

Under this model, the law is not primarily aimed towards a resolution of existing private conflicts than it is towards solutions. As Simon writes:

[49] *Ibid.*, at 156–161.

[50] For a similar understanding of the role of the citizen in legal processes, see Selznick and Nonet's conception of 'civility' under responsive law. P. Selznick and P. Nonet, *Law and Society in Transition: Towards Responsive Law* (Washington: Octagon, 1978).

[51] For a famous account, see A. de Tocqueville, *Democracy in America* (London: Penguin, 2003). The important side question here is whether the emphasis on associational democracy in the context of the US limits the applicability of experimentalist theories to the EU. Does the EU have a 'civil society', or a tradition of interaction between 'lower-level groups' and public policy, or has this effect been stunted in the European case by the comparatively stronger historical role of the state?

> Pragmatist practice is problem solving. A legal claim is a suggestion of a problem that calls for a public solution. From the pragmatist point of view, the most important difference between solutions and rights is that solutions to problems cannot be derived analytically. They are best derived deliberatively, and experimentally.[52]

The law must provide the conditions for the experimental and deliberative building of policy solutions. Under the pragmatist vision, law is not only reactive: it must provide the foundations for an experimental testing and building of policy solutions. It must encourage actors themselves to take responsibility for animating and elaborating legal programmes.

In doing so, experimentalist literature outlines three potential roles for modern law. First of all, Courts play a role in destabilising or re-evaluating existing knowledge. In a near-exhaustive study of the example of child welfare reform, Sabel, Simon and Noonan have outlined the efforts of courts to suspend programmes or services underperforming in relation to their mandates.[53] The example of the European Court could also be used here – the ECJ brings new issues, or new understandings of legal problems, to the table, which must somehow be reconciled with an existing, nationally defined body of jurisprudence. Law breaks down old certainties, encouraging cognitive re-evaluation, while at the same time, incentivising participants to construct *new* knowledge. Law has an essentially cognitive or communicative function in the sense that it both imparts information (i.e. encourages a reflexive attitude on the part of its participants) and carries it (i.e. is open to future re-evaluation of those understandings *on the basis of information that only the affected actors themselves hold*).[54]

Secondly, the Court must play a role in inducing the parties to a particular problem or dispute to negotiate (rather than impose a settlement of its own making). The guiding assumption of the experimental approach is that a negotiated and commonly agreed outcome (one based on a common pooling of information) is always preferable to a solution imposed by courts alone.[55] Here, DDP speaks to its 'polyarchical' aspects – the job of the legal system is not only to 'execute' given

[52] Simon, n. 46 above, at 177.

[53] K. Noonan, C. Sabel and W. Simon, 'Legal Accountability in the Service-based Welfare State: Lessons from Child Welfare Reform' (2009) 34 *Law and Social Inquiry* 3.

[54] See C. Sabel and J. Zeitlin, 'Learning from Difference: The New Architecture of Experimentalist Governance in the EU' (2008) 14 *European Law Journal* 3 at 303–305.

[55] Simon, n. 46 above, at 185–186.

norms, but to delegate the task of *framing* legal provisions to lower-level actors, who must themselves negotiate and deliberate their meaning.

Finally, legal institutions have a role to play in ongoing monitoring and review. Legal decisions are not treated as one-off incidents; their purpose is not only to return the parties to their normative starting positions. Instead, norms are seen as revisable, and therefore requiring *structures for revision*. As Simon puts it:

> Just as every default rule is regarded as no more than a starting point to be readily discarded as better options are discovered, every negotiated consensus is a starting point for a continuous effort at implementation.[56]

Again, we return here to an issue discussed under the first procedural heading. The law is not regarded as something settled in advance of its application; but deemed open to revision in light of the expectations and preferences of legal participants. The challenge, again like proceduralisation, is to lay down a structure through which forms of 'revision', 'negotiation' and 'consensus building' can take place.

As 'a revision structure', law under DDP essentially engages in a trade-off. On the one hand, it delegates decision-making power, or encourages lower level actors to 'experiment' with policy solutions. It encourages the very forms of diversity which have been seen – through much of the new governance debate – as debilitating to the attempt to provide the EU with a more robust 'social dimension'.

'In a deliberative polyarchy, local – or more exactly, lower level actors – are granted autonomy to experiment with solutions of their own devising within broadly defined areas of public policy.'[57]

A founding premise of deliberative approaches has thus been that public discussion is not undermined by a retreat to more sectional identities, but potentially benefits from the working through of common positions in situations of diversity. The very recognition of diversity – 'the politics of difference' – can allow a truly public and general law to reach normative and social spaces that were previously closed off to it.

Such an attitude permeates DDP's view of experimentalism – and even of the prospects of EU integration itself.[58] Law should see deliberation – in the words of Iris Marion Young – 'as a resource for democratic communication'.

[56] *Ibid.*, at 187. [57] See Gerstenberg and Sabel, n. 45 above, at 291–292.

[58] See, for example, Sabel and Zeitlin's treatment of enlargement, n. 54 above, at 319–323.

> While not abandoning their own perspectives, people who listen across differences come to understand something about the way that proposals and policies affect others differently situated. They gain knowledge of what is going on in different social locations and how social processes appear to connect and conflict from different points of view. By internalising such a mediated vision, participants in democratic discussion and decision-making gain a wider picture of the social processes in which their own partial knowledge is embedded. Such a more comprehensive social knowledge better enables them to arrive at wise solutions to collective problems to the extent that they are committed to doing so.[59]

This is experimentalism's broader normative hope. Perhaps the fracturing of society – its division along functional, normative, and territorial lines – need not mean an end to truly 'public' forms of law-making, but can mean a form of law in which citizens themselves can articulate the meaning of the law in their own personal context. The diversity of modern societies – and of a European polity – does not stand in the way of collective solutions, but instead forces rule-makers to consider the impact of rules on *all* actors, as a precondition for effective reform.

The second aspect of the trade-off, however, is the opportunity that such delegation provides for 'the centre'. It is not only the case that lower level actors are encouraged to experiment with policy solutions, but also that 'the results' of such experimentation are to feed back into the objectives and procedures of the policy community as whole.

'In return' for the granting of decisional autonomy, lower level actors must also, in the words of Sabel and Gerstenberg:

> Furnish central or higher level units with rich information regarding their goals as well as the progress they are making towards achieving them, and agree to respect in their actions, framework rights of democratic procedure and substance as these are elaborated in the process of experimentation itself. The periodic pooling of results reveals the defects of parochial solutions, and allows the elaboration of standards for comparing local achievements, exposing poor performers to criticism from within and without, and making of good ones (temporary) models for emulation.

Here, both the problem and the opportunity arise. On the one hand, the second aspect of Sabel and Gerstenberg's definition of DDP speaks to its 'polyarchical' elements. Diversity is seen not as a route to self-referential discourses, but as an opportunity for mutual learning. The

[59] I. Marion Young, 'Difference as a Resource for Democratic Communication', in Bohman and Rehg, n. 42 above, at 403–404.

separation of decision-making sights is an experimental advantage, so long as opportunities exist for both 'central' institutions, and other actors (like neighbouring states) to learn from the experiences of each other.[60] If polyarchy is truly 'deliberative', the sharing of experience can indeed expose parochial solutions to external criticism, and reinforce examples that take account of their impact on others.

At the same time, the idea of 'granting' autonomy 'in exchange' for information sits uneasily with our perception of what a polity like the EU is supposed to mean. In the areas in which Sabel, Zeitlin and other exponents of deliberative approaches have identified experimental forms of governance, the EU is not in a position to 'grant autonomy to lower level units', but instead has had its capacity to intervene intentionally limited. The Treaties have placed the lower level actor itself (i.e. the member state) in a sovereign position, able to determine the extent of their legislative commitments, and the role of the EU in mediating them.

Under DDP, this position is subtly reformed. Lower level actors are not given autonomy only for its own sake, but in order to increase the cognitive capacity of central institutions. They are used as experimental 'sites', able through their separate endeavours, to create a better strategy for the policy-making community as a whole. This strategy is one constantly open to challenge and reformulation, yet one that suddenly finds itself radically divorced from its original national or 'local' home. To this extent, DDP does not only mean the dispersal of decision-making capacity, but also presents opportunities for recentralisation (albeit on a 'deliberative' or 'dynamic' basis). Areas that were closed off to central intervention through their complexity, or distance, now become subject to the purview of central institutions.[61] We do not have to switch perspective all too radically to see DDP as suffering from 'a problem of hierarchy' akin to the one observed under the procedural approach.

[60] 'In conventional views of deliberative decision-making, the goal is consensus and reflective equilibrium. In the EU, by contrast, deliberative decision making is driven at least as much by the discussion and elaboration of difference.' Sabel and Zeitlin, n. 54 above, at 274.

[61] This gives weight to considerations that the OMC – and the DDP approach – could lead to moves towards procedural or functional centralisation (precisely in spite of its devolutionary rhetoric). For an exploration of this in the context of new governance, see S. Smismans, 'New Modes of Governance and the Participatory Myth' (2008) 31 *West European Politics* 5; for a more theoretical treatment, see P. Kjaer, '3 Forms of Governance; 3 Forms of Power', in E. Erikssen, C. Joerges and F. Roedl, *Law, Democracy and Solidarity in a Post-national Union* (London: Routledge, 2008).

This perspective becomes relevant as we move onto the next sections. To what extent is DDP not just an interesting theoretical framework, or a way for Europeans to access academic discussions on the other side of the Atlantic, but a model able to inform discussions about the EU? And, furthermore, does the tension just described – between DDP's 'centre' and its 'periphery' – belie other problems in the experimentalist framework? As with the procedural approach, the next two sections will explore experimentalism, as a model that both carries explanatory potential, and displays important normative challenges.

3.2 The 'experimentalist architecture' of governance in the European Union

As we have already discussed, the DDP framework has a transatlantic origin. One might expect then that its application to the EU would be something of a theoretical hangover. There are plenty of objections to the use of experimentalist ideas in the European context. Its commitment to deliberation, for example, seems more robust in the US context, than in a European public space in which common media and institutions, and a common language, are absent. How can European law make use of the opportunity that deliberative polyarchy suggests – of new spaces for deliberation and accountability between peers – when some of its cultural preconditions are lacking? Here, we are talking of something the US has – a common 'background frame' or, in Habermasian terms, a 'life-world' – that in Europe, has only ever existed in embryonic form.

In spite of this limitation, proponents of DDP have insisted that the EU is not just a 'foreign' example to which experimentalism might apply, but central to its conceptual advances. The EU is not an 'outlier', but a 'front-runner'; a paradigm case.[62] It is so precisely because it lacks many of the features which make a 'traditional' view of accountability and the rule of law feasible.[63] In the European case, precisely the lack of a sovereign parliamentary authority, and the presence of extensive 'gaps' between European law as it exists in

[62] Sabel and Zeitlin, n. 54 above, at 278.

[63] See C. Sabel and W. Simon, 'Epilogue: Accountability without Sovereignty' in G. de Burca and J. Scott (eds.), *Law and New Governance in the EU and the US* (Oxford: Hart, 2006) at 398–400.

directives and regulations, and EU law as it has been applied in distinct national legal systems, makes clear lines of authority between those who 'make' the law and those who are responsible for applying it difficult. One cannot forward a normative vision of European law which simply copies the visions of 'legality' that are assumed to exist at the national level.

At the same time, this has not diminished the need for transnational solutions. Still states face significant interdependencies, or collective action problems that require a pooling of common information. These demands are evident in the areas where mechanisms like the OMC have been developed. The call for transnational responses to regulatory problems has not abated, even if the available mechanisms to render such action legitimate are not easy to find.

In response to this dilemma, these states have turned to an experimentalist framework; one that neither concentrates action in the hands of a supra-national executive – whose cognitive capacity and steering mechanisms are woefully inadequate to solve problems invoking 'the dense complexity' of several national contexts – nor completely disperses decision-making authority to states living in an ever more integrated and interdependent polity. There is being developed 'an underlying architecture of public rule-making in the EU'; one that runs beneath or parallel to the official 'constitutionalised' relationship between the EU and its member states.

In short, we can see evidence of precisely the type of 'trade-off' that animated Sabel and Gerstenberg's original definition of 'DDP'.

> In this decision-making design, framework goals (such as full employment, social inclusion, 'good water status', a unified energy grid) and measures for gauging their achievement are established by joint action of the Member States and EU institutions. Lower-level units (such as national ministries or regulatory authorities, and the actors with whom they collaborate) are given the freedom to advance these ends as they see fit.[64]

This is the first part of the trade-off – the functional granting of autonomy. In the OMC example, it can be analogised to the system of national reporting, where the EU sets overall objectives, but

[64] Gertsenberg and Sabel, n. 45 above, at 273.

encourages governments to design their own solutions in delivering them.[65]

The second element of the trade-off is represented by other aspects of the OMC procedure:

> But in return for this autonomy, they must report regularly on their performance, especially as measured by the agreed indicators, and participate in a peer review in which their results are compared with those pursuing other means to the same general ends. Finally, the framework goals, metrics and procedures themselves are periodically revised by the actors who initially established them, augmented by such new participants whose views come to be seen as indispensable to full and fair deliberation.

The second part of the new compact is the obligation incumbent upon states participating in OMC procedures to report on their performance, and submit it to evaluation according to common benchmarks. The delegation of authority is also to have a reflexive dimension, feeding back in to the common objectives, and even leading to potential revisions in the way the procedures of the method themselves are laid out. Here, there is – on its face at least – an eerily close fit between DDP's original design and the OMC's 'official' enumerated procedure as it has developed via the Lisbon strategy.

DDP has sought to identify in the method both 'directly-deliberative' and 'polyarchical' elements. It is seen as polyarchical for reasons that we have already given – because the rejection of classical instruments also entails some rejection of an explicit legal hierarchy.[66] There is no expectation that the sharing of common objectives, or even a common procedural frame, will lead to uniform outcomes. There would be little

[65] It must be noted there is a shifting 'object of analysis' in respect of applications of DDP to the example of 'new governance'. In recent literature – like Sabel and Zeitlin's exhaustive article – 'experimentalism' is generalised. It includes, but is not exhausted by the OMC itself. One can therefore only see all of its features – its 'common architecture' – if we combine the OMC with other policy mechanisms. The problem of course with this 'architectural' approach is that – in any one area – a vital ingredient of the DDP approach may be missing. Inclusion – the subject of our case study – is a prescient example. While later in Sabel and Zeitlin's article, they talk about 'penalty default' rules as possible incentive mechanisms for parties who otherwise would not negotiate, it is difficult to see how – in an area like inclusion, where an explicit legal competence is lacking – this mechanism could operate effectively. On penalty defaults, see Sabel and Zeitlin, n. 54 above, at 305–309.

[66] 'The goal here too is mutual correction not uniformity'. J. Cohen and C. Sabel, 'Sovereignty and Solidarity: EU and US' in J. Zeitlin and D. Trubek (eds.), *Governing Work and Welfare in a New Economy* (Oxford University Press, 2003) at 347.

point to 'mutual learning' or to peer review structures, if the outcome of mutual learning was simply to 'relearn' that which is already known.

It is seen as 'directly-deliberative' for similar reasons. Peer review not only provides possibilities for integrating different perspectives, but also to encourage actors to see their perception of problems as cognitively open. A state's 'interest' in a particular policy is not treated as fixed or given, but open to readjustment in light of other experience, and in light of having to justify one's position *in relation to others*.[67] Part of the challenge the OMC undertakes is to encourage actors 'to question their initial representation of the issues which they confront, and even more precisely, to reconstruct the definition of those issues with the other actors concerned'.[68] Law – and EU law – must not only take forward particular legislative priorities, but encourage the construction and reforming of collective knowledge.

The task of course is to see where, under the OMC, this capacity lies. We can only start with a presumptive scepticism. To begin with, there is a potential contradiction. How can law both 'carry' particular understandings of problems, and 'disentrench' them at the same time? Much has been made – in the OMC example – of the rise of a discourse on 'active' welfare policies (both in labour markets, and in social inclusion) which could back up Sabel and Zeitlin's claim that the OMC contains a capacity for cognitive re-evaluation.[69] We can imagine therefore that the method has 'guided' national policies by creating a new common policy vocabulary.

The problem with this, however, is that the more the vocabulary is effective, the less it would seem to create possibilities for a re-evaluation of existing knowledge. Is there not a possibility that the method itself could not 'destabilise' but instead 'entrench' particular policy paradigms? If the capacity of DDP to 'frame' national policy is truly acted

[67] Indeed, this is an aspect that is seemingly common to both DDP and the procedural approach. In Deakin and de Schutter's account they thus argue that: 'Central among the conditions of success for the OMC and related processes are mechanisms which function as incentives for actors to reflect upon the extent to which their understanding of the problem which is to be overcome, and their own position, may be context dependent.' Deakin and de Schutter, n. 38 above, at 4.

[68] *Ibid.*

[69] See e.g. J. Zeitlin, 'The Open Method of Co-ordination in Action: Theoretical Promise, Empirical Realities, Reform Strategy' in J. Zeitlin and P. Pochet (eds.), *The Open Method of Coordination in Action: The European Employment and Social Inclusion Strategies* (Bern: Peter Lang, 2005) at 450–457. See also S. Bernhard, n. 134 below.

upon, the 'polyarchy' upon which it is also based could potentially be under threat.

Overcoming this scepticism depends on other elements. It depends, for example, on the ability of the method to encourage states to view the issues which the method is said to 'coordinate' as common problems. It depends equally on the capacity to create a robust peer review structure; one in which common understandings – framed in the European objectives, and restated in national reports – are not treated as given, but subjected to public scrutiny, and even revised on the basis of each state's experience. To this extent, the success of deliberative polyarchy depends not only on robust institutions and procedures, but also on the political commitment and will of the involved actors to take the process of policy coordination seriously.[70]

These initial scepticisms again must be addressed in the particular – through the case study in social inclusion, which will be the subject of the fourth chapter. They belie, however, other problems – inner tensions between the commitment of DDP to the dispersal of normative authority and the danger that 'experimentalism' could lead to centralisation, or an implicit concentration of social power.

3.3 *Experimentalism and the rule of law*

I would like briefly to document three (interrelated) problems (many of them documented by the architects of the 'experimentalist' project themselves). These problems will be described as: (i) the problem of power, (ii) the problem of hierarchy, and (iii) the problem of stability. A number of them, as we will later see, are also shared by the other two approaches.

(i) The problem of power

Simon already recognised the problem of power in his original 'Claiming Rights' article in a final discussion of 'interest representation'.[71] Experimental regimes rely, as we have seen, on the ability to harness cognitive resources, and encourage deliberation among

[70] See A. Héretier, 'New Modes of Governance in Europe: Policy-making without Legislating?' in Héretier (ed.) *Common Goods: Reinventing European and International Governance* (Lanham: Rowman and Littlefield, 2002) at 202–203. See also, A. Héretier and M. Rhodes, 'Governing in the Shadow of Hierarchy: New Modes of Governance in Regulation' in Héretier and Rhodes (eds.), *New Modes of Governance in Europe: Governing in the Shadow of Hierarchy* (Basingstoke: Palgrave MacMillan, 2010).

[71] Simon, n. 46 above, at 209–211.

stakeholders. In a complex and diverse polity, solutions cannot be imposed from above, not only because of legitimacy problems, but because of the lack of the necessary pool of technical and social information. The delegation of authority to key stakeholders is a means of increasing law's responsiveness. The vital question is over who these stakeholders are to be. As Simon recognises, 'legal pragmatism has little to say about who has standing to participate in stakeholder negotiations and how the views of different participants are to be weighed in decision-making'.[72] Answering this question is both crucial, and difficult.

Simon himself suggests a presumption of inclusion over exclusion (as well as for consensus over voting). Similarly, the Habermasian understanding relies on an idea that all those with a stake in the outcome of a legal programme have a legitimate say in its formulation. Reading participation requirements broadly would seem the only way of safeguarding a vital political commitment – that individuals should have access to the law, and to public policy, on an equal basis.

The problem – one recognised in democratic theory for centuries – is that the participation of all those affected has surely been overtaken by the rise of mass democracy. It is certainly unrealistic in a national democracy; even more so in a European one.[73] A limitless form of participation – the more it is successful – increasingly places pressure on the ideals of direct deliberation and exchange between individuals on which deliberative theory also rests. It makes the deliberative 'working through' of policy solutions more difficult.

One can see this – as was briefly developed in the last chapter – through the example of comitology. In part, its success in creating forms of deliberative exchange, and decision-making through consensus, is based on the 'socialisation' of the involved actors; the fact that they can coalesce around a limited, and functionally specialised, problem-to-be-solved.[74] The more, however, the process is opened up, the more it would seem to call for, not direct, but indirect forms of representation (i.e. a retreat to 'representative' or 'liberal' models of democracy, and with it, a retreat from the experimentalist ideal to a more distanced or hierarchical one).

There is a second and connected problem. Even if we 'solve' the first obstacle, i.e. even if we can assume that all with a legitimate interest are

[72] *Ibid.*, at 209. [73] See Scheuerman, n. 18 above, at 87.
[74] See Joerges and Neyer, n. 108 below, at 291–292.

to be included, real inequalities between participants are likely to persist. The very removal of hierarchy experimentalism suggests makes other forms of hierarchy, e.g. the divisions within participants as regards power, wealth and resources, more potent.[75] More organised actors, with access to greater resources, are not only likely to exert formal influence on the process, but are also more likely to carry the necessary 'know-how' to frame an argument that is convincing to others.[76]

Here, an old critique of formal law returns with a vengeance. Does the formal equality to participate which experimentalism provides merely mask more important disparities of power that are now free to be valorised through the rhetoric of 'open and deliberative' policy-making?[77] In doing away with the 'victim perspective' Simon so derides, experimentalism opens itself up to a criticism from the perspective of power of which it is well aware.[78] It has not yet offered an adequate response.

(ii) The problem of hierarchy

The second problem relates to central institutions, like courts and legislatures: what exactly is their role under an 'experimental' regime? Simon admits that experimentalism 'makes courts less central', yet insists that they still have an important 'destabilising' role. At the same time, in the horizontal model of accountability he espouses, courts and legislatures seem to be squeezed out. Under a 'rolling' or iterative rule regime, accountability, as we have seen, is not seen 'backwards', to the original legislative mandate, but 'forwards' and

75 For an expansion, see M. Greven, 'The Informalization of Transnational Governance: A Threat to Democratic Governance' in E. Grande and L. Pauly (eds.), *Complex Sovereignty: Re-constituting Political Authority in the 21st Century* (University of Toronto Press, 2005) at 272–275.

76 Arguably US politics provides a good example. Candidates that are better financed have more money to run ads and even *personally* to contact voters in influential early voting states (e.g. through the primary system). They thus are able to appear as more 'genuine', 'personable', etc. than their less organised opponents.

77 See D. Kennedy, 'Remarks on New Governance', Paper Presentation to the Workshop on New Governance, Harvard Law School, February 2005.

78 There is certainly an explicit reference to this in Simon's conclusion to 'Claiming Rights': 'Legal liberalism has been centrally pre-occupied with imbalances of power and wealth and with background entitlements that determine people's options in the event that negotiation fails. It would be reckless to ignore its warning that search for collective goals risks coercing the most vulnerable or under-appreciating their interests.' Simon, n. 46 above, at 212.

'sideways', to peer review institutions.[79] Are courts and legislatures merely to be considered as one of these peer actors, playing an ongoing review function, or do they have some more constitutive role?

Sometimes this latter function is alluded to. As we have described, in experimentalism, courts are there to 'induce parties to negotiate'. They have a role in 'creating conditions' for free negotiation. They may even – if the first objection is to be addressed – have a role in hearing and defining who the relevant participants in any concrete legislative process should be. Under all of these functions, Courts have a role to play – in a similar manner to the procedural approach – in setting the terrain over which the experimental game can be played.

It is hard to imagine, however, how central institutions could fulfil any of these tasks without returning to some of the forms of legal hierarchy that experimental approaches explicitly try to reject. Surely the 'conditions for free negotiation', for example, are provided through the procedural rules of the court, the authority of the judge, the rules of judicial evidence, and the other elements of the existing legal apparatus? Equally the idea of 'inducing the parties to negotiate' relies upon the court as a background institution, able to step in, and utilise old 'legalist' models where negotiated compromise breaks down, or else, to use Sabel and Zeitlin's term, as a 'penalty default' where one party is unwilling to deliberate with the other? In basic terms: can experimentalism survive without hierarchy, and if it requires hierarchy, is it really experimental?[80]

(iii) The problem of stability

Finally, there may be a problem in the way experimentalism approaches its temporal dimension. William Scheuerman has explored this problem in an explicit critique of DDP.[81] He associates the primary

[79] Sabel and Simon, n. 63 above.

[80] The additional difficulty is that there seems to be something of a conflict between the main protagonists of the theory on this question. Whereas on the one hand, Sabel and Zeitlin's work tends to mirror the approach of 'turtles all the way down', i.e. revisable standards, even at the procedural level, Sabel and Simon's work on child welfare sees the reforms conducted in Alabama and Arkansas as complementary to an existing federal legislative scheme. There remains some question: are all norms truly to be seen as 'rebuttable' presumptions, or are we still governing 'under the shadow' of another legal or federal hierarchy?

[81] W. Scheuerman, 'Democratic Experimentalism or Capitalist Synchronisation: Critical Reflections on Directly-Deliberative Polyarchy' (2004) *Canadian Journal of Law and Jurisprudence* 17.

challenge of regulatory law as 'time and space compression'; the increasing rapidity of capitalist relations of exchange and hence the difficulty of regulating modern society through the ordinary procedures of a liberal democracy (which are long and burdensome precisely to ensure that relevant political institutions and actors can be consulted on any proposed change).[82] What, in systems theory (as we will see in section 4) appears as a *functional* gap between different systemic contexts, or under proceduralism, appears as a *rationality* gap between the rule and its application, appears here as a *temporal* gap – 'Legislators and administrators may find themselves debating complex issues and potential objects of regulation whose contours suddenly alter before their eyes.'[83]

Law is faced, in this situation, with a paradox. Either it could accept the gap, and with it, downgrade law's relevance as a force capable of regulating social life, or capitalism's worst excesses. Courts could, as Weber's formal paradigm suggested, merely confine themselves to the formal guarantee of individual rights. Or else, it 'synchronises state economic regulation in accordance with the temporal imperatives of high-speed capitalism'. Either law refuses to 'catch up' with society, or it does so precisely by sacrificing its own 'normative character', i.e. its presence as an institution that is in some way *independent* of the activities it is attempting to regulate.[84]

As Scheuerman points out, the 'inflexibility' and temporal inefficiency of the legal medium so derided by many economic critics of regulatory law is precisely what provides it with its liberal character; it is what may allow political debate, the entry of other views, and the review of decisions on grounds of their undermining of individual or group rights, to take place. The move in favour of 'capitalist synchronisation' could then be a move against the tradition of locating the legitimacy of law in popular assent and political deliberation.

While experimentalism, or DDP, presents itself as a way out of this paradox, it too attempts to 'synchronise' regulatory law with the economic structures of global capitalism. It does so by mimicking the preference of economy for the constant adaptation of rules, and their benchmarking according to 'performance'.[85] An early Marxist prediction was that capitalist economies were like bicycles – if one stops pedalling, one is also likely to fall off. Economies require new markets,

[82] See Scheuerman, *ibid.*, at 90. [83] *Ibid.*, at 105. [84] *Ibid.*, at 106. [85] *Ibid.*, at 110.

new goods and new technologies in order to create wealth; perhaps a similar adaptive quality is needed in law.

Scheuerman's suggestion is that perhaps law does not and should not evolve in this way. Our commitment to law and to liberal democracy may suggest that the constant perturbations of the modern economy precisely requires a legal system that is more stable or static, or at the very least, some kind of trade-off between constancy and adaptation. In his eyes, therefore, the link drawn in experimentalism between law and economy:

> seems eerily reminiscent of the troubling Schmittian view that liberal democratic political and legal institutions (in this case, Parliaments and the rule of law) necessarily rest on a specific mode of capitalism, and that with the decay of that earlier capitalist 'stage', so too must traditional liberal democratic structures suffer decline.[86]

In this sense, law's commitment to particular values (e.g. the bundle of norms over prospectivity and stability in rules that we call 'the rule of law') is not something that evolves just as surrounding social conditions evolve, but carries its own entrenched dynamic or character. We commit to particular legal institutions to protect us from the uncertainty of a game in which the rules are constantly changing.[87] To this extent, the insecurity that economic globalisation has brought to our working lives (the fear that our jobs will be lost, or savings devalued, with little warning) is not offset under an experimental regime, but carried over from the economic sphere, into the constituent rules of social and political life.

One feels that this may be a more fundamental critique of experimentalism than the other two criticisms. It does not simply point to potential internal inconsistencies, or particular groups that are left out, but critiques the very idea of legal evolution in the face of societal change, upon which all three 'inside theories' rest. In combination with the other criticisms it points to an important tension within 'inside' theories. While they all attempt to reconcile law with the diversity and rapidity of modern economy and society, to what extent do they do so at the cost of other important legal or political values? To what extent – even if we can succeed in conceptualising new governance as intra-legal in some important sense – are constitutive elements of legality in the EU

[86] *Ibid.*, at 124.

[87] *Ibid.*, at 126–127. This is also (see section 4.3) part of the Luhmannian critique of reflexive law.

being overlooked? Once again, these tensions should be kept in mind when considering both the merits of 'experimental' theories, and their use to describing (and even more *defending*) the EU's own 'governance turn'.

4. Governance as reflexive law

4.1 The use of reflexive law

By now, we can identify some points of similarity that have emerged between 'inside' approaches to the law–governance relationship. These common starting points will be used in the last section of this chapter to derive some shared elements of 'inside' conceptions of governance in the EU (features that will then be applied to the example of the OMC SPSI). To take an example of such a common foundation, both proceduralisation and DDP situate the development of 'new governance' in a complexity problem pertaining to modern societies, and to post-national legal orders like the EU in particular. This complexity potentially undermines some of law's traditional ethical and operational commitments, e.g. to relative stability and clarity in rules, reimagining the role of 'central' legal institutions, like courts, in the process.

Given this fact, perhaps the introduction of a third approach is pointless. Much of what I will say about reflexive law bears similarities to Habermasian proceduralisation (and to Sabel and Simon's model as well). This is unsurprising – the founders of the reflexive project – Günther Teubner and Helmet Willke – found their own theoretical inspiration in the essays by Habermas, Wiethölter and others that have already been extensively described. Isn't the introduction of reflexive law therefore just 'filler'; another excuse to go on a theoretical ramble, or to 'cover' further aspects of the dense and unfolding new governance literature?

The argument of this section, however, will be that – on the contrary – reflexive law adds a vital piece to the puzzle; one that much of the debate over new governance and the OMC has overlooked. Adding this element, however, requires a switch in perspective. The use of systems theory involves thinking about governance as responding not just to a challenge of vertical differentiation (i.e. different relationships between a European 'centre' and a national 'periphery'), but also to problems with horizontal differentiation (i.e. the steering of different functional sub-systems such as law, politics, science and so on that each carry particular rationalities and discourses of their own).[88] To what extent has European law mimicked the deficit of regulatory law in the nation state, i.e. over-estimated its ability to govern social systems with quite different operational logics? In Luhmann's famous phrasing, to what extent does Europe have 'a problem with steering'?[89]

Law's steering problem emerges from a basic fracture in modern societies. While it may have once been feasible to integrate individuals with reference to grand ethical or religious narratives – to carry, so to speak, a common normative language – communication in modern societies involves speaking in a way that is specialised. In order to 'deepen' the range of available meanings – to scientists, teachers, bankers, and even to lawyers – 'narrower' or more specialised discourses have emerged in specific fields. These discourses exclude any reference to 'general' social communication.

In law, the increasing 'materialisation' Habermas observed under the welfare state has been accompanied by internal *differentiation* – the development within the legal system of 'autonomous, positive, highly formalized and professionalized law'.[90] This development has been mimicked in other social systems – politics, economy, religion and so on – which, in order to become more complex, have increasingly separated themselves from the communication of 'the outside'.

The problem occurs when we switch to the perspective of regulatory law. Such law-making has greater ambitions than simply to refer to itself; it attempts to guide society towards socially ameliorative outcomes. One system (law) is attempting to communicate with another. How though is such communication possible? As Günther Teubner has famously argued:

> External demands are not directly translated into internal effects according to the stimulus-response scheme. They are filtered according to specific selection criteria into the respective system structures and adapted into the autonomous logic of the system. In terms of environmental influence on law, this means that even the most powerful social and political pressures are only perceived and processed in the legal system to the extent that they appear on the 'inner screens' of legal reality constructions. Conversely, legal regulations are accepted by

[88] S. Smismans, 'Reflexive Law in Support of Directly-Deliberative Polyarchy' in Deakin and de Schutter, n. 15 above, at 105.

[89] N. Luhmann, 'Limits of Steering' (1997) 14 *Theory, Culture and Society* 1.

[90] G. Teubner, n. 3 above, at 20.

> environmental systems only as external triggers for internal developments which are no longer controllable by law.[91]

This single paragraph contains the essence of Teubner's famous 'trilemma' of regulatory law. In a society in which law does not regulate society from an Archimedean point, but is 'one system among others', direct regulatory intervention is likely to lead to ineffective or unanticipated outcomes.[92] If law, economy, culture, science and so on all have autonomous and distinct rules of operation and selection, any direct communication from one to another is likely to lead to one of three outcomes: the colonisation by law of other systems, the pollution of law by its outside, or no effect.[93] The 'materialisation' of law fails, not because it is out of touch with the normative demands of its citizen – the Habermasian thesis – but because of its own hubris; the arrogant assumption that a central legislator can create a blueprint for social life comprehensible across all functional boundaries.

The plea of reflexive law – the response to this dilemma – is therefore first and foremost, a plea for legal humility. Certainly, deregulation, or 'alternatives to law' are, as Teubner puts it, 'not seriously considered as a counter-strategy. If it is correct that juridification in the welfare state is part of an epoch-making thrust of development then it cannot be reversed by mere political decision, let alone by an isolated decision about more or less law. The "floods of law" cannot be stemmed by dykes or dams; at best it can be channelled.'[94] Reflexive law therefore sets itself up as an opponent, not only of material law-making, but also of the Hayekian demand for a return to a formalist or market-driven legal order.[95]

How though is this 'channelling' to be conducted? In spite of the difficulties of regulating society under conditions of systems closure:

91 *Ibid.*, at 20–21.

92 'The greater the complexity and inter-dependence of the object area of control, the more difficult it is to identify distinct reference points, and to isolate them from each other'. G. Bechman, 'Reflexive Law: A New Theory Paradigm for Legal Science?' in A. Febbrajo and G. Teubner (eds.), *State, Law and Economy as Autopoietic Systems* (Milan: Giuffre, 1992) at 420.

93 To quote the famous dictum: 'Every regulatory intervention which goes beyond these limits is either irrelevant or produced disintegrating effects on the social area of life or else disintegrating effects on regulatory law itself.' Teubner, n. 3 above, at 21.

94 *Ibid.*, at 12.

95 On reflexive law as a 'third way' between deregulation and re-regulation, see J. Paterson, 'Reflecting on Reflexive Law' in M. King and C. Thornhill, *Luhmann on Law and Politics: Critical Appraisals and Applications* (Oxford: Hart, 2006) at 20–22.

> It is not impossible to invent a theoretical way out of the paradox. If the overall problem is one of exceedingly high complexity, then the overall solution must lie in complexity reducing and complexity processing mechanisms and institutions. And if the specific problems are consequences of the functional differentiation and specialisation of various sub-systems, specific solutions must consist in the creation of inter-linking structures and inter-mediating processes which make compatible, and re-integrate, the divergent sub-rationalities of the different parts.[96]

Willke and Teubner's 'way out' thus consists of both internal and external elements. The legal system must avoid society's 'disintegration'.[97] Even if one cannot overcome the distinct modes of operation of each system (in the vernacular of system's theory, its 'coding'), law must still be used as an inter-linking or coordinative social structure. This speaks to reflexive law's external dimension. Systems must be encouraged not only to democratise their internal procedures, but also to reflect on the impact of their action on the priorities and strategies of other social fields. Law must awake social systems precisely to their interdependence, i.e. to a realisation that they live in a world where the capacity of each to achieve their goals depends on the knowledge and cooperation of others.[98] As Teubner argues:

> Law must make the institutions concerned sensitive to the social effects which their strategies for the maximization of a specific rationality trigger.[99]

This 'sensitivity' also though depends on reflexive law's internal role. The other task of the legal system is to avoid society's 'over-integration', or ensure that systemic boundaries are not diluted. We have already seen – through Habermas' thesis of 'the colonisation of the life-world' – a danger that Luhmann terms 'de-differentiation'; the blurring, or overriding of systemic boundaries, and with it, a retreat to impersonal and

[96] H. Willke, 'Three Types of Legal Structure: The Conditional, the Purposive and the Relational Program' in Teubner (ed.), n. 4 above, at 289.

[97] This distinction is taken from Willke, who observes the role of his 'relational programming' as to avoid 'over-integration on the one hand, and dis-integration on the other'. Willke, *ibid.*, at 291.

[98] Teubner thus insists that: 'one can talk of reflexive Law if, and only if, the legal system identifies itself as an autopoietic system in a world of autopoietic systems and faces up to the consequences'. G. Teubner, *Law as an Autopoietic System* (Oxford: Blackwell, 1993) at 97. NB: this self-identification, however, may precisely be where the weaknesses of the reflexive approach lie (see Luhmann's criticisms of reflexive law, below).

[99] Teubner, n. 3 above, at 38–39.

intrusive forms of legal intervention.[100] A reflexive form of law-making depends crucially not only on granting but on *protecting* the autonomy of social systems; on ensuring the continued ability of each sphere of life to carry a distinct social role of its own (without the spectre of being 'totalised' by other political or legal imperatives).

As a result, reflexive law's 'internal' dimension suggests a trade-off between values relating to autonomy on the one hand and to integration on the other.[101] Left to their own devices, systems can often stagnate. In economy, we call this 'market failure' – the circumstances under which the very operation of a free market undermines its own preconditions, or privileges certain actors over others. Legal discourses over 'access to justice' and 'regulatory failure' attest to similar phenomenon within the system of law. While the central 'steering' of social systems is impossible, their abandonment to mere 'self-reflection' poses difficulties of its own.

In response – again a point of similarity with the other approaches of this chapter – law must retain a procedural role. Whereas the law 'no longer takes responsibility' for the achievement of substantive outcomes, it must be more ambitious about its institutional and discourse-enhancive capacities.[102] This speaks to reflexive law's final 'internal' task – to encourage 'reflexion' within social sub-systems, i.e. the presence of competing positions and information, the inducement of mutual learning, and due consideration of the relationship to the system's 'outside'.[103] Law 'integrates' not in the classical sense – i.e. through combining dense and distinct perspectives into a single regulatory framework – but through the building of a common reflexive capacity.

There are some similarities between these dual aspects of reflexive law and existing attempts to theorise EU governance. While certainly not emerging from a systems-theoretical tradition, the theory defended by Christian Joerges and Jurgen Neyer – of 'deliberative supranationalism' – shares some common ground with the reflexive view. Joerges and Neyer's theory argues that EU integration should be

[100] On the colonisation thesis, see Habermas, n. 4 above, at 216; on de-differentiation, see N. Luhmann, *Law as a Social System* (Oxford University Press, 2004) at 162–165.

[101] 'Reflexive law combines aspects of control with that of integration'. Bechmann, n. 86 above, at 425.

[102] G. Teubner, 'Substantive and Reflexive Elements in Modern Law' (1983) 17 *Law and Society Review* 2 at 254.

[103] See Willke, n. 96 above, at 290–293.

understood as a response to constitutional failure – the impossibility of adequately defending national sovereignty in a polity (like the EU) that is functionally interdependent.

> The legitimacy of governance within constitutional states is flawed in so far as it remains inevitably one-sided and parochial. The taming of the nation-state through democratic constitutions has its limits. If (and indeed because) democracies pre-suppose and represent collective identities, they have very few mechanisms to ensure that 'foreign' identities and their interests are taken into account within the decision-making process.[104]

While this problem has led to doctrines of 'supremacy' and 'direct-effect', deliberative supra-nationalism calls for a re-evaluation.[105] The role of EU law should not be to establish a legal order with primacy over the orders of the member states. Instead, it would do better to follow some of Willke's and Teubner's recommendations. Under conditions of territorial and functional differentiation:

> No single actor or organization or sub-system can generalize its own specific rationality or world-view and declare it binding for all the others. No single individual or corporate mind can construct an adequate internal map of the overall complexity of society; nor can it 'understand' all parts and the intricacies of their operations.[106]

As Joerges and Neyer themselves put it, supra-national steering requires that 'the interests and concerns of non-nationals should be considered even within the national polity'.[107]

Their answer (once more) is for a more humble role for European law. They call for a form of law-making that is less a substantive legal discipline in its own right than a form of 'conflict of laws'. European law – as a set of conflict rules – must try to delineate operational rules of competence and procedure that all parties can accept. It must primarily seek to render national policy discourses more sensitive to the operational norms and preferences of other jurisdictions.

[104] C. Joerges, 'Deliberative Political Processes Revisited: What Have we Learnt About the Legitimacy of Supranational Decision-Making' (2006) 44 *Journal of Common Market Studies* 4 at 789.

[105] See C. Joerges, 'Re-conceptualizing the Supremacy of European Law: A Plea for a New Supra-national Conflict of Laws' in B. Kohler-Koch and B. Rittberger (eds.), *Debating the Democratic Legitimacy of the European Union* (Lanham: Rowman and Littlefield, 2007).

[106] H. Willke, 'Societal Guidance through Law?' in Teubner and Febbrajo, n. 92 above, at 358.

[107] Joerges, n. 104 above, at 790–791.

> What supremacy requires then, is the identification of rules and principles that will ensure the co-existence of different constituencies and the compatibility of these constituencies' objectives with the common concerns they share. It is precisely about these issues that Community law needs to lay down a legal framework which structures political deliberation.[108]

While deliberative supra-nationalism takes as its starting point national rather than functional boundaries, this is certainly part of Willke and Teubner's meaning. In a society marked both by differentiation and interdependence, the challenge is not to achieve 'unity'; to integrate society under a common framework. The challenge instead is to insert – into otherwise self-referential discourses – criteria of action that encourage the consideration of others.[109]

4.2 *Reflexive law in the EU*

'Deliberative supra-nationalism' is a concept that has already been extensively applied to problems of EU governance. The concept of reflexive law, however, has had a very different trajectory. As with its related ideas (e.g. Wietholter's 'proceduralization' and Kirchheimer's 'juridification') the origins of reflexive law are in the domestic sphere, with the clearest application being the development, in continental Europe, of a complex system of 'co-determination'.[110] The concept's godfather, Teubner himself, did not much consider the European case, instead preferring to jump to the global and international arenas.[111] Does this tell us something; that ultimately, reflexive law has little explanatory purchase in the specific example of the EU?

The parameters of existing debates on 'new governance' in some sense support this suggestion. The most popular thesis about the

[108] C. Joerges and J. Neyer, 'From Inter-governmental Bargaining to Deliberative Political Processes: The Constitutionalisation of Comitology' (1997) 3 *European Law Journal* 3 at 294.

[109] The challenge is thus one of: 're-introducing the consequences of actions of social subsystems into their own reflection structure'. Teubner, n. 102 above, at 257.

[110] On the genesis of the concept, see Teubner, n. 3 above, at 33–37. It is unsurprising therefore that labour law has been the area in which the few essays applying the reflexive law concept to the EU have emerged. See e.g. R. Hobbs and W. Njoya, 'Regulating the European Labour Market: Prospects and Limitations of a Reflexive Governance Approach' (2005) 43 *British Journal of Industrial Relations* 2; C. Barnard, S. Deakin and R. Hobbs, 'Reflexive Law, Corporate Social Responsibility and the Evolution of Labour Standards' in Deakin and de Schutter, n. 15 above.

[111] See e.g. G. Teubner, 'Global Bukowina: Legal Pluralism in the World Society' in Teubner (ed.), *Global Law Without a State* (Aldershot: Ashgate, 1997).

OMC's origins is that it represents a 'constitutional compromise'; a trade-off between different levels of authority.[112] Reflexive law's instinct – that the main fracture in modern societies is not territorial, but functional, would seem to go against this characterisation. It would seem to add nothing to a debate which is primarily focused on the ongoing impasse between federalist and intergovernmental conceptions of the EU polity.[113]

The use of reflexive law depends on whether or not we can move beyond seeing the OMC in these terms only. As well as responding to constitutional limitations, the genesis of the OMC – as the first chapter of this book has suggested – can precisely be read as functional; its crisis is not just one of 'where ultimate authority' in the EU legal order lies, but also over the functional purposes of EU integration; over the various conflicts and reconciliations between integration's 'social' and 'economic' aspects. Once we switch to this perspective, the insights of reflexive law may become relevant once again.[114]

These insights suggest that the EU too may have 'a problem with steering'. At the territorial level, traditional legislative instruments have proceeded on the basis that common EU norms can effectively be 'translated' into the legal systems of the member states (with the Court and Commission playing an enforcement role).[115] At the horizontal or functional level, it is equally assumed that Europe's legal system can carry forward complex interventions into other spheres of life (e.g. break down private monopolies or, in the case of social law, stipulate 'minimum conditions' for health and safety in the workplace). One of the guiding assumptions is that EU law is still able to 'speak to' other territorial or functional spheres.

How though do we see this act of legal communication? Along both its territorial and functional dimensions, as will be seen, it can be seen not only as a 'translation' of normative authority, but also as a potential example of 'self-reflection'; a language that is simply 'adapted into the

[112] J. Zeitlin, 'Social Europe and Experimentalist Governance: Towards a New Constitutional Compromise?' in G. de Búrca (ed.), *EU Law and the Welfare State: In Search of Solidarity* (Oxford University Press, 2005).

[113] It would thus be possible to argue (although there is little time to expand upon the argument here) that reflexive law could be seen as a supplement (along a different functional axis) to the deliberative supra-nationalism concept.

[114] See Smismans, n. 88 above.

[115] See, on this, the formulation of the 'Classical Community Method' provided in *European Governance: A White Paper*, COM (2001) 428 final, at 8.

autonomous logic of the system'. EU law has not escaped, but remains potentially bound by, the normative closure of systems.

At the first territorial level, this problem was already identified in the last chapter. The Union's numerous deficits relating to compliance and implementation illustrate that national legal orders cannot be assumed to be mere 'appliers' of the law. They often take on board or legislate only for those norms (or aspects of norms) that they deem 'cognisable' within the national setting. The metaphor of 'translation' comes up against the significant diversity of national political or legal cultures.

This deficit also emerges at the second functional level. European social law is in effect attempting a double move; it not only has to step into the domestic sphere, but into the social one as well. It must overcome both differences between states, and the differences between the various organisations and rules that characterise processes of collective bargaining, workers' councils, industrial tribunals and so on; all of which have a distinct language and expertise beyond the capacity of any 'central' official. In such circumstances, how can a common European law use the legal system to reorganise areas of life that have distinct procedures of their own? At the functional level too, the 'crisis' of social regulation in the nation state would only seem to be heightened when we step into the European arena.

Reflexive law's answer to this dilemma was to induce internal and external 'reflexion' structures within social systems. Even if systems (or states) are presupposed as self-referential, they must be awakened to their interdependency. The system of economy, for example, is not expected to respond mechanically to external stimuli, but law may play a role in encouraging the economic system to reflect on its linkages and effects on other parts of society, e.g. on the relative distribution of resources, or the quality of the environment. We are to recognise that the system is 'normatively closed', but also that it is 'cognitively open', i.e. that each part of society is still dependent on information held elsewhere.[116]

As much as it may be naive to consider the OMC as a fully 'reflexive' mode of governance, part of this rationality (as the first chapter attempted to illustrate) is evident within the Lisbon strategy. While the proponents of the 'constitutional compromise' thesis are right to suppose

[116] Teubner, n. 98 above, at 70.

that the method was mainly developed in those areas of social policy where the competences of the EU were limited, it was also inserted into a larger economic and social discourse.[117] Lisbon was designed (and recently, reformed) as a series of overlapping 'pillars'; the achievement of any one having clear effects on the options available to the other.[118] To give one example, the rationality for creating a comprehensive EES was not only to tackle employment challenges, but also to minimise the potential risk those challenges could carry for the Euro-area (e.g. through discouraging governments to run up inflationary deficits).[119] The Council's 'integrated guidelines for jobs and growth' have consequently sought to link the course of employment reforms to the terms of the Stability and Growth Pact (a link strengthened through the recent '2020' reforms).

This element to Lisbon opens the door to a reflexive reading. One can see aspects of both the internal and external dimensions of the Teubner/Willke approach. Externally, the method displays features that encourage both governments, and different areas of action, to internalise or reflect upon the needs of each other. The OMC-inclusion, for example, has – as one of its founding objectives – 'effective and mutual interaction between the Lisbon objectives of greater economic growth, more and better jobs and greater social cohesion'.[120] States are asked, not only to compare their social reforms to those of other states, but also to consider the interrelation between social policy, and other areas of policy-making.

If we move to reflexive law's internal dimension, we can observe the adoption by the Lisbon strategy of elements of a 'self-regulatory' vocabulary. At its founding, the Lisbon process described the role of the EU as a 'catalyst', 'mobilising the resources available on the market as well as in the Member States'.[121] The rhetoric of new governance has been deployed to present the Union (and the Commission in particular) as an intermediary actor, 'building partnerships' between different

[117] As the first chapter also addressed this is, of course, part of the critique offered by the method's sceptics. See C. Joerges and F. Rödl, 'Social Market Economy as Europe's Social Model?' (2004) *EUI Working Papers (Law)* 8 at 25.

[118] Presidency Conclusion, Lisbon European Council, 23–24/03/2000, [24]–[34].

[119] See D. Trubek and J. Mosher, 'New Governance, Employment Policy and the European Social Model', in J. Zeitlin and D. Trubek (eds.), *Governing Work and Welfare in a New Economy* (Oxford University Press, 2003) at 35–38.

[120] *Common Objectives in Social Inclusion and Social Protection* (European Council, 2006) at Point B.

[121] Presidency Conclusion, n. 118 above, at [44].

levels of governance.[122] The EU is further cast as having an internal procedural role; laying down annual reporting cycles, and incentivising (through instruments like the Community Action Programme) the entry – into the policy-making process – of non-governmental actors. To this extent, the 'centre' can be seen as 'an external trigger' for domestic reflection and reform.

The 'added value' of reflexive law as an analytical template for the OMC rests on these elements. It rests on its ability to describe something that the other two approaches do not – namely the role of the method, not just as a potential intermediary between national and European levels, but between different functional fields. The OMC is more than a new means of decentralising decision-making (if indeed it decentralises decision-making power at all). It is deeply embedded within a larger social discourse – about the relative balance and interdependence of social, economic and fiscal policies.

At the same time, this characterisation begs as many questions as it answers. Most crucially, does the method really operate according to its enumerated 'design'? Quite clearly, reading and analysing a series of Communications from the European Commission is more than inadequate. 'Reflexivity' could just as easily be part of the OMC's ideology, as it could be an element of its practice. What is the reality of the reflexive discourse that the adoption of the Lisbon strategy points us towards? This is a part of the task that the following two chapters will take up.

There remain, however, other obvious tensions within the reflexive approach. In the first chapter, I argued that the flip side of 'reflexivity' was 'colonisation'; the heightened risk that the integration of the social and economic fields could easily degenerate into a relationship of functional domination.[123] This thesis is not only suggested by literature within new governance, but was also suggested by reflexive law's most formidable critic – the architect of modern systems theory himself. To what extent – as Luhmann put it – does new governance illustrate larger 'problems with reflexive law'?

[122] 'Mobilisation and collective effort are the key elements of the partnership. The challenges are common challenges and affect our model of development. We have to rise to them together – after all, everyone's individual input is essential to ensure collective success. The scale of the challenges is such, and our economies so interdependent, that no Member State is capable of facing up to the task alone.' Commission Communication: 'Working Together for Jobs and Growth: A New Start for the Lisbon Strategy', COM (2005) 24 final at 14.

[123] See Chapter 1, section 5.3.

4.3 Some problems with reflexive law

Reflexive law – like the OMC itself – can in some sense be seen as a *via media*. Those who have attempted to apply its insight to pressing regulatory problems have often used it to forge a middle path between either deregulatory, or intrusive and hierarchical, regulatory structures.[124] The attempt by Teubner to forge a version of system theory that is not fatal to the concept of 'societal guidance through law' has led to a theory of legal development that sits between – to repeat Bechmann's phrasing – the 'over-integration' of society on the one hand, and its 'disintegration' on the other.

The attempt to build a middle path, however, is never an easy one. One is opened up to criticism from both sides. On the one hand, reflexive law can be criticised from proponents of material law-making; as a naive political effort to dress up the dissolution of purposive legal intervention in a more conciliatory political language. Similarly, in the EU, any devolutionary effort through the instruments of 'new governance' can easily be read as a retreat to intergovernmental bargaining.[125] We 'solve' the impasse between national and European action; or 'social' and 'economic' visions of the European polity, not by a new breakthrough, but by repackaging an old political compromise in new language.[126]

The flip side of such a view is that reflexive law can be refuted from the other side; as over-intrusive. If separate systems in society will not respond to the external stipulation of their substantive ends, why should the steering of their internal 'procedures', or their 'reflexive' view of other fields of action, be any different? Similarly, in the EU case, for every critique from those who have seen – in the OMC – a threat to the EU's existing legislative power, we have seen many more from those who argue that Lisbon's discourse on 'partnership' is designed to turn fields where member states carry exclusive competence into an increasing relationship of functional equality between the EU and member state levels.[127]

[124] See e.g. the application of the reflexive law concept to (i) self-regulatory associations (J. Black, 'Constitutionalising Self-Regulation' (1996) 59 *Modern Law Review* 1; (ii) occupational health and safety (J. Paterson, *Behind the Mask: Regulating Health and Safety in Britain's Offshore Oil and Gas Industry* (Aldershot: Ashgate, 2000).

[125] See e.g. the suspicious early treatment of the OMC in the Commission's *White Paper on Governance*, n. 115 above, at 22.

[126] A. Moravcsik, 'The European Constitutional Compromise' (2005) *EUSA Review*.

[127] C. Möllers, 'European Governance – Meaning and Value of a Concept' (2006) 43 *Common Market Law Review* 2.

These two attacks allow the idea of 'reflexivity' under the OMC to be reinterpreted. What if the 'integration' of functional and territorial fields the OMC suggests is not – in the language of Chapter 1 – 'reflexivity', but 'colonisation'; an attempt not to reconcile the boundaries between national and European integration, or between different functional objectives, but instead, to elevate one discourse over another? What if Lisbon does not integrate social and economic policies under a single roof, but 're-calibrates' welfare regimes in implicitly neo-liberal directions (where doing so under an explicit political decision would be impossible)?[128] These are among the criticisms that the present OMC has attracted.

This 'colonisation' critique can be developed through Luhmann's own account of reflexive law. It is no mere aside to register the fact that Luhmann himself saw little common ground between Teubner's approach, and his own.[129] On the contrary, he posited reflexive law as at odds with the main premises and outcomes of any belief that modern societies must reproduce themselves under conditions of functional differentiation. The theory of self-referential systems, he argued, was invented as a definition of life that is 'rigorously inflexible'.[130] If the barriers between social systems are indeed autopoietic barriers, not only are the possibilities for a form of 'general social communication' undermined, but also for the types of decentralised steering that Teubner suggests as its alternative.

The problem is one summarised by Michael King. The reflexive approach wants to have its cake and eat it. It wants to believe in a theory of autopoietic systems, 'while at the same time observing ways in which law might improve its performance through better relations with other systems'.[131] It seeks a discourse between different functional systems, yet what if *the very basis of there being systems* is that 'a common discourse', or a singular means of communicating between one system and another, is absent?

In the absence of such a discourse, how can 'reflection' be anything other than a rhetorical exercise? Under such a sceptical view, we do not 'integrate' the expectations and needs of the others; we simply 'self-reflect', constructing the other only through the boundaries

128 See Offe, n. 39 above.

129 See N. Luhmann, 'Some Problems with Reflexive Law' in Teubner and Febbrajo, n. 92 above.

130 *Ibid.*, at 390.

131 M. King, 'What's the Use of Luhmann's Theory?' in King and Thornhill, n. 95 above, at 43.

of one's own understandings. Luhmann himself puts the problem succinctly:

> Reflexive law can only be self-reflexive law. Only in the manner in which it reproduces itself can it take account of the fact (and perhaps take more account of the fact) that society (and hence also law itself) reproduces itself autopoietically.[132]

We can develop this insight through an analogy to the OMC itself. The last section attempted to identify some common ground between the OMC's discourse on mutual learning, and the second aspect of the Teubner/Willke definition of reflexive law; the idea that self-referential systems must be sensitised to the demands and externalities of others. Mutual learning – under its official EU definition – implies publicising externalities, and learning from best practice. It is designed to encourage states to consider the impact of their social and monetary policies on outsiders; or even to adjust their programmes in light of practices developed elsewhere. Along its functional dimension, the 'design' of the Lisbon strategy can be seen in a similar light – as encouraging the adjustment of social policies in light of the demands of other policy fields.

How though is this practice of 'adjustment' conducted? What can be posited as the building in of a reflexive capacity could as easily be characterised as 'self-reflection', i.e. the selective mimicking of those policies from the outside that most readily meet with the plans and criteria of selection of the host state, or the particular field in question in any case. Metrics, and best practice 'examples', are read according to a distinct national discourse, and in light of existing programmes, to the extent that there is no 'reflexive' relation; but simply the *overlaying* of external information onto existing practice.[133] What is defended as a free-wheeling discourse, in which experience is shared, simply becomes a common vocabulary (of 'active inclusion', 'social cohesion', 'budgetary stability' and so on) that is quickly retranslated into an entrenched national or functional discourse.

The alternative of such a 'self-reflection' of course – if we are to take the presence of systemic boundaries seriously – is that the reflexive exercise is *too* effective. The state subjected to mutual learning, or policy

[132] Luhmann, n. 100 above, at 397–398.

[133] See – for a similar argument in the context of private law harmonisation in the EU – P. Legrand, 'Against a European Civil Code' (1997) 60 *Modern Law Review* 1.

field 'streamlined' into the Lisbon strategy – takes too literally its instruction to be 'other-regarding'. It begins to reorient its policies entirely according to the 'paradigm' that the European example of 'best practice' has provided.[134] Social policy begins to understand *itself* – and its primary functions – in terms of its contribution to Lisbon's growth and competitiveness targets. 'Reflection' induces the gradual erosion of the differences between social fields.

We are left with the paradox that the distinction between 'reflexivity' and 'colonisation' draws us towards. The very call for a more reflexive form of governance is precisely what induces, and makes pressing, the possibility for the OMC to 'colonise'; to integrate features that were previously able to govern themselves autonomously. Awakening systems to their interdependence – or in the case, of the OMC, awakening states to their coexistence in an integrated polity – is a crucial exercise, yet – as Luhmann's objection makes clear – it is also a precarious one.

The point of this discussion is not to fetishise the paradoxical nature of reflexive law, or the OMC (although such a move has become very fashionable).[135] After all, the paradox of systems closure was one of which Teubner and Willke were very aware. Any 'middle approach' to both reflexive law and the OMC is likely to leave certain constituencies unsatisfied, or even to lead to inconsistencies.

The purpose instead is to carry out two tasks. First of all, Luhmann's objection links the challenges reflexive law faces to problems we have also identified in the other main 'inside' approaches. The common element would seem to be this: to what extent – if the move to reflexive law is predicated on a radical closure or complexity deficit in modern societies – does a move to 'softer', 'procedural' or more iterative modes of governance simply fall into the same trap? Does it not simply redraw hierarchical boundaries, albeit at a higher, more abstract, or more reflexive level (through language that is often vague or lacks any clear definition or fixed meaning)? Are there not only common starting points, but also common tensions, which draw together the procedural, experimental and reflexive views of modern law, and indeed of modern 'governance'?

[134] See (on the use of this argument in the case of social inclusion) S. Bernhard, 'The European Paradigm of Social Exclusion' (2006) 2 *Journal of Contemporary European Research* 1.

[135] See e.g. O. Perez and G. Teubner, *Paradoxes and Inconsistencies in the Law* (Oxford: Hart, 2006).

Secondly, the paradox is meant to suggest that any true resolution or analysis of the dilemma can only be truly carried out in the particular. It should not only be a question of applying theoretical constructs (with quite distinct historical trajectories) to the EU example; but also a question of whether 'new governance' and the OMC really carries the common features that have been ascribed to it. One should not take for granted, but instead test the OMC's 'reflexive' role, and capacity.

While this more empirical task will be the function of the next two chapters, it is to this first element – reconstructing the commonalities of the three approaches – to which we now must turn. To what extent can the definitions, features and tensions outlined in this chapter allow a more holistic 'internal' definition of the law–governance relationship to emerge? And finally, where might the limits of such a definition be drawn?

5. Common problems, common solutions and common tensions

The answers which the three approaches outlined above provide to the dilemmas of regulatory law reflect the quite different starting points, and even methodologies, of each theory. At one level, they should not be drawn together. Systems theorists talk a quite different language to those advocating a deliberative or communicative concept of law. It is because of these differences that the chapter has expanded upon each account separately.

At the same time, it is remarkable how – in spite of these differences – important common elements emerge. These can be identified either in terms of the challenges each approach attempts to overcome, the solutions they prescribe, or the tensions or difficulties that they evidence. In the section below, the chapter will conclude by developing five features of a 'procedural' approach to the law–governance relationship; features that will be used to analyse the present OMC process in social inclusion and protection. To what extent do the three approaches not only respond to common problems, but create a basis for testing the claim that 'new governance' can be described from the 'inside' of legal categories, or as part of a 'transformation' in EU social law and policy?

5.1 Common problems – the ambivalence of 'materialisation' in modern law

This mapping exercise must begin with a bringing together of the problems of 'materialisation' of modern law that each account tries to overcome. The use of 'social regulation' or 'regulatory law' has become an embedded element in the legal system. The faith of individuals in law (and in EU law) depends not just on the formal pedigree of rules (e.g. judicial independence, or respect for the rule of law) but also on their ability materially to advance social life. Law carries heightened expectations and, with it, faces far greater administrative and technical burdens than at any point in its history. The 'materialisation' of law – as much as certain policy-makers in the EU would like to pretend otherwise – is a more or less permanent part of Europe's political and social identity.

One can only grasp the solutions which 'inside' theories attempt to offer if one is also able to see this 'materialisation' of law as ambivalent. Both normatively and cognitively, the common starting point of all 'inside' approaches is that the use of law to 'steer' social life has been a problematic and normatively ambiguous exercise.

Cognitively, this steering ability may depend on information, and administrative capacities, that central institutions lack. In the 'experimental' view, this is because of temporal difficulties – e.g. the conflict between relative stability and clarity in rules, and the 'accelerated' demands of modern economy and science; in the procedural one, it is because of the gap between 'central' and 'local' levels of governance. Either way, the unproblematic 'translation' of legal norms into the local context, or the objective 'execution' and 'application' of common norms, has become increasingly difficult to achieve. It is not difficult to extend this insight to the EU case. With a small and confined administrative bureaucracy, EU law has commonly relied on the administrative and judicial resources of its member states in order to achieve normative effects in its laws. Cognitively, the materialisation of European law has only ever been a halting and partial exercise.

If these difficulties were not enough, 'inside' theories have posited a series of further normative deficits. Under material law-making, individuals – and states – are commonly treated as 'clients'. The law does not respond to their needs; instead it demands that individual needs *respond to the law*. Law is increasingly cut adrift from the normative reasons and discussions of the parties to whom it applies. Not so shockingly – in the EU case at least – law is not seen as popularly 'owned' but as another cog in the administrative machinery.

This 'client' relationship is even more problematic in the European case. We are dealing not only with another legal subject, but with a sovereign state, with a distinct constitutional framework and political culture of its own. The attempt to steer *this* framework not only opens up new cognitive difficulties, but the perception that EU law could be undermining foundational social commitments. If 'materialisation' strategies are difficult at the national level, they may be downright objectionable in a European environment where bonds of common identity and social solidarity remain precarious. In simple terms – a new legal strategy is called for.

5.2 *Common solutions – five common features of the 'procedural turn'*

If these are the problems, how can one respond to them? What draws the approaches together is also their rejection of one particular answer to the problem. If material or hierarchical forms of law-making are unwanted, this does not mean that the answer can be found within re-regulatory strategies or within the realm of 'alternatives to law'. The answer to Europe's 'steering problem' does not lie in a full retreat from law-mediated rule (as much as 'new governance' has often been conceptualised in these terms). As Teubner has put it, 'the already completed functional differentiation of societies with welfare state structures does not permit alternative to law; at best it admits alternatives within law'.[136]

If the problem of modern law is its tendency to treat individuals as 'clients' or addressees, the true alternatives must lie in creating conditions both for the opening up of the law to new contextual information, and in the opening up of legal procedures to facilitate possibilities for legal *authorship*. The law must enlist, harness and 'guide' the cognitive resources, and normative reasons, of the individuals to whom European norms apply.

This inevitably involves a balancing of law's 'substantive' and 'procedural' roles. Substantively, the goal of 'societal guidance through law' is not given up on. Instead, it is up to local decision-making bodies, and even functional sub-systems, to themselves take responsibility for legal outcomes. Legal norms – including, for example, the objectives, targets and indicators of the OMC – are not be treated as a final word on any given policy solution, but as 'rebuttable presumptions' that have to be justified (and even reframed) in light of a local context. The substantive delegation of authority is not only a 'devolution' but designed reflexively, i.e. with the intention also of increasing the knowledge and expertise of future rule-making, and of other decision-making sites.

Procedurally, law does not devolve power only, but also reasserts its steering capacities at a secondary level. Law cannot presuppose either

[136] Teubner, n. 3 above, at 12.

that, internally, the devolution of decision-making power will lead to fair or informed decision-making procedures, or that, externally, it will lead to a full respect for the external impacts of one's action on others. Law's procedural role thus comprises a legal system – a parameter of obligations (whether soft or hard) – capable of inducing both internal deliberation, and external reflection. A procedural law is designed to awaken legal actors, both to the possibilities for material self-determination that even post-national law still implies, and to the danger of allowing deliberation to become instrumentalised.

We can map these 'common solutions' through five elements of a procedural or 'inside' approach to the law–governance relationship; one that sees, in new governance, possibilities for legal 'transformation'.[137] Each speaks to a different – yet vital – element of the three 'inside' approaches.

(i) Law as cognitive

Firstly, the idea of law as cognitive implies a communicative concept of law. Law not only implements 'given' and 'objective' normative rules, but is open to future elaboration. This act of elaboration involves both the 'destabilisation' of existing understandings of problems, and the construction of new ones (based on information held at more local levels). Given the cognitive limitations inherent in post-national decision-making, law must attempt to take on board, and make use of, the informational resources of its surrounding regulatory environment. Deference to local forms of knowledge is not a sign of law's weakness, or its 'corruption', but is seen as the only way of achieving regulatory objectives in a manner conducive to the 'public autonomy' of individuals and states alike.

(ii) Law as adaptive

Secondly, law's cognitive character implies its adaptive or non-essentialist quality. Law is open to change in light of the experience and needs of those to whom it applies. This entails two vital capacities. On the one hand, law must downgrade expectations of substantive uniformity. In a diverse regulatory environment, the guiding assumption is that common norms must leave some 'room for manoeuvre'. Diversity is seen not as an obstacle to effective law-making, but an experimental advantage, allowing the law-making process access to practice and information that would otherwise be closed off.

[137] See Sabel and Simon, n. 63 above.

This, of course, implies a second capacity – the capacity to 'learn'. It implies that the relation between 'local' application discourses, and a common reflection on goals, objectives and procedures can be dialectical in nature, with local practice 'feeding in' to broader policy discussions among a wider group of constituents. The distinction between the 'political' framing of rules, and their 'legal' execution, is thus broken down.

(iii) Law as participative

The 'dialectical relation' which emerges from this erosion carries certain preconditions. What if the vacuum left by the erosion of legal hierarchy is quickly filled by other forms of social or economic power? A law that reflects only the opinions of a select few cannot aspire to 'cognitive openness', nor to an adequate learning capacity. The closing off of law-making procedures is likely to be fatal to the notion that procedural law can do a qualitatively better job of treating individual citizens as the 'authors', rather than 'addressees', of the law.

Law's 'dialecticism' also thus requires that the legal medium is opened up. The role of law 'as participative' not only implies that law *itself* must include competing understandings, but also that law provide the conditions for effective deliberation elsewhere. Law must break down barriers to access to the policy-making process, not only as a means of guaranteeing its legitimacy, but also in order to buttress its effectiveness. Without the resources that affected actors themselves can provide, regulatory law is likely to descend into the 'trilemma'; to create legislation that not only 'misses' its target, but produces unwanted or disintegrating side effects.

(iv) Law as reflexive

This capacity for 'disintegration' refers to the fourth, and penultimate, common aspect – law as reflexive. Inside theories reject traditional understandings of legal integration. The purpose of procedural law is not to integrate individuals around a uniform set of values. In the OMC example, a convergence of goals or ideas is not designed to lead to eventual 'policy convergence'. As well as avoiding 'disintegration', *over-integration* is also something which inside theories set themselves against. If we are to achieve unity in a polity like the EU, it must also be – to repeat a trendy new motto – a 'unity in diversity'.[138]

[138] This, of course, would have been – were the aborted Constitutional Treaty to have been adopted – the Union's official motto.

Law is integrative – under inside readings – in a more reflexive sense. It recognises the autonomy of local or national decision-making bodies. Yet at the same time it encourages them to be other-regarding. Law must build in a reflexive capacity, both between national, and between functional discourses, if the externalities which social policy coordination has produced are to be managed. Law is 'integrative' not in the sense of creating an 'ever-closer union' but in encouraging otherwise self-regarding policy actors (both within national governments, and within functional fields of action) to reflect on the consequences of their action on others.

(v) Law as procedural

Law as procedural is both an accumulation of, and an addition to these four aspects. Cumulatively, it speaks to the basic distinction upon which all four parts rest – the distinction between substance and procedure. Law is not to second guess substantive outcomes, but to encourage the affected actors themselves to design and deliberate policy solutions in keeping with the normative and social context in which they find themselves. This discourse must be 'guided' through rules of access and deliberation that reduce internal manipulation, and encourage reflection on the practice of others ('reflexive law').

In addition, however, it speaks to the most vital normative aspect of a 'procedural paradigm' in law; an aspect that is at once its most optimistic promise, yet at the same time, opens the procedural account to numerous accusations of naivety, or worse, manipulation. It suggests that 'new governance' could not only represent a 'steering technique', or a more effective problem-solving procedure, but a means of opening-up European law. It suggests that the central role of law in driving forward the integration process may not only be something conducted according to judicial fiat, but a mechanism of 'entry' for individuals into the law-making process.

The optimism of this 'procedural' reading of the law–governance relation lies in the idealistic hope that the erosion of legal hierarchy new governance suggests is not carried out simply to circumvent burdensome decision-making procedures, but to allow European citizens greater access to a legal order that has spread to regulate almost every aspect of their public lives. While this may be a highly ambitious presupposition, this 'democratising' role may be one aspect of why the 'new governance' debate has attracted so much academic and institutional attention.

5.3 *Common tensions – reintroducing hierarchy? The politics of governance and the politics of law*

As was stated in the introduction to this chapter, the five 'common features' outlined in the last few sections represent proceduralism in its best light. They both generalise and idealise. They generalise in the sense that the effort to construct a 'new governance theory' of law involves drawing together theoretical approaches that have distinct methodological origins. They idealise because the leap from procedural and experimental theories to the practice of new governance, remains an intimidatingly high one. In the following chapters, an important task will be to ground this idealising task; to ask whether it adequately describes the OMC as it stands (at least in one of its most important policy fields – social protection and inclusion policy).

Before that begins, however, we can already decipher some important lessons. The very design of inside theories – as well as revealing aspects which make the analogy to new governance useful – also reveal common tensions. The basis of these tensions are the very elements which have made the debate over proceduralism and reflexive law, and the EU's own 'turn to governance', such exciting and well-documented phenomena. The rush to 'erode hierarchy', delegate decision-making power, and encourage a reflexive 'dialectic' between 'rules' and their application to particular factual contexts has led to questions over how procedural law can be reconciled with some of the foundational value commitments of the EU's legal order.

The central problem which this chapter has tried to identify is over the question of 'hierarchy' (broadly defined). The phenomenon of 'new governance' illustrates both its explicit removal and its potential reintroduction. In all of the approaches under discussion, substantive legal 'steering' is rejected, on the basis, either that the steering capacity of the centre is limited, or that it could act to the detriment of functional and political diversity. In its place, more 'decentralised', 'iterative' or 'reflexive' forms of legal intervention are to be encouraged. In the OMC case, substantive harmonisation is ruled out under open coordination in favour of a convergence of goals, preferences and ideas. 'Law' is to act largely at an abstract, or second-order level; as a forum within which substantive disagreement is still possible, or even encouraged.

By now, however, it is clear that this supposed dissolution of hierarchy is question-begging. Firstly, to what extent do precisely those factors which made material law-making impossible (i.e. functional, territorial and normative differentiation) also apply at a more abstract or procedural level? If we cannot gain agreement on, for example, the substantive goals of European social policy, what makes it any more likely that we will gain agreement on its procedures? How can we achieve a common understanding of the indicators and targets by which 'policy successes' and 'policy failures' in EU social policy are to be identified? We are left with the possibility, either that supposedly 'procedural' norms will elevate one substantive vision over another, or that they will be sufficiently 'normatively empty' as to have no guiding effect whatsoever (i.e. liable to be 'retranslated' into the self-referential discourse of each state, or each social system). These are significant dangers.

Each option produces its own distinct pathologies. Firstly, there is the danger that supposed 'devolutions' of normative authority will mask other forms of social power. We remove formal legal hierarchy only to find other types of hierarchy in its place. What is presented as 'deliberation' may in fact privilege more powerful and organised voices. To take the OMC example, hierarchical steering is not conducted through imposing substantive principles of public law, but achieved through creating common understandings of problems, or strict procedural rules, that 'guide' actors to decisions already centrally agreed upon (but presented as part of an 'evolving' and 'deliberative' local discourse). The power of the 'centre' is not removed; instead central institutions gain access to 'local' and 'experimental' discourses; discourse that were previously granted their own autonomy. One can see this challenge in countless objections to the method on the grounds that it infringes on competences properly held within the national welfare state itself.

The other possibility is what Luhmann captured through his idea of 'self-reflection'. If the removal of legal steering does not create new hierarchies, it may simply conceal that the old one has effectively been left in place. Neither states, nor other functional spheres of action, 'learn' from the benchmarks, guidelines and indicators that the method sets down; but simply take in whatever is most suitable for their own plans. Here again, proceduralism has a masking effect. It implies that 'governance' is going on; that Europe is building an adequate response to its present social malaise; when, in effect, we are left with the same old inertia. It provides an image of social solidarity that is in fact overlain by an empty or rhetorical series of social commitments.

These pathologies lead to an overriding scepticism. One wonders whether, underneath the 'official structure' of the OMC laid down at Lisbon, and the five features enumerated above – features that give meat to the idea of governance as an intra-legal phenomenon – there is a 'politics of governance'. One wonders if we can see the recreation of the hierarchies, and political power relationships, that proceduralism's dispersal of normative authority was meant to displace.

The question is put presciently by David Kennedy:

> The new governance literature also seems, at least to my ears, in full retreat from what might be called the 'linguistic' or 'self-reflective' turn in legal scholarship. The tradition that would see these alternatives, hard and soft, as claims, postures, justifications, rhetorical performances rather than as useful policy alternatives to be selected and deployed as needed . . . Lost is the historical and cultural randomness of the regulatory system, and its porousness to instrumentalization from without. What are the stakes, not constitutionally, but actually – for this round, this conflict, this rule, this standard? Who, for example, benefits from policy failure, from governmental gridlock – from governance deficits, democracy deficits, from old governance, or for that matter, from 'new' governance?[139]

Kennedy's plea is for politicisation; for a realisation that the move towards new legal and regulatory strategies do not simply represent the substitution of one 'mode of governance' for another (or the evolutionary triumph of a particular 'form of law'), but also represent part of a *political* strategy; a way of distributing and legitimising power. The key is that this strategy is not concealed, but contestable; that the abstract goals, indicators and targets of the OMC are not treated as an 'insider's secret' – something to be determined through technical or expert advice – but as elements that are open.[140] The 'turn to governance' will, under this critical reasoning, only be a normative plus for European societies if it does not replace one secretive discourse with another, but opens up the future of European social policy to substantive contestation.

One does not have to accept Kennedy's conclusions. Certainly the purpose of this book is not to dismiss the method as mere power politics, just as I do not wish to take for granted the theoretical constructions which have dominated the new governance debate so far. As the first chapter argued, while the method may be capable of instrumentalisation, this is so from a variety of political positions. If there is a danger that 'law' has become stylised in the new governance debate, we should avoid a political stylisation of the concept of governance itself.

[139] D. Kennedy, n. 77 above, at 7. [140] *Ibid.*, at 8.

What the 'politics of governance' does require, however, is a process of unmasking. One cannot, as the introduction to this book argued, treat the theoretical models explored in this chapter as a 'natural order of things'; instead they represent imperfect attempts to make sense of complex and shifting phenomena. Their very failures to capture new governance methods – their inner inconsistencies and contradictions – do not just represent 'failures', but may provide opportunities to uncover and even reform the pathologies and paradoxes of contemporary new governance methods.

It is to this empirical and critical task that the next two chapters must now turn. In the first case, Chapter 4 will use the 'common features' outlined in this chapter to analyse an expansive OMC process – in social protection and social inclusion. This study will illustrate that the method – even in less 'prescriptive' domains, like that of social inclusion policy – is no mere 'paper tiger', but has shaped the terrain on which EU-level social policy decisions are taken. At the same time, the use of the OMC SPSI cognitively and procedurally to shape the policy discourse of its participants draws us towards some of its most central legitimacy deficits. Returning to the 'problem of hierarchy', the method's purported dispersal of normative authority has tended to conceal its inability to include democratic input in its procedures (or indeed any significant level of substantive contestation at all). In short, the 'common features' outlined in this section may have framed new governance's failures, as well as its achievements.

Finally, Chapter 5 will conclude by arguing that the application of the procedural model demands significant changes to its constructive logic. We can neither assume that the OMC can be perfected, in the words of Jonathan Zeitlin, by applying the logic of new governance and experimentalist theory 'to itself', nor by bringing the method under the roof of a rigid constitutional hierarchy. Rather reforms to 'new governance in the EU' should focus on a more robust politicisation of its procedures – the use of a 'constitutional' frame, not to cement judicial review, but rather to create opportunities for individual and parliamentary scrutiny of the indicators, objectives and recommendations that make up the normative infrastructure of open coordination as it stands.

Kennedy's 'plea for politicisation' illustrates the promise and the pitfalls of 'governance as proceduralisation' – on the one hand, procedural theory has allowed the positive construction of new governance in terms of its relationship to an evolving legal ideal in the EU; on the other, it illustrates how evolution and 'transformation' need not be a process of progressive liberation, but also one where old pathologies of central steering and exclusion may reassert themselves. This is a danger of which future attempts to build a 'theory of new governance' must be aware.

4 Assessing the procedural paradigm: the case of the OMC SPSI

1. Introduction

In the third chapter, the focus was on the development of an 'inside' approach to the law–governance relationship. Inside theories treat governance as an intra-legal phenomenon, or as part of a process of decentring which has also altered our view of the nature and institutions of law. This shift was characterised through three headings – proceduralisation, experimentalism and reflexive law. All three approaches point to a common challenge to which European law has had to respond – the functional and territorial complexity of the European polity, and the regulatory environment within which methods like the OMC SPSI must live.

Together, these 'inside' approaches have produced major conceptual innovations. They may even have contributed towards overcoming what Neil Walker has described as the methodological nationalism of much of European legal scholarship.[1] They have sought to evaluate law not from within a 'given' statist framework, but in light of the distinct features of the European polity. They have based their evaluation of methods like the OMC not on the mythical standards (criticised in the second chapter) of a 'hard', 'determinate' or 'uniform' legal order, but on the basis of structural limits already implicit within the EU's legal system. In this manner, they have allowed inside approaches to provide a positive definition of the law–governance relationship, rather than

[1] M. Zurn, 'On the Conceptualization of Postnational Politics: The Limits of Methodological Nationalism', Paper presented to Workshop on Global Governance, Robert Schuman Centre, Florence, April 2001.

one that solely posits governance in opposition to 'traditional' legal categories (whatever that may mean).

At the same time, there is something about these approaches that remains unsatisfactory. First of all, they pose one obvious question – beyond the usefulness of 'proceduralisation' as a conceptual framework, does it accurately describe the fields of action to which it is commonly – even ubiquitously – applied? Do the taken for granted assumptions of the OMC as an experimental or procedural regime, based on iteration, concrete problem-solving, and 'multi-level governance' really hold water? In simple terms, beyond the (by now, quite commonplace) empirical studies of the *policy impacts* of the method – one has to enquire whether there is a basis in practice for the *legal and political relationships the OMC is said to constitute.*

Secondly, one wonders, even if these approaches have an explanatory potential, what has been their normative impact? The promise of proceduralisation is not just to reflect the law as it stands, but also to point forward; to forge legal institutions that are both relied upon by social actors, and *accepted* by them. The procedural account is both a description of an outlying reality, and an attempt to renew traditional normative concepts – like accountability, democracy and the rule of law – in a new post-national setting. Does it succeed, or are the tensions and ambiguities outlined in the third chapter again lurking in the background?

The chapter will approach the OMC with both of these sets of questions in mind. On the one hand, it will attempt to consider the OMC SPSI in light of a particular analytical template. This template – developed in the third chapter – comprised five features: law as cognitive; law as non-essentialist; law as participative; law as reflexive; and law as procedural. Are these features evident in the OMC SPSI, and if not, what other legal relationships or rationalities are emerging in their place?

On the other hand, this template will not be taken as 'given', but reconsidered and tested in light of the particular features of social inclusion and protection. The subject of the chapter will not only be the explanatory potential, but also the normative failings, of 'inside' approaches to law. The methodology for the chapter will therefore be inductive rather than deductive; attempting to use the experience of the OMC SPSI to re-evaluate, and reposition, the theoretical model into which so many evaluations of the OMC so far have tried to fit.

The chapter will argue that – while the OMC as it stands contains evidence of all five elements – they rarely emerge in the forms that one would expect, either evidencing contradictions between different procedural values, or recreating precisely the hierarchies that the introduction of the OMC was intended to break down. The final section of the chapter will therefore reassess 'inside' approaches, pointing towards both different readings of the law–governance relationship, and possible reform agendas (the principle subject of Chapter 5).

1.1 *Methodology*

The main source of information for this assessment will be the evaluation of the OMC SPSI carried out by the Commission in 2005–06. The evaluation asked governments, NGOs and the social partners to give their opinions about two processes – the OMC for social inclusion, and the OMC process on pensions (amalgamated, from 2006, into the present OMC SPSI). According to the Commission's official Communication, the purpose of the questionnaire was to canvass views on, 'the extent to which the processes have been effective in promoting policy coordination and the dissemination of good practice, and any changes to be introduced in order to improve them'.[2]

In practice, the questionnaire was organised around a series of specific questions. The questions asked, and a full list of respondents, can be found in Annex 1 at the end of the book. These either addressed matters of a general nature (i.e. the 'added value' of the OMC in the social inclusion domain, or its relation to the European Employment Strategy) or particular procedures or institutions (i.e. the use of joint reporting, the format of the National Action Plans (NAPs), the value of peer review, and the extent of actor mobilisation in each policy 'strand').[3] Responses were received from all twenty-five of the governments then participating in the OMC, as well as European 'umbrella' organisations of social NGOs, the social partners, and organisations representing regional and local authorities. In this sense, the most habitually involved actors in the present OMC SPSI were consulted. The wealth of critical information available in this chapter attests to the comprehensiveness of the responses themselves.

2 Commission Staff Document, 'Evaluation of the Open Method of Coordination for Social Protection and Social Inclusion', SEC (2006) 345 at 2.

3 See Annex 1.

At the same time, the questionnaire contains limitations. Firstly, its evaluation of 'streamlining' – the reform carried out following the mid-term review of the Lisbon strategy in 2004 – as well as subsequent reforms conducted following the Commission's 2008 social agenda, is quite premature. Although the respondents were asked for their opinions on the reforms undertaken in light of Lisbon, it may be a number of years before a more measured assessment of their impact can be conducted. As a supplement, the chapter therefore includes more recent evaluations in the specific context of the 'streamlining' measures.

Secondly, the evaluation still excludes certain actors. Key institutions at the European level (for example, the Economic and Social Committee, and the Committee of the Regions) were not consulted. Equally, while some governments asked national parliaments for an opinion in preparing their answers, there was (perhaps in a manner indicative of the OMC in a broader sense) no systematic attempt to engage parliaments and other representative bodies (particularly at local or regional levels).

While these limitations do not make the value of the responses negligible, they suggest two things. Firstly, that the evaluation conducted in this chapter is partial, and should not be read as an exhaustive synopsis of the OMC as it stands. The very reading of the method according to 'five features of a procedural regime' suggests an engagement with some, but not all aspects, of the contemporary OMC SPSI. The analysis that I will conduct is carried out with the specific intent of uncovering normative and procedural relationships, leaving some questions – e.g. over the extent to which the OMC has promoted forms of 'policy convergence' – unanswered.

Secondly, it suggests a need to engage with a wider body of literature. While the information offered by the respondents is fairly candid, it was still given as part of an official evaluation, with its results (in summary form) disseminated publicly. In light of these caveats, the assessment will include a number of other sources:

- the 'Joint Reports' of the Commission and European Council adopted in 2007 and 2008;[4]
- the 'Joint Inclusion Memorandums' on social inclusion adopted for the ten new member states in December 2003;[5]

[4] All EU-level reports (joint reports, country profiles, and implementation reports) can be found here: http://ec.europa.eu/employment_social/social_inclusion/jrep_en.htm.

[5] The Memorandums involved bilateral agreements between the new member states and the Commission on preparatory steps for inclusion in the OMC process. See: http://ec.europa.eu/employment_social/spsi/enlargement_en.htm.

- Synthesis Reports of the European Network of Independent Social Inclusion Experts;[6]
- Evaluations of National Reporting conducted by select Non-Governmental Organisations (EAPN, and European Public Social Platform);[7]
- a 2005 Evaluation on the Implementation of the Peer Review Programme;[8]
- a Commission Evaluation of the Community Action Programme to Combat Social Exclusion 2002–06;[9]
- the Operational Guide for Peer Review and Assessment 2008;[10]
- two Commission statements on its 'Social Agenda 2005–2010' and 'Renewed Social Agenda 2008';[11]
- the Work Programmes of the Social Protection Committee;[12]
- the Commission's Guidelines to National Governments for the Preparation of their NAPs for 2006–08;[13]

6 Under the framework of the Community Action Programme, a network of independent experts has been funded to report on national developments and conduct thematic studies. Reports are given twice a year and contain analysis of recent trends and developments in social inclusion with a view to feeding into the 'Joint Reports' produced by the Commission and Council. See www.peer-review-social-inclusion.eu/policy-assessment-activities.

7 These documents are:
  (1) a report on 'Social Services and Social Inclusion' by the European Social Network (including preliminary reports on implementation of the 2006 round of NAPs), see www.socialeurope.com/inclusion/alldownloads/esn_social_services_report.pdf;
  (2) a report on 'Local Authority Involvement' by the European Public Social Platform on the first round of the NAPs/incl. (2001–2003);
  (3) a report by EAPN: 'The 2006–2008 National Reports on Strategies for Social Protection and Social Inclusion: What Do They Deliver for People in Poverty?', see www.vides.org/ita/download/EAP_NOMC06_reportfinal_en.pdf.

8 See 'Peer Review in Social Inclusion. Final Report: Implementation of the Peer Review Programme 2005' (2006).

9 *Evaluation of the EU Programme to promote Member State co-operation to combat social exclusion and poverty* (Luxembourg: Office for the Official Publications of the European Communities, 2007). The executive summary is here: http://ec.europa.eu/employment_social/social_inclusion/docs/evaluation_summary_en.pdf.

10 See www.peer-review-social-inclusion.eu/peer-reviews.

11 Communication from the Commission on 'the Social Agenda' COM (2005) 033 final; Commission Communication on 'A Renewed Social Agenda: Opportunities, Access and Solidarity in 21st Century Europe' COM (2008) 0412 final.

12 See http://ec.europa.eu/social/keyDocuments.jsp?type=0&policyArea=750&subCategory=758&country=0&year=0&advSearchKey=Work+Programme+&mode=advancedSubmit&langId=en.

13 See http://ec.europa.eu/employment_social/social_inclusion/docs/2006/guidelines_en.pdf.

- the Council Resolutions setting up the committees of the OMC SPSI;[14]
- Relevant Opinions and Studies of the Social Protection Committee;[15]
- empirical academic studies of the OMC inclusion process.[16]

Structurally, this material will form the basis of two sections. The first will analyse the five features developed in the third chapter in turn. To what extent are they evidenced in the OMC SPSI as it stands? The second will assess the lessons of the evaluation for the method's future development. How might this assessment have a bearing on, or lead to, a re-evaluation of the relationship between new governance and law? The question of how we can respond to this evaluation will be the subject of the next (and final) chapter.

1.2 The Europeanisation of social inclusion: the structure and evolution of the 'OMC SPSI'

While Chapter 1 described the foundational functional and procedural origins of the OMC in a broader sense, it is important to give some specific background on the development of the OMC SPSI.[17] The initial mentions of social inclusion in the European domain came through the Union's 1974 Social Action Programme. Following its failure, the Union's action in the social inclusion domain was largely restricted to soft pleas for member states to respect 'fundamental' social entitlements (see e.g. the 'solemn declaration' on the rights of workers agreed in 1989), or the funding of pilot 'poverty' programmes, designed to

[14] See e.g. Council Decision 689/2004/EC 'Establishing a Social Protection Committee' (repealing Decision 436/2000/EC) [2004] O.J. L 314; Decision 1672/2006/EC 'Establishing a Community Action Programme for Employment and Social Solidarity – Progress' [2006] O.J. L 315.

[15] See e.g. the Opinion of the SPC on the Commission's 'streamlining' communication; the report of the (brilliantly named) 'Working Group on the Mutual Interaction between the Common Social Objectives and the Strategies for Growth and Jobs' (Social Protection Committee, 2007).

[16] Although I have drawn on a number of empirical evaluations, including work conducted in the context of the 'new-gov' project (coordinated at the EUI), the chapter also draws on two significant academic compendiums: Jonathan Zeitlin and Philippe Pochet's *The Open Method of Co-ordination in Action: The European Employment and Social Inclusion Strategies* (Bern: Peter Lang, 2005); and Eric Marlier, Anthony B. Atkinson, Bea Cantillon and Brian Nolan's, *The EU and Social Inclusion: Facing the Challenges* (Bristol: Policy Press, 2007).

[17] See also, K. Armstrong, *Governing Social Inclusion: Europeanization through Policy Coordination* (Oxford University Press, 2010) at 54–95.

allow 'information, coordination, assessment and the exchange of experiences at the Community level'.[18]

Given the constraints of the Treaty structure, little more was possible. Successive treaties, culminating in the Treaty of Nice, accompanied efforts to beef up the Union's 'social objectives' with ever more strident refusals to contemplate legislative harmonisation.[19] Even the provision of funding for such purposes was placed in serious doubt. In *UK v Commission (Social Exclusion)*, the ECJ limited the capacity of the Commission to provide budgetary resources for programmes that could not be backed up by legislation.[20] This certainly included the social inclusion example. It seemed that these restraints would restrict European efforts to tackle social deprivation for the foreseeable future.

At the same time, social inclusion and protection policy also faced a series of 'Europeanising' pressures. In the first case, just as the massive unemployment, and significant social spending to counter it described in Chapter 1 could endanger the anti-inflationary policies needed to guarantee the viability of the euro, the spiralling costs of healthcare, pensions and other social transfers, represented a similar threat in the social inclusion field. The proportion of national GDP spent on health, pensions and other social protection policies dwarfed that invested in employment benefits in most of Western Europe. As a result, social inclusion had the potential to create significant negative externalities between European states.

In the second case, the European Court set important yardsticks for the Europeanisation of social inclusion through interpreting EU citizenship provisions, and the Treaty's articles on free movement, as necessitating a degree of openness in national welfare states. Free movement provisions – originally intended as neutral with regard to social benefits – were read by the courts as necessitating cross-border portability of particular social entitlements.[21] Labour could not be equated

[18] Council Decision 457/89/EEC 'Establishing a Medium-Term Community Action Programme Concerning the Economic and Social Integration of the Economically and Socially less privileged groups in Society' [1989] O.J. L 224, Art. 2(c).

[19] On Treaty, and other legal constraints to harmonisation social exclusion policy, see K. Armstrong, 'Tackling Social Exclusion through the OMC: Re-shaping the Boundaries of EU Governance' in T. Borzel and R. Cichowski (eds.), *The State of the European Union* (Oxford University Press, 2003).

[20] Case C-106/96 *United Kingdom of Great Britain and Northern Ireland* v. *Commission of the European Communities* [1998] ECR I-02729.

[21] See Case 75/63, *Mrs M. K. H. Hoekstra (née Unger)* v. *Bestuur der Bedrijfsvereniging voor Detailhandel en Ambachten* [1964] ECR 379; Case 100/63, *J. G. van der Veen, widow of J.Kalsbeek* v. *Bestuur der Sociale Verzekeringsbank and nine other cases* [1964] ECR 565.

with capital – a decision to move across borders would not only rest on a relative judgement of the available economic dividends, but also on the likely social risks. A worker who had accumulated significant entitlements under an occupational pension scheme in one state was unlikely to give that up if extinguished upon moving to another. The 'closure' of the welfare state was in this sense also a barrier to the full exercise of economic freedoms.

As such, social 'outsiders' were entitled to escalating levels of benefits in the domestic sphere, to be compensated by insurance schemes in the original country in which entitlement had been earned (a system politically codified as early as 1971 by Regulation 1408/71/EEC).[22] The original 'coordination' of social protection systems therefore, while a political initiative, was prompted and enforced by the Court's ambitious reading of the very terms of the EC Treaty.

In recent years, we have seen the development by the Court of additional 'Europeanising' pressures in other social policy domains. In health, the Court argued in cases such as *Kohll* and *Decker* in the late 1990s, that refusals on the part of a national health insurer to reimburse health or dental services sought abroad were in violation of the free movement of services, and that the need for prior authorisation from the host state could be invoked only in cases of a serious threat to the financial viability of the national system.[23] The political sphere has essentially been forced to play 'catch-up' to a court forwarded de-territorialisation of social welfare,[24] with the Commission outlining in 2008 a proposed directive 'on the application of patient's rights in cross-border healthcare'.[25]

These pressures meant that while – as with the employment case – legislative action was ruled out, soft coordination mechanisms for

[22] For more, see M. Ferrera, *The Boundaries of Welfare: European Integration and the New Spatial Politics of Integration* (Oxford University Press, 2005) at 99–104.

[23] See Case 158/96 *Kohll v Union des Caisses de Maladies* [1998] ECR I-1931; Case C-120/95 *Nicolas Decker v Caisses de Maladie de Employés Privées* [1998] ECR I-1831. For a more in-depth treatment of the impact of the ECJ on the Europeanisation of health policy, see T. Hervey and J. McHale, 'Health Law and the European Union' (2007) 13 *European Law Journal* 5; S. L. Greer, 'Uninvited Europeanization: Neo-Functionalism and the EU in Health Policy' (2006) 13 *Journal of European Public Policy* 1; E. Mossialos, G. Permanand, R. Baeten and T. Hervey, *Health System Governance in Europe: the Role of EU Law and Policy* (Cambridge University Press, 2010).

[24] See D. Martinsen, 'Social Security Regulation in the EU: The De-Territorialization of Welfare?' in G. de Búrca (ed.), *EU Law in the Welfare State* (Oxford University Press, 2005).

[25] COM (2008) 414 final.

social inclusion were put in place long before the Lisbon European Council's formal codification of the OMC. Particularly notable were two pieces of soft law created in the early 1990s – Council Recommendation 92/441/EEC 'on common criteria concerning sufficient resources and assistance in social protection systems', designed to establish a degree of convergence among the member states on the minimum standards and overriding objectives of social protection reforms, and Recommendation 92/442/EEC 'on the convergence of social protection objectives and policies', created 'to encourage and organize, in liaison with the Member States, the systematic exchange of information and experiences, and the continuous evaluation of the national provisions adopted'.[26] The basis of the later OMC – that common action on social inclusion was necessary, but that it should be conducted through a process of benchmarking and peer review – were thus already in place by the early 1990s.

Later moves developed and codified the political intentions captured in the recommendations (for an overview, see Annex 3, 'History and Development of the OMC SPSI (1997–2010)). In terms of providing a treaty basis, both the Treaties of Amsterdam and Nice boosted the Union's social competences. Article 136 of the Amsterdam Treaty – agreed by a new generation of centre-left leaders – for the first time listed 'combating social exclusion' as an objective of the Union. Article 140 of the Treaty also formalised the Commission's prior monitoring efforts by requesting the Commission to 'encourage cooperation between the Member States, and facilitate the coordination of their action as regards social policy'.

Decisively, two later European Councils, at Lisbon and Nice in 2000, provided the final pieces of the jigsaw. At Lisbon, the European heads of government matched (or tempered!) their famous 'growth and competitiveness' target with an equal agreement to 'make a decisive impact on the eradication of poverty' by 2010.[27] To do so, they agreed to extend the basic structure of coordination and review established by the European Employment Strategy to the domain of social inclusion.

The overriding objectives of the process were agreed later in the year at Nice. These objectives clearly stated that the new OMC procedure was to be a 'multi-dimensional' process, aiming to facilitate individual access to employment, goods and services, help the most vulnerable,

[26] Council Recommendation 442/92/EEC, Art. 1.

[27] Presidency Conclusions, Lisbon European Council, 23–24 March 2000 at [32].

and mobilise all relevant bodies through 'the participation and self-expression of people suffering exclusion'.[28]

In terms of its procedures, the new process was structured around six main steps (summarised in Annex 4). The first two involve the development and agreement of overall objectives and indicators. The indicators for the process are developed by a specialist sub-group within the Social Protection Committee, made up of national and Commission experts. The objectives are more abstract, co-agreed by the Commission and the European Council. The most recent set of objectives, agreed in 2006, created three overall goals through which each of the pensions, health and social inclusion 'strands' of the OMC SPSI should be guided. These were:

(1) 'Social cohesion, equality between men and women and equal opportunities for all through adequate, accessible, financially sustainable, adaptable and efficient social protection systems';
(2) 'Effective and mutual interaction between the Lisbon objectives of greater economic growth, more and better jobs and greater social cohesion, and with the EU's Sustainable Development Strategy';
(3) 'Good governance, transparency and the involvement of stakeholders in the design, implementation and monitoring of policy'.

The next step involves national reporting. Following the agreement of the objectives, the Commission adopts guidelines to be sent to the national governments before the drafting of their national plans. These plans differ depending on the stage in the three-year 'reporting cycle' in which they fall. In the first year of each cycle, member states must draft 'strategy reports', laying out the present 'social situation' in each member state (supported with reference to EU data), and setting out detailed legislative plans. Governments are encouraged, in these initial plans, to set strategic targets for themselves, to be met by the end of the three-year cycle.[29] The setting of specific national targets will become mandatory in the context of the 'Lisbon 2020' strategy, which has for the first time, established a specific poverty target for the Union – to lift 20 million people out of poverty by 2020.

In the second and third years, lighter 'implementation reports' are required; designed to comment on progress following the initial report,

[28] *Common Objectives for Social Inclusion*, Nice European Council, 12 December 2000, Point 4(a).

[29] This innovation is a recent addition (beginning from the 2008–2010 cycle). See Commission Communication, 'A Renewed Commitment to Social Europe: Re-enforcing the Open Method of Coordination for Social Inclusion and Social Protection', COM (2008) 418 final at 5.

set out new developments, and indicate potential legislative and non-legislative responses. The Commission sets out relatively detailed guidance at the start of each cycle over how national reports should be structured, while leaving the member states to decide which non-governmental and regional bodies are to be consulted during the drafting process.[30]

Following the submission of the reports, the final two steps involve extensive peer review and reporting at the EU level. Peer review is conducted through a divided structure.[31] The principal 'reviewing' body is the Social Protection Committee, who is responsible for reviewing national reports, and preparing submissions to the Commission and Council on national plans. In the second case, however, the OMC SPSI also contains a second *peer review and assessment* programme, sponsored through the Community Action Programme for Social Solidarity – 'Progress'. This programme is designed to allow 'concrete' examples of best practice found in particular member states to be reviewed and disseminated in a more in-depth manner (through a number of thematic meetings per year). Country peer reviews represent, in effect, the OMC's official 'day out', with national representatives (and select invited NGO participants) visiting a country experimenting with a policy solution deemed to be innovative or exportable to other national contexts.

Finally, the Commission and Spring European Council, having analysed the national reports, and taken account of the 'benchmarking' undertaken through peer review, must then adopt their own annual 'Joint Reports'. These include both a general analysis of common trends and concerns across the Union as a whole, as well as a country-specific analysis. While these parts may contain (mildly) critical comments, the Council is not empowered (as they are in the EES) to make specific recommendations to states on changes to their legislative plans (even if informally, soft pressure can be exercised through the peer review process).[32] The agreement of the Joint Reports effectively signals the end of the annual cycle, and the beginning of the new one.

[30] See Commission, n. 13 above.

[31] For a more detailed description and analysis of peer review in the OMC SPSI, see M. Dawson, 'EU Law Transformed? Evaluating Accountability and Subsidiarity in the "streamlined" OMC for Social Inclusion and Social Protection' (2009) 13 *European Integration Online Papers* 1 at 6.

[32] For a comparison of the basic procedures of the EES, and OMC SPSI, see E. Radulova, 'Variations on Soft EU Governance: The Open Method(s) of Coordination' in D. De Bievre and C. Neuhold (eds.) *Dynamics and Obstacles of EU Governance* (Cheltenham: Edward Elgar, 2007) at 10–13.

This description of the OMC SPSI is one that could be easily garnered by any observer willing to take the time to look at a smattering of Commission documents, or indeed the website of the Commission DG for employment and social affairs. It represents the method's 'official description'. As a result, it has been heavily relied upon for much academic analysis of its activities.

At the same time, it contains a number of blind spots. As we will see, while for example, the Social Protection Committee (SPC) is designed as a peer review institution, engaged in comparative scrutiny and analysis of national plans, it rarely displays this function. While the 'experimental' and 'reflexive' approaches described in the last chapter rely on peer review as a functional substitute for parliamentary forms of accountability, the contemporary SPC sees its role in quite different terms, less scrutinising, than generalising national plans, and in doing so, building indicators and policy recommendations for the future. This is just one example (of many to be explored) in which a proper description of the social inclusion process, and an analysis of its theoretical templates, requires scratching beneath the surface.

To truly 'describe' the OMC, and indeed to evaluate the normative and procedural relationships it has introduced, requires moving beyond the realm of policy documents, and into an analysis of the views and opinions of the very participants of the OMC SPSI themselves. The remainder of the chapter will do so through analysing the five features of a procedural approach to 'new governance' in light of the questionnaire data. How do the individuals with the power and capacity to frame open coordination in Europe see the OMC – both its political potential, and its normative weaknesses?

TESTING FIVE FEATURES OF A PROCEDURAL APPROACH TO THE OMC

2. Law as cognitive – the need to gather and incorporate new information. Information is not treated as 'given' but as retrieved from those to whom the law applies

2.1 The 'paradigm' of social inclusion in the EU

The first feature of a procedural or 'inside' approach developed in Chapter 3 was the idea of law as cognitive. This cognitive dimension suggests that law is an information gatherer and disseminator. It not only 'commands' particular outcomes, but also carries, and seeks to draw out, new understandings of problems. Law is 'cognitively open', in the sense that its success in regulating society depends on an ability to seek out new information from its environment. In the context of new governance, it must treat the national contexts to which it applies not as uniform, but as a diverse constituency, whose *very diversity* may itself create new opportunities for adaptation, and policy learning.

This dimension to the OMC is reflected in the first question asked by the Commission through its evaluation: what is the 'added value' of the OMC? What difference has the introduction of OMC in social inclusion made to national policy-making and, in particular, what understandings of social exclusion exist in 2006 (after two rounds of national reporting) that did not exist before?

In answer, the responses highlight a number of 'common understandings' that the introduction of the OMC has brought. On the one hand, few respondents named specific policies that had arisen as a result of carrying through OMC objectives. These objectives were sufficiently broad that most national reforms could potentially be attributed to them. Governments in particular, have defended their prerogative to develop autonomous social policies through the insistence that the OMC process has played a limited role in prescribing *solutions* to social inclusion problems.[33]

Even if, however, the diagnostic capacity of the method has often been limited, there is a common feeling that the orientation of policy-making has nonetheless changed. In an analysis of European policy on social inclusion, Stefan Bernhard captures this idea through Habermas' 'paradigms'.[34] Policy learning in the OMC is 'voluntary' in the sense that there are no sanctions for states who fail to take European objectives seriously. At the same time, the dissemination of information is not voluntary – all states have to describe and evaluate national practices in light of certain definitions and objectives defined at the European level, and repeated through peer reviews, Committees and seminars.[35] These

[33] Slovak Republic at 1. NB: country names or abbreviations below will represent the names of evaluation respondents. While the Commission's own (highly partial) summary of the evaluation was cited above (n. 2 above) the specific responses were requested specifically by the author and are held only on file. References to the responses are by page number, unless stated.

[34] S. Bernhard, 'The European Paradigm of Social Exclusion' (2006) 2 *Journal of Contemporary European Research* 1.

[35] *Ibid.*, at 44–45.

understandings can become an implicit template of knowledge that actors begin to use or rely upon.

This idea of the 'paradigm' seems to be borne out, in limited ways, through the responses. While the OMC has not led to a convergence in policy *outcomes*, it is seen as nonetheless contributing to a common understanding of the *causes and nature* of social exclusion. The responses indicate a changed perception of what social exclusion means. While different states often disagreed, for example, on whether social exclusion should be seen as 'multi-dimensional', or whether it should be primarily associated with low income, there seems now to be a broad-based consensus that social exclusion should not only be considered in monetary terms, but also in relation to access to a wider range of goods and services. 'Social exclusion' has moved from a traditional Anglo-Saxon definition (one where exclusion means 'exclusion from the market') to one where the broader position of the individual in society is seen as the central indicator.

This shift is apparent even in the response of the UK government (long considered by the European left as a liberal, Anglo-American 'Trojan horse'). In discussing indicators, the UK government complains in its response about the excessive use of quantative data, at the expense of qualitative indicators, able to measure non-monetary elements, such as housing and child welfare.[36] They particularly highlight the case of pensioner poverty – in measuring such poverty, indicators based on income alone can be misleading; they have the capacity to ignore either the potentially exorbitant costs of care and support services, or the impact on the health and well-being of elderly persons of non-monetary factors (e.g. the ability to foster and maintain contact with family members).[37] Even among more 'liberal' or 'Anglo-Saxon' states, we have seen an increasing understanding of inclusion as meaning not only an imperative to reform social assistance policies, but also to consider the access of individuals to housing, employment, education, and all those other factors which have a bearing on their 'social well-being'.

More generally, 'multi-dimensionality' is seen as a strong common message. For Latvia:

> The OMC has verified that the multi-dimensional approach used in solving the problems of poverty and social exclusion is the right one; in the case of

[36] UK at 10. [37] *Ibid.*, at 11.

> pensions, a common understanding has been created, for example, on the 'inter-connectedness' between pension systems from the one side and economy and employment from the other.[38]

A recognition of the 'nested' quality of social protection and inclusion reforms, and their interdependence with other policy areas, is here seen as one of the method's distinct achievements.

As a second and related example, a number of respondents mention the use of the method to more closely integrate social inclusion and labour market policies. Following the presence of 'making work pay' as a distinctive strand of the original Nice objectives, they talk about the link between poverty and involvement in the labour market as part of a common 'pool of information' about inclusion/exclusion that the OMC has created.[39] Thus, for Hungary:

> The OMC has helped in strengthening the link between employment policy and social policy, as well as moving from a passive social policy towards an active one, focusing on labour market integration.[40]

Here, while there is no overall consensus about the substantive policy mix needed to tackle exclusion problems, we can see, firstly, a common acknowledgement that the causes of these problems stem from something more than low income (and that hence an integrated government programme is called for) and secondly, an emerging link between 'the activation' discourse present in the EES, and the idea that providing opportunities for work should be a key lever in fighting social exclusion. To this extent, the EU discourse has cognitively succeeded in carrying forward and disseminating particular categories and understandings, even if the policies attached to them vary. Cognitively, the method has had some success in penetrating a social policy discourse previously seen as belonging almost exclusively to the national level.

[38] Latvia at 2.

[39] As well as Hungary below, see the Netherlands and Ireland as examples of this more liberal view. For the Netherlands, the practical orientation of inclusion policies under the OMC has been to 'attract more people to the labour market, increase the supply of labour and generate more investment in human capital', Netherlands at 7. For the Irish government, 'the analysis in the NAPs and the overview in the Joint Inclusion Reports have been helpful in understanding the causes and consequences of social exclusion, and in understanding the importance of social inclusion as a productive factor in the European economy', Ireland at 3. At the time of the responses, both countries were led, unsurprisingly, by centre-right governments.

[40] Hungary at 1.

2.2 *Setting the agenda*

The second sense in which the OMC may be seen as 'cognitive' relies on its role in 'Europeanising' particular policy agendas. Many respondents indicate that the need to establish and disseminate national action plans has succeeded either in keeping inclusion policies on the national agenda, or giving them a higher priority.[41] The most influential social NGOs, like EAPN, note something similar at the EU level, where the inclusion process has focused attention on social inclusion at a time where the need to spur greater economic growth had begun to grab the headlines.[42]

This 'agenda-setting' role may not only be about 'putting issues on the table' but also encouraging states to engage in a common reflective exercise. In a contribution by David Friedrich and Milena Büchs on the OMC's national impact in Germany, one of the most important consequences of the method's introduction is seen as the very recognition that social exclusion and poverty are recurring problems. Whereas Germany, since the Kohl era, had tended to assume that its efforts to introduce minimum income schemes had removed structural deprivation as an endemic problem, the comparisons afforded by the method between states, could be observed as 'waking it up' from a fatalistic form of complacency.[43]

Several aspects of the OMC could encourage this reflective function. The first phase demanded of states by the guidelines issued by the Commission on the preparation of national action plans is to survey and comment upon the social situation in their own state. Member states are to 'give a synthetic overview of the economic, social and demographic context that needs to be taken into account when setting priorities and developing policies'.[44]

Secondly, states are encouraged to conduct this exercise through a comparative lens – comparing the nature and extent of exclusion problems in their state with the social situation of others. The OMC can be

[41] 'La MOC est plutôt perçue favorablement en ce qu'elle donne une *meilleure visibilité* à la lutte contre la pauvreté et l'exclusion sociale'. Belgium at 4.

[42] EAPN at 1. They observe this as being a particularly important factor given the cooling effect of the blocking efforts by the UK and German governments against the 4th Poverty Action Programme.

[43] M. Buchs and D. Friedrich, 'Surface Integration: The National Action Plans for Employment and Social Inclusion in Germany', in Zeitlin and Pochet, n. 16 above, at 267.

[44] Guidelines on Preparing National Reports 2006–2008, n. 13 above, at 3.

'cognitive' not simply in the sense of 'carrying' normative understandings, but also in encouraging re-evaluation, both internally and between different national contexts.[45] This reflective capacity – as will be discussed in later sections – may in fact be an important precondition for effective reform.

2.3 *Cognitive gaps*

The two elements described above indicate that the OMC has a cognitive capacity. The evaluation's respondents see the OMC as introducing a distinct vocabulary and set of priorities into the national social policy sphere. The responses also, however, indicate that this has been limited by other problems (many of them expanded upon in other parts of this chapter). In particular, the respondents tend to see a close link between the awareness raising potential of the OMC and both its *openness* and *visibility* as a process.

These two aspects of the OMC refer to its capacity both to relay and to absorb social information. In order to relay information, the method has to be something that is visible to more than the usual suspects of 'Europeanised' officials. It has to enter into, and become part of, a larger policy-making discourse. In order to absorb information, it must be open to, and reflect upon, the practice of its environment. Law must not only be a transmitter of norms, and but also open in its content.

The responses suggest severe limits in both cases. In terms of visibility, it is regularly reported in the responses that there is 'no great political interest' among the general public in the OMC, or that participation is 'passive'.[46] Only those with a specific sectional interest, i.e. groups representing particular causes, tend to get involved. In the words of the Belgian response:

> Elle demeure trop limitée à un cercle restreint de responsables politiques et administratifs 'européanisés', directement en charge de sa mise en œuvre sur le plan national.[47]

[45] An example of the latter given in one empirical study is France. While France has traditionally talked about inclusion in the context of a republican tradition, the references in the Joint Reports to the integration of ethnic minority migrants means that (as one interviewee put it) 'today we speak about ethnic problems in the context of social inclusion in a slightly different way than 10 years ago'. See J. Buchkremer and S. Zirra, 'Europeanization of Social Policies: The Influences of OMC/Inclusion on National Institutions in Germany, France and Italy'. Paper Presentation, ESPAnet conference, September 2007, at 10.

[46] Estonia at 7. [47] Belgium at 12.

If information is being relayed, it is to a sectional, not a general, public.[48]

In terms of openness, the ability to receive information may be limited by the method's participative shortcomings. While peer review procedures, for example, can be seen as a way of gathering and accessing new information, a number of social NGOs argue that their potential is limited through a consistent emphasis on national governments as the main 'reviewing' actors. The implications of limited participation are seen by these respondents not only as detrimental to the personal lobbying capacity of their institutions, but also to the ability of the method itself to gather, and benefit from, the experience of those further down the policy chain. In the words of AGE, 'NGOs can provide invaluable insights into what works, and what does not work on the ground. This knowledge is not being fully accessed in the current programme'.[49]

Opening up participatory boundaries is in this sense not only important in order to boost the *legitimacy* of the process, but also to be able to tell whether the 'experiments' tested through the method are actually working. As ATD Fourth World put it, 'common understandings of the causes and nature of social exclusion are likely to be of little use – or may even be misleading – if they leave the experience of those living under poverty out of the equation'.[50]

Here, some examples of better practice also emerge. In the case of Belgium, efforts have been made to include socially deprived individuals in the process of creating indicators (for example, in order to establish factors which have presented barriers to social inclusion in the past).[51] As a second example, FEANTSA (a transnational NGO representing the homeless) indicate their role in providing indicators and data sets for housing, developed under the European Typology on Homelessness and Housing Exclusion (ETHOS).[52] In

[48] See 'Deliberative polyarchy and executive governance', section 4.5 below.

[49] AGE at 13.

[50] ATD Fourth World make this point directly – 'Partnership with people who have direct experience of poverty in the development of indicators would result in new insights on what needs to be measured in order to establish whether or not policies are having an impact, or indeed, the desired impact. *If the knowledge that people living in poverty possess is left out of the equation then inevitably the full picture will not be understood.*' ATD Fourth World at 5.

[51] *Ibid.*, at 5–6.

[52] 'ETHOS is an example of a concrete contribution of service providers to the advancement of the OMC process in this specific area of policy and demonstrates just how important it is to have social and political deliberation when elaborating indicators.' FEANTSA at 5.

both instances, the resources of non-governmental organisations are posited as pathways to boosting the method's cognitive capacity. In the present OMC SPSI, however, it seems that they are being underutilised. The ability of the OMC to 'carry knowledge' depends on its capacity to go beyond the usual suspects of national and European administrators.

2.4 Destabilising knowledge?

So long as the OMC remains participatively closed, it seems likely that the normative messages it is effectively able to 'carry' will also be limited. An OMC comprising only a narrow band of European and national officials could succeed in establishing a 'common pool of knowledge', but only one closed off to the preferences of actors lower down the policy chain. Those 'common understandings of problems' that it imparts are not subject to critical reflection, but have already been determined and enumerated in advance.

This criticism emerges in defence of an important element of the 'cognitive dimension' of a procedural approach to law. Legal frameworks should not only carry, but also 'destabilise' existing knowledge. An important argument of the experimental approach in particular was that, in a diverse polity, law cannot reflect an underlying equilibrium, but instead must be attuned to the needs of different states, and different fields of action. It must be able, both to bring different perspectives into a common discourse, and subject otherwise taken for granted assumptions to critical scrutiny. Can the method not only carry and absorb, but also undermine embedded patterns of social knowledge?

In practice, the method's ability to carry out this function depends on a number of institutions. The responses speak to the role of 'Joint Reporting' by the European Institutions in this way. In their Joint Reports, the Commission and Council survey 'the social situation' in the member states, including a critical analysis of social protection reforms in each country. They also include a statistical analysis of the social situation across the EU as a whole.

While these reports could potentially play a role in subverting 'given' assumptions about social inclusion reform, they rarely take on this role. Most often, Joint Reports are descriptive, attempting to outline common patterns among member states. In this sense, the institutions themselves commit an error to which they frequently accuse member states: they evidence a practical inability to carry out strategic thinking or analysis.[53]

This can have both positive and negative elements. Positively, even a mere descriptive report can have destabilising effects. It is impossible, for example, not to draw some conclusions about social protection reforms, and their relative success, from the annexes to the Joint Reports. These annexes comparatively analyse the range of 'at risk of poverty' rates across the EU, linking them to employment and inequality levels, and breaking down poverty risks by gender, and by age. As a specific example, the Report draws a clear link (with serious political implications) between those states that have invested heavily in key social services and those that have favourable poverty rates.[54]

> A comparison between the standard at risk of poverty rate and the hypothetical situation where social transfers are absent, other things being equal, shows that such transfers have an important re-distributive effect that helps to reduce the number of people at risk of poverty.[55]

What may be more important is the conclusions drawn from this move. Here, the need to evidence political neutrality (the traditional image of the Commission as depoliticised) has had a limiting effect. Rather than critique dominant positions, the Commission and Council have used joint reporting as a way of searching for consensus among the member states. This consensus has been used as a basis for the common objectives and indicators, and as a way of identifying possible avenues for future rule-making (in the form, either of policy priorities for the future, or soft law norms).

This search for consensus suggests that the role of the EU institutions can be inverted. They do not 'destabilise', but precisely *stabilise* existing knowledge, allowing common patterns of thought and reform to be used as a basis for joint action in the future. While minority positions are seen as deviations from the norm, the patterns of a majority of states can lead to changes in the overall objectives of the inclusion process, or alternatively, provide a basis for future law-making.

There is time here to develop only one example. In the 2005 and 2006 Joint Reports, the use of 'active inclusion' policies was identified by the Commission as a common theme among national plans. Following a

[53] A 'Golden Nugget' in this regard may be an opening line of the section of the 2008 Joint Report on child poverty: 'If children are poor, it is generally because they live in poor households.' With analysis like this, one wonders why child poverty remains such a pressing issue among European states. Joint Report 2008, n. 4 above, at 4.

[54] Joint Report 2007, n. 4 above, at 14. [55] *Ibid.*, at 15.

wide-ranging consultation in 2006, the Commission has since sponsored workshops and academic studies into active inclusion policies, identifying an opportunity to establish a 'virtuous circle' between social inclusion, and labour market reform.[56] In early 2007, the Commission even passed 'soft law' on the matter, enacting a Communication and Recommendation on 'taking forward the active inclusion of people furthest from the labour market'.[57]

This represents an early instance of the way in which the 'cognitive capacity' of the method has been used. The lessons of 'law as a cognitive medium' become fractured – while the OMC has certainly carried 'common understandings' of particular problems (like the understanding of 'active inclusion' contained in these reports), there remains the danger that these understandings are not open to reformulation and adaptation, but used primarily as a way of driving forward the ordinary legislative process. 'Common understandings' are not open to question, or seen as opportunities more closely to connect social inclusion reforms with the experience of actors operating 'on the ground', but instrumentalised in pursuit of a common, overarching 'social agenda'.

The cognitive dimension to law seems to provide both a threat and an opportunity – while it has provided a means to pool information, and increase awareness about the social inclusion process, there remain significant limits, many of which are tied to aspects to be discussed in this chapter. It is to one of those – the need for 'flexibility' in rule-making – that we now must turn.

3. Law as adaptive – the need for flexibility in rule-making. Law is not self-delineating, but must be considered in terms of the situation and context in which it is it is to be applied

3.1 The challenge of diversity

The larger discourse about 'flexibility' in the context of proceduralisation carries certain assumptions. It refers back to what was described in

[56] On these activities, see: http://europa.eu/legislation_summaries/employment_and_social_policy/social_inclusion_fight_against_poverty/em0009_en.htm.

[57] Commission Communication 'On Modernising Social Protection for Greater Social Justice and Economic Cohesion: Taking Forward the Active Inclusion of People Furthest from the Labour Market, COM (2007) 620 final.

the last chapter as a 'common problem' for reflexive, procedural and experimental approaches to law. This is the functional complexity, and temporal rapidity, of modern societies. Social conditions, particularly in post-national settings like the EU, are sufficiently complex, and shifting in their complexity, that rules are quickly rendered irrelevant or out of date. This drives the need for more flexible or iterative norms.

In the context of the OMC process in social inclusion, a different problem arises. In some sense, the challenge social inclusion policies respond to is a long-standing one. Since Karl Marx's famous diagnosis in *Das Kapital*, and its revolutionary response, states have been in the business of attempting to 'correct' the worst excesses of the market. The basic objectives of social policy – far from being on a tumultuous journey of change – remain the same: to protect the social dignity and autonomy of the individual.

The challenge in the EU context may thus be altered. While most European states have attempted to 'decommodify' the labour market through building systems of social protection, they have not gone about it the same way. Some have based their systems of welfare provision on principles of universalisation and compulsory membership, whereas others have given a larger role to the family or to the voluntary sector. Some have funded their welfare systems through general taxation, whereas others have relied more heavily on private provision and market principles.[58] For each state, 'the welfare state' has meant not just a particular organisational model, but a deeply embedded set of institutional, political and normative commitments.

This diversity has left European law in an unusual situation. Just as economic and social interdependency have been increasing, so the call to respect the distinct social conditions and welfare institutions of each state have become more vocal. It is in the context of this simultaneous demand, first for common action ('unity') and second, for respect for national traditions ('diversity') that the need for flexible ways of conducting regulation in Europe has arisen.

The respondents to the Commission's evaluation largely share the view that the OMC was designed to achieve this balance. It is seen less as an attempt to 'centralise' power than as a means of devolving legislative responsibility to the national level. The OMC is variously described in the responses as 'a proper translation of the principle of subsidiarity'

[58] G. Esping-Andersen, *The Three Worlds of Welfare Capitalism* (Princeton University Press, 1990).

and as an instrument 'able to respect the specific cultural, social and economic conditions of each country'.[59] While the introduction of the OMC may not therefore represent an absolute abandonment of central steering power, it is recognised as creating a presumption that European policies are embedded within, and conditional upon, distinct preconditions operating at the national level.[60] This account would seem to support an 'intergovernmental' reading of the present OMC. No doubt some national respondents support the method for this reason.

Others, however, see the embrace of diversity differently; as a productive factor for the creation of a *European* response to social inclusion problems. In particular the structural divergences between European states potentially increases the experimental potential of EU policy-making. In US literature, this has been described as the advantage of using regional or state governments as 'laboratories' for policy learning.[61] Successful reforms in one state can be emulated by others, whereas states can learn to steer clear of policy failures. Diversity is seen not as an obstacle to law-making, but as an opportunity to challenge given knowledge, fostering real innovations in the process.

While the language of 'experimentalism' has yet to become part of the European vernacular, there is some evidence that actors within the OMC SPSI support this usage. In the case of pensions, for example, AGE write that:

> In contrast to what international financial institutions like the World Bank used to do, [the OMC] has not sought to impose a single pension reform model in Europe. The 'objective-oriented' approach of the OMC on pensions allows for policy-makers from different EU Member States to assess different reform proposals, get involved in a mutual learning process and exchange good practice, instead of getting bogged-down by nation specific semantics.[62]

[59] Denmark at 3; Czech Republic at 2; CEEP at 1.

[60] In this context, see the Commission's description of its role under the Social Agenda 2010: 'The Agenda combines the consolidation of a common European framework with the implementation of diversified measures to respond to specific needs. In this way, it supports the motto of "unity in diversity", which is proclaimed by the Draft Constitutional Treaty.' Commission Communication 'On the Social Agenda', COM (2005) 033 final at 3.

[61] See Justice Brandeis (dissenting) in *New State Ice Co.* v. *Liebmann*, 285 US 262, 311 (1932): 'It is one of the happy incidents of the federal system that a single courageous state may, if its citizens choose, serve as a laboratory; and try novel social and economic experiments without risk to the rest of the country.'

[62] AGE at 4.

In this case, the OMC is seen not only as spreading legislative power, but also as treating the law-making process as open to new ideas. 'Flexibility' in this context implies that policy solutions are not handed down from on high, but capable of adapting to and learning from local practice.

In the case of pensions, as with other social protection policies, successful reform may depend on combining a pool of common knowledge with an awareness of demographic, financial and social factors that are specific to each state. The promise of a 'flexible' OMC, according to the respondents, may lie in precisely this ability not only to encourage, but also to learn from, devolutions of legislative power.

3.2 *Flexibility v. participation?*

The advantage of flexible policy-making is that it allows new issues to be put on the table. In a social inclusion process where the nature of poverty, and the policy tools available to combat it, are in a state of fluctuation, there may be advantages to a more long-term approach.[63] As such, the OMC SPSI has been framed not as a single legislative intervention, but as an iterative process. National administrations (in theory at least) are to use their experiences of policy implementation, and the knowledge of non-governmental actors, to readjust legislative plans on an ongoing basis. This cognitive openness to new information is what makes the method a 'flexible' legal instrument.

There may, however, be costs to flexibility. Its immediate consequence is that the time frame for reporting under the OMC is relatively short. The formation of national 'action' or 'implementation' plans, and their submission to, and evaluation by, the Commission, should all take place within a year. While this time frame may be an advantage for governments intent on 'speeding up' the legislative process, it poses obvious challenges to the claim that the method can encourage broad levels of participation. A vocal minority within the responses argue that the OMC has given up on such requirements precisely in order to guarantee greater 'flexibility' in its approach to regulatory reform.[64] On the one hand, respondents like the city of Copenhagen complain about being given only five days to respond to the Danish NAP. On the

[63] This advantage is summarised by FEANTSA: 'The Flexibility of the OMC is an advantage in this respect since the objectives can be modified in accordance with evolving situations/problems, and target areas where Europe has not performed well.' FEANTSA at 8.

[64] See e.g. CEMR, s. 5; SOLIDAR at 4; Eurocities at 5.

other, a number of national respondents note the complete exclusion of parliaments from the process, whose burdensome legislative procedures are designed precisely to allow legislative acts to be properly debated and scrutinised.[65]

Where there is not exclusion, participation often comes at a point where its practical effect is limited. One of the most common complaints offered is that – while consulting key NGOs is common practice – this has often occurred relatively late in the NAP process.[66] Consultation often takes place at a point when the strategic objectives, priorities and targets of each plan have already been set. The 'inclusion' of the non-governmental sector has therefore often been treated as a formality rather than as a means of guaranteeing the openness of law to new, or critical, social information.[67]

In such circumstances procedural 'iterability' may come at a cost. Whereas on the one hand, 'flexibility' in law-making is sought as a means of allowing access to new forms of knowledge, on the other, the constant drive for renewal may make public involvement more difficult (or alternatively, more selective).[68]

3.3 *Is there such a thing as a 'dialectical' OMC?*

The tension between flexibility and participation is an important one for 'procedural' or 'inside' theories. They rely on an accommodation between these virtues. Flexibility is pursued in order to keep rules more attuned to their environmental conditions, while, at the same time, the very ability of law adequately to reflect social conditions depends upon

[65] Eurocities at 10.

[66] This is a conclusion, for example, of a report by European Public Social Platform on Local Authority Involvement in the preparation of NAPs: 'The drawing-up of NAPs and the process of consultation is very complex and requires a lot of resources. In the short time period offered by the national authorities it is almost impossible to go into a very extensive analysis in a sufficient time period to give a balanced and serious assessment', n. 7 above, at 10. See also, in the responses, Malta at 6; Hungary 7–8.

[67] See also 'Law as participative', sections 4.1–4.2 below.

[68] In this context, many of the respondents favour a compromise solution. While flexibility is sought in *policy-making*, i.e. in adapting European goals to the domestic political context, it is rejected at the procedural level, where attaining stability and clarity in the rules under which the OMC SPSI is governed is considered important. This argument is made most forcefully by the non-governmental respondents, who argue for a code of conduct; or clearer timetable for reporting; for national administrators, and contributors from 'civil society' to follow. See (among national respondents) Hungary at 11; Belgium at 19; France at 7; (among NGOs) CEMR, s. 4; AGE at 11; SOLIDAR at 4.

the inclusion of new actors, and the information that they can bring to the table.

According to advocates of the first 'procedural' approach, this tension is to be resolved by seeking a 'dialectical' relationship between European objectives and their application to a national context.[69] Not only is it the case that the meaning of the law depends on its application to a 'local practice', but also that the experience of law-application should be reflected in future rule-making. Law should be open to adjustment in light of both changing priorities, and a concrete reflection on what 'works', and what does not at more local levels.[70] A feedback loop between local experience, and the common priorities identified at the European level, is vital. In the method, this function is fulfilled by certain institutions. The Social Protection Committee, as we have described, critically reviews national action plans, and also plays a role in drawing up the 'Joint Reports' adopted by the Commission and Council in subsequent years. The 'Roundtable on Social Exclusion' sponsored by the Council Presidency is another example of an institution designed to 'feed in' the experience of stakeholders into annual discussions about the focus of European social policy (conducted at the Spring Council itself).

Troublingly, the responses indicate that – while such institutions may have an important deliberative function – they often fail to produce any such dialectic between 'local' and 'European' priorities. To take the Roundtable on Exclusion as an example, the UK notes that – while the Roundtable has seen 'a community of actors emerging' – '[it] has not been a consistently effective means of driving the process forward, or assisting the transition from process to outcome'.[71] In effect, while it has allowed social NGO's, and those with direct experience of poverty, to share their experiences with others, there is little evidence that its outcomes have been reflected in the strategic decisions of subsequent Councils. The exercise has been used as an opportunity to share

[69] See J. Lenoble and O. De Munck, 'Transformations in the Art of Governance', in O. De Schutter, N. Lebessis and J. Paterson (eds.), *Governance in the European Union* (Luxembourg: Office for Official Publications of the European Communities, 2001) at 40–42.

[70] This is also clearly a part of experimentalist literature – in its language, deliberation should be 'polyarchical'; the delegation of power to the 'periphary' is conducted not in opposition to, but in order to increase the cognitive resources or organisation capacity, of the 'centre'. J. Cohen and C. Sabel, 'Directly-Deliberative Polyarchy' (1997) 3 *European Law Journal* 4.

[71] UK at 18.

information, not to update European priorities and objectives in light of concrete experience on the ground.

Often the root of this problem can be something as banal as differences in the officials assigned to each process. As Jenny Buchkremer has argued, in some member states, the officials who contribute to peer review processes under the SPC are often not the same individuals who implement policy, or take strategic decisions over national reporting.[72] Whereas the lack of any link between the Roundtable and the Spring Council would seem to limit the 'filtering up' of local to European experience, the difficulty of identifying common officials would also seem to count against any 'filtering down', from common European deliberations and concerns, to the setting of national policy priorities.

So long as those who 'deliberate' and set policy at the European level are effectively insulated from discussions and experiments in reform going on at national and local levels, 'flexibility' in the OMC would seem unlikely to go beyond guesswork; the selective adaptation of rules according to the opinions of national and European administrators. In so much as the 'procedural approach' relies on a dialectical relationship between the formation of European norms, and their 'application' to a local context, there is plenty of evidence that the promise of the procedural approach remains unfulfilled. The OMC very much remains an imperfect model for dialectical or 'responsive' rule-making.

4. Law as participative – the need to enlist and vocalise new actors. Law is not 'handed down' from a higher political authority, but articulated and framed by those most affected by its rules

By now, there are a number of studies that have looked at the extent to which high levels of participation are evident in the OMC, both in the EES and in the various strands of the OMC SPSI.[73] The general tenure of

[72] See Buchkremer, n. 45 above, at 7. It is interesting to note that the same problem can pertain below the level of the state. In Germany again, national federal authorities may draw up the strategic plan but, lacking the competence in a federal system, have limited power actually to implement it.

[73] See e.g. C. de la Porte and P. Pochet, 'Participation in the Open Method of Coordination: The Case of Employment and Social Inclusion' in Zeitlin and Pochet, n. 16 above; P. Nance and C. de la Porte, 'The OMC – A Deliberative-Democratic Mode of Governance?: The Case of Employment and Pensions' (2004) 11 *Journal of European Public Policy* 4; A. Horvath, 'Analysing Deliberation as a Legitimating Principle of the OMC: A Conceptual Framework and Analysis', Paper Presentation, Workshop on Democracy, the Rule of Law and Soft Modes of Governance in the EU, University of Roskilde, November 2006.

these studies is that – while there are still significant gaps – the OMC process in social inclusion has been relatively successful in allowing new relationships to be established between national administrators, and the non-governmental sector. Levels of participation are perceived to be higher and broader in the social inclusion process than they are, for example, in the heavily 'corporatist' EES.[74]

While this section will cast some doubt on this participative claim, there are good reasons to believe that the very effectiveness of the method in achieving structural and political reform requires the taking on board of new actors. The constitutional template upon which social inclusion policies work in the EU is a polity in which the capacity to enact social assistance reforms has often been devolved to local or regional levels. Achieving the Lisbon commitment of the Union to lift 20 million out of poverty by 2020 therefore relies on more than the 'usual suspects'; it requires the habituation of European objectives and indicators into each and every level of governance. 'Participation' is not just a route to more legitimacy, but may also be an important precondition for policy effectiveness.

As with the other parts of this chapter, however, there is always a flip side of the coin. The relevant question for those seeking to learn about participation in the OMC is not just: is there participation? This question alone is problematic in the case of the OMC SPSI. There is plenty of evidence in the responses of disaffected participants, or of the tokenistic nature of participation in the inclusion process as it stands.

There are also two further questions that are important. Firstly, how is participation conducted? It is not sufficient that other actors are 'consulted' on the nature of reform proposals, but also that they should have a say in shaping how norms under the OMC evolve. Does actor involvement translate into policy change, or is it used merely to legitimise decisions that have already been taken? Secondly, who participates? Real participation relies on a broad ethic of involvement, not one in which participants are either selected, or placed within particular confines. It requires both that participation is incentivised, and that these incentives allow critical scrutiny of the dominant executive actors of the OMC to be carried out. To what extent are these elements present in the current process?

[74] J. Zeitlin, 'The Open Method of Coordination in Action: Theoretical Promise, Empirical Realities, Reform Strategy' in J. Zeitlin and P. Pochet, n. 16 above, at 468–470.

4.1 Participation as structural entry

According to the responses, the structure of participation in the OMC process as it stands tends to coalesce around two models. The first is to mix a centralisation of decision-making at national and federal levels with the input of certain 'invited' participants. The design for this structure is represented by the common (indeed, almost ubiquitous) model of a working group, coordinated by a national labour or social affairs ministry, and including non-governmental organisations in the drawing up of the national strategy reports.[75]

The second model is to directly delegate decision-making responsibility downwards. As an example, the Spanish government recognise three different levels of actor participation, and has created different institutions to represent them.[76] At the federal level, cross-departmental coordination is facilitated by an interministerial Commission, while at the local level, the Commission for social services within the Spanish Federation of Municipalities and Regions has been given specific responsibility to monitor, review and report upon regional and local policy. A further body – the 'Working Group for Social Inclusion and Employment' – is entrusted with fostering civil society involvement. As an example of its work, the Spanish government cites a questionnaire sent to 500 civil society organisations on the preparation of the 2003–05 NAP, with a rolling out of this practice to 1,500 participants for the 2006–08 round.[77]

The creation of new structures like this one – while certainly not ubiquitous among the respondents – heralds some of the more positive elements of the OMC's development to date. It is widely recognised among the respondents that – while much work remains to be done – the creation of the OMC has encouraged governments to establish closer relationships with the non-governmental sector. In most cases, this has led to the development of new structures for NGO participation.[78]

[75] According to the responses, a version of this model is employed by: the UK, Hungary, Finland, Lithuania, the Slovak Republic, Austria, Cyprus, the Czech Republic, Estonia, Greece, Latvia and Portugal.

[76] Spain, 7–8. [77] *Ibid.*, at 8.

[78] See, as three examples, Ireland's development of an Office for Social Inclusion, the UK's creation of the 'Social Policy Task Force', and Greece's 'National Committee for Social Protection'. For a summary, see the Commission's own evaluation summary, n. 2 above, at 21–22.

It is thus common for NGO respondents to claim the method as 'opening doors' or as giving non-state actors (in the words of EAPN) 'a certain legitimacy to lobby'.[79] NGO involvement no longer simply depends on goodwill, or informal contacts with government departments, but upon (in Kerstin Jacobsson's words), 'the legitimate claim to voice' that the leverage of a formalised EU process has brought.[80]

To this end, national governments have been forced in their national reports explicitly to comment on the steps they have taken to secure non-governmental involvement in the drawing up of their plans; a capacity which the Commission can then review as part of the third 'mobilisation' objective of the inclusion process. The existence of this objective – according to one social NGO – has 'helped promote consultation at the national level where this was not necessarily part of the received political system'.[81]

This 'structural entry' advantage may be particularly important in new member states. AGE, the platform of NGOs for the elderly, for example write that:

> While the experience of AGE's members have differed in the context of the OMC on social inclusion, one of the most important and tangible successes of the Method has been to provide a clear and open structure for national policy-making where no such structures existed before. This has been particularly felt in some of the new Member States, where thanks to the Open Method, older people's associations have been able to engage with governments, sometimes for the first time, on the situation of older people at risk of poverty and social exclusion.[82]

Whereas in old members of the club, procedures for consultation are often established, or based on corporatism, the Joint Inclusion Memorandum, signed by the accession states in late 2003, indicates a different picture in the new Europe. There is a recognition that many states have emerged from a heavily 'top down' tradition in managing government policy. As such, NGO involvement in the past 'had tended to be limited or haphazard'.[83]

[79] EAPN Report, n. 7 above, at 28. See also, ATD Fourth World at 7.

[80] K. Jacobsson, 'Trying to Reform the "Best Pupils in the Class?" The Open Method of Coordination in Sweden and Denmark' in Zeitlin and Pochet, n. 16 above, at 131.

[81] AGE at 10. See also, Kenneth Armstrong's conclusion in the UK context: 'without the driving force from Europe to work with civil society and other actors, it was unlikely that the DWP [Department of Work and Pensions] would have developed a willingness to engage with NGOs.' Armstrong, n. 86 below, at 92.

[82] AGE at 3. [83] Joint Inclusion Memorandum, n. 5 above, at 36.

The presence of a transition period in the institutional culture of the new member states may have provided the method with a window of opportunity to influence policy-making practice. For ATD Fourth World, in states where there had been little previous activity in social inclusion, the process had 'created a whole new dynamic, bringing different people and groups together both horizontally and vertically'.[84] A similar claim is repeated in the national responses. The Hungarian government, for example, describes its preparation of a Joint Inclusion Memorandum as, 'the first time ever that the Hungarian government has initiated a dialogue with experts and civil society organisations on the issues of social exclusion'.[85] In particular, they describe a contrast between the absence – in the past – of a tradition of involving victims of social deprivation in national planning, and the recent representation of socially excluded people through Hungarian social NGOs.[86]

This window has even – in some states – emerged in Western Europe. In a recent contribution by Kenneth Armstrong, for example, he describes how the devolution in 1999 of some legislative power to Scotland, Northern Ireland and Wales has created possibilities for using the OMC process as a springboard to establish cooperative relationships with devolved administrations.[87] During discussions in 2003 about proposed changes to the format of the inclusion process, the UK government defended the NAP process, arguing that it had allowed it to develop a more participatory approach to policy-making, including better and more integrated relationships with Britain's new regional administrations.[88] In short, in states where new institutions are being developed, we may see examples of adapting the participative rhetoric of the OMC to domestic models.

The second major advantage is more bottom up. The method may have provided incentives and funding for greater organisation on the part of the NGO sector itself (particularly at the EU level). For many

[84] This is in contrast to their experience in old member states, where participative structures were 'already in place'. As such, 'the outcomes of national processes and consultation structures did not automatically feed into the EU level reporting mechanisms as they should have done.' ATD Fourth World at 2–3.

[85] Hungary at 6. [86] *Ibid*., at 9.

[87] K. Armstrong, 'The Europeanization of Social Exclusion: British Adaptation to EU Co-ordination' (2006) 8 *British Journal of Politics and International Relations* 1, 90–91. See also, UK at 17

[88] K. Armstrong, 'How Open is the United Kingdom to the OMC Process on Social Inclusion', in Zeitlin and Pochet, n. 16 above, at 296–300.

NGOs, low levels of involvement are not necessarily always the product of secretive public bureaucracies or a closed legislative process, but simply follow from a lack of resources. The politics of social inclusion is undoubtedly a complicated business, requiring organisations with the capacity to devote significant time to monitoring (and even understanding) national decisions. Fully contributing to the OMC requires sending people to seminars and meetings, and combining lobbying functions with the other, more substantive tasks for which social NGOs receive charitable funding.

In order to alleviate this burden, the development of the OMC has gone hand in hand with efforts to increase the levels of funding available to the NGO sector. The community action programme on social solidarity (Progress) was founded with the explicit objective of 'developing the capacity of key European level networks to support and further develop Community policy goals and strategies on social protection and inclusion'.[89] In order to apply for funding under Progress, NGOs must have a 'significant European dimension'.[90] This normally means they must form themselves into networks, bringing different national bodies together into an overall 'umbrella organisation'. This may have provided two advantages – firstly, it has allowed the NGO sector to self-organise, and to create a European voice for groups (e.g. children and the elderly) who were previously represented only at the national level; secondly, it has given these bodies the funding to effectively lobby both the Commission and national governments for changes they see as favourable to the groups they represent.[91]

While this structural entry advantage to the NGO sector is by no means uniform across all member states, there is sufficient evidence to conclude that the OMC has played a role in breaking down formal participative boundaries. It may be necessary to look beyond this formal account in order to see its participative limits.

[89] Council Decision 1672/2006/EC 'Establishing a Community Action Programme for Employment and Social Solidarity – Progress' [2006] O.J. L 315, Art. 5.

[90] *Ibid.*, at Art. 9.

[91] An example in the first case may be EAPN Malta, who note the development of transnational networks among NGOs. 'Member organisations of EAPN Malta (currently there are 46 such organisations) are benefiting from direct experiences in other countries. Some NGO representatives had the opportunity to meet counterparts abroad and locally. This experience of cross-fertilisation is helping Maltese NGOs to share experiences with other countries.' Malta at 2.

4.2 Who is participating?

The formal account of participation in the OMC is that the process is open to all those who are affected by its outcomes. Already, this contains a half truth. The Committee structures that determine things like the indicators that measure poverty, or the decisions over funding of the Community Action Programme are not 'presumptively open to all', but largely closed, comprising a select number of national representatives and Commission officials.[92] We have to search past this - to the national level - to see where the structural openness of the OMC really lies.

Even here, participation depends on a number of factors. Particularly, it depends on the willingness of several processual 'gatekeepers' to include non-governmental opinion. At a more formal level, the gatekeepers are national governments, who must ultimately decide to what extent 'civil society' opinion should be represented in national reports. These governments are also, of course, in control of any legislative initiatives that arise from the process of submitting national strategy reports.

At a more informal level, the Commission itself could be said to be a second 'gatekeeper'. Engagement often relies - as the previous section has discussed - on participants who have the resources and information to engage in the process fully. These resources are often practically provided through Progress funding, which is allocated under a committee comprising Commission and national representatives. To this extent, even if the process is formally 'open', it is 'controlled' at several levels.

The questionnaire itself is an excellent example. On the one hand, the evaluation on which this chapter is based displays an admirable degree of inclusiveness. The wealth of information that it has been able to draw upon is a direct consequence of the breadth of the questionnaire's respondents. There is important input from a cross section of European civil society, including national governments, social partners, regional organisations and social NGO's. In addition, national

92 This is made clear, for example in the rules of procedure of the Progress Committee: http://ec.europa.eu/employment_social/progress/docs/rules_en.pdf. According to those rules, the Committee is confined to a single national representative for each country, and, in certain circumstances, invited 'expert' participants, or representatives from third countries. According to Art. 14 (on transparency!), 'the Committee's discussions shall be kept confidential'.

governments were themselves advised to prepare their responses as 'mini-NAPs', inviting contributions from non-state actors or social partners, and collating this information into a general report.[93] The responses thus represent a broad cross section of European opinion.

On the other hand, there are clear limits to the representativeness of the sample of opinion available. It is notable that the evaluation was not conducted under an open invitation but involved a series of contributions granted by the Commission itself. From the seven main social NGOs that responded to the questionnaire, only one (ATD Fourth World) does not presently receive Commission funding.

The role of participation at the sub-state level is also ambiguous. While most national governments consulted non-state actors in preparing their national responses, few relayed this information comprehensively. While two governments (Malta and the UK) used the questionnaire as an opportunity to canvass domestic opinion, the most common use of input from social NGOs or regional bodies was to substantiate the claims or policy positions of the national government itself.

The questionnaire represents a larger danger – so long as participation is dependent upon the discretion of executive actors, what guarantee exists that the opinions of non-governmental actors will be represented faithfully, or that some participants will not be favoured over others? In the last chapter, this was described as the problem of hierarchy; how can equal participation be granted under conditions of formal or informal inequality? If this problem is present in the evaluation, it is also a key tension within the OMC SPSI itself.

Historically, the origins of the problem can be traced through the early development of the OMC for social inclusion. Caroline de la Porte, in an analysis of the steps leading up to the Nice Council, charts a history of exchanges and alliances between the Commission and social organisations.[94] Social NGO's, like EAPN (the European Anti-Poverty Network) have been partially funded by the Commission since the end of the second pilot 'poverty programme' in 1989. When we talk of the participative potential of the OMC, we are often talking about precisely such organisations.

[93] See the Commission summary, n. 2 above, at 3.

[94] C. de la Porte, 'The Emergence of the OMC in Social Inclusion', Paper Presentation, ESPANET conference, 24 August 2005.

To return to a question posed at the beginning of this section, for what purpose is 'participation' being encouraged? As well as pointing at a regular exchange of officials between the DG Social Affairs and EAPN, de la Porte discusses the active lobbying EAPN undertook in the late 1990s for greater EU competences on social protection issues.[95] Since then, EAPN have been active participants in the OMC, using their branches in a number of member states to monitor national governments, and press them on implementing obligations reported in the national action plans.

The alliance between EAPN and the Commission has in this sense not only been a way of boosting the OMC's legitimacy, but also a means of carrying out functional tasks the Commission could not carry out on its own.[96] In the words of Kerstin Jacobsson:

> Engaging other actors, including civil society actors, has also been a way of putting pressure on governments to live up to the commitments in the common guidelines and objectives.[97]

This problem makes it difficult to gauge real levels of involvement. Given that many of the Social NGOs who respond to the questionnaire rely heavily on the funding available through the Community Action Programme, they all have a vested interest in keeping the process going. It would be unsurprising if such organisations wanted to maintain a cooperative rather than adversarial relationship with national and European officials, who one day could have an important say in whether or not transnational funding for their organisations can continue.

The potential effects of this are that – while the procedural model relies on the use of lower-level actors, and other states – to hold central administrations accountable, NGOs are being asked to do so in circumstances that could potentially endanger the viability of their organisations. Paradoxically, while the very purpose of the Community Action Programme is to create and involve transnational organisations in the OMC – and to level an otherwise prejudicial playing field – it may at the same time make critical scrutiny of its processes more difficult.

95 *Ibid.*, at 4–5.

96 Arguably, the possibility of alliance building or 'partnership' is even a legitimate part of funding decisions under 'Progress'. Under its founding mandate, it is authorised to provide funding only to partly Europeanised organisations, i.e. those that have 'a strong European dimension'. Decision No 1672/2006/EC, n. 5 above, at Art. 9(2).

97 K. Jacobsson, n. 80 above, at 131.

The problem that remains is: what about those actors who are not useful? What about organisations who represent a threat to the policy ambitions of the Commission, or the plans of national governments? Even within an evaluation often based on the responses of 'established' European actors, there remains plenty of evidence that some respondents have advantages over others. While this includes some of the social organisations that have been the focus of this section, the main protagonists in this regard are two specific excluded categories – regional and local authorities, and national parliaments and assemblies.[98] While these two groups can easily be dismissed as the 'usual suspects' of traditional legislative procedure, their conceptual and practical exclusion may come at a serious cost to the democratic aspirations, and to the effectiveness, of OMC procedures.

4.3 *Excluded groups: the local level*

The traditional structure of European law treats the primary addressees of European norms as states. Federal governments have the duty to negotiate international provisions, and are also charged with their implementation. The OMC – while proclaiming itself as an instrument of 'multi-level governance' – often follows this basic structure. Strategic decision-making and reporting is assumed to be the prerogative of the federal government. This structure is designed to create a complementarity between decision and implementation – governments take on obligations because they also have the authority to see them through.

In the case of the OMC SPSI, this 'dualist' framework tends to break down. For social inclusion and protection policies, the competent actors to enact reform have often been local or regional governments. The rise of the OMC has been accompanied by attempts to devolve power over social protection policy to regional levels in a number of countries.[99] While federal governments thus remain the competent 'Europeanised' actors – able to decide on a national 'strategy' for inclusion policy, send representatives to EU-level committee and commit to common targets

[98] I will focus on these two categories. It must be noted, however, that there are a number of NGOs who also voice objections. See e.g. European Disability Forum, 4: 'In some countries, organisations have been excluded from the process of the OMC. There is a lack of interest in communication with civil society and there is a lack of economic support to facilitate involvement of national and local NGOs).' See also (on the potential paternalism of the inclusion process vis-à-vis children and young people) Eurochild at 4.

[99] See, as two important examples, 'devolution' in the UK, and the new Title V of the Italian Constitution.

or indicators – they do not at the same time have the capacity to ensure that a common strategy is acted upon. Federal structures are stuck in what the Kok report described as the 'implementation gap'; the gulf between aspiration, and the political will or authority to produce material change.

This 'gap' presents both a threat and an opportunity. In positive terms, the existing problematisation of relationships between federal and regional government could allow the OMC to emerge as a 'constitutional opportunity' to re-engage relationships between different levels of governance. The best example of this provided in the responses is the development in some states of 'local action plans', where OMC-style reporting is used to coordinate the activities of different regional bodies. In countries like Belgium and Spain, the possibility of a coherent strategic national plan clearly depends on information and resources available at the national level.[100] They have therefore developed local reporting mechanisms as an opportunity both to keep tabs on what regional administrations are doing, and to subtly influence their strategic priorities. Belgium, in their response, thus describes the primary advantage of the Method in these terms:

> La MOC a joué un rôle important pour mobiliser certaines administrations qui ne seraient jamais impliquées spontanément. Dans notre État fédéral composé de neuf gouvernements, la MOC a suscité la mise sur pied d'un réseau compose des représentants de tous les niveaux de pouvoir et instauré une collaboration permanente entre ceux-ci à propos du PAN Inclusion, collaboration élargie aussi à d'autres compétences liées à l'inclusion sociale. La MOC a engendré la *creation d'instruments* qui jettent des ponts d'une part entre les entités fédérées et d'autre part entre le niveau politique, les partenaires sociaux, le monde scientifique et la société civile.[101]

For precisely the same reasons, however, the method can also be represented as a constitutional threat. While depicted as 'constitutionally neutral', in not legally redefining the parameters of local, federal and European competences, the method's practice of preparing a plan for 'national action' at the level of the federal government, and of enumerating a set of common *EU* objectives, is hardly consistent with the move in many states to devolve social inclusion policy. What is now a 'collaboration permanente' was previously a power held and driven by

[100] Belgium at 11–12; Spain at 4. [101] Belgium at 3–4.

governments at the local level, and protected by a parameter of legal obligations.

The OMC has replaced this legally defined relationship, with one in which national governments are effective gatekeepers.[102] It is they who have the capacity to influence those parts of the process operating at the EU level, and they who get to decide whether or not, and which, regional input should find its way into national reports. The evidence from the responses is that this gatekeeper function has had a limiting effect. For the CEMR (Council for European Municipalities and Regions), for example:

> Experience from the first round of the NAPs on social inclusion have revealed that, while central governments have stepped-up their efforts to consult with the regional level, in most cases, this consultation process has not been formalised and rarely allows genuine consultations from regions to the design and delivery of anti-poverty measures.[103]

Regional and local involvement exists, but is ad hoc, or 'consultative', varying wildly from one member state to another.[104]

While, in some states, this deficit is merely 'business as usual', in others it has been perceived as a more serious threat. In Germany, for example, from the formation of the EES in 1997, the Länder governments have been among the OMC's most fervent critics. In a comparative study of the employment and inclusion OMC's, Milena Büchs and David Friedrich report that:

> In general, the local administrative level takes a rather reserved position towards the EES and the OMC, fearing that the EU gains influence in areas where it does not have competencies. They are also opposed to the government taking further decisions which cannot be influenced by local authorities but which have to be carried out by them.[105]

In such circumstances, the 'bottom up' logic of the OMC is inverted. Local actors do not see themselves as 'authors' of the process; or as actors who have to elaborate rules according to their own conditions; but as 'addressees' of norms created and decided upon at a higher

[102] Thus according to Eurocities, the method's principle deficit is 'mainly due to the fact that the OMC has so far largely been confined to coordination between the national and the European levels'. Eurocities at 3.

[103] CEMR, s. 10.

[104] On member states variation in local involvement, see the findings of European Public Social Platform, n. 7 above.

[105] See M. Büchs and D. Friedrich, n. 43 above, at 259.

political level. The 'non-bindingness' of the OMC does not mean a more intense and integrated relationship with regional governments, but often one in which existing constitutional procedures – including the duty to respect a particular sphere of legislative action – are ignored.[106]

In the context of this harsh political assessment, there are a few signs of either a clearer recognition of the problem, or possible suggestions to overcome it. In the former category, the Commission and Council have recently become more activist in urging governments to take local actors more seriously. In one of the few critical parts of their 2007 Joint Report, for example, they observe that:

> While the key role played by regional and local authorities tends to be emphasised, only a few Member States report on new or additional arrangements to better articulate the priorities set at national level with the responsibilities of regional or local authorities.[107]

The main respondents representing local authorities – Eurocities and CEMR – also make some suggestions for the devolution of decision-making power. Eurocities suggest an expansion of the local action plan idea with 'partnership frameworks between national, regional and local authorities to ensure consultation and dialogue in the national action planning process, and coordination and integration between national and local action planning'.[108]

Such a move – they argue – could put regional governments back at the heart of decisions over strategic reform only if they simultaneously carry a voice in European decision-making. They thus argue that not only should local actors be able to send representatives to the main peer review institutions (the European Roundtable and the Social Protection Committee), but they should be aided by explicit procedural requirements for national governments to set out a timetable for consultation with all stakeholders, reported and monitored through the NAP.[109] Here, the suggestion moves beyond the 'reflexive' idea of applying the procedures of the OMC to the local level, and towards a more rigid procedural commitment to guaranteeing broad participation.

[106] 'The rights of Member States and the Regions for legislation in the field of social inclusion and anti-poverty policies should be left untouched. The OMC may be in conflict with the principle of subsidiarity, which should have first priority.' German association of counties in European Public, in European Public Social Platform, n. 7 above, at 11.

[107] 2007 Joint Report, n. 4 above, at 59. [108] Eurocities at 9. [109] CEMR, ss. 5–6.

In both cases, the reassertion of local involvement is seen as essential both to the legitimacy of a process overtly driven by executives, and the effectiveness of reform strategies that still do not reach down into the very sites at which social inclusion policy is applied. Addressing these gaps may require the method to move beyond the image of 'the gatekeeper' which – to date – it has consistently evoked.

4.4 *Excluded groups: parliament*

If executives are the gatekeepers of the present OMC – and indeed of many legislative processes – we might expect parliaments to be the guardians. In most constitutional democracies, parliaments play a role both in proving popular input into the legislative process, and in holding governments to account. Parliaments 'stand in' for an electorate unable to devote the time and energy to pass or vet general legislation. As we saw, under the experimental model this accountability role for parliament was re-evaluated. While the 'rule of law' model of accountability finds its legitimacy through connecting executive action to a 'popular will', in a diverse polity like the EU, accountability has to be found 'without sovereignty'.[110] It may have to be found in circumstances where the expertise of national representatives is limited, yet where a European 'public sphere' is yet to be found.

In such conditions, experimentalist theories, like those forwarded by Charles Sabel and Bill Simon, argue that our best hope may be to seek accountability in a different direction. If law cannot look backwards for its validity – to the decision of an original law-giver – it has to look sideways; it must gain its legitimacy from the scrutiny of peers; those with the direct knowledge and expertise to properly hold executive action to account.[111] In the words of John McCormick, the absence of an ability to appeal outwards to a *Sozialstaat* may lead us instead to the *Sektoralstaat*; to the critical scrutiny and deliberations of 'micro' policy communities.[112] The practical effect of such an approach is that – while 'peer review', and the opinions of specialists (like the 'network of independent experts' funded under the Community Action Programme), has become a central part of the OMC's policy discourse – the exclusion of parliaments has not only become commonplace, but

110 C. Sabel and W. Simon, 'Epilogue: Accountability Without Sovereignty' in G. de Burca and J. Scott (eds.), *Law and New Governance in the EU and US* (Oxford: Hart, 2006).

111 *Ibid.*, at 400.

112 J. McCormick, *Habermas, Weber and the Transformation of the European State* (Cambridge University Press, 2007).

even something backed up by serious academic justifications. Parliamentary procedures are seen as too arcane, too protracted, and too uninformed to meet the challenges that a pan-European social inclusion policy has to offer.[113]

This is not only, however, an academic justification, but one that has found favour among national governments. The responses indicate that parliaments – previously the sole actor with the ability to give policy proposals the 'force of law' – have been relegated to the role of 'another participant'; rarely given the chance to provide input into national action plans. Under the procedural approach, it becomes either a further enumerator of revisable 'framework norms', or itself a peer review institution, 'feeding in', or providing information, for national strategy reports. To this extent, the challenge the OMC offers to traditional law-making is truly radical.

If so, it is too radical for many of the respondents. The lack of involvement for parliaments is seen as perhaps the single most significant challenge to the OMC's legitimacy. It is mentioned as a serious deficit by no fewer than twelve respondents.[114] Where there is parliamentary involvement (as there is in Cyprus, the Czech Republic, Finland, Germany, Hungary, Latvia, Luxembourg, the Netherlands and Sweden), it is frequently described as 'consultative' or 'not very significant'.[115] The NAP is something that is 'submitted' to the national assembly, not something that requires its approval.

Here, parliaments suffer from the 'gap' that the description of the OMC as 'non-legal' has produced. In countries like Denmark – where governments are constitutionally obliged to seek a parliamentary mandate in order to negotiate European legislation – the NAP is seen as a 'government document', and therefore one which does not require the formal assent of parliament (but only its opinion).[116] A safeguard designed to protect both parliamentary sovereignty, and the erosion of national competences, has been partially eroded as a result of the self-description of the method as an extra-legal process. Recent innovations introduced by the Lisbon Treaty – such as the 'yellow' and 'orange' card procedures in which parliaments can check the consistency of

[113] See J. Zeitlin, n. 74 above, at 488.

[114] Eurocities at 11; European Disability Forum at 8; AGE at 11; ATD Fourth World at 2; SOLIDAR at 5; EAPN at 6; FEANTSA at 4; UK (NGO respondents) at 17; Hungary at 7; Slovak Republic at 3–4; Austria at 5; Greece at 8.

[115] Hungary at 7. [116] K. Jacobsson, n. 80 above, at 112–113.

legislation with the principle of subsidiarity – seem unlikely, given that they only apply to legal acts, to plug this gap.[117]

What are the effects of this erosion? The most significant may be that it reinforces the method's normative critics. In particular, it has added to a perception that the OMC continues to be largely an extension of cooperation between executives (national and European).[118] In a contribution on the attitude of the Dutch government to the OMC process in the context of the Netherlands, Jelle Visser summarises this position:

> A somewhat high handed 'we know best' attitude influences not only the approach to Europe, but is also found in relation to the Social Partners and NGOs. They are invited to participate, of course, but only to help deliver a package of policies the direction of which is pre-defined in detailed coalition agreements. This re-assertion of the 'primacy of political direction' and the 'authority of the state' over the messy entanglements of corporatism in industrial relations, no less than in the governance of labour markets, social security, pensions, health and social assistance, has become stronger after 2002. Rather than restoring the primacy of politics through electoral competition, parliamentary control, political debate or public involvement, it strengthened the authoritarian and elitist element in Dutch politics, in which the state likes not to learn from but teach Europe and its citizens.[119]

This attests to a common attitude among governments – that the NAP is still 'theirs'; an opportunity to set out and defend government policies, rather than a document that is provisional, or potentially open to revision in light of practice.[120] It is in this context that the objections to parliamentary exclusion can be understood.

The rejection of parliaments can thus be seen more cynically as an attempt to shield public policy in Europe from institutions that could hold decision-makers in check. The European Parliament – in a recent resolution – suggests this through the claim that soft law has been used largely 'to avoid the involvement of the democratically elected

[117] See Protocol 1 of the Treaty on the application of the principles of proportionality and subsidiarity.

[118] Austria at 5.

[119] J. Visser, 'The OMC as Selective Amplifier for National Strategies of Reform. What the Netherlands Wants to Learn from Europe', in Zeitlin and Pochet, n. 16 above, at 209.

[120] 'It becomes clear that the government regards the NAP as presenting its own policy strategy and not as a document in which the pros and cons of policy approaches are discussed and different viewpoints of actors integrated.' Büchs and Friedrich, n. 43 above, at 258–259.

Parliament and legal review by the Court of Justice'.[121] The exclusion of parliaments on the grounds that the OMC is 'non-binding' is seen here as a rationalisation for an illegitimate grab for power.

While the respondents to the questionnaire are less dramatic in their conclusions, they still argue that the exclusion of parliaments represents a missed opportunity. The entry of the European Parliament into the circle of Council and Commission decision-making that currently produce the 'Joint Reports', and the use of national parliaments to vet NAPs, is forwarded as a way both of engaging a wider public, and as a means of subjecting executive action to critical scrutiny.[122] Here, rather than return to a 'parliamentary' model for legitimating the OMC, the suggestion is simply to use the critical resources for scrutiny parliaments have to offer. Parliaments are not to be seen as 'decisive actors', capable of making final statements on policy, but as further players, who are in a unique position to hold national and European executives to account. They can sit in the OMC as critical rather than hierarchical actors.

This may present several advantages. In the first place, it could fight the perception that the OMC is purely an intergovernmental process. It could bring the method into the kind of public arena that the national parliament in particular is said to represent.[123] It could therefore be seen as a way of providing general input into an OMC that is, in practice, too often the concern of a limited number of 'Europeanised' or sectoral policy actors.[124]

Secondly, it could serve to politicise a procedure whose politics (as the final section of this chapter will explore) is often hidden. It may allow the procedures of the OMC to be open not only to input considered 'helpful' by national and European administrations, but even to suggestions antithetical to its basic assumptions and objectives. If the model of

[121] European Parliament Resolution 'On the Institutional and Legal Implications of the use of "soft law" instruments', 2007/2028 (INI).

[122] 'The European Parliament could debate specific policy issues in the relevant Parliamentary Committees and Inter-groups, and review progress of Member States towards the Common Objectives. Efforts to democratise the OMC should also focus on National Parliaments. This can be done with systematic Parliamentary debates on the NAPs/incl. before the annual Spring European Council'. FEANTSA at 5.

[123] Eurocities at 11.

[124] 'Elle demeure trop limitée à un cercle restreint de responsables politiques et administratifs «européanisés», directement en charge de sa mise en œuvre sur le plan national.' Belgium at 12.

dynamic accountability is serious about 'destabilising knowledge', it must also be open to the kinds of contestation (even from heavily Eurosceptic actors) that the parliamentary traditions of countries like Denmark and the UK have to offer.

In practice, the omens for this involvement are not particularly good. While there is little evidence of trends towards greater domestic parliamentary involvement in the OMC, the Commission's 2005 Communication on streamlining offered only a vague commitment to 'explore' methods for engaging the European Parliament; the Commission's 2008 Communication on the OMC also produced few further commitments.[125] This is now an exploration that has gone on for eight years, without any tangible results. One wonders whether there is real political will behind engaging bodies which will only slow up the pace of 'reform'.

At the same time, parliaments offer a general perspective, and a critical capacity, that cannot be satisfied fully either by endless efforts at cross-departmental coordination, or a renewed effort at non-governmental involvement. They may not, as Jonathan Zeitlin argues, be a 'panacea' for the OMC's participative failings, but neither is their involvement likely to further 'narrow' the policy-making process.[126] For a method that suffers from low visibility, and the constant danger of depoliticisation, the possibility of a new relationship with parliaments may be a means of forwarding rather than limiting the method's participative potential (a potential that will be explored further in the following chapter).[127]

4.5 *Deliberative polyarchy and executive governance*

Most of the theoretical models discussed in the third chapter relied on participation or actor deliberation as a means of securing both the legitimacy and the effectiveness of supra-national decision-making. In terms of legitimacy, local and NGO involvement was a way of securing a new basis for democratic participation. In terms of effectiveness, the taking on board of new actors was to be less a barrier than a springboard for opening up law to new knowledge, and with it, to the particularities

[125] Commission Communication on 'Working together, Working better: a new Framework for the Open Coordination of Social Protection and Social Inclusion Policies in the EU', COM (2005) 706 final at 9.

[126] J. Zeitlin, n. 74 above, at 488.

[127] See Chapter 5, section 7.

of its surrounding environment. It is with this hope in mind that the EU's first codified coordination process was labelled an 'open' method of coordination.

While the limited evidence of the responses indicates that participation is not – as Stijn Smismans has suggested – a 'myth', the limits of actor mobilisation in the present OMC are clear.[128] While, on the one hand, it has succeeded in encouraging and funding NGO participation – and even creating structural opportunities for non-governmental involvement – it has failed to challenge the executive actor as the dominant 'gatekeeper' of European law, providing executives, both national and European, with new steering opportunities.[129]

The principle concern here must be over the implication of this move for the democratic accountability of European law. The more the method operates as an 'insiders' club', the less the range of opportunities available to subject it to critical scrutiny. This can either be a general scrutiny – outwards to a currently 'passive' European public – or a 'dynamic' one – to policy communities like the ones currently being created through the five-year Community Action Programme. Unfortunately, this community may not be an independent body of expertise but one whose very future is tied up with the success of the process, and even with their capacity to serve the interests of its dominant actors.

While experimental or procedural approaches to law attempt to marry the devolution of decision-making with policy coordination by a central authority, what if this process of polyarchical engagement does not result in the sharing of authority, but the reassertion of control? What if the dominant 'participant' in the OMC is not the embattled NGO, but the executive actor – 'gatekeeper' of the process, and guardian of its future direction? The spectre of executive governance may be the underside of the OMC's progressive and participatory narrative.

[128] S. Smismans, New Modes of Governance and the Participatory Myth (2008) 31 *West European Politics* 5.

[129] This would seem to be at the heart of the objection of Christian Joerges to the OMC's development: the method means 'executivism'; an elevation of functional concerns over law-mediated rule. See, on this, both my analysis of William Scheuerman in Chapter 3, section 3.3 ('the problem of stability'), and (from Joerges himself) C. Joerges, 'What is Left of the European Economic Constitution?' (2004) *EUI Working Papers (Law)* 13, 29–34.

5. Law as reflexive – the need to encourage reflexivity in law-making. Law must play a role in encouraging the integration and internalisation of competing territorial and functional discourses

5.1 *Varieties of integration: encouraging functional and territorial reflexivity*

The 'inside' theories explored in the third chapter do not rely on a shared ethical community as a precondition for establishing legal obligations. Nor do they presuppose that supra-national law-making is oriented towards a common 'telos' for action. Law refuses to be 'integrative' in the common meaning of that word – it does not, for example, seek to bind individuals into what Jurgen Habermas has described as the 'demos' – the myth of a national 'community of fate'.[130]

At the same time, post-national law-making not only retains but requires an integrative dimension. Unable to rely on a 'given' ethical or functional consensus, the capacity of law to bring different individuals, states or institutions into a common normative framework may be ever more vital. In a recent essay on legal theory and European integration, Neil Walker has described this as such:

> What makes law central, namely the weakness of its cultural supports and political steering mechanisms, also makes law precarious. What makes law a window of change and a key to innovation, namely the unfinished and shifting nature of the European journey, also exposes law to overreach and disappointment.[131]

This could just as easily be inverted – what makes common law-making so difficult to achieve also makes it more essential. The more the conditions for law are absent, the more it may be needed, precisely in order to bring together what would otherwise be disparate, self-regarding or atomistic.[132]

[130] J. Habermas, 'Why Europe Needs a Constitution' (2001) *New Left Review* 11 at 15

[131] N. Walker, 'Legal Theory and the European Union: A 25th Anniversary Essay' (2005) 25 *Oxford Journal of Legal Studies* 4 at 592.

[132] In Habermas' words: 'The question is whether modern law is just a means for the exercise of administrative or political power or whether law still functions as a medium of social integration. In this regard, I side with Emile Durkheim and Talcott Parsons against Max Weber; today legal norms are what is left from a crumbled cement of society. If all other mechanisms of social integration are exhausted, law yet provides some means for keeping together complex and centrifugal societies that would otherwise fall into pieces.' J. Habermas, 'A Discursive Foundation for Law and Legal Practice' (workshop paper (unpublished) – EUI, June 1998).

The integrative function of a procedural approach to law builds on this insight through 'bringing together' not in order to reduce, but to establish and deliberate differences. The law is a mechanism that, in so much as it cannot 'reflect' common preferences, must bring divergent positions into a common discourse. This discourse both 'carries' competing normative messages, and (in de Búrca and Scott's words) 'seeks to explore different ways for securing their fruitful interaction'.[133]

In the first chapter, this idea was advanced through the concept of 'reflexivity'.[134] If we cannot choose between competing priorities or objectives, we must provide ways of integrating and managing them; we must encourage self-regarding discourses to be opened up to, and reflect upon, the priorities of others.[135] Law integrates in so much as it subjects public action to the scrutiny of those situated from a different point of view. It is to this integrative element of law – and not the ability to create a common 'end point' – that the reflexive function of law speaks.

'Difference' under the OMC manifests itself in a number of ways. The most obvious in the European context is differentiation into nation states. The OMC SPSI must address difference in national social protection systems, each of which is 'embedded' within a particular historical and cultural context. These systems are to be 'integrated' not through the imposition of a common social model, but through the creation of institutions (for example, country peer reviews) through which different approaches to inclusion policy can be deliberated. The integrative capacity of the method is here targeted at encouraging autonomous *national* systems to be 'other regarding'.

There is, however, also a second set of differences to which the OMC is addressed. The set of policies and institutions that make up the present EU are not only territorially, but also functionally divided.[136] The

[133] de Búrca and Scott, n. 110 above, at 6. [134] See Chapter 1, sections 5.1–5.3.

[135] In the context of relationships between states, Christian Joerges' conception of 'deliberative supra-nationalism' may be a close relative of this position. In a world that is simultaneously diverse and interdependent, law must be oriented towards developing 'second order' rules – or, under the language of private international law, 'conflict of laws' principles – which all actors can legitimately agree upon. See C. Joerges, 'Deliberative Supra-nationalism: Two Defences' (2002) 8 *European Law Journal* 1.

[136] See S. Smismans, 'Reflexive Law in Support of Directly-Deliberative Polyarchy; Reflexive Deliberative Polyarchy as a Normative Frame for the OMC' in S. Deakin and O. de Schutter (eds.), *Social Rights and Market Forces: Is the Open Coordination of Employment and Social Policies the Future of Social Europe?* (Brussels: Bruylant, 2005).

European legal space comprises a series of functional discourses and policy fields, each of which carries its own set of priorities. In the area of social protection, this includes the reduction of poverty; in employment, it means decreasing the rate of joblessness across the EU; in fiscal policy, it concerns budget deficits, and so on.

In the field of international law, Martti Koskenniemi has described this phenomenon as 'fragmentation'; the presence of international law not under a single unifying frame, but a series of 'boxes', with their own internal vocabulary.[137] How can this differentiation be dealt with – how can the OMC play a role both in securing the autonomy of different policy fields, and in encouraging them to recognise and manage functional interdependencies between each other?

The emergence of the OMC through a multi-pillared Lisbon strategy suggests an attempt to carry out this task. While the 'streamlined' OMC SPSI is to retain its functional autonomy, it is designed in such a way as to 'feed in' to policies in employment, education and fiscal design, just as reforms in those areas are to 'feed out' towards the inclusion process.[138] To what extent have these changes – potentially oriented towards a 'functional reflexivity' of law – been successful?

5.2 *The integration of states – the use and limits of peer review*

The capacity for critical reflection – and its realisation through structures of peer review – is a vital ingredient in the model of 'dynamic accountability' developed by Sabel and Simon. In their model, peer review structures act as functional substitutes for a now moribund parliamentary authority. They provide an opportunity for officials – those who have the requisite knowledge and resources – to subject the plans of other states to critical scrutiny.

To this extent, peer review carries an 'integrative' capacity in two senses. Internally, it is designed to encourage member states to consider the expectations and demands of others, externally, it forces them to justify policy failures, or their inability to meet the common European objectives. In Kerstin Jacobsson's words (analysing the Nordic case):

> Externally, the OMC does exert a certain pressure on the Member States. As a minimum, governments have to actively defend their positions if they are not willing to conform to the common norms and they have to

[137] See M. Koskenniemi and P. Leino, 'Fragmentation of International Law? Post-modern Anxieties' (2002) *Leiden Journal of International Law* 15.

[138] Commission Communication (on 'streamlining'), n. 124 above, at 4.

> 'think twice' before introducing measures that go against [these] norms.[139]

Against this view, the responses commonly reconceptualise the role of peer review in the OMC. Most states, rather than view peer review seminars as opportunities to critically evaluate the plans of other countries, see their 'central goal' as mutual learning, and the exchange of information.[140] The country peer reviews are viewed as opportunities to learn from, or adapt, foreign practices, while one of the primary benefits of the SPC is conceptualised as the informal administrative networks between officials that it has created.[141]

The objectives of the peer review process, set out in the 'operational guide to peer review and assessment', reflect this:

> The aim of the Peer Reviews is to implement a *mutual voluntary learning process* through which Member States and the Commission can develop a systematic exchange of experiences and evaluation of systems, policies, programmes or institutional arrangements that can be considered as good practice.[142]

The very founding objectives of the peer review process are not to build-in a capacity for accountability and critical evaluation, but instead to allow for transnational learning. The label of peer review is in many ways a misnomer – peer reviews do not 'review'; they largely 'disseminate' or 'report'. They aim towards the generalisation of existing approaches – particularly those that are deemed successful, or exportable to other countries – rather than towards a more accountable form of governance (in which justifications for policy failures are demanded or expected).

On the one hand, this aspect of peer review is mourned. Countries like Italy and the Netherlands see peer review as 'watered down'.[143] According to the Dutch government, peer reviews will be successful 'only when member states dare to be open, honest and critical to one another'.[144]

[139] K. Jacobsson, n. 80 above, at 133.

[140] Slovenia at 5; Netherlands at 6; Latvia at 8.

[141] 'It should not be underestimated that the OMC promotes the creation of national and international networks. These networks identify persons in charge of the relevant authorities and agencies, enabling formal and informal exchanges of experience.' Austria at 6.

[142] Operational Guide, n. 10 above, at 3 (my emphasis).

[143] Italy at 11.

[144] Netherlands at 6.

On the other hand, some respondents argue that the contribution of peer review to creating closer links between administrations, and providing possibilities for policy learning, is itself an important contribution. The second strand of the experimentalists' great hope for peer review is that it can allow the pooling of common knowledge, and a deliberative working through of policy solutions.

In this regard, peer review processes potentially share some of the features that Joerges and Neyer have ascribed, in their famous essay, to the system of 'comitology'.[145] There are two features in particular that are worthy of mention. The first is the ability to bring together different kinds of expertise, and different territories, into a common discussion about regulatory reform. The second is the creation of a 'problem-solving mentality', able to temporarily transcend the strategic interest held by each 'representative' actor.

There is some evidence to suggest that peer reviews carry both of these features. While on the one hand, they have – as the first section argued – infused a common vocabulary among European policy-makers; creating cognitive institutions like the 'network of independent networks' to discuss and evaluate policy ideas; on the other, they are seen in the responses as allowing a more 'concrete' reflection on common problems. For the Netherlands:

> Among the different initiatives of the OMC, the Peer Review Programme received most support and interest from the involved ministries. The advantage of this Programme is that the issues are concrete and that mutual learning is the central goal. It is easier to mobilise government partners, local authorities, NGOs and public opinion on concrete issues, such as homelessness or integration of immigrants.[146]

Against the excessive abstraction of the original Lisbon and Nice objectives – with their vague commitment to 'making a decisive impact on poverty by 2010' – country peer reviews allow for the pragmatic appraisal of reforms. They have created a community of policy actors that approach inclusion policy in Europe not only with the intention of forwarding a 'given' national interest, but to find answers to concrete problems.

At the same time, the potential for Committee structures to carry out this regulatory function depends on certain factors. It depends, for

[145] C. Joerges and J. Neyer, 'From Inter-Governmental Bargaining to Deliberative Political Processes: The Constitutionalization of Comitology' (1997) 3 *European Law Journal* 3.

[146] Netherlands at 1. See also, Spain at 9.

example, on the ability of actors to be open and honest in their deliberations; on the diversity of available opinions, and on a means of disseminating the information (and even common positions) that the actors eventually agree to. Here, the responses indicate that these conditions are often lacking. Firstly, enlargement is commonly mooted as a problem. The need for a Constitutional Treaty in 2003 was often justified by governments on the basis that, in an enlarged club, new institutional rules were needed, in order to avoid a breakdown in decision-making. The responses indicate something similar in this case. Enlargement is seen by some respondents as making the reaching of consensus opinions within committees, and deliberative exchange within peer reviews, more difficult. For the Finnish government, for example, 'with the increased number of Member States, the [peer review] process has become heavier, and this limits the handling and capacity to make use of, information'. For Denmark, enlargement makes the present process 'unsustainable': 'It is more difficult to go into depth when so many countries meet at one time.'[147] It may be something of a paradox that while enlargement has brought forward a need for more differentiated policy-making, accompanied by processes of horizontal review, it also precisely stands in the way of making mutual learning a feasible and useful exercise.

A second problem relates to transparency. One of the conclusions of Jacobsson and Vifell's analysis of committee deliberation under the OMC is that there is something of a trade-off between deliberation and transparency.[148] The capacity to be 'open, honest and critical with one another' in part depends on ensuring that committee proceedings are private. There is some evidence of this aspect too. If we look into the 'Operational Guide' for peer review, strict caps are placed on the number of invited participants precisely in order to allow for 'in depth discussion and exchange'.[149] The 'deepening' of expert-based discussions is predicated upon a 'narrowing' in the range of available participants.

The practical effect of this move is a feeling among the actors of the OMC SPSI that the process is opaque. For Eurocities, there is a need, under peer review, for 'more transparency regarding who is invited, how and why'.[150] A number of NGO respondents claim that peer review

[147] Denmark at 7.

[148] K. Jacobsson and A. Vifell, 'Integration by Deliberation? On the role of Committees in the OMC', Paper Presentation, Workshop on 'The Forging of Deliberative Supra-nationalism in the EU' (Florence) February 2003, at 21–23.

[149] Operational Guide, n. 10 above, at 11. [150] Eurocities at 13.

structures systematically exclude them.[151] At the same time, governments with a more prolonged history of 'open government' see the closed nature of peer review as suspicious; or even as potentially undermining recent efforts by the Union to bring itself closer to its citizens. In this context, the Finnish government argue for a more open SPC where 'the use of written procedures and video conferences should be promoted systematically'.[152]

There is no easy answer for this problem. Some of the solutions suggested in the responses potentially compound the problem. Denmark, for example, suggest responding to enlargement through creating smaller working groups focused on specific themes.[153] While this indeed may allow for more of a 'deliberative focus' to discussions, it would again seem to result in 'narrowing'; the exclusion of more affected actors.

The common lesson may be that integrating national policies and administrations through peer review is a potential double-edged sword. While, on the one hand, it lays open the capacity of open coordination to create a forum for debate and policy exchange, it also potentially undermines the commitment to real accountability, or to an open and transparent legislative process. This may be one of the key dilemmas of an 'integrative' OMC. The commitments of the process to 'coordinate' and, at the same time, to remain 'open' may potentially work against one another. The reconciliation attempted by procedural theories – between a law-making process that is to be simultaneously 'deliberative' and 'open' has not often, in the case of the OMC SPSI, been successfully realised.

5.3 *Functional integration – the 'colonisation' thesis revisited*

The second 'variety of integration' most commonly associated with the OMC is functional. As the last chapter has described, a type of 'functional integration' has been forwarded through the reforms proposed by the Commission under its 'streamlining' Communication in 2005. The Communication argued for the 'feeding in' and 'feeding out' of inclusion, employment and fiscal reforms. In this sense, it recognises the mutual interdependence of policies in social protection and inclusion, and those in other domains such as the fiscal policies able to pay for them. The streamlining reform thus upholds the idea of 'multi-dimensionality' identified as the respondents as part of the 'common vocabulary' the OMC SPSI has introduced.

[151] E.g. European Disability Forum at 7; AGE at 12–13; Eurochild at 5.
[152] Finland at 1. [153] Denmark at 7.

At the same time, streamlining raises the question of whether the 'integration' of the OMC SPSI with other elements of the Lisbon strategy could be considered a 'subordination of the social', or an attempt to strip the OMC of its functional and procedural autonomy. This section is an opportunity to return to a vital question (posed in the first chapter) – is the method a reflexive medium, or instead an instrument for the 'functional colonisation' of social policy by other (economic) discourses?

The need for functional integration is in part a consequence of the EU's very definition of social inclusion. In its 1993 Green Paper on Social Policy, the Commission argued that social exclusion:

> Does not only mean insufficient income. It even goes beyond participation in working life; it is manifest in such fields as housing, education, health-care and access to services. It affects not only individuals who have suffered serious set-backs but social groups, particularly in urban and rural areas, who are subject to discrimination, segregation, or the weakening of the traditional forms of social relations. More generally, by highlighting the flaws in the social fabric, it suggests something more than social inequality, and concomitantly, carries with it the risk of a dual or fragmented society.[154]

The responses broadly support this idea – that social inclusion policy has an 'embedded' quality. To take one example, for AGE, the policy tools necessary to ensure the social inclusion of the elderly depend not just on pension reform, but on the retirement age, and the extent of employment and payroll taxes in any given country.[155] 'Adequacy' in pensions cannot be defined without the specific knowledge of the labour market, and the available resources in the budget, that actors operating under other processes, e.g. the 'Integrated Guidelines' for jobs and growth, can provide.[156] A more integrated functional relationship is necessary for the objectives of either process to be fully acted upon.

[154] Commission Green Paper on European Social Policy: Options for the Union, COM (1993) 551, November 1993, 20–21.

[155] AGE at 16.

[156] As a further example from pensions, the policy cycle of pensions, employment and social assistance is discussed as an important part of the 2007 Joint Report. A mixture of early retirement and poor employment rates for those between 55 and 70 has often led to pressure on incomes for the elderly, or on public pension schemes. This in turn has created problems with pensioner poverty that have to be met by governments through increasing the available funding for minimum income programmes. There is in this way a recognised and reciprocal relationship between fiscal, employment and social protection policies. Joint Report 2007, n. 4 above, at 3.

This supports what was characterised in the first chapter as the reflexive view. The reflexive integration of the various strands of the OMC takes the autonomy of each process as a precondition for ensuring that distinct policy priorities can be pursued. At the same time, it also assumes that the need to incorporate, internalise, or otherwise take regard of the objectives of other processes is implicit if each particular process is to achieve *its own* objectives. This is recognised in the responses as part of the OMC's social potential. Just as it has broadened our definition of social inclusion so it has – at the national and European levels – encouraged 'social' and 'economic' actors to talk to one another. Indeed, its first contribution – recognised and consistently repeated in the responses – is that it has made such a discourse possible by giving social actors a political voice.

The very presence of the OMC is thus seen as a means of balancing the highly economic or 'productivist' focus of EU discussions on social protection reform to date. Austria gives an example in the case of pensions:

> At the European level, it is of great importance that it was possible to include the social component in the European discussions on pension reforms. Prior to the introduction of the OMC, the discussion at the European level was restricted to the Ministers of Finance debating the long-term financial viability of pensions systems. The actual purpose of the pension system i.e. safeguarding an appropriate and secure income for retired people, thus fostering social cohesion and clearly reducing poverty and social exclusion in old age, was somewhat relegated to the background.[157]

The method has put social issues on the table – at national and European levels – and given social as well as economic actors a legitimate reason to be involved in the policy debate.

The most important question may be whether these actors are talking on an equal footing. The streamlining communication attempted to secure this through the idea of 'feeding in' and 'feeding out'. The objectives and guidelines of the OMC SPSI and the 'integrated' European employment and fiscal reform strategies were to be synchronised in a partial sense, with national governments asked to consider the relationship between employment, social protection and fiscal reform in the preparation of their national reports.[158]

[157] Austria at 2. See also, Spain at 20.
[158] Communication (on 'streamlining'), n. 124 above, at 7.

If this was the hope, however, the weight of evidence available in the responses, and in other supporting reports, can only lead to the conclusion that – as it stands – the policy of 'streamlining' has been a failure. There is neither (i) consistent evidence of feeding in and feeding out between the different coordination processes, nor (ii) an equal and balanced synergy between them.

The first evidence to substantiate this conclusion comes from an analysis of the guidelines issued for the 'integrated' employment and fiscal strategies. If there really was feeding in and feeding out, one would expect to see references to social inclusion in the guidelines offered under both processes. In both cases, however, 'feeding in' and 'feeding out' are limited. An important example is the proposed Integrated Guidelines for 2008–10. While the Guidelines include as their third objective 'determined action to strengthen and reinforce social inclusion', and a demand that 'strengthened interaction is needed with the OMC in Social Protection and Social Inclusion', the Guidelines *themselves* carry few references to these objectives.[159]

While the first six guidelines, for example, all seek to embed employment reform in fiscal stability, either to ensure that employment policies (under guideline 6) 'contribute to a dynamic and well functioning EMU', or that they (under guideline 5) 'promote greater coherence between macro-economic, structural and employment policies', only two, out of a total of twenty-four, guidelines actively use the language of social inclusion. Guideline 17 does so by incorporating the third 'social cohesion' objective of the EES, while guideline 19 asks member states to 'ensure inclusive labour markets, enhance work attractiveness, and make work pay for job-seekers, including disadvantaged people and the inactive'. While the links to fiscal policy are clear, references to social inclusion appear 'somewhere in the back'.

Given this disparity, it is perhaps unsurprising that national governments have often disregarded social inclusion goals when reporting on employment and fiscal policy. A 2007 analysis of 'National Reform Strategies' by Jonathan Zeitlin suggests a widespread failure at the national level to draw on social inclusion objectives in employment reporting, with only ten member states including social cohesion or inclusion objectives among their domestic priorities. Even fewer

[159] Commission Communication to the Spring European Council on 'Integrated Guidelines for Jobs and Growth (2008–2010)' COM (2007) 803 at 27.

reported extensively on employment measures they had put in place to achieve them.[160]

To confirm this, the 'network of independent experts' 2006 synthesis report on feeding in and feeding out highlighted 'a disturbing lack of commonality between the NRPs and the National Reports on Strategies for Social Protection and Social Inclusion'.[161] The national Lisbon reports, and the Integrated Guidelines were said to pay scant attention to the Social Inclusion and Protection OMC, either subsuming social inclusion reform under their categories (i.e. considering inclusion goals only in the context of 'jobs and growth'), or ignoring the processes altogether.[162]

Here, a further charge emerges. It is not only that there is a lack of 'feeding in and out', but that there is one without the other; a recalibration of welfare policies to meet the needs of EMU and the employment process, but without any influence the other way around. Thus, for EAPN, while, 'it is clear that the economic and employment processes, whether "wrapped" in the NRP [national reform programme] or not, dominate and constrain the social processes (feeding in)'; on the other hand, 'there is little evidence of poverty proofing of strategies or measures in other dimensions of the Lisbon process (feeding out)'.[163] It may not just be that there is a lack of integration, but – where integration does occur – it is one-way traffic; designed not to encourage 'reflexivity', but the functional elevation of one discourse over another.

This is a fairly common feeling among social NGO respondents to the evaluation. A recent report by EAPN, examining 'feeding in' from the implementation reports for the Community Lisbon strategy towards the OMC SPSI concludes:

> Most EAPN national networks point out that the implementation reports remain *overwhelmingly economic* and with little evidence to show how this economic vision of Lisbon can deliver social justice, decent jobs and a

[160] As such, 'experience with the operation of the re-launched Lisbon strategy during the first two years demonstrates that the effectiveness of this mutually re-enforcing feedback between its social, economic and employment dimensions has remained decidedly limited, with wide variation across Member States'. J. Zeitlin, 'Strengthening the Social Dimension of the Lisbon Strategy' (2007) *La Follette Working Papers* 22 at 2.

[161] Network of Independent Experts, Second Term Synthesis Report, n. 6 above, at 4.

[162] The problems associated with feeding in and out are also recognised by the SPC itself – see e.g. the Report of the Working Group on the Mutual Interaction between the Common Social Objectives and the Integrated Guidelines for Jobs and Growth, n. 15 above, at 2–3.

[163] EAPN Report on 2006–2008 National Inclusion Strategies, n. 7 above, at 23.

> better life for people currently experiencing poverty and social exclusion ... From the national responses it is clear that there is little evidence of a clear link with the policy priorities and measures of a streamlined OMC SPSI. For most groups, this was above all evidence of subservience to Lisbon and the imposition of 'growth and jobs' priorities.[164]

In this context – rather than enlarge the scope of the policy areas 'social voices' can contribute to – streamlining has had the opposite effect, 'narrowing the political debate' to a discussion of growth and jobs.[165]

In the context of employment, this charge is again repeated by the network of independent experts. While – in the Integrated Guidelines – inclusion policies are often evaluated according to whether they can achieve higher employment rates, or balanced budgets, there is little evaluation the other way around:

> A cause for concern is the relative lack of attention to whether economic policies, especially those that target competitiveness, are contributing to or decreasing income inequalities and to raising the income of those at risk of poverty and social exclusion.[166]

It is perhaps then of little surprise that so many of the respondents to the evaluation raise a concern about 'less visibility' for the OMC after streamlining; for an OMC that is either 'a low priority' or 'a less important or supplementary process' than the Lisbon reports, or the 'Integrated Guidelines'.[167] The 'colonisation' thesis here returns as a practical and vocal concern that the OMC SPSI is being left behind (or worse, in a servient relationship to other functional fields of action).

In its place, there is a plea for a new kind of relationship – one in which social inclusion is freed from an implicit hierarchy. While some of the suggestions made by the respondents in this regard are relatively obvious, others attempt to take what I have characterised as the 'reflexive' ideal in law seriously.

These remedies pertain to both the European and the national levels. At the EU level, the present level of integration between committees (described in the responses as 'sporadic' or 'non-existent') should be addressed, say some respondents, through a broadening of their respective agendas.[168] The SPC itself has recently suggested:

[164] EAPN Report on 'Implementing the Lisbon Strategy', n. 171 below, at 3.
[165] *Ibid.*, at 5. [166] Network of Independent Experts, n. 6 above, at 5.
[167] European Disability Forum at 5; Czech Republic at 8. [168] Czech Republic at 9.

> Joint SPC-EMCO-EPC meetings aimed at discussing issues concerning the dynamic interplay of the three policy areas and to improve mutual understanding – as well as to cooperate in the preparation of common opinions – ensuring equal footing to all Committees in relation to the evaluation of both the NRPs and the NSRs.[169]

So long as each committee is only subject to the information of its own set of 'socialised' actors, it may succeed in creating a deliberative forum for policy ideas, only to find itself insulated from 'outside' sources of information. The integration of the business of each committee could have the effect – firstly, of incentivising the consideration of other goals, and second of giving 'social' and 'economic' voices an equal say in EU decision-making. While one would expect each committee to display a degree of specialisation, this should not – if we are to take the idea of a 'multi-dimensional' inclusion process seriously – preclude it from considering its agenda in light of other objectives.[170]

At the national level, this argument is mirrored through a second suggestion. EAPN, in their response, mourn the 'one-sided' development of the Lisbon process, principally because it has left certain questions unanswered. It has failed, for example, to provide (or even ask for), 'evidence of the impact of growth (or indeed lack of growth) on the delivery of better jobs or quality of life'.[171] Processes like the Integrated Guidelines have operated on the basis of untested, or self-regarding, assumptions about the relationship between fiscal, employment and social inclusion policy.[172]

To counter this, instruments are needed to test and internalise the impacts of reform measures on the priorities of other fields. The 2008 Joint Report mandates the use of 'social impact assessments' in which coordination processes in employment, social inclusion and fiscal reform include explicit requirements for states to report on 'external effects', e.g. the impact of fiscal restructuring on poverty, or of pension

[169] SPC Working Group on Mutual Interaction, n. 15 above, at 18–19. See also, Estonia at 9.

[170] Estonia at 9; European Disability Forum at 7.

[171] 'Making Lisbon deliver for people experiencing poverty: EAPN response to 2006 Implementation Reports on the National Reform Programs' (EAPN, 2007) at 5.

[172] Even the SPC outlines this challenge: 'the challenge for pro-growth and higher employment policies is that they cannot be assumed to lead automatically to improved social cohesion. They need to be underpinned by provisions for the most vulnerable groups and by modern and social protection systems in order to deliver social progress.' SPC Working Group on Mutual Interaction, n. 15 above, at 2.

reform on the principle objectives of the EES.[173] In a similar vein, EAPN and the Network of Independent Experts talk of 'poverty proofing'; encouraging an inclusion-related 'litmus test' for Lisbon reforms.[174]

In these examples, 'integration' is promoted in a key, but also in a partial, sense. Going back to the start of this section, it is not seen as an attempt to eliminate differences. It is precisely in the context of resistance to the amalgamation of the OMC SPSI with other elements of the Lisbon process that the suggestion for 'poverty proofing' is made. Social inclusion is seen as a distinct field, which should not be subsumed under similar mechanisms in employment, education and fiscal reform. Part of what we do when we 'integrate' is to secure the *autonomy* of each field of action (an autonomy which impact assessment is designed to take seriously).

'Integration' also, however, carries a second meaning. It entails the linking of functional discourses; recognising that social inclusion is not a segmented policy field but one that requires reflection upon the goals of others. In introducing 'poverty proofing' we are attempting both to respect functional autonomy, and encourage the reflexive consideration of an outside often based on organisational principles other than ones own.

Both territorially and functionally, the OMC is engaged in a tenuous search for integration, yet one that constantly faces the danger, either of 'centralising' decision-making power, or elevating discourses that must be approached on equal terms. While the vocabulary of 'feeding in' and 'feeding out' may capture this problem, it has masked a more complex and imperfect reality. 'Social Impact Assessment' – as the following chapter will further explore – may provide a better solution.

6. Law as procedural – the need for an 'institutional' or 'procedural' understanding of law. Law does not stipulate substantive ends, but carries and contains processes of policy deliberation and exchange

6.1 Law as procedure

The idea of law as procedure refers primarily to the first theoretical approach outlined in the third chapter. It comprises elements of all four 'components of a procedural regime' outlined in this chapter so far. In

173 2008 Joint Report, n. 4 above, at 9.
174 EAPN Report, n. 7 above, at 24; Network of Independent Experts, n. 6 above, at 20.

particular, it symbolises and embodies the role of law as a structuring rather than substantive framework. In the absence of a common agreement on the idea of a 'European social model', law must provide the procedural mechanisms through which the attempt to negotiate, and learn from, different policy positions, is conducted.

It can only do so by providing a framework for action which does not second guess its eventual outcomes. Many of the processes that make up what we know as 'the OMC' are in fact formalised in this way. This need not take the form of a treaty basis, as exists for the EES under Article 128 EC, but can also take the form of loose procedural rules. In this context, the OMC – while often characterised in the 'new governance' literature as an 'extra-legal' regime – contains a cacophony of informal rules and procedures, designed not to bring the method within the larger body of European law, but to provide a framework within which policies, objectives and indicators can be elaborated.

As well therefore as the Council decisions, setting up and enumerating the role of the various OMC committees, and the Community Action Programme, problem-solving processes like the country peer reviews work under an 'operational guide'.[175] The guide is effectively a code of conduct; it is designed to create rules which can allow for a practical exchange of ideas, ensuring that the results of peer reviews are properly disseminated. It enumerates and caps the invited participants, describes (in depth) their responsibilities, and produces requirements for reporting and dissemination.

This would seem to stem from a certain Habermassian premise. In order to create an uncoerced and productive discourse, a certain parameter of surrounding legal obligations may be needed, either to 'frame' political discourse in ways that allow others to participate, or to reduce inequalities of power. As an example discussed in the previous section, the guide places a cap of thirty participants on each peer review 'to allow for in depth discussion and exchange', and thus to ensure that the review process can be a properly deliberative exercise (rather than a mere mechanism to disseminate given policy messages).[176] Formalisation is seen as a precondition for effective exchange.

It is still possible to see the OMC in this context. Some member states – when discussing how the rules governing the method as it stands – recognise that, even if the strategic priorities of the method might change, a core level of stability in its secondary features i.e. over the

[175] Operational Guide, n. 10 above. [176] *Ibid.*, at 11.

requirements incumbent upon states in reporting, is needed. Some national governments thus argue for procedural stability 'so that the ways in which the reports have to be prepared can be foreseen'.[177] For the NGO respondents, this should include clear timetabling commitments for the consultation of non-governmental actors.[178] Here, proceduralism means seeing law, and the use of procedural rules, as a route to – rather constraint upon – the mechanisms of policy exchange and ongoing review upon which the OMC SPSI relies. Rules – even if not backed up by the hierarchical force of a European Court – can play a role in guiding actors through the policy-making process, creating expectations about how the main institutions of the method will operate.

Finally, rules potentially play a role in giving the OMC a more secure footing. While most of the respondents see the method as relatively habituated within domestic policy-making, one is also struck by the frequency of significant doubts about its future. The dithering of the Barrosso commission over the OMC's ongoing role within the Lisbon Strategy has only contributed to this feeling.[179] In this context, some respondents suggest 'anchoring' the method through soft law. For EAPN:

> As a general point this present time of uncertainty has shown how vulnerable the social aspects are within the EU. There is a need to institutionalise the OMC on Inclusion and to give more certainty to its continuance. As there appears not to be a treaty base for such an approach maybe it can be achieved by a joint Council and Parliament decision. Such a decision would signify a real commitment to achieving social progress at EU level and provide the stability needed to ensure confidence in the OMC processes on Social Protection and Social Inclusion.[180]

Even for a process nearly a decade old, the commitment of the Union to reflecting and advancing a 'social dimension' to its activities is seen as tenuous. A move to a formal anchoring of the method, and an outline of its dominant procedures – even without the formal backing of the Treaty – could be a means of securing a more lasting institutional

[177] Hungary at 7. See also Austria at 6–7. [178] Solidar at 4; AGE at 11; EAPN at 12.

[179] This dithering included suggestions by some within the Commission to abolish the OMC SPSI in its entirety. More formally, it is represented through the almost complete absence of social inclusion from the strategy outlined in the Commission's first response to the Kok report – 'Working Together for Jobs and Growth: A New Start for the Lisbon Strategy' COM (2005) 24 final.

[180] EAPN at 7. See (for similar recommendations) Austria at 7; Belgium at 19.

commitment (a 'constitutionalisation' route explored in the next chapter).[181]

6.2 *The implementation gap*

The 'procedural' account given above mirrors much of the academic work on the OMC to date. This work has often focused on the 'mechanics' of the method. It has analysed – as indeed much of this chapter has – the procedural mechanisms under which social inclusion policy has evolved in the European level. The EU institutions have copied this approach. Responding to suggestions of a severe 'implementation gap' in the Lisbon process to date, the Commission's first instinct upon the publication of the Kok report was to issue their streamlining communication, suggesting the procedural 'synchronisation' of the inclusion process with other fields. As of writing, we await how the Commission will respond to possible amendments to the OMC SPSI in light of its Lisbon 2020 reforms.

There is, however, another, more substantive element to the OMC SPSI. It is also about achieving change. It is about outcomes. While it is little surprise that lawyerly respondents should focus on the 'rules of the game', there is an actual 'game' to be played too. In this context, the presence of the OMC 'as a mere procedure' faces some hostility in the responses. The emphasis upon 'procedure' may either mask or ignore two important elements. Firstly, it may divert attention from the need for substantive change; secondly, it may conceal implicit forms of politicisation.

In terms of the first point, some social NGOs argue for a more prescriptive strategy.

For the ETUC (the principal EU-level trade union), for example:

> Bolstering the OMC process does not mean embarking on a procedural approach ... ETUC supports an OMC that cannot be reduced to a mere framework for close cooperation on social protection based on exchanging experience, learning from each other and benchmarking performance in an attempt to identify best practices, even though there are always lessons to be learned from exchanges between Member States. After all, in ETUC's view, such an approach would be too weak and ineffective bearing in mind the challenges to be faced, both as regards the fight against social exclusion and in terms of the future and quality of pension and long-term healthcare systems.[182]

[181] See Chapter 5, sections 2–4. [182] ETUC at 3.1–3.3.

Here we see a version of the familiar argument of Fritz Scharpf and Adrianne Heretier that the 'soft' norms of the OMC are inadequately robust to deal with the seriousness of the social challenges the EU must face.[183] For respondents like ETUC, coordination is useful only as a route to hard law, or only so long as, 'it results in *upward convergence*, and consequently in an improvement of social policies'.[184]

Among the national respondents, Belgium also mentions the difference between an employment and fiscal coordination process that carries a clear treaty basis and the OMC SPSI, which gains its legitimacy only from the continued commitment of the member states to its enactment. In their words, 'cette différence d'assise juridique joue en défaveur du social'.[185] While others reject the idea that the procedural nature of the OMC means it should be abandoned in favour of hard law, they contend that there is a danger it retreats into a mere reporting exercise, or an inter-institutional discourse. The respondents therefore warn that national strategy reports often represent 'reporting requirements' where past achievements are listed; not strategic documents where future priorities and legislative commitments are identified. CEMR summarise this concern: national reports 'often have the character of a report rather than of an action plan containing a strategic approach involving all departments and all levels of governance'.[186]

Parts of the charge are admitted by some governmental respondents. For Estonia, 'the national action plans seem to be documents that are reports in nature rather than national strategic policy papers'.[187] In other cases, the problem arises from national reports perceived to be 'owned' by a particular government department, and used simply to present its strategy, rather than integrate or develop other suggestions.[188] Thus, for EAPN, as long as policy energy under the national strategy report is devoted primarily to looking backwards – at policies already decided upon – rather than forwards, to what might come in the future – there is likely to be little incentive for governments to use the

[183] For a further discussion of these objections, see Chapter 2, section 3.2.
[184] ETUC at 3.5 (my emphasis).
[185] Belgium at 17. See also, the Czech response: 'It is high time to limit the searching for new initiatives, paths, tools etc. and start, on the national, regional and local levels, to thoroughly realise the already existing tasks.' Czech Republic at 10.
[186] CEMR, s. 1. [187] Estonia at 9–10.
[188] Again, this is a conclusion of Büchs and Friedrich in the German context, n. 43 above, at 258–259. See also, Hungary at 7–8.

procedural input of other actors (to monitor and review existing policies, or update them in light of changing conditions):

> In most Member States, monitoring and implementation are rudimentary because the NAPs/incl. *do not drive policy but report it.*[189]

Here, procedural requirements appear as a 'checklist'; they represent boxes to be ticked, rather than opportunities for policy-making (or for the creation of a new community for its enumeration). The danger is that procedure is fetishised; that we make the assumption that – if the correct frameworks are in place – everything else will work out too.

If there was a clear political message from the Kok report it was that this outcome should not be taken for granted. Not just a procedural framework, but a clear political commitment on behalf of all actors to take that frame seriously, is required to translate the lofty ideals of the OMC SPSI into real change.[190] In the words of FEANTSA, it may be 'time to start the second phase – implementation'.[191] Both the existence of an adequate framework, and the capacity and will on the part of political actors, may be a necessary foundation for the success of the method in meeting its poverty and social inclusion goals.

6.3 *The politicisation of procedure*

The idea of law as procedure suggests that – if significant diversity exists at a substantive level – it can be accommodated through procedural rules that all parties can agree upon. It seems to be clear that all of the states who submit national reports under the OMC SPSI accept, and have habituated, the procedural guidance given by the Commission over the basic structure and strategic priorities to be addressed through their reports. There is a common template that 'guides' reform, even if the specific means by which measures are to be enacted is left open.

If we look, however, into the parts of the evaluation that question the indicators and objectives of the OMC, it is clear that these elements are not seen as depoliticised or merely procedural or abstract in nature. This applies particularly in terms of indicators. In so much as indicators allow cross-sectional evaluations of particular national practices, the 'success' of measures, or the relative 'importance' of action in one area or another is seen as following from the kinds of indicators used.

189 EAPN Report on 'National Strategies for Social Inclusion 2006', n. 7 above, at 26 (my emphasis).

190 Kok report, n. 179 above, at 39.

191 FEANTSA at 3.

In a *material* sense, this means that different actors tend to read indicators in different ways, fighting over the inclusion of the group that they most closely represent. As an example, whereas ETUC argue for indicators and objectives that are largely independent of competitiveness and growth targets ('ETUC believes that whereas growth and competitiveness are key factors for development, they are not ends in themselves'),[192] for UNICE (the employers federation), both the overall objectives of the OMC, and the criteria for evaluating their fulfilment, should be economically oriented ('policy orientations defined at EU level should fully respect the fact that economic sustainability should be the aim of reforms').[193]

Some evidence of a similar battle exists between governments. Denmark and Finland (countries with significant success in integrating women into the labour market) both argue that 'a more systematic treatment of gender and gender equality perspectives' is missing in the indicators.[194] They further argue that the monetary and quantative focus of the present indicators ignores or undervalues certain non-monetary aspects of the Scandinavian welfare state, e.g. heating benefits, free public transport, free personal care for the elderly and so on.[195]

Similarly, in Italy, the reliance of Italian families (who often pool income among an extended group) on undeclared income means that there is a significant difference between the 'at risk of poverty rate' used at the EU level and the one preferred by the Italian government (which is based on consumption). The differences are significant – whereas the Italian government register a poverty rate of 12–13 per cent, the EU statistic is closer to 20 per cent.[196] This disparity is a source of anxiety that, in the debate over relative performance – over which countries have practices to 'learn from' and which not – Italy might be systematically undervalued.

[192] Instead they ought to be seen as 'means for developing more, higher quality jobs'. ETUC at 2.1.

[193] UNICE at 3. [194] Denmark at 5.

[195] As an example to the contrary, the Czech Republic – a centre-right government at the time of its response – sees the present indicators in the opposite light; as carrying an excessively qualitative focus that could obscure their real purpose: 'From the viewpoint of further work, it appears useful to concentrate on indicators from the thematic area "making work pay" – on the attractiveness of work and material deprivation. We consider the testimonial value of indicators resting on subjective evaluations in general to be questionable.' Czech Republic at 3–4.

[196] Italy at 7. See also, Marlier *et al.*, n. 16 above, at 50.

In both of the above examples, the choice over 'which indicator' is seen not only as a technical matter but as a source of *political* disagreement. The choice of indicator is not merely something that can be decided through the integration of expert or technical advice, but involves either elements of political sensitivity, or the potential elevation of some social models over others.[197] It is perhaps for this reason that the SPC's first indicators report in 2001 argued that: 'it is important that the portfolio of EU indicators should command general support as a balanced representation of Europe's social concerns'.[198]

The 'primary' indicator mentioned above – of 'at risk of poverty' rates – can be used to illustrate the point further. At the moment, it considers an individual as 'at risk of poverty' when holding an income below 60 per cent of the median income.[199] It thus measures relative poverty – the extent to which individuals and households are 'falling behind' the general standard of living enjoyed by the population as a whole.

While this indicator is a long-standing part of the OMC SPSI, its relativity also makes it highly contestable. As a relative measure of poverty, it is arguably more punitive towards those states with fast-growing economies than those whose economies are growing slowly; it potentially penalises states like Ireland, who have seen rapid economic growth, yet must quickly compensate those at lower levels in order to avoid a sharp increase in observable rates of poverty (even if, measured in other absolute terms, the income of these groups may have, in fact, risen).[200]

[197] This would seem to mirror Joerges and Neyer's observation that, as much as comitology may represent an 'expert' decision-making structure, this does not insulate it from questions of a normative or ethical nature. Instead, 'judgements on the social acceptability of risks require a balancing of benefits and costs which cannot be meaningfully performed without the help of experts but which, at the same time, must also pay due regard to normative, political, and, occasionally, ethical considerations.' Joerges and Neyer, n. 145 above, at 278.

[198] SPC 'Report on Indicators in the Field of Poverty and Social Inclusion' (Social Protection Committee Indicators Sub-Group, 2001) at 2.

[199] SPC Report on 'Portfolio of Over-arching Indicators in the Streamlined Social Inclusion, Pensions and Health Portfolios' (Social Protection Committee Indicators Sub-Group, 2006) at 17.

[200] A second example – referred to in the ISG's 2003 report as a source of political contestation – is measurement over 'in work poverty', i.e. the extent to which a more 'streamlined' OMC should seek to measure the impact of employment on at risk of poverty rates. 'Mid-year Report from the Indicators Sub-group to the SPC' (Social Protection Committee Indicators Sub-Group, 2003) at 6–7.

The purpose here is not to contest the indicator, but merely illustrate how – in the very measurement of social exclusion – we are also making choices about what 'poverty' or 'exclusion' means; choices that have a direct bearing on how the future framing of social inclusion objectives is carried out. Although the measurement of indicators can be seen as a way of creating frameworks for action and evaluation, it also involves substantive political decisions.

This is evident not only at the material level (in terms of *which aspects of poverty* indicators should measure) but also in terms of *to whom indicators should apply*. The responses also elicit disagreements over both the *territorial* and the *personal* scope of indicators. While territorially, the respondents argue over whether they should be framed at state or sub-state levels (or even point up the way towards the performance of the EU as a whole), personally, they differ over how indicators should be disaggregated, e.g. according to gender, class, race, or family unit.

Unsurprisingly in this context, we again see a high degree of sectionalism – NGO respondents argue for the promotion of indicators that would better reflect the needs of the social 'voice' they represent.[201] As two examples, AGE, argue for an additional measure for poverty among those over 80; while CEMR request 'the adoption of new EU-wide local and regional indicators enabling de-centralised governments to compare and improve their performance'.[202] The scope of indicators is contested in so much as it has the capacity either to highlight or to shield information relevant to particular at risk groups.

Each decision in this regard has clear consequences. As CEMR point out, the decision to consider indicators primarily in national terms has had the effect of masking serious regional disparities (where a lack of progress in one area is concealed by better performance elsewhere).[203] At another level, the original 'road not taken' of an overall EU-level target for poverty reduction – a target which now appears in the renewed 'Lisbon 2020' strategy – could have contributed to a neglect for the 'European dimension' of social inclusion (including for the issues of cross-border migration that represent one of the OMC SPSI's founding justifications).[204] Decisions that may otherwise appear as technical or procedural in nature – habitually agreed on the basis of

[201] Additional to the examples below, see Eurocities at 4; European Disability Forum at 4; FEANTSA at 3.

[202] CEMR, s. 7; AGE at 7–8.

[203] CEMR, s. 3; See also, in the national responses, Greece at 4; Hungary at 3.

[204] EAPN at 5.

recommendations from a 'sub-group' of the SPC – may implicate a high degree of substantive choice.

The question – one also implicated by other sections of this chapter – is: who chooses? Who chooses the ambit of indicators, and with it the evaluative basis through which the comparison of 'European social models' is to be conducted? Who chooses which organisations will be represented in national action plans? Who chooses which NGOs will receive the necessary funding to make an impact on the formulation of European guidelines? Who chooses how the heterarchical processes of 'coordination' in the EU will be organised?

The answer – in the case of indicators, as with other elements of the OMC SPSI as it stands – is executives; both the sub-group of 'expert' opinion provided through the SPC, and the Council (which tends to habitually adopt the committee's recommendation). Beneath the 'heterarchy' that proceduralism is supposed to represent there remains a political hierarchy, for whom the very characterisation of the method as a 'non-binding' or extra-legal process serves a purpose of normative insulation.

The politicisation of procedure suggests that beneath the attempt to use the OMC to promote heterarchical negotiation and learning, there remains a politics – either a series of substantive choices over which kind of social inclusion strategy European states should adopt, or an implicit hierarchy – a situation in which executive negotiation is forwarded under the slogan of 'participatory governance'. As the final chapter will argue, it may be beneficial to address this politics not through a further attempt to perfect and deepen the method's 'multi-level' rhetoric, but through a reflexive *constitutional* frame.

7. Assessing the procedural paradigm – proceduralism and the politics of governance

It is evident from the responses that elements of what I have termed 'the procedural approach' are not only an analytical template, but by now a part of the very policy vocabulary of the OMC's dominant actors. The repetition of reporting cycles, and of other elements, such as the reports of the Commission, and the network of 'independent experts', have led to a common assumption that the method should operate as a flexible, integrative and participative structure. It is recognised, in this sense, as qualitatively different from other forms of EU decision-making.

The method is not, however, seen as a 'paper tiger'. The very fact that actors argue so much over their involvement, and over the content and scope of indicators, suggests that the process and its outcomes still matter. While the method is a 'voluntary' decision-making process, it is seen by all actors as something that imposes meaningful obligations upon them. The method should not therefore be summarily dismissed. Whether or not it is producing particular policy responses, it has been habituated and relied upon by European governments and NGOs, and altered the relationships between them.

At the same time, it is precisely *because* it is no 'paper tiger' that some of the normative implications of the procedural approach should be taken seriously. What is the 'policy vocabulary' that the OMC is creating? And what kind of institutional and political exclusions belie the method's description of itself as a process of 'soft law'? The language of proceduralism is in evidence, but its practice is precarious. The categories of proceduralisation and multi-level governance can have a masking effect – using an abstract and technical vocabulary that obscures the political choices devising an open coordination process for social policy entails.

This comprises two potential 'hidden' elements. The first of these is inner tensions or contradictions. These tensions were discussed in the last chapter as the problems of 'power', 'hierarchy' and 'stability'. Many of these problems – areas where the very philosophy of decentred governance *begins to work against itself* – are apparent in the present OMC SPSI. To take just one example, while the OMC has sought to fill gaps in political accountability through an appeal to civil society involvement, this involvement has effectively been controlled and mediated by the very executive actors it is meant to hold accountable. The problems of a procedural or 'inside' approach – that relies on actor participation, but is unable to specify how it can be brought about – are here realised within the realm of 'new governance' itself.

The second 'hidden' element is examples of political contestation. The rhetoric of the method as a coordinative procedure is underlain by real political conflict – particularly over the material and personal scope of the indicators through which national social policy is to be compared and evaluated. While the method is presented as a 'constitutional compromise' that neither institutionalises nor abandons 'the European dimension'; that neither elevates, nor dilutes economic commitments; and that neither sacrifices nor entrenches particular models of social policy-making; it carries real political effects.

These political consequences – the 'politics of governance' – suggest both the usefulness and the limits of proceduralisation as a descriptor for OMC-like methods. While on the one hand, the politics of the OMC defies its 'procedural' description, on the other, it suggests the capacity of new governance to carry and reflect different political programmes and preferences. The challenge may be to ensure that this 'politics' is defined not only by executive actors, but by a wider body of public opinion.

Addressing this challenge will be the subject of the next and final chapter. As we will see, the most natural solution for any lawyer faced with the problems of political arbitrariness brought by the present OMC is to place new governance under a constitutional frame. The possibility of creating an overarching constitutional framework for methods like the OMC – including concrete participation requirements, and rights of access for individuals to documents and information – brings the capacity to break the 'insiders loop' of the present OMC SPSI: one where administrators are accountable not to external political opinion, but largely to themselves.

While there are certainly merits to such a legal solution, it also contains significant limits. While one vision of 'constitutionalism' sees the role of constitutional discourse as placing a circle of protection around the private autonomy of the individual, one wonders if this is the role we are really searching for. A set of administrative law remedies alone – given the restrictive rules of standing to be explored in the next chapter – seems unlikely to address either the social imbalances the introduction of the OMC has brought, or the problems of elitist citizenship and voice, listed in this chapter, that have done so much to undermine the method's wider legitimacy. If, as the next chapter will argue, we require a 'constitutional' grounding of the OMC, it must be one that takes the task of providing political input and substantive contestation into the indicators and recommendations of 'new governance' more seriously.

The chapter will conclude by offering three suggestions for an enlarged 'republican' constitutionalisation of OMC-like methods. If one of the key problems of the contemporary OMC lies in its inability to foster real deliberation and scrutiny of its dominant indicators and objectives, a solution must lie in institutions able to subject otherwise technocratic decisions to popular scrutiny.

Three such institutions – the scrutiny role of the European Parliament, the development of the European Ombudsman as an avenue to provide non judicial means for addressing problems of intransparency and accountability in new governance, and the advantages and disadvantages of 'social impact assessment' – will be explored. In all three cases, while the reforms suggested do not provide a catch-all solution to the OMC's present ills, they could significantly enhance the capacity of new governance processes to step beyond the close circle of administrative elites to which they are presently bound. In this sense, the chapter will be devoted to exploring avenues to ensure that the 'transformations' of European law being undertaken via the new governance project contribute not just to the effectiveness, but to the wider political legitimacy, of European law-making.

5 Constitutionalising new governance

1. Introduction – what does it mean to 'constitutionalise' new governance?

If economists seek to resolve every pressing problem of public policy with a market-based solution, the response of the lawyer to most public problems is to 'constitutionalise' them away. From the great early social contract theories of Locke and Hobbes on, the Constitution has been seen as a vehicle to tame arbitrary forms of political power, and place them under popular control. It is the response of the cool-headed lawyer to a society that would otherwise be awash with irredeemable competition and conflict.[1]

Given this natural impulse, it is little surprise that we, as lawyers, should seek to 'constitutionalise' new governance. As the last chapter has shown, processes like the present OMC SPSI face numerous deficits. They are overrun with unaccountable forms of executive power. They furthermore privilege forms of taken-for-granted knowledge that in fact shield important substantive political preferences. They have failed to promote decentralised forms of participation or 'learning', and even undermined those institutions, like courts and parliaments, that could act as an effective check on executive activities. The OMC seems a particularly apt target to be brought under the realm of 'law's empire'; the procedural safeguards and political controls that constitutionalism the world over has offered.

[1] This is indeed Locke's original justification for man's emergence from the state of nature – to find an impartial adjudicator for conflicts which would otherwise spin out of control (i.e. because *nemo iudex in causa sua*, no man can be judge in their own cause). J. Locke, *Two Treatises on Government* (Cambridge University Press, 1967) at [13].

This impulse, however, is tempered by something else. Bar the notion that 'constitutionalising' new governance is an urgent task, it is not at all clear, however, what it would involve. What form would such a constitutionalisation take, and what should its primary mission be? A further problem is that the game of constitutionalism is awash with what Neil Walker has called 'nominalism', i.e. the problem of trying to find – within the constitutional box – an array of effects and meanings that differ, or that may even contradict each other.[2] This ambivalence is captured by the one attempt to constitutionalise the OMC, already tried – the Constitutional Convention's working group on Social Europe (urged on by two influential academic commentators) proposed a partial constitutionalisation of the method, yet internal divisions (returned to in section 2) led to the absence of any explicit general provision on the method within the draft Treaty.[3] Even if such a provision *had* been created, it is unclear what effect it would have had on the method's wider political standing (bar the pyrrhic victory of being mentioned in a now dead constitutional text). Following from this development, what do we now do, or mean, in 'constitutionalising' the method, or indeed other new governance forms?

This final chapter will be aimed at exploring, and eventually advocating, a number of constitutional options. To begin, it may be useful to offer some reservations. As we have said, constitutionalism seems an impulsively desirable task; yet one cannot take its merits for granted. Not only is the constitutionalisation of the method an unclear project in a descriptive sense, but it is also a normatively ambivalent one. The placing of legal parameters around new governance could contribute to remedying some of the deficits outlined in the last chapter; at the same time, it could equally produce pathologies of its own. The next section will introduce the concept of 'juridification' precisely in order to capture this ambivalence.[4] While on the one hand, this chapter will argue that we need to move beyond the view of law as a pesky obstacle to a more perfect and

[2] N. Walker, 'Constitutionalism and New Governance in the European Union: Rethinking the Boundaries' in G. de Búrca and J. Scott (eds.), *Law and New Governance in the EU and the US* (Oxford: Hart, 2006) at 18–19.

[3] See G. de Búrca and J. Zeitlin, 'Constitutionalising the Open Method of Coordination: What Should the Convention Propose?' (2003) *CEPS Policy Brief* 31.

[4] As well as references below, see, for a general overview, G. Teubner, 'Juridification: Concepts, Aspects, Limits, Solutions' in Teubner (ed.), *Juridification of Social Spheres: A Comparative Analysis in the Areas of Labour, Corporate, Antitrust and Social Welfare Law* (Berlin: de Gruyter, 1987).

experimental 'governance architecture' for the EU, on the other, the legal remedies available to the OMC are themselves severely limited.

The creation of mechanisms of judicial review or accountability for OMC structures does not represent an unqualified good, but one that depends on other constitutional efforts. In this vein, sections 2 to 5 will explore both the strengths and limits of legal reform strategies that aim to use ordinary legal institutions and remedies to 'perfect' or place boundaries upon new governance procedures. This will include, firstly the use of a documentary constitutional frame for the OMC (section 2), secondly, the incorporation of the Charter of Fundamental Rights as a means to limit deregulatory tendencies tied to the adoption of a 'reformed' Lisbon agenda (section 3), and thirdly, the development, already nascent within the EU order, of procedural rights in other 'new governance' procedures, such as the right to access to documents, to reasoned decision-making, and to participation (section 4). While, in combination, these strategies could go some way to remedying problems of executive dominance and limited participation in the OMC as it stands, they are alone insufficient (section 5). If the current practice of the ECJ in cases invoking 'social Europe', or the restrictive bases of individual standing before European courts, are anything to go by legal efforts are as likely to 'juridify' new governance, or reinforce its elitist tendencies, as they are to improve its procedural and democratic legitimacy.

Instead, constitutionalism under new governance should be seen in broader terms. The problems of the current OMC do not simply concern abuses of due process rights, nor can they be solved by strengthening individual legal remedies alone. Instead, we need to conceptualise the failings of new governance in expressly *political* terms. While the OMC has been claimed as an instrument to legitimise EU action through decentralised rule, advancing a debate over Europe's social future in the process, its preference for benchmarks, indicators and secretive committees, and the encasement of the OMC within the Lisbon strategy, has led to precisely the opposite – a form of managerialism that disincentivises broad public involvement in its procedures. The advances of experimentalist theory, in seeing the method as a route to matching the rapid pace of modern social regulation, has not only led to a 'dynamic' cycle of policy exchange, but provided potentially dangerous justifications for the exclusion of the political actors and public fora that could properly scrutinise and contest the OMC's development. Rather than displace law in favour of political negotiation, the present method has too often left political discussions themselves hidden or out of reach.

To this end, in its final parts (sections 6 to 9), the chapter will propose a political or societal vision for the constitutionalisation of new governance. This vision will focus on reform strategies for the OMC that seek to use legal and political institutions not just to provide individual remedies, but increase opportunities for the political contestation and public scrutiny of new governance procedures. The 'constitutionalisation' should be seen in terms of forcing open, and demanding justifications from, a process that has used its iterative nature to insulate precisely the debates over the place of social policy in the EU order that it was originally intended to advance.

The mainstay of this strategy (explored in section 7) will be the reintegration of European and national Parliaments. Only by opening up the OMC to general political bodies may the twin threats of technocratic domination on the one hand, and 'juridification' on the other, be avoided. The chapter, however, will conclude with two final suggestions. First it will (in section 8) introduce the European Ombudsman as an institution able to mandate administrative oversight of the bodies of the OMC while avoiding the very adversarial approaches to the enforcement of social and political rights that animated the governance debate in the first place. Lastly, the chapter (in section 9) will explore recent suggestions to expand the practice of 'impact assessment' to the social OMCs as a means of encouraging both functional reflexivity between different coordination processes, and wider political reflection on the necessary trade-offs between the Lisbon competitiveness goals, and the OMC SPSI's social priorities (a debate that has so far been largely lost in the mist). As the chapter will argue, only a broad constitutionalisation of 'new governance' can hold out the prospect of rendering its processes consistent with the social, legal and political guarantees the Treaties of the European Union were designed to offer.

2. Juridification and the Convention for the future of Europe

One could hardly revisit the issue of constitutionalisation under new governance without acknowledging Europe's abortive attempt to establish a documentary constitution in the early part of this decade. The constitutional project itself included a failed attempt to include a generic provision on the OMC within its draft text – a failure that frames our present analysis. This constitutional enterprise evoked two types of ambiguity that are central to the research question of this chapter – first a normative ambiguity: is constitutionalism desirable, and for what reasons? Secondly, a conceptual ambiguity – what would constitutionalisation entail, and what would its effects and mechanisms really be?

Within the Convention itself, the issue of constitutionalising the OMC particularly invoked the first normative question. The degree of constitutional inclusion was the object of significant disagreement among members of the Convention's working groups. The positive case for constitutional inclusion, urged on by two influential academic commentators, centred on increasing the method's credibility and viability.[5] Already by 2003, it was apparent that processes like the EES had failed to produce the degree of political inclusion and transparency that was originally expected. To remedy the deficit, the Convention's Working Group on Social Europe favoured a type of constitutional inclusion for the OMC able to 'improve its transparency and democratic character, and clarify its procedure by designating the actors involved, and their respective roles'.[6] As we have already seen in the last chapter, a number of the OMC SPSI's present participants have indicated their enthusiasm for such a provision, either in a renewed constitutional project or (more realistically) in a future reform treaty for the EU (a hope not reflected in the now-ratified Lisbon Treaty).[7]

This inclusion would aim towards remedying the problems of voluntarism and executive 'gatekeeping' that characterise the OMC to date, by providing the actors involved in its processes with relatively clear expectations about how each reporting cycle would proceed. If one of the tasks of law is to remove the procedures governing political life from arbitrary decision-making, providing boundaries for political negotiation 'in advance', a constitutional enumeration of the OMC could achieve precisely this task. This would meet with a core goal of the proceduralist approach outlined in Chapter 3 – namely, that broad participation in new governance procedures will not come by itself; law instead must provide the conditions for its effective realisation.[8]

[5] See de Búrca and Zeitlin, n. 3 above.

[6] Final Report of Working Group XI on Social Europe, CONV 516/1/03 REV 1 (2003) at [44].

[7] See 'law as procedural', Chapter 4, section 6. Incidentally, the European Parliament also indicated, at the time of the Convention, its support for such a provision. See the Resolution of the European Parliament on 'Analysis of the Open Coordination Procedure in the field of Employment and Social Affairs, and Future Prospects' 2002/2223 (INI) at 2.

[8] See O. de Schutter and S. Deakin, 'Reflexive Governance and the Dilemmas of Social Regulation' in de Schutter and Deakin (eds.) *Social Rights and Market Forces: Is the Open Coordination of Employment and Social Policies the Future of Social Europe?* (Brussels: Bruylant, 2005) at 3.

Constitutional inclusion – in opening the doors for a broader legal engagement with new governance – could go the same way towards advancing that task.

At the same time, important doubts remain. Firstly, it is not obvious what constitutional or treaty inclusion would do bar put in writing what is already contained in a plethora of Commission and other soft law documents (namely the repeated, yet unheeded, insistence that the OMC should be based on broader participation and transparency). To constitutionalise the OMC is one thing, to provide its actors with the means to judicially enforce constitutional commitments is quite another. A more thorough engagement with the specific mechanisms that would be available to excluded actors under future Treaty revisions will be a core purpose of later sections of this chapter (sections 3 to 5).

For now though, a second objection may be even more pressing. The Constitutional Convention contained the seeds of a powerful case against the constitutional specification of OMC procedures. To take this excerpt from the Convention's Working Group on Economic Governance:

> There is a large measure of support within the Group for including, for the sake of clarity, the basic objectives, procedures and limits of the open coordination method, where the European Parliament and the European Commission should also have a role to play, in the Constitutional Treaty, but in a manner which does not undermine the flexibility of the method (which is one of its main advantages) and which does not have the effect of replacing or circumventing 'Community' procedures or policies. It is recommended that it should include a provision allowing for a wide-ranging consultation process, in particular with the social partners. However, some members of the group consider that the informal character of the open coordination method should be better preserved by keeping it outside the Treaty.[9]

Here, we have indications of an opposite feeling – constitutional inclusion would not increase the legitimacy of the process, rather it could reduce or rigidify the very features of adaptability, and the flexible 'tailoring' of political procedures to the needs of specific fields, that has been one of the method's distinct contributions.[10] The specification

[9] Final Report of Working Group VI on Economic Governance, CONV 357/02 (2003) at 5. See, for a similar view, Working Group on Social Europe, n. 6 above at [42].

[10] This is the basis for de Burca and Zeitlin's argument that, 'a generic provision for constitutionalising the OMC should not seek to prescribe in detail the respective roles of particular actors in its procedures'. See n. 3 above at 3.

of particular actors to be involved in each process, rather than allow a more diverse public to come forward, could cement the cosy and cooperative relationship between national and Commission officials, and select NGOs, that already characterises a number of OMC processes. This is an objection that deserves to be taken seriously – what are the possibly unwanted side effects that squeezing new governance within a constitutional or treaty-based frame could produce?

We can explore some of these effects, and their ambivalences, through an important socio-legal idea – the concept of 'juridification'.[11] For Habermas, as we saw in Chapter 3, the spread of law in modern society is a story of the simultaneous 'guarantee', and 'denial', of political freedom. Whereas law has, on the one hand, been used to assert popular control over public life, it is at the same time a common instrument of bureaucratic domination; it has been used to expand state power, or intrude upon spheres of life that were once relatively protected from legal, or other forms, of state control.

This 'juridification of the polity', for Habermas, has taken hold in four separate 'thrusts' of activity.[12] The first two concern the establishment of what we might call the classical rule of law, in which both citizens and political authorities are bound by a legal order, while the third and fourth concern its 'democratisation', firstly through the rise of popular sovereignty, and secondly, through the attempt to democratise the economy itself through the provision of social rights. In each case, the spread, growth and densification of the law is an assertion of popular power by what Habermas terms the 'lifeworld' (the realm of normative and political communication) against the 'system' (the sphere of life dominated by functional imperatives). In its freedom-providing form, law is used to limit or restrain impersonal media (such as money and power) in favour of a sphere of life in which normative reasons, and societal cohesion, remain relevant factors in political life.

Juridification also, however, carries another meaning. The promotion of social rights and economic goods also involves increasing the demands that we place upon law. Law is no longer simply expected to resolve private disputes, but to achieve a form of distributive justice,

[11] For a comprehensive account of this concept, see two sources: (i) the essays in G. Teubner (ed.), *Juridification of Social Spheres: A Comparative Analysis in the Areas of Labour, Corporate, Antitrust and Social Welfare Law* (Berlin: De Gruyter, 1987); (ii) L. Blichner and A. Molander, 'Mapping Juridification' (2008) 14 *European Law Journal* 1.

[12] J. Habermas, 'Law as Medium and Law as Institution' in G. Teubner (ed.), *Dilemmas of Law in the Welfare State* (Berlin: De Gruyter, 1986) at 203–210.

and economic prosperity, that overwhelms prior legal forms. Ironically, precisely the medium designed to safeguard the 'lifeworld' from systemising tendencies, can itself become systemised, or be used to assert impersonal and colonising forms of social control.[13]

The outcome of this systemisation – as reflected in twentieth-century legal theory – is two contradictory tendencies.[14] While on the one hand, law is increasingly called upon to manage functional tasks, lawyers are at the same time endowed with a professionalised and positivistic sense of their social role. The job of the lawyer is no longer to carry forward particular public goods, but to safeguard 'the law', understood as a system of rules divorced from their social and political context, or from 'external manipulation'. The ambiguity of juridification is that law's very attempt to inject political control and meaning into the exercise of public power can lead to its 'depoliticisation'; the treatment of legal rules as if they were ends in themselves, rather than one means (among many others) of achieving political justice, or social integration.[15] As Habermas himself puts it, 'it is now the very means of guaranteeing freedom which endangers the freedom of the beneficiary'.[16]

Juridification here represents what Judith Shklar describes as a 'legalistic attitude' – one where political actors are overtly defensive or passive, or refuse to take responsibility for decision-making.[17] Instead, we place responsibility in following legal procedures – or particular processual 'hoops' – alone, deeming this sufficient to fulfil our political responsibilities. The advance of law thus means the simultaneous evacuation of politics, understood as the responsibility to respond to pressing challenges, or advance a political dialogue over how they should be tackled.

The lesson of this simultaneous provision and denial of freedom can be extended to the question of new governance's constitutional boundaries. On the one hand, the establishment of legal controls can be a mechanism both to enumerate basic legal accountability in new

[13] Habermas labels this form of regulatory law, 'law as a medium'. See Habermas, *ibid.*, at 209–214.

[14] This – the basis for Teubner's 'regulatory trilemma' – is explained in more depth in Chapter 3, section 4.1. See also Teubner, n. 4 above, at 20–21.

[15] On this interpretation of juridification as de-politicisation, or the expropriation of conflict, see E. Christodoulidis, *Law and Reflexive Politics* (Alphen aan den Rijn: Kluwer, 1998) at 96–101.

[16] Habermas, n. 12 above, at 209.

[17] J. Shklar, *Legalism: Law, Morals and Political Trials* (Cambridge, MA: Harvard University Press, 1986).

governance, and to forge mechanisms of popular influence. If the problem of the OMC is one of the imposition of rules, and modes of understanding, that are insulated from external scrutiny, or driven by functional or 'expert' logics, then a 'freedom-providing' form of juridification would be oriented towards laying down rules of access, transparency and participation able to render the OMC's supposed commitment to an open form of rule meaningful. Juridification, in this sense, entails the use of law to impose political control on systems of governance whose pursuit of particular goals can eventually blind them to the constituencies they are designed to serve (an agenda developed further in section 4).

On the other hand, the entry of law into new governance could precisely deprive its processes of political meaning. In what position, for example, is the European Court of Justice to decide the levels of social provision twenty-seven different European states are able to achieve, or to pronounce on the necessary boundaries between the Lisbon goals of growth and competitiveness on the one hand, and national demand for social protection on the other? The danger is that law's articulation of these conflicts does not insert into them a degree of political openness but instead rephrases them as merely procedural disputes. What if law – and indeed later sections will show that this is no mere hypothetical conundrum – becomes blind to the social effects of its commitment to enforce treaty, and other EU law, obligations?

Both of these tendencies are evident in the discussions of the Constitutional Convention. While the camp in favour of constitutional inclusion saw the legal enumeration of new governance as a means of reclaiming popular control and political accountability from closed EU elites (of which the members of the Convention were of course themselves part), opponents saw, in constitutional inclusion, the threat of removing from new governance precisely what made it normatively useful – namely its ability to achieve tasks where law's capacity to act had run out. The 'juridification' of new governance could mean both the provision of political freedom through law, or the freezing of OMC processes in the name of a more perfect and coherent legal order.

While the duality of 'juridification' does not provide a template for how the OMC could or should be conceptualised, it can provide a greater awareness of both the potential and limits of a legal frame for new governance processes. As we will see, this ambiguity of law's use applies not only to the documentary constitutional project, but also to more ordinary and achievable legal remedies.

3. Solidarity and the use of fundamental rights

3.1 Social rights under the Charter

One of the concrete shifts which anticipated the development of a documentary constitutional project, and indeed one of the instruments through which a 'constitutional' frame for the EU has been advanced, was the agreement in 2000 of an EU Charter of Fundamental Rights. A number of scholars have suggested the use of the Charter as a means of remedying some of the obvious deficits suffered by the OMC to date.[18] This possibility has been given further impetus by the Charter's binding legal status under Article 6 of the TEU following the ratification of the Lisbon Treaty. How could the Charter supplement new governance's 'constitutional moment'?

The use of fundamental rights can be envisaged both in a classical and a functional sense. Classically, like many other rights instruments in the domestic context, the Charter has been advocated as a way of protecting individuals, and other affected parties, against abuses of institutional power.[19] This is reflected in a number of provisions, particularly the extensive articles enumerated in the Charter's Chapter V (on political and citizenship rights). In service of this goal, the Charter includes, in Article 41, a right on the part of EU citizens to good administration, including 'the right of every person to be heard before any individual measure which may affect him or her is taken'. It also includes, in Article 42, a right of access to Community documents, and in Articles 39 and 40, political rights to stand and vote in European and municipal elections. While many of these rights simply

[18] For examples of this argument, see S. Smismans, 'How to be Fundamental with Soft Procedures? The OMC and Fundamental Social Rights' in G. de Búrca and B. de Witte (eds.), *Social Rights in Europe* (Oxford University Press, 2005); G. de Búrca, 'New Modes of Governance and the Protection of Human Rights', in P. Alston and O. de Schutter (eds.), *Monitoring Fundamental Rights in the EU* (Oxford: Hart, 2005); N. Bernard, 'A New Governance Approach to Economic, Social and Cultural Rights in the EU' in T. Hervey and J. Kenner (eds.), *Economic and Social Rights under the Charter of Fundamental Rights of the European Union* (Oxford: Hart, 2003); O. de Schutter, 'The Implementation of Fundamental Rights through the Open Method of Coordination' in de Schutter and Deakin (eds.), n. 8 above.

[19] See de Búrca, *ibid.*, at 28–31.

codify entitlements already established by ECJ case law, or by the Treaties, their commitment to greater transparency, and political involvement, could go some way to 'concretising' the soft calls for a broader and more open OMC that we find in numerous Commission documents.

The more innovative use of the Charter, however, relies on a second, functional deployment. This use concerns applying the Charter negatively, as a means of balancing the economic focus of the Lisbon strategy, or otherwise safeguarding the use of the OMC to trigger regulatory competition between EU states.[20] If one of our concerns with the OMC is that it could lead to 'unlearning', or the implicit erosion of fundamental welfare commitments under the guise of economic coordination, the Charter could act as a counterweight, using the legitimacy claims of enumerated social rights to encourage a more reciprocal relation between the method's economic and social dimensions.

The legal basis for this argument rests in the rights elaborated in the Charter's Chapter IV (on solidarity). This contains formal entitlements, in Article 31, to fair and just working conditions (including maximum working hours, and annual leave), in Article 34, to basic social security and social assistance, and in Article 33, to adequate maternal and paternal leave. The Charter provides a hospitable environment for social rights insofar as it was part of a recognition by the Community that traditional distinctions between 'negative' and 'positive' duties in human rights protection are obsolete.[21] Against some objections, the Charter's founders declared that its four founding values – of human dignity, freedom, equality and solidarity – were 'indivisible' in the Charter's preamble, thus avoiding the consignment of social rights (long observed in the EU's history) to a separate, and less binding, rights regime.[22]

In this, the Charter invites an effort on the part of the Court, and other EU institutions, to read EU norms in light of social values, including the commitment to universality in the provision of social services that defenders of a 'European Social Model' propound. There are some

[20] See (in support of this use) A. Adronico and A. Lo Faro, 'Defining Problems: The OMC, Fundamental Rights and the Theory of Governance', in O. de Schutter and S. Deakin, n. 8 above, at 52; O. de Schutter, n. 18 above at 318; S. Smismans, n. 18 above at 222.

[21] B. de Witte, 'The Trajectory of Fundamental Rights in the European Union' in de Burca and de Witte, n. 18 above, at 159.

[22] But see the distinction utilised in the Charter between 'principles' and 'rights' (below).

indications that the Court – in the course of the last decade – has begun to heed this call. In a number of important decisions in the mid-1990s the Court relied on the 'solidarity principle' – as enshrined both in the Charter, and the preamble of the EC Treaty – to shield important welfare institutions from the perceived deregulatory pressures of internal market law.[23]

The ECJ did so by making a distinction between undertakings which were economic in nature and those which were designed to compensate individuals regardless of their social or generational status. In *Poucet & Pistre*, for example, a public insurance scheme for the self-employed was held not to be an economic undertaking for the purposes of EC competition rules because it was both compulsory and universal (i.e. not based on the financial status or health of the individual at the time of making a claim), and redistributive.[24] Similarly, in *Sodemare*, an Italian rule outlawing profit-making companies from applying to run care homes was said to be 'based on the principle of solidarity, as reflected by the fact that it is designed as a matter of priority to assist those who are in a state of need owing to insufficient income, total or partial lack of independence, or the risk of being marginalised'.[25] The use of the language of social inclusion in these cases is notable. Here, social rights were relied upon to limit the applicability of a scheme of economic entitlements that could otherwise have undermined the universal nature of national social assistance.[26] This is precisely the negative use of social rights that the second functional aspect of 'Charterisation' implies, i.e. to limit the functional domination of the method by economic actors. Perhaps the Court's jurisprudence could similarly act as a limit on deregulatory tendencies within the present-day OMC.

[23] See Case 263/86 *Belgian State v Humbel* [1988] ECR 5365; Joined Cases C-159/91 and C-160/91 *Poucet and Pistre* [1993] ECR I-637; C-70/905 *Sodemare* [1997] ECR I-3395; Case C-67/96 *Albany* [1999] ECR I-5751.

[24] As such, 'it follows that the social security schemes, as described, are based on a system of compulsory contribution, which is indispensable for the application of the principle of solidarity, and for the financial equilibrium of those schemes.' *Poucet & Pistre*, *ibid.*, at [317].

[25] *Ibid.*, at [29]. This case can be contrasted with another, Case C-238/94 *FFSA*, in which the insurance scheme concerned was supplementary and based on capitalisation (i.e. members received out of the scheme in proportion to what they put in). As a result, 'solidarity' was deemed inoperable. For a discussion of both cases, see Barnard below.

[26] See C. Barnard, 'EU Citizenship and the Principle of Solidarity' and M. Dougan and E. Spaventa, 'Wish you weren't here . . . New Model of Social Solidarity in the European Union', both in Dougan and Spaventa (eds.), *Social Welfare and EU Law* (Oxford: Hart, 2005).

3.2 *The paradoxes of Charterisation*

Both these uses of the Charter rely on the perception that the 'soft' OMC and 'hard' Charter could be mutually reinforcing (they are thus in keeping with some of the 'hybridity' theories discussed in the second chapter). On the one hand, politically independent social and political rights could act as a hard barrier against an OMC process that – dependent on the impetus of powerful political actors and narratives – could lead to backsliding on 'fundamental' social and procedural commitments. On the other hand, the OMC offers possibilities for the elaboration of fundamental rights themselves.[27] Fully integrated within OMC procedures, the OMC could play a role in transferring fundamental rights from static, negative or pre-political standards into proactive and positive policy instruments, relying not on Court intervention by rich or self-serving individuals, but upon a broad process of political reform. The OMC could thus elaborate or 'realise' the positive dimension of Charter rights, just as negatively, the Charter could act as a 'final instance limit' on an OMC process too flexible and iterative to take social and political rights seriously.

One wonders, however, whether the converse is also the case. The interaction of the OMC and the Charter could be mutually destructive; indeed the positive argument for the Charterisation of the method contains fairly obvious flaws in its constructive logic. There is a first paradox. How can fundamental rights act simultaneously as a depoliticised, independent check on the activities of OMC-like methods and as an instrument that is *realised* through the processes of new governance themselves? If the OMC truly is an instrument liable to problems of political manipulation, or functional constraint, then all the more reason to insulate fundamental rights from its ambit. Conversely, if fundamental rights are sufficiently 'soft' that they are animated only by the politically reflexive operations of new governance, how can they then be in any sense useful as a 'buttress' against the OMC's supposed deregulatory tendencies? As one hesitant proponent of 'Charterisation' has put it:

> One wonders whether new modes of governance, with their emphasis on non-binding non-justicable instruments and on coordinating and informational mechanisms, are appropriate for the area of human rights protection, given that what is generally said to differentiate 'rights' in law from other claims of interest is the availability of a legal remedy, usually a remedy which can be individually enforced, and usually in judicial proceedings. Is there a

[27] See Smismans, n. 18 above, at 231–235; de Schutter, n. 18 above, at 334–343.

> risk that the shift towards new modes of governance for the protection and implementation of human rights undermines the idea of a core content, rendering the standards of protection ultimately fluid and flexible?[28]

While on the one hand, the use of the OMC to 'flesh out' fundamental rights (that would otherwise be announced by judicial fiat alone) could subject them to tendencies towards political majoritarianism and abuse, on the other, the use of rights to 'limit' the OMC could precisely stand in the way of the use of 'new governance' as a flexible, differentiated and iterative set of policy instruments. In both cases, we see a return of what was described in the last chapter as 'the problem of hierarchy' – the paradoxes that the attempt to legally or constitutionally ground experimental political processes implies.[29]

Even, however, if we were to ignore this paradox, to what extent is the Charter actually applicable to OMC-like methods? The Charter's architects were careful to avoid a repeat of the problems encountered by the signatories of the EC Treaty itself, whereby a Treaty designed largely to restrict and delimit the power of *European* institutions became a vehicle primarily to vet *national* legislation.[30] As such, the Charter contains a notorious set of 'horizontal' clauses in Article 51, which limit its use either to expand the Union's competences, or to alter the level of rights protection enjoyed in the domestic sphere.

This places in doubt the binding status of social rights, particularly, for our purposes, the right to social security and assistance enumerated in Article 31. Given that the Treaties explicitly exclude legislative harmonisation in the field of social assistance, how can we square the Charter's social commitments with its equal insistence (under Article 51(2)) that it cannot be read as expanding the EU's competences?

The Constitutional Convention, adopting the Charter into its text in 2003, simply added to this confusion. Fearing the effects of a binding Charter on national social autonomy, a number of delegates to the Constitutional Convention insisted on the addition of an additional article within the draft text, enumerating social rights as 'principles' rather than 'subjective rights'.[31] Whereas the latter could be relied upon by individuals directly, the former were judicially cognisable only in

[28] See de Búrca n. 18 above, at 31. [29] See Chapter 5, section 3.3.

[30] On this rather infamous insight, see M. Cappelletti, M. Seccombe and J. Weiler, *Integration Through Law: Europe and the American Federal Experience* (Berlin: De Gruyter, 1986) at 29–35.

[31] See Article II-112(5), Draft Treaty Establishing a Constitution for Europe. On the motivations and debates underlying this distinction within the Constitutional

'informing', 'guiding' or 'aiding' the interpretation of measures taken by the EU institutions or the member states to implement Charter rights.[32] This distinction has caused considerable academic consternation, not least because it clearly violates the original rejection by the Charter's drafters of the attempt to enumerate social rights in the language of 'principles' rather than direct obligations. In this way, the supposedly 'indivisible' Charter has become another part of a familiar story – one that continues into the current 'Reform' Treaty – of the international confinement of social rights to a less authoritative normative sphere.

In the case of the OMC, the situation is further complicated by the wording of Article 51(1). It states that the provisions of the Charter are addressed to the member states only 'when they are implementing Union law'. This limitation sits uneasily, however, with the non-legislative nature of OMC provisions. As we have seen in Chapter 1, the OMC was declared judicially non-binding precisely to allow national governments some flexibility in incorporating EU objectives, the precise details of which may vary from one national context to another.

However, even if we are to stretch OMC obligations far enough to declare them an element of Union law, how can we determine whether acting under the OMC involves 'implementing' such obligations or not? There are no obvious evaluative criteria. How can one identify which, for example, of the national measures designed to 'implement' obligations under the OMC SPSI draw their inspiration solely from the domestic sphere, and which are driven by the need to respect EU-level commitments? In many ways, the method was precisely designed to explode these distinctions, with governments forming their policies through multiple influences (including through cross-national mutual learning, adjusted to the domestic context). This leaves those proposing a 'Charterisation' of the method with an uncomfortable choice. We either place the OMC outside the Charter's ambit, removing its ability to check its procedures *ex post*, or we declare *all* national efforts listed under national action plans part and parcel of 'implementing Union law', thus leaving both the 'non-binding' nature of OMC recommendations, and the wording of Article 51 itself, meaningless. Such an interpretation would not only involve significantly stretching the OMC's

Convention, see B. Bercusson, 'Social and Labour Rights under the EU Constitution' in de Burca and de Witte, n. 18 above, at 170–180.

32 On the ambiguous nature of the rights/principles distinction (including in the present Treaty), see D. Damjanovic and B. de Witte, 'Welfare Integration Through EU Law: The Overall Picture in Light of the Lisbon Treaty' (2008) *EUI Working Papers (Law)* 34 at 20–25.

original design, but also provoke significant resistance among the member states.

Finally, we must enquire into the institution that would be charged with enforcing potential violations of the Charter. Even if all of the practical obstacles listed above could somehow be resolved, they would still require judicial invocation by a sympathetic court. We have to be sure we are dealing with an ECJ willing to take seriously its role in using social rights – or the 'shield of solidarity' – to avoid problems of regulatory competition, or indeed the usurpation of the OMC by Lisbon's growth and competitiveness agenda, and actors.

If once this was a realistic hope, however, there are plenty of indications that the Court has begun to move away from its 'solidarity' jurisprudence. In several landmark recent cases concerning conflicts between collective action and the market freedoms, the Court has placed itself at the centre of a fierce academic debate.[33] Whereas, in cases like *Poucet & Pistre* and *Albany*, the Court had exempted institutions based on 'solidarity' from the scope of competition rules (on the grounds that the application of the four freedoms would negate their social purpose), through the case of *Viking Lines* (and other recent jurisprudence), the Court considerably restricted this reasoning.

The facts of the case are by now familiar to each and every labour lawyer (national or European), and were briefly discussed in the first chapter. It may be useful to briefly recount them. The plaintiff in the case, Viking, was a shipping line who had attempted to reflag its company in order take advantage of cheaper pay and conditions in another member state. This action was resisted by a Finnish Union firstly through the threat of strike action, and secondly through the issuance of a trade union circular, forbidding future collective negotiations with Viking in other member states. In considering the conflict between rights of collective action and freedom of establishment invoked by the case, the Court undertook a number of radical moves. While the social objectives of trade union activities designed to restrict 'social dumping' were explicitly recognised, this was not considered sufficient

[33] For the three most significant judgments, see Case C-341/05 *Laval un Partneri Ltd v Svenska Byggnadsarbetareforbundet and Others* [2007] ECR I-11767; Case C-438/05 *The International Transport Workers' Federation & The Finnish Seamen's Union v Viking Line ABP & Ou Viking Line Eesti* [2007] ECR I-10779; Case C-346/06 *Rechtsanwalt Dr. Dirk Rüffert v Land Niedersachsen* [2008] ECR I-1989.

to render the market freedoms inoperable. Instead, fundamental social rights, and the economic rights enumerated in the Treaty, had to be 'reconciled' through an act of judicial balancing.[34]

As Joerges and Rödl have argued in a series of recent essays, this move entails a number of potentially restrictive effects.[35] Not only did the case subsume collective labour law – an explicitly national competence, and even a *fundamental social right* in a number of member states – under the scope of EU rules (thus limiting the use of social rights to negatively 'shield' the national welfare state), but it also involved treating the Finnish Union as a public entity (rather than as one partner engaged in an ongoing negotiation over acceptable terms and conditions of employment).[36] This latter action has gained considerable attention among labour lawyers; fearful that the Court's jurisprudence may, somewhat ironically, have a constraining effect on the 'Europeanisation' of efforts by trade unions to restrict pan-European forms of social dumping through transnational resistance strategies.[37]

The consequences of *Viking* (and the later cases of *Laval* and *Rüffert*) – as Rödl and Joerges admit – cannot yet be fully assessed.[38] The act of judicial 'balancing' of social and economic entitlements could yet lead future courts to read efforts by unions and other collective agencies to defend social entitlements more generously. Equally, there is certainly merit to *some* of the Court's actions. As Loic Azouli has argued in an influential recent essay, the Court's rulings in *Laval* and *Viking* signal its intent to move from a 'conflictual' to a

[34] To quote a crucial paragraph, the Court observes that, 'it is sufficient to point out that, even if, in the areas that fall outside the scope of the Community's competence, the Member States are still free, in principle, to lay down the conditions governing the existing and exercise of the [social] rights in question, the fact remains that, when exercising that competence, the Member States must nevertheless comply with Community law'. *Viking*, n. 33 above, at [40].

[35] C. Joerges and F. Rödl, 'Informal Politics, Formalised Law and the Social Deficit of European Integration: Reflections after the Judgements of the ECJ in Laval and Viking' (2009) 15 *European Law Journal* 1; C. Joerges and F. Rödl, 'On the Social Deficit of the European Integration Project and its Perpetuation through the ECJ Judgements in Viking and Laval' (2008) *RECON Online Working Papers* 6.

[36] This was a significant move in both cases. See *Laval*, n. 33 above, at [85]; *Viking*, n. 33 above, at [61].

[37] See e.g. B. Bercusson, 'The Trade Union Movement and the European Union: Judgement Day' (2007) 13 *European Law Journal* 3 at 294–295; N. Reich, 'Free Movement v Social Rights in an Enlarged Union: The Laval and Viking Cases before the European Court of Justice' (2008) 9 *German Law Journal* 2 at 160.

[38] Joerges and Rödl, n. 35 above, at 19.

'consensual' approach to the relation between social and economic rights in the EU.[39] In the first chapter, I described this as law's reflexive role – the use of law not to choose, or establish a hierarchy between different sets of values – but to seek to develop each harmoniously or with a reflexive awareness of the other. This approach could yet be used to extend this reflexivity into the practice of the OMC.[40]

As it stands, however, the judgments, at the very least, should urge some caution in relying on the Court's deployment of social rights as a means of limiting or constraining the Union's dominant economic narratives. In these cases at least, social rights are deployed not only to protect the national welfare state's autonomy, but rather to legitimise the attempt by the Court to evaluate national social policies at the EU level, and thereby judicially elaborate where the boundaries between a free European market, and a national welfare state, should lie. The prospect of this Court moving unequivocally to protect the national social state through the invocation of the Charter, while normatively compelling, seems a distant hope.

In combination, these objections can only leave us sceptical. They question the very feasibility of using the Charter to remedy some of the challenges outlined in the last chapter. We can add to this considerable question marks over the *desirability* of using the Charter in this way. After all, why should the question of the necessary and desirable boundaries between European economic rights and the national welfare state in any case be a question that the European judiciary should largely decide? The aforementioned critique of 'juridification' applies as strongly here as it did to the process of placing the OMC under a documentary constitutional frame. Whereas on the one hand, the introduction of a human rights register could potentially protect minorities sidelined in the OMC's game of policy learning and legal change; it could at the same time, simply hand power from one closed circle of elites to another – an EU judiciary particularly poorly placed to answer the questions that the OMC's role in the wider Lisbon strategy poses.

Perhaps the more useful deployment of fundamental rights could be, not as a 'hard', 'constitutional' backbone to the OMC, but as a *political*

[39] L. Azoulai, 'The Court of Justice and the Social Market Economy: The Emergence of an Ideal and the Conditions for its Realization' (2008) 45 *Common Market Law Review* 5 at 1347–1350.

[40] For a suggestion along these lines, see M. Dawson, 'The Ambiguity of Social Europe in the OMC' (2009) 34 *European Law Review* 1.

foundation for the method. Beyond these judicial strategies, the Charter, and the language of fundamental rights, could be deployed *non-judicially*. This is suggested by the Commission's advocacy of an approach which, I will argue in later sections, should be applied to the social OMC's – the 'mainstreaming' of fundamental rights across other areas of EU policy.

This political approach to fundamental rights can, in part, be read from the text of the Charter itself. While Article 51 states that the Charter does not establish any new Union powers, it urges the EU institutions not only to respect the rights it contains, but also to 'promote their application'. While in this sense, competence questions may limit the Charter's use to legislate for the protection of social rights at the EU level, it could still be used to encourage measures in other fields to respect, or take heed of, Charter rights. As Bruno de Witte has put it:

> Thus the question is not so much whether the EC and EU may gain *extra* legislative powers under the Charter for the promotion of social rights (they do not), but whether the *existing* legislative and other powers of the EU will be re-oriented and infused with a range of different values and policy considerations after the enactment of the Charter.[41]

This function is partly being fulfilled through the Commission's promise to include a statement on the impact on fundamental rights of all the legislative initiatives it proposes from 2005. In 2008, the Commission also proposed extending the mainstreaming approach to the guidelines of the OMC.[42] This would involve encouraging guidelines in separate OMC strands, as well as bodies like the EPC and SPC, to consider the objectives and promotion of fundamental social rights when formulating common recommendations (and to report on this requirement). In this capacity, the role of the Charter seems not to be as a constitutional safeguard of the OMC's procedural integrity; but rather as an instigator of political and institutional reflexivity. This political function will be returned to in section 9 of this chapter.

This use, however, is certainly less than what is hoped for by the most optimistic proponents of the OMC's Charterisation. Their argument is not merely that the Charter can 'prompt' political elaboration, but also act as a procedural and social safeguard against the OMC's worst

[41] See de Witte, n. 21 above, at 166.

[42] Commission Communication, 'A Renewed Commitment to Social Europe: Re-enforcing the Open Method of Coordination for Social Inclusion and Social Protection, COM (2008) 418 final at 6.

deregulatory excesses, providing in the process, a greater harmony between the method's economic and social dimensions. In the words of Maurizio Ferrera:

> This codification can contribute to shifting gradually the centre of gravity of the EU political production towards some middle point between the safeguard of 'freedoms' and the stabilization of 'entitlements' – the two sides of life chances in the European tradition.[43]

There is little indication in the Charter's practice that such a use is even possible. While the Charter remains relatively enfeebled in its enforcement mechanisms, we see little indication that either the actors of the OMC, or the Court, are willing to take its social provisions seriously. Under present conditions, we may have to look elsewhere – even towards more 'ordinary' and 'long-standing' legal remedies – when considering how the social and procedural shortcomings of the present social OMCs can be addressed.

4. The good Court

Additional to the question of the normative good of 'constitutionalising' the OMC, either through the Charter or a documentary constitutional frame, we also have to enquire into its effectiveness. Bar its symbolic impact, it is not obvious what the outcome of endowing the OMC with a 'general procedure' would be. In some ways, the effects we are looking for in 'constitutionalising' new governance could be achieved *without* embarking on a broad project of constitutional or treaty-based reform, or even through providing an extra layer of fundamental rights upon a European polity already overloaded with rights-based commitments. The existing treaties contain a number of provisions designed to guarantee the transparency, responsiveness and accountability of European law in its 'ordinary' guises.

These provisions are part of what has been labelled an emergent 'European administrative law'.[44] This discipline in some sense brings European law, and its guardian Court, 'back to its roots'. In imposing basic rules of procedure on the administration of EU rules, the Court is cast less in the role of an offensive pioneer, forging a supra-national

[43] M. Ferrera, *The Boundaries of Welfare: European Integration and the New Spatial Politics of Social Protection* (Oxford University Press, 2005) at 243–244.

[44] See P. Craig , *EU Administrative Law* (Oxford University Press, 2006).

legal order replete with realisable individual rights, than in a defensive role, attempting to hold the European institutions to their original institutional mandates. To what extent could this body of norms address the deficits outlined in the last chapter?

One important reform proposal has suggested its use for precisely this purpose. In an essay published in 2007, Joanne Scott and Susan Sturm have attempted to forge a middle course between the original view of law as external to new governance processes, and the spectre of 'juridification', or a legal imperium over OMC-like procedures.[45] In doing so, their essay argues for a renewed understanding of national and European courts. They argue that the critique of courts implicit in the new governance project is of a traditional, liberal understanding of the role of the judge under regimes of domestic administrative law. Under this view, courts are impartial assessors of whether an individual has acted within the scope of a particular rule, or an agency within the mandate bestowed upon it by parliament. The Court's decision is both all or nothing, and determined through a hierarchical relationship to the parties involved. In the first case, it either decrees that the individual or agency fell within its entitlement or not; in the second, it gives 'the last word' on the specific issue of whether or not the action concerned is permissible (a judgment which actors must then 'obey').

> Once the Court rules on the applicability of legal norms in a particular case, extended interaction (either with the Court or with the relevant institution) questioning the meaning and implementation of the legal norm suggests failure – failure to articulate a precise enough rule, failure to embody the ideal of dispassionate adjudication or failure to achieve compliance with the applicable rule.[46]

In their model, however, precisely this type of interaction is to be positively welcomed. Courts are not to act as a final arbiter of the meaning and interpretation of norms; instead they are to engage in, and instigate, an ongoing institutional dialogue about the relationship

[45] J. Scott and S. Sturm, 'Courts as Catalysts: Re-thinking the Judicial Role in New Governance' (2007) 13 *Columbia Journal of European Law* 3. For more traditional examples of proposals to reintegrate the OMC 'under the shadow' of conventional Community law, see V. Hatzopoulos, 'Why the Open Method of Coordination is Bad for You: A Letter to the EU' (2007) 13 *European Law Journal* 3 at 337–341; F. Scharpf, 'The European Social Model: Coping with the Challenges of Diversity' (2002) 40 *Journal of Common Market Studies* 4 at 662–665.

[46] *Ibid.*, at 569.

between 'formal law' and its implementation through 'new governance' itself:

> Courts can (and we argue that they should) choose to structure that relationship explicitly, to influence both the way normative activity occurs in other arenas, and the capacity of the judiciary to learn from (and sometimes to incorporate) the process and outcome of normative activity in other areas. This is a reciprocal process of interaction, rather than one where the causal arrows go only in one direction.[47]

On the one hand, in keeping with the proceduralist school, law is to create certain baseline conditions for adequate deliberation within new governance processes. On the other, it is not enough for law simply to 'regulate' new governance *ex post*. Instead, the Court is encouraged to actively *learn from* efforts within the realm of new governance to recreate legal values. Where these processes have shown themselves capable of introducing new variants of transparency, accountability and reasoned decision-making, these practices should be mandated, rather than usurped by traditional legal procedures.[48] The metaphor they use to describe this role is the court 'as a catalyst', i.e. as an instigator of a process of institutional reflection designed not only to move new governance in particular pre-set directions, but to 'discover' practices of accountable governance that can influence not only the realm of the OMC and other new governance methods, but also the monitoring role of the European Court itself.

In practical terms, they point to a number of examples upon which such a model could be based. While these examples offer a starting point, they will be expanded upon significantly in order to give a broader account of the use of European courts, either to act as a procedural monitor of OMC-like processes, or to take on what Scott and Sturm have described as the ECJ's embryonic 'catalyst' role. The Court, and the treaties, could promote legal values like transparency, accountability and reasoned decision-making in new governance through four possible Channels: (i) through the expansion of participation rights; (ii) through demanding an improved information basis for decisions under new governance; (iii) through a general duty to give reasons for decisions; and (iv) through the creation of requirements for transparency and access to documents.

[47] *Ibid.*, at 570. [48] *Ibid.*, at 571–575.

In the following four sections, we will analyse these elements in turn, before turning in the following part to their (extensive) limitations. While judicial review may have a role to play in the new governance saga, the deficits of the existing Court may in fact make many of its most important due process guarantees inoperable.

4.1 *Expanding participation rights*

A first possible advantage judicial review could bring to new governance would be to enhance the commitment of processes like the OMC SPSI to 'the involvement of stakeholders in the design, implementation and monitoring of policy' (its third 'overarching' objective). The voluntary nature of these rights – as observed in Chapter 4 – has not only often limited the OMC to a sectional or 'elitist' public, but even ensured that those who do participate are indebted for their involvement to the very executive actors whose conduct they must review.[49] The OMC's 'gate-keeper problem' has not only inhibited the legitimacy and effectiveness of its processes, but directly fostered the perception that it is restricted to an 'insider's club' of mutually self-serving administrative actors.[50]

One possible means of overcoming this arrangement would be to transform the method's vague commitment to 'the widest possible mobilisation of stakeholders' into concrete and realisable legal entitlements. What if the explanatory burden in justifying participation in OMC procedures was shifted from the regional assembly or NGO, trying vainly to make its case for inclusion, to the national or European executive, able to exclude only in circumstances of an overwhelming public interest?

Already, the Court's standing rules have significantly shaped the contours of who may participate in new governance procedures. The classic example in this regard is the *UEAPME* case, which concerned rights of participation under the social dialogue.[51] The applicant, UEAPME (an organisation representing small businesses) was involved in the initial Commission consultation over the adoption of the 1996 Parental Leave Directive (the first piece of legislation to be adopted directly by the social partners). In spite of UEAPME's consultative role,

[49] See Chapter 4, section 4.2. On the problem of 'elitist citizenship, see P. Magnette, 'European Governance and Civic Participation: Beyond Elitist Citizenship?' (2003) 51 *Political Studies* 1.

[50] See C. Harlow and R. Rawlings, 'Promoting Accountability in Multilevel Governance: A Network Approach' (2007) 13 *European Law Journal* 4.

[51] Case T-135/96 *UEAPME v Council* [1998] ECR II-2335.

it was subsequently excluded from the formal negotiations between the social partners over the directive's content. UEAPME argued that their exclusion affected the validity of the Directive, insofar as it violated their right to participate as an essential procedural requirement.

The Court rejected UEAPME's objections. In particular, they argued that, while there may be a right to consultation, this should be distinguished from the *negotiations* stage, at which more limited participation could be justified. At this stage, the involvement of UNICE – a body that also represented small businesses – met, in the Court's opinion, the participation requirement contained in the dialogue's Treaty provisions.

At the same time, the judgment is notable for the Court's insistence that the Commission and Council were under an obligation to:

> Ascertain whether, having regard to the content of the agreement in question, the signatories taken together, are sufficiently representative. Where that degree of representativity is lacking, the Commission and Council must refuse to implement the agreement at Community level.[52]

While UEAPME did not meet the test, the Court here established that a certain bar of participation would have to be met as a precondition for considering the agreement in question legitimate. At the same time, the Court – rather than establish that standard itself – referred the question back to the Commission and Council (thus declining finally to decide the question of representation itself). As a result of the case, UEAPME lodged an appeal, which eventually resulted both in an agreement between UEAPME and UNICE over the former's legitimate claim to represent European small business, and a commitment by the Commission to more frequently update its list of consulted social partner organisations.[53] As Scott and Sturm put it, while in this instance, 'the Court does not itself establish the criteria for adequate participation', at the same time, 'it requires *the deliberative process* to define and apply those criteria'.[54]

Such a requirement could be part of the OMC's constitutionalising project. While an over-specification of the necessary actors involved could have the perverse effect of reinforcing the 'insider's club' effect, a court willing to place a justificatory burden on institutions (like the Commission) seeking to deny actor involvement could have a

[52] *Ibid.*, at [90].
[53] See the report of the IST/Universite Catholique de Louvaine, *Report on the Representativeness of European Social Partner Organizations* at 41.
[54] Scott and Sturn, n. 45 above, at 578 (my emphasis).

benevolent role. In such an environment, those wishing to exclude interested organisations would at the very least be under an obligation to explain that exclusion in light of a general Union interest, while not precluding an effective judicial remedy to those cut out. This could be a first move in encouraging actors within the process to take their participative commitments more seriously.

4.2 Decision-making – improving the information basis

A second role for judicial review of new governance processes could lie in attempts by the Court to force political actors to reflect on the information basis for their decisions. Undoubtedly, the OMC relies on a significant body of technical and scientific knowledge. This is embodied in the indicators and metrics through which relative rates of poverty, unemployment and social cohesion in the member states are measured. In reality, these indicators do not simply 'measure' social inclusion; they also act, as the last chapter has argued, as a background template through which national social policies can be comparatively evaluated. They thus constitute an important part of the knowledge basis upon which decisions over the direction of EU social policy are made.

At the same time, they pose a dilemma. On the one hand, indicators have to encompass a wide variety of social schemes, and diverse national political preferences. Detailed scientific knowledge of these systems, and of the data available to engage them, is essential for a meaningful exercise in comparative benchmarking to take place. On the other hand, there is an equal danger of going too far in the other direction. Such indicators – as the last chapter also argued – have the capacity to hide or displace normative discussions that ought to be held in the open. While 'technical expertise' creates a template upon which peer review and mutual learning can operate, *too much deference* to scientific opinion can either lead to the implicit favouring of one social model over another, or lead to a situation in which the coordination of social policy becomes a purely 'managerial' exercise, devoid of political content.[55]

[55] On this danger, i.e. that either scientific expertise gain a 'trumping' power, or that 'expert knowledge is substituted or 'overruled' by the problem perceptions of the layman', see C. Joerges, 'The Law's Problem with the Governance of the European Market' in C. Joerges and R. Dehousse (eds.) *Good Governance in Europe's Integrated Market* (Oxford University Press, 2002) at 22–24. See also, C. Joerges, 'Scientific Expertise in Social Regulation and the European Court of Justice: Legal Frameworks for De-nationalized Governance Structures' in C. Joerges, K. H. Ladeur and E. Vos (eds.), *Integrating Scientific Expertise into Regulatory Decision-making: National Traditions and*

In the area of consumer protection, and the regulation of environmental risk, the Court has developed an approach which could go some way to providing the balance we are searching for. As such, the effort to encourage an adequate consideration of 'external' advice could be an important contribution of the Court to safeguarding the legitimacy and effectiveness of the OMC. Where the EU institutions, particularly the Commission, have established advisory bodies to enable them to make technical evaluations, e.g. over the safety of particular products, the courts have been faced with a similar dilemma to the one sketched out above. On the one hand, the Court must recognise that risk regulation involves important cultural and political considerations, on the other; it also must hold the EU institutions to their commitment to take scientific advice seriously. How can the Court simultaneously provide the Commission and Council with the discretion properly to carry out *political* functions, while ensuring that scientific advice is not subordinated in the name of placating powerful interests, or public hysteria?

The Court has thankfully shown a willingness to address this balance head on. Many of the relevant cases concern matters of high political sensitivity. This is particularly so for a series of judgments decided in the late 1990s concerning the explosive issue of BSE. During the period, the Commission responded to widespread public anxiety over the spread of the disease by banning British beef exports.[56] This move was predictably contested by British farmers, who argued that the ban was based on public panic rather than sound scientific evidence. The conflict came to the fore in the case of *National Farmers Union*, where the Court read the inclusion into the Treaty of the 'precautionary principle' as providing the Commission with a margin of discretion in putting consumer safety first, particularly when considerable uncertainty over risks to the public prevailed.[57] At the same time, the Court followed its reasoning in an earlier case, *Angelopharm*, in which it had asserted that any ban 'should be founded on scientific and technical assessments

European Innovations (Berlin: Nomos, 1997). See also the criticisms offered in section 6 below.

56 See Cases C-157/96 *National Farmers Union and Others* [1998] ECR I-2211; Case C-180/96 *R United Kingdom* v. *Commission* [1996] ECR I-3903.

57 While the principle has not been defined under the Treaty, the Commission established its own quasi-working definition under a 2000 Communication: 'recourse to the precautionary principle presupposes that potentially dangerous effects deriving from a phenomenon, product or process have been identified, and that scientific evaluation does not allow the risk to be determined with sufficient certainty'. See Commission Communication 'On the Precautionary Principle' COM (2000) 1 final at 4.

which must themselves be based on the results of the latest international research'.[58] While political discretion in such cases was deemed vital, this discretion still had to meet a minimum threshold of scientific consultation.

This requirement was further tightened in two almost simultaneous decisions, which concerned banned antibiotics.[59] For a number of years, antibiotics had been used by farmers to lower rates of infection in animals (but erroneously conceived by a number of member states, particularly Denmark and Sweden, as carrying a risk to the effectiveness of *human* antibiotic use). Here, the Court displays a similar political deference in one sense – it argued, in *Pfizer*, that 'the Community judicature is not entitled to substitute its judgement of the facts for that of the Community institutions'.[60] The Court seemingly displays a reflexive awareness of the 'juridification' concerns explored in the previous section – that political institutions can and should not be expected to defer to scientific *or* judicial reasoning in cases where a wide range of political or cultural factors are in play.

In another sense, however, the Court holds the Commission to a higher standard. This political deference is predicated, the Court makes clear, on particular conditions, particularly that decisions are based on a scientific risk assessment. As the Court puts it, 'that risk assessment task must be entrusted to experts, and the advice they provide must match standards of excellence, independence and transparency'.[61] Here, the assessment did not meet that standard – the comitological committee carrying out the assessment was neither 'independent', nor was it 'transparent' (because its findings were not published, with minority scientific opinions inadequately taken into account). The Court makes clear in the case that the Commission is under a justificatory burden in such cases – while it has discretion in seeking to protect the public from undue risk, it must explain its consideration of scientific evidence, its opinion of its quality, and its reasons for possible departures from it.[62]

Through such examples, the Court has begun to engage in a more dialogic relationship to new governance processes. In particular, we see instances in which it has encouraged political actors, and expert-based

58 Case 212/91 *Angelopharm* v. *Freie Hansestadt Hamburg* [1993] ECR I-171 at [31].

59 Cases T-13/99 *Pfizer Animal Health* v. *Council* [2002] ECR II-3305; T-70/59 *Alpharma* v. *Council* [2002] ECR II-3495.

60 *Pfizer*, *ibid.*, at [169]. 61 *Ibid.*, at [157]–[159]. 62 *Alpharma*, n. 59 above, at [198]–[199].

bodies, to engage in a dialogue over the necessary threshold of risk, and how producers and consumers can adequately meet that threshold.[63] This function is embodied in a final case, *Technische Universität Munchen*, in which the Commission's decision to impose a duty on a microscope imported from abroad was overturned on the basis that there had been an inadequate integration of relevant scientific advice.[64] What is most interesting in this example is the morphing of the duty to consult technical opinion into a larger participative right for the affected parties. The Court ruled that crucial to its decision was the failure on the part of the Commission to consult the affected party himself on the purpose and use of the relevant instrument. In the words of the Court:

> It is the importing institution which is best aware of the technical characteristics which the scientific apparatus must have in view of the work for which it is intended . . . The right to be heard in such an administrative procedure requires that the person concerned should be able, during the actual procedure before the Commission, to put his own case and make his views known on the relevant circumstances, and where necessary, on the documents taken into account by the Community institution.[65]

In keeping with the Habermassian idea – that only the addressees of the law *themselves* can articulate how that norm is to be framed in light of its environmental context – the Court insisted that meeting basic information requirements also required a degree of interaction with the parties directly affected.

We can see here the links between different administrative protections. The need, in certain cases, to base decisions under new governance on relevant expertise may in this case provide a wider judicial rationalisation for broader participation in the very framing of OMC-like, and other new governance, methods, as well as for access to documents and other due process rights. It is to one of these rights in particular – to be given *reasons* for decisions – that we must now turn – to what extent has the Court not only demanded *ex ante* consideration of certain factors, but *ex post* explanations for its decisions?

[63] This, of course, is in keeping with Scott and Sturm's view of the Court's 'catalytic' function; that the Court should not simply create procedural 'hoops' to be jumped through but incentivise, through dialogue, the creation of accountability structures within the relevant political institutions themselves. See n. 45 above, at 582–587.

[64] Case C-269/90 *Technische Universität München* v. *Hauptzollampt München-Mitte* [1991] ECR I-05469.

[65] *Ibid*., at [24]–[25].

4.3 *Decision-making – the duty to give reasons*

Just as the courts have encouraged new governance institutions to base their decisions on a threshold of independent advice, so the Court has played a role in expanding its duty to give adequate justifications for those decisions. This heading of administrative law certainly carries a more secure legal basis than the interpretive games with which the Court pushed the incorporation of scientific advice. Whereas, in cases like *Angelopharm*, the duty to consult experts was said by the Court to be based 'on the nature of things and apart from any provision laid down to that effect', the duty to provide reasons for decisions has a more secure basis: ex. Article 253 of the EC Treaty, which demanded that Community legislation and decisions 'state the reasons on which they are based'.[66] From this quite categorical provision, the Court has gone even further, expanding reason-giving into a general principle of Community law. The reasons for its move are clear – reason-giving can be a vital tool for the courts insofar as it allows both individual legal actors to assess the likely success of a particular claim, and the Court itself to uncover the mechanisms that underlay decisions by the Community institutions. The Court laid out this dual reasoning in the *WWF* case, where it argued that the purpose of the principle was to:

> On the one hand, permit the interested parties to know the justification for the measure in order to enable them to protect their rights; and, on the other, to enable the Community judicature to exercise its power to review the legality of the decision.[67]

To what extent does this rationale apply to the OMC? While on the one hand, non-binding methods like the OMC SPSI are not intended to be policed by legal remedies, such a duty could still serve important uses. In an OMC context, the duty to give reasons (e.g. for country-specific recommendations under the EES, or indicators adopted under the OMC SPSI) may expose self-interested decision-making, or at least forces the European institutions to consider the relationship between proposed measures and a general community interest.

In a normative guise, this argument has been forwarded by Cass Sunstein – reasoned decision-making can uncover 'rent seeking' or

[66] *Angelopharm*, n. 58 above, at [33].

[67] Case T-105/95 *WWF UK* v. *Commission* [1997] ECR II-313 at [66]. See also (in establishing reason-giving as a general principle of Community law) Case C-76/01 P *Eurocoton and Others* v. *Council* [2003] I-0000.

factionalist behaviour, or the 'capture' of regulatory processes by the interests that they are trying to regulate (also a danger that applies in the new governance case).[68] Where self-serving policies are being pursued, they can more easily then be exposed by external observers (such as media, NGO or ordinary citizen participants).

Perhaps the application of judicial review can improve accountability in new governance, not by increasing its steering capacity, but instead through encouraging explanations and justifications (beyond mere references to the common norms and interests of a closed circle of administrative decision-makers). The 'catalytic court', even if it can and should not substitute its own judgement for that of the political actors of new governance itself, may at least provoke a process of dialogue and reflection able to make regulatory decisions more cognisant of a broader 'public' interest.

4.4 *Facilitating transparency through access to documents*

The contributions of the Court outlined above themselves depend on a final factor, which is the general transparency of new governance procedures, and access to the information on which their decisions are based. Some of the rationalisations that animate the judicial attempt to encourage institutional reason-giving also apply in advancing access to documents. While this access now has a legal basis both in EU legislation, and through the Treaty itself (even, e.g., through Article 1 TEU), these moves were themselves prompted by a Court seeking to make its task of supervising the Community institutions easier.

Without basic information on institutional decisions, or access to the documents that underlie them, how can an individual seek an effective legal remedy, or identify a breach of his or her rights? Furthermore, how can the Court itself assess the validity of such claims? Faced with these obstacles, the Court used early decisions to encourage the institutions to develop open practices. In the case of *Zwartveld*, for example, the Court forced the Commission to provide information to a magistrate conducting a fraud investigation in a particular member state (an early example of inter-institutional cooperation between national and European courts to advance freedom of information).[69]

[68] See C. Sunstein, 'Legal Interference with Private Preferences' (1986) 53 *University of Chicago Law Review*.
[69] Case C-2/88 *Zwartveld and Others* [1990] ECR I-3365.

There are though other political reasons for more open access to documents – reasons which apply forcefully in the case of OMC-like methods too. The decision by the Commission to draw up a code of conduct on access to information in 1993, and the insertion of general rights of access into the Amsterdam Treaty (through Article 255 EC), have to be understood in light of the legitimacy crises of the post-Maastricht period. As numerous poll findings testified, the EU was seen during the decade as an increasingly bureaucratic, paternalistic and secretive organisation (a realisation that eventually prompted the Laeken declaration, and the documentary constitutional project). As a result, all three of the institutions adopted, in 2001, provisions on access to Community documents (through Regulation 1049/2001/EC). While there remain (to be discussed in the next section), significant holes in its framework, the regulation potentially heralded in a new beginning, through stating, in Article 2(1), that 'any citizen of the Union, and any natural or legal person residing or having its registered office in a Member State, has a right of access to documents of the institutions'.

At the same time, the question of the regulation's effectiveness also relies on the 'exceptions' under which access could be restricted. This includes circumstances where release of documents would (Article 4(3)) 'seriously undermine the institution's decision-making process'. This exception seems particularly broad – left unchecked it could be used to block almost any inconvenient request. Almost all document requests are likely to involve some investment of time and effort on the part of the institution concerned; while more contentious requests could lead to the disclosure of information that could make decision-making more difficult (for example, by exposing internal dissensus within the Commission, or between member states).

At the same time, these exceptions have been read by the Court quite narrowly. In the case of *Carvel*, the Court urged that – even in circumstances where the Commission could be justified in invoking one of the exceptions contained in Article 4 – it must still carry out 'a balancing exercise . . . between the interests of the citizen in gaining access to its documents and the need for confidentiality in its proceedings'.[70] This

70 Case T-194/94 *Carvel and Guardian Newspapers Ltd* v. *Council* [1995] ECR II-2765 at [64]. For an almost identical piece of reasoning in relation to Council documents, see Case T-174/95 *Svenska Journalistforbundet* v. *Council* [1998] ECR II-2289 at [113].

balancing is suggested by the wording of the Regulation itself, which suggests that limitations on freedom of access can be outweighed by reasons of 'an overriding public interest in disclosure'. The Court's policing of transparency has thus not only enforced the requirements of the Regulation, but also attempted to prompt institutional practices where documents can and will be restricted only where compelling reasons for their refusal can be given.

The relevance of this provision to the OMC, and other new governance processes, is clear. Not only does the lack of transparency identified in the last chapter defy the categorisation of the OMC as an 'open' process; it potentially produces a structure of policy-making where gross miscalculations, self-serving decisions, or political manipulations of technical advice, go unheeded. The application of judicial review to OMC-like methods – in enforcing concrete rights of information and access – could serve as a basic precondition for holding its dominant actors in check.

5. Governing in law's shadow?

The development of a 'European administrative law' is surely one of the distinct achievements of the European legal order, one that it is in the habit of trumpeting.[71] Through enforcing requirements of transparency, openness and access to justice, the ECJ has gone some way towards making the European institutions accountable not just to each other, or to the national orders they attempt to regulate, but to the European public itself.[72] To shield the sphere of new governance from reaping the benefits of these achievements would surely only increase public suspicion of its activities. If it is good enough for ordinary European law – for the regulations and directives that have built the EU order – surely it is good enough for the fields in which OMC-like methods operate as well.

While one could argue that the application of judicial review would, as an influential earlier essay put it, involve 'squeezing new governance into law's existing categories', this argument should be viewed with

[71] One is not in short supply of examples. For a famous statement, see Advocate-General Tesuaro – 'the obligations of the Member States and of the Community institutions are directed above all . . . to the creation of rights for individuals'. Joined Cases C-46/93 & C-48/93 *Brasserie du Pecheur SA* v. *Germany; the Queen* v. *Secretary of State for Transport ex parte Factortame Ltd* [1996] ECR I-1029 at [39].

[72] C. Harlow, *Accountability in the European Union* (Oxford University Press, 2002) at 190.

some suspicion.[73] Surely we could introduce some level of judicial review without diluting, or 'juridifying' the other achievements of the new governance project, or the reasons that have called it into existence, namely the desire for flexibility and differentiation in the agreement and adoption of EU laws. While the existence of persistent welfare diversity, and rapid changes in social preferences and technologies, provide a good reason to be sceptical of the success of EU-wide *social* standards, it is questionable whether such diversity stands in the way of basic *procedural* rights.

Surely all European states can agree – or can at least find few acceptable reasons to disagree – with the idea that citizens affected by decisions under new governance have a right to a statement of reasons for decisions, or access to the basic documents through which those processes are governed? It seems feasible that limited forms of judicial review of new governance – under the four headings discussed above – could be designed without collapsing the whole project of open coordination in on itself, or undermining the conceptual justifications for its emergence. Instead, greater procedural rights may be a 'last best hope'; a necessary means of ensuring that limited participation and executive dominance do not fatally undermine the legitimacy and effectiveness of the OMC in the future. Scott and Sturm's imagery of the 'catalytic court' speaks to this desire: for a Court that is willing to take both the strengths and the limits of its role in encouraging forms of accountable and participatory decision-making seriously.

At the same time, there are reasons to suggest that a judicial strategy for governance reform – on its own – will do little to solve the deficits of opaqueness, executive dominance and functional bias outlined in the last section. In some sense they could reinforce them – not opening up new governance to new participants, but further retrenching the patterns of executive dominance, and even social subordination, countenanced in the fourth chapter.

The capacity of judicial review effectively to 'constitutionalise' new governance in fact relies on two important conditions. First of all, the idea that law can 'open up' the OMC relies upon a system of EU law that is itself an open medium. Is this the case, or are there barriers to access to judicial remedies such that the administrative procedures outlined above are effectively inaccessible? Alternatively, are there reasons to

[73] J. Scott and D. Trubek, 'Mind the Gap: Law and New Approaches to Governance in the European Union' (2002) 8 *European Law Journal* 1 at 18.

suppose that – while such remedies may be available in certain cases – when applied to the OMC, and other new governance processes – they are effectively closed off? As we shall see, both of these restrictions apply – the problems with judicial review of new governance do not lie solely in the attitude of the Court to its processes, nor in possible juridifying tendencies, but at a prior stage: in terms of access to justice (and standing before the Court) itself.

Secondly, the notion of broadening the OMC through legal interventions depends on the type of actors able to make use of judicial remedies. While part of our complaint against the OMC was that it is too often the preserve of a sectional public, focused on their self-interest, and lacking the will or legitimacy to address broader political questions, what if the very same conditions apply to those able to pursue judicial review? If this were the case, rather than improve the method's participative or deliberative shortcomings, judicial review could have the perverse effect of narrowing new governance processes further, or constraining their capacity to reach or represent new constituencies. Rather than – as the social participants demanded – 'broaden the Lisbon debate' – a more court-centric OMC could reorient the dialogue of new governance around a smaller set of economic actors (by placing, for example, strict parameters around who is, or is not, considered sufficiently 'representative' to engage in its processes). In the next sections, we will address these two assumptions in turn.

5.1 Standing and access to justice

As we saw in the last chapter, the problem of the gatekeeper is one of the key obstacles to the creation of a participatory OMC. In the last section of this chapter, participation rights were put forward as one possible solution to this problem. Laying down more clearly a procedural framework, enforced by the European courts, over who is entitled to participate in OMC procedures could potentially preserve flexibility in policy-making, while reinforcing procedural rights of access for disenfranchised participants.

The problem with this solution is that EU law has a gatekeeper problem of its own. Its infamous rules on standing have severely restricted the possibilities for individual or associational access to the European courts. At the same time, the presence of the OMC as a 'soft', flexible and multi-level instrument makes seeking judicial alternatives at the national level, extremely difficult. As a result, individual actors cut out of the insiders' club face a dilemma – those that have the greatest need to judicially challenge their exclusion are precisely those that have the least capacity to do so.

Complicated and expansive rules on standing to seek judicial review are not unique to the European courts, but apply across a wide swathe of jurisdictions. Their justifications are clear – restrictive rules on standing allow courts to avoid overly time-consuming or frivolous claims, and focus on cases of particular need, where contentious points of law are at stake (for example, where judgments by the European Court could have an important framing role on national courts). In many ways, such rules are even more justified in the European case – not only is the jurisdiction of the ECJ particularly wide (covering over 450 million inhabitants) but most claims can be brought and dealt with before national courts. As a result of these factors, the treaties place a high burden on applicants attempting to seek justice *á la europeéne*. As the treaties put it, while the EU institutions, and national governments, all have a privileged right of standing, this right applies to EU citizens only where a decision or act is of 'direct and individual concern' to them, or where a decision is of 'direct concern' provided that it falls within the narrowly defined category of 'regulatory acts' which do not require implementing measures.[74]

The problem with this test is less the wording of the Treaty than the Court's reading of it. Through the strict formula it set out in its *Plaumann* decision, the Court created one of the enduring contradictions of the EU legal order. On the one hand, judicial principles like supremacy and direct effect have been elaborated on the back of the need to provide individuals with realisable rights and forge a community of citizens. This judicial battle has not only driven the process of political integration but been recognised by the member states through the rights to a judicial remedy enshrined in both the EU Charter (discussed above) and Articles 6 and 13 of the ECHR.

On the other, the ECJ has perplexingly refused to follow the administrative law practice of national constitutional courts in liberalising

[74] Article 263 TFEU (ex. 230 EC). The exact meaning of the term 'regulatory act' remains unclear but may be clarified by the pending *Inuit* case before the ECJ (Case T-18/2010 R, *Inuit Tapiriit Kanatami and others*, Order of the President of 30 April 2010). On its face, however, one would question whether this slight liberalisation of standing rules through the Lisbon Treaty would have any bearing on the argument developed below – norms created under the OMC, e.g. Council guidelines and objectives, do not seem 'regulatory' in nature but are often of general application. Furthermore, they do require national implementation.

standing rules in order to take account of new constituencies. It has stuck doggedly to the interpretation of Article 263 set out in *Plaumann*, whereby to meet the 'direct and individual concern' test, the decision would have to affect the individual or group concerned 'by reason of certain attributes which are peculiar to them or by reason of circumstances in which they are differentiated from all other persons'.[75] In effect, by the wording of this formula, an individual has reason to raise judicial review only where the measure in question affects them in a way that clearly distinguishes that applicant from *all other* potential applicants – a prohibitively high hurdle. Not only must the decision concern the applicant directly, i.e. pass onto them a particular cost or burden which alters their legal position, but it must do so in a way which is specific to them, and does not apply also to a general class of people.

While the Court has been given several invitations to relax its standing rules, it has consistently turned them down. In a famous failed attempt to change the Court's mind, Advocate-General Jacobs argued, in the *UPA* case, for a more liberal test (based on whether or not the contested measure could have a 'substantial adverse effect' on individual interests). The Court argued instead that it was bound by the terms of the Treaty; as such, 'it is for the Member States, if necessary, in accordance with Article 48 EC, to reform the system currently in practice'.[76] Similarly, in its *Jégo Quèrè* decision, while the Court of First Instance cited both the provisions of the Charter and the ECHR in support of its proposition that a relaxation of standing rules was necessary to provide individuals with a direct legal remedy, the ECJ itself rejected this reasoning on appeal, claiming that it would render the notion of 'direct and individual concern' meaningless.[77] They again in the ruling placed the onus for reform not on their own backs, but on that of the member states – thereby conveniently ignoring that the strictures of Article 263 were not brought by the Treaty itself, but by the Court's *own* interpretation of its provisions. The dogmatism with which the Court has reiterated its *Plaumann* formula continues to place obstacles in the way of individuals seeking to challenge institutional malpractice through the EU courts.

[75] Case C-25/62 *Plaumann* v. *Commission* [1963] ECR 95 at [107].
[76] Case C-500/00 P, *Union de Pequenos Agricultores* v. *Council* [2002] ECR 6677 at [45].
[77] Case T-177/01 *Jégo Quèrè et Cie SA* v. *Commission* [2002] ECR II-2365 at [38].

At the same time, the opportunities for affected groups to seek remedies through *national* courts (the ECJ's preferred alternative) are also limited. First of all, in order to raise such an action, an individual would have to intentionally violate an EU rule (perversely, seeking justice would then require a hopeful act of law-breaking). Secondly, they would have to rely on the discretionary judgment of national courts to use the preliminary reference procedure (with the national court itself framing the relevant questions for which the ECJ is to be consulted). In effect, the national route to enforcement is no less restrictive (a problem which the 'soft' nature of national efforts to incorporate OMC recommendations or objectives will only add to).

The effect of the Court's standing rules are particularly problematic in the OMC case given that the parties most often claiming access to the process are not individuals but associations or non-governmental interest groups. The very phrasing of *Plaumann*, i.e. that the greater number of persons affected by such a measure, the less likely standing is available to *any one of them*, makes it particularly difficult for such groups to make a case for adequate standing. Other cases suggest that such groups are likely to be considered only where closely involved in the procedures leading up to the decision (thus doing little for organisations who have been explicitly *excluded* from that process).[78]

A good example of this dilemma is the *Greenpeace* case, which involved the question of standing for several environmental groups (including Greenpeace, as well as local residents) to challenge a Commission decision to provide financial assistance for the construction of two power plants in the Canary Islands (a decision that was reached without carrying out an independent environmental impact assessment).[79] Predictably, the Court found that the parties involved were not 'individually affected' by the measure, but instead had an interest that could not be individuated from any other resident or claimant. Ironically, the more pressing the claim, or the more it affects a broad swathe of the population, the less the rights in question are justicable.

The problem faced here in the case of environmental law applies with equal force to the areas in which methods like the OMC operate. By their very nature, problems of unemployment and social exclusion are diffuse problems – they are likely not to affect one person individually, but a wide range of individuals with a mutual and common interest for or

[78] See e.g. Case C-313/90 *CIRF* v. *Commission* [1993] ECR I-1125.

[79] Case C-321/95 P, *Stichtung Greenpeace Council* v. *Commission* [1998] ECR I-1651.

against particular decisions. The most vocal participants in processes like the OMC SPSIs, and the most successful in monitoring national efforts to meet OMC obligations have been social NGOs rather than 'directly affected' individual participants. In such cases, the lack of 'group' or 'associational' grounds of standing not only excludes these groups, but potentially leaves *all* applicants without an effective remedy.

By contrast, the courts have been much more willing to afford standing in cases where a direct and individual cost can be attributed to a decision.[80] In cases involving matters such as state aid, other competition decisions, and the provision of structural funds, standing rules have been relaxed significantly on the basis that a direct financial interest is at stake. The beneficiaries of these rules have predictably been corporations, who have used EU remedies to either challenge competitors, or limit political intervention in their financial holdings.

While the problems of executivism within the OMC, and the future direction of European social policy under the Lisbon strategy, are no less pressing, the complainants are quite different – they generally object to process decisions not on the basis of an individual interest (a violation of one's property or other rights), but through recourse to a general interest, and furthermore, on behalf of others – in many cases those excluded persons for whom the ECJ might as well sit in another universe. To this extent, judicial review, rather than open up the doors of OMC procedures, may only place new barriers in the way of a properly participatory process. The beneficiaries of judicial review – as the next section will explore – may not be the genuinely excluded, but a narrow caste of sectional, and already privileged, interests.

5.2 *Standing and political participation*

Often rules on standing have been crystallised into a particular view of participation rights in new governance processes themselves. Not only then does the Court's jurisprudence in this area have a bearing on who can seek judicial remedies, but it also inflects how the Court sees legitimate participation in other processes, including in the field of new governance. This refers to the second assumption of the 'catalytic

[80] For two general discussions, see D. Chalmers *et al*, *European Union Law: Texts and Materials* (Cambridge University Press, 2010) at 418–427; J. Corkin, *A Manifesto for the European Court: Democracy, De-centred Governance and the Process-Perfecting Judicial Shadow* (EUI Thesis, 2006) at 377–382.

court' – Scott and Sturm's thesis not only turns on the question of who can seek access to justice, but on how the Court views questions of participation and access in non-judicial processes.

Unfortunately, the Court's rules on standing have often formed into a restrictive view of 'participation' and rights to access and voice in a more general sense. To capture this ambivalence, we would do well to return to the *UEAPME* case. While the Court does indeed recognise through the case, a right on the part of employer organisations to participate in the social dialogue, it argued that this right did not extend to all organisations.[81] The Court particularly relied on the exclusion of the European Parliament as necessitating a 'representativity' test among the social partner organisations now taking its legislative place. As such:

> The parties to the agreement can only be regarded as representing the people if they possess between themselves sufficient cumulative representativity, hence the duty of the Commission and Council to ensure the representativity of the social partners.

The Court's ruling was that – to meet the test of a representative democracy – the social partners would need to be properly representative of the constituencies they served.

There are though distinct problems with equating the Social Dialogue with a representative model of democratic law-making. Notwithstanding the fact that collective bargaining at the national level fulfils a quite different function than that of being a 'surrogate' for national parliaments, the Court, in assessing, whether the social partner concerned was sufficiently representative, applied a strict test.[82] The Court deferred to the Commission's own advice in its 1993 Communication 'Concerning the Implementation of the Protocol on Social Policy'.[83] This required the social partners involved to meet three overarching criteria: firstly, comprehensive organisation at the EU level, secondly, to be sufficiently integrated at the national level to negotiate agreements representative of *all* EU member states, and thirdly, to have adequate structures and resources effectively to participate in the process.[84]

[81] See *UEAPME*, n. 51 above, at [72]–[80].

[82] On the former criticism, see N. Bernard, 'Legitimising EU Law: Is the Social Dialogue the Way Forward? Some Reflections around the UEAPME case' in J. Shaw (ed.), *Social Law and Policy in an Evolving European Union* (Oxford: Hart, 2000).

[83] COM (93) 600 final. [84] *Ibid.*, at [24].

It is difficult, however, to see how any participants – beyond a highly selective group of organisations – could meet this test. While these criteria were put in place in order to maximise the effectiveness and universality of any eventual agreement, the requirement that the body concerned carries an organisational capacity in each and every member state seems, in a Union of twenty-seven, to be an impossibly high hurdle.

Ironically, these tests seem to preclude precisely the 'bottom-up' organisations originating in the domestic context that the OMC's experimentalist proponents argue is the mark of the OMC's very innovation. The demand for a pan-European presence also conveniently excludes both those organisations at the national level who may be sceptical of a pan-European anti-poverty or employment strategy, or those who may have been cut out of the game of seeking transnational funding under the Commission's Community Action Programme. To this extent, judicial review, rather than undercut the cosy relationship between Commission DGs, and select European NGOs and social partners that was outlined in the last chapter, may reinforce that bond, either through making the 'entry' of other participants impossible, or through legitimising what was once a bare exclusion of inconvenient parties as a necessary means of 'safeguarding the representativity of the process'. In truth, full representativity – in the sense of taking *critical*, as well as supportive, voices on board – may be better served by removing such requirements altogether.

Other due process rights listed in the last section may fare no better in this respect. A good example is EU rules on access to documents. It would seem that access to documents could be a first starting point in creating a more honest and open relationship between the executive and non-executive actors within the OMC. It could serve an important accountability function in the sense that it could allow gross errors of judgement, or nepotistic decision-making to be exposed, or at least ensure that such decisions were made under the knowledge that such exposure *could* occur (the idea of 'governing in law's shadow').

There are, however, two distinct problems with this use of access rules. First of all, who is applying for documents? It is clear that, rather than be oriented towards greater involvement in the political process, claims for documents are often animated by a narrower and more selfish interest – to allow the applicant, most often a corporate or individual economic actor, more easily to seek a judicial remedy or advance their case against the European institutions (for example, in circumstances where the Commission has taken a company to court for anti-competitive practices). As the Commission notes in its 2008 report (covering the course of requests in 2007):

> As in past years, the overall picture that emerges from analysis of access applications is that a large proportion of them relate to Commission monitoring of the application of Community law. In a very large number of cases access was applied for in order to obtain documents likely to support the applicant's position in a complaint concerning, for example, an alleged infringement of Community law or an administrative or judicial action.[85]

This is confirmed if one examines the relevant statistics. In 2008, individual members of the public account for just 17 per cent of all requests. Journalists account for less than 3 per cent. At the same time, interest groups, corporations, lawyers and academics together make up just under 60 per cent of all requests.[86] While one would like to think that a band of lonely PhD researchers could act as an effective check on new governance activities, these numbers suggest that many, if not most, information requests are used by a public more keen on safeguarding their finances, advancing their interests, or publishing their theses than holding actors like the representatives of the SPC in check.[87]

Secondly, the EU's document regime contains a number of exceptions in which decisions by the institutions to refuse requests for documents are not only discretionary but *mandatory*. The most important for our purposes may be the exception contained in Article 4(5) of Regulation 1049/2001, which concerns access to national documents. The article states that 'a Member State may request the institution not to disclose a document originating from that Member State without its prior agreement'. While this seems innocuous enough, both the institutions and the Court have read the provision as going beyond a mere notification requirement.

[85] Commission Staff Document, 'On the application in 2007 of Regulation EC No. 1049/2001 Concerning Access to Community Documents', COM (2008) 630 final, at 6–7.

[86] Report from the Commission, 'On the application in 2008 of Regulation EC No. 1049/2001 Concerning Access to Community Documents', COM (2009) 331 final, at 13.

[87] There is one other notable element that gives cause to be pessimistic in the OMC case – the lack of requests in the substantive areas in which the OMC operates. In 2007, access requests to the DG Social Affairs represented only 3.7 per cent of all requests (with the competition, customs and internal market DG's representing a far higher total – 25 per cent combined). *Ibid.*, at 16.

In the case of *IFAW* v. *Commission*, the Court argued that the intention of the Regulation was to leave more or less untouched national freedom of information rules. This left the member states in a 'special position', whereby they held an effective veto over any Commission decision to release documents emerging from the domestic context. In keeping with this, the Court argued that:

> The Member State is under no obligation to state the reasons for any request made by it under Article 4(5) and, once it has made a request, it is no longer a matter for the institution to examine whether non-disclosure of the document is justified in, for example, the public interest.[88]

If the purpose of judicial review under new governance is to prompt an inter-institutional and public dialogue over violations of basic rights of due process, it is clear that such rationalisations – that even a statement of reasons to refuse a document is unnecessary – leave this dialogue effectively shut down. This limitation may be particularly significant in the OMC context – given its differentiation between different levels of governance, many of the most important documents – e.g. information on the decisions and outcomes of country peer reviews – originate in the national context (yet are still used to prompt EU-level recommendations and discussions). The member state exception remains a significant further barrier to a more transparent OMC procedure.

While these cases may provoke pessimism, there may still be some light at the end of tunnel to resuscitate this particular part of the 'catalytic' thesis. In a recent case, the Court of First Instance has argued that 'Article 4(5) of Regulation 1049/2001 cannot be interpreted as conferring on the Member States a general and unconditional right of veto'.[89] Instead, the Court stated that, where a member state refuses to disclose a particular document, it is 'obliged to state reasons for that objection' (a duty which the Court argued applied to the EU institutions too).[90] As a result of this decision, an amendment to the Regulation, proposed in 2008, suggests including a reason-giving requirement in Article 4(5).[91] Such a change – while both limited, and dependent on

88 Case T-168/02 *IFAW* v. *Commission* [2004] ECR II-1435 at [59].

89 Case C-64/05 P, *Sweden v Commission* [2007] ECR I-11389 at [61]. 90 *Ibid.*, at [85].

91 See Commission Proposal 'For a Regulation of the European Parliament and the Council regarding public access to European Parliament, Council and Commission Documents' COM (2008) 229 final.

national approval that has not yet been forthcoming – could go some way to limiting the use of exceptions to justify a wholesale exclusion of OMC, and other Commission document, requests.

These and other limitations, however, demand a re-evaluation of the notion that EU administrative law could easily remedy the challenges of accountability, opacity and arbitrary power described in the last chapter. While – on paper – the Court's arsenal to demand explanations and information from new governance officials is strong, its own barriers to access, and its myopic misreading of participation under new governance processes themselves may render many of EU law's most important remedies either meaningless, or available only to a select and privileged group.

6. Politicisation and 'republican' constitutionalism

Many of the legal remedies outlined in the first part of this chapter have spoken to liberal uses of constitutionalism. The liberal view is of a European polity that not only forms a collection of state interests, but is used to serve the interests and autonomy of individual citizens.[92] This liberal view points towards a particular understanding of law's social and constitutional functions – to limit manifestations of state power that go beyond the authority the legislature has been invested with, or that infringe upon individual rights. Most European constitutional frameworks (written or otherwise) in this way lay out the rights and responsibilities of the state's principal political actors, including express areas in which state authority runs out (or is subject to more severe procedural boundaries).

Liberalism is, however, one among many constitutional traditions in the EU. As Fritz Scharpf has observed, European thought has been equally influenced by a second republican tradition.[93] This vision rejects the view of the individual as somehow 'prior' to society. This view of the 'unencumbered self' is particularly lacking in its failure to explain the significant linguistic and cultural contexts *through which*

[92] This is indeed the Hayekian justification of the European project – that a community of private economic individuals can limit the use of state authority to infringe basic economic rights. For an elaboration of this view (and opposing corporatist visions) see G. Morgan, *The Idea of a European Super-state: Public Justification and European Integration* (Princeton University Press, 2005) at 70–88.

[93] F. Scharpf, 'Legitimacy in the Multi-level European Polity' (2009) 1 *European Political Science Review* 2 at 2–3.

individual identity is formed.[94] Society is made up of more than a collection of individuals, but is a political community itself; as such, it recursively imbues individuals with a particular understanding of their own personhood.

This view of the self leads republicans towards a different vision of law's social role. Constitutional law is seen as more than an attempt to limit state power in the name of a sectional interest; but also as a means of seeking collective self-determination *through law*. The Constitution provides not just individual remedies, but the necessary links between the exercise of public power, and processes of collective will formation, to ensure that law can both reflect and advance a common or collective interest.

These dual visions carry their own distinct critiques of the new governance project. The liberal complaint against OMC-like methods was the object of most of the legal and administrative remedies outlined in the last section. By this view, the OMC, as much as it has been marketed as an 'open' coordination process (or a 'deliberative polyarchy') has too often been used not to disperse power, but override constitutional protections that would otherwise limit executive dominance, or protect individual rights. By this liberal view, the function of the OMC's 'constitutionalisation' would be to reassert individual rights of due process – basic entitlements to voice, access and information – that have been dangerously subverted (as outlined in section 4 of this chapter).

Many of the OMC's participants, do not, however, see the method's failings in these terms. Instead, they voice their complaints in what might be termed republican political language. When voicing, for example, complaints about the 'managerial' and 'functionally biased' nature of the OMC SPSI's indicators, or the 'unjustifiable' exclusion of national and European parliaments, participants do not conceptualise their exclusion in terms of individual rights, but in terms of the goals and constituencies that the OMC SPSI is meant to advance.[95] Their dominant objection is that, under a 'closed' OMC procedure, the use of law to connect public power to the general goals and interests of Europe's citizens is being undermined.

[94] See M. Sandel, 'The Procedural Republic and the Unencumbered Self' in G. W. Smith (ed.), *Liberalism: Critical Concepts in Political Theory* (London: Routledge, 2002).

[95] For the first objection, see Chapter 4, section 5.3 ('the colonisation thesis re-visited'); for the second, see section 4.4 ('excluded groups: parliament').

The republican objection focuses upon two complaints in particular. The first can be explained through the work of an important practitioner and theorist of administrative law, Carol Harlow. Throughout her academic career, Harlow has been interested in the concept of accountability.[96] In the EU, however, she sees a perversion of some of its most important aspects.[97] While the obligation of the Commission to act as a relatively depoliticised servant of the 'general Community interest' has obliged it to seek accountability in abstract notions of administrative efficiency and 'good governance', the intergovernmental nature of the Council has created a scenario where administrations are accountable largely to each other, rather than to the public mandates on which they are elected. While we see administrative and technical forms of accountability in abundance – a feast that experimental approaches to governance feed upon – *political accountability* is distinctly lacking.

While the OMC contains numerous opportunities for sectional actors to advance the causes of the particular functional constituency they serve, this process, rather than serve the input of 'general' electoral bodies, is seen as a replacement for it.[98] It is difficult, however, to see what could possibly justify such an exclusion. If the indicators and objectives of the OMC really carry a 'framing' role in the orientation of national and EU-level policy – and the political disagreements within bodies like the SPC suggest that they do – the body responsible for providing democratic and popular input into EU law – the European Parliament – ought to have a say in their formulation. Only such general bodies, as section 7 will argue, can both save the method from descending into a 'mini-politics' of petty factionalism, and carry the legitimacy to say where the necessary boundaries between socially protective and competitiveness enhancing policies should lie.

The second objection concerns the *managerialism* of OMC processes.[99] The metrics of the OMC not only encourage 'smaller' political discussions but often have the effect of presenting as 'technical' or beyond the reach of political enquiry, questions that may be both vital for the future orientation of social policy in the EU, and the source of

[96] C. Harlow and R. Rawlings, *Law and Administration* (London: Butterworths, 1997).

[97] C. Harlow, *Accountability in the European Union* (Oxford University Press, 2002) at 178–189.

[98] *Ibid.*, at 190.

[99] See also, M. Dawson, 'Transforming into What? New Governance and the "Managerial Sensibility" in Modern Law' (2010) *Wisconsin Law Review* 2.

significant political disagreement.[100] In the case of new governance, this danger is manifest. The real failures – outlined in the last chapter – to use the OMC to encourage functional 'reflexivity' or a balanced synergy between the OMC's social and economic dimension – indicate all the more why the procedural rules and indicators new governance processes offer must not be taken for granted but instead be subjected to robust empirical analysis and political scrutiny. There is a real possibility that the OMC could slip further into a 'managerial' mindset – one where its rules are not seen as deriving from popular experience and input, but better left to the benevolent guiding hand of functional 'experts', and other networks of mutual interest.[101]

A republican vision of 'constitutionalising' the OMC must also speak to these concerns. Rather than see the question of indicators and recommendations under the OMC, or the content of national reports, as merely 'administrative', or leave their fate to an abstract series of limited judicial remedies, it would focus on opportunities to *politicise* the method, or to reinsert links between new governance and processes of popular will formation and scrutiny that have gone dangerously astray.

In the final sections of this chapter, we will turn to two further possible proposals to achieve this task: firstly, the development of non-judicial remedies through the European ombudsman; and secondly, the use of social impact assessment to encourage forms of functional reflexivity able to rebalance relationships between fiscal and social coordination that have too often been one-sided. While these remedies contain deficits of their own, together they may constitute a vital first step in politicising, or exposing to public forms of scrutiny, a method too easily dominated by a sectional and privileged set of voices.

7. Reintegrating parliaments: governance under the shadow of politics

Both the most vital, and the most obvious, step in any politicisation of OMC procedures is surely the reintegration of Europe's general political institutions – national and European parliaments. This reintegration would have as its target both the lack of political accountability

[100] See Chapter 4, section 6.3.

[101] M. Koskenniemi, 'International Law: Constitutionalism, Managerialism and the Ethos of Legal Education' (2007) 1 *Journal of European Legal Studies* 1.

inherent in the 'insider's club' of agreeing the OMC's indicators, and the need for a broader legitimisation of EU activity in areas of social and employment policy that invoke the very future of the European welfare state.

The need for parliamentary inclusion – as the last chapter has noted – is no mere academic demand; but supported by a broad swathe of the method's most important participants.[102] Notably it is demanded by the European Parliament itself. Just as the Parliament's institutional power has grown, so have the ferocity of its demands for greater involvement in soft law procedures. In 2003 the Parliament was relatively circumspect, recognising that the OMC is 'not intended to replace legislative work' and even that 'Parliament's role is considerably constrained by the time limits attached to the procedure'.[103]

In this sense, the Parliament began with an ambiguous relationship to the method. While, on the one hand, it called on the Commission and Council to 'take greater account of Parliament's observations when establishing guidelines', on the other, it accepted the 'external' thesis outlined in Chapter 2 – namely, that the OMC was sufficiently 'soft' and 'marginal' to warrant limited parliamentary oversight of its activities.[104] The EP allowed the OMC to expand into new areas in its early life without viewing this as a usurpation of its hard-won prerogative to act as the co-legislator of an increasing number of Community rules.

By 2007, that view had considerably changed.[105] In signalling its opposition to the OMC's expansion, it is clear that the Parliament now sees the OMC as a serious institutional threat. In its most recent resolution on soft law, the Parliament has insisted that legally:

> The use of soft law is liable to circumvent the properly competent legislative bodies, may flout the principles of democracy and the rule of law under Article 6 of the EU Treaty, and also those of subsidiarity and proportionality.[106]

At the same time, politically:

[102] See Chapter 4, section 4.4.

[103] European Parliament Resolution on 'Analysis of the Open Coordination Procedure in the field of Employment and Social Affairs and Future Prospects', 2002/2233 (INI), Points C and I.

[104] *Ibid.*, at 7.

[105] Resolution of the European Parliament 'On Institutional and Legal Implications of the Use of Soft Law Instruments', 2007/2028 (INI).

[106] *Ibid.*, at Point X.

> Soft law tends to create a public perception of a 'super-bureaucracy' without democratic legitimacy, not just remote from citizens, but actually hostile to them, and willing to reach accommodations with powerful lobbies which are neither transparent, nor comprehensible to citizens.[107]

On the one hand, the OMC is deemed a direct contravention of the European order's most basic constitutional principles. On the other, its expansion is deemed 'bad political business', entrenching ever further the idea of the EU as a distant and opaque political regulator. What was once an accommodation between the Parliament, Commission and Council over the method's structure has threatened to descend into institutional warfare.

According to the Parliament, there can only be one answer. Either soft law should be increasingly circumscribed in its use, or the Commission must be called upon to 'discuss with the Parliament how it may be consulted before the Commission adopts soft law instruments, in order to enable proposed soft law measures to be scrutinised and to avoid any misuse of power on the part of the executive'.[108] This seems a reasonable request; a call for an olive branch (or 'inter-institutional agreement') whereby proposals for minimal oversight of the Committees and recommendations of the OMC would be hammered out.

In spite of this call for a cessation of hostilities, however, the Commission has continued to stick to its guns. In its response to the EP resolution, the Commission has argued that 'operators and citizens have generally recognised and appreciated the benefits in terms of speed and flexibility that such [soft law] instruments may have'. As such, the idea of greater parliamentary involvement via an institutional agreement is unnecessary:

> Under an OMC, the Community's institutional character and Treaty-based decision procedures do not apply, and it is therefore not possible to have the corresponding institutional guarantees. By contrast, whenever action is undertaken according to Treaty competencies, normal procedures apply and guarantee that the European Parliament can play its proper role.[109]

In such reasoning, the Commission relies on the 'external thesis' to completely bypass the Parliament's main objection, namely that the

[107] *Ibid.*, at Point Y. [108] *Ibid.*, at 17.
[109] See the Commission's response at www.europarl.europa.eu/oeil/DownloadSP.do?id=13809&num_rep=6798&language=en at 2.

externality of the OMC to the constitutional guarantees and architecture of the Treaty is *precisely the problem*, rather than a reason for the Parliament to remain unruffled by new governance's continued advance.

What lies behind the Commission's intransigence? It is notable that legal academia has not only censured this idea – of the 'speed' of new governance demanding parliamentary exclusion – but provided justifications for it. These can be explored through another debate involving the 'parliamentarisation' of new governance procedures – the debate over the role of the EP within the Community's comitology system.

This debate emerges from a paradox of the EU's development in the late 1990s. While on the one hand, the European Parliament was gaining in legislative power, particularly through the development and expansion of co-decision, on the other, the Parliament found itself consistently blocked, particularly by the Council, from gaining oversight over the comitological committees, who had responsibility for elaborating and specifying the rules which it has co-agreed.

This was often justified on the basis that its general form of oversight was unsuitable for the technical, self-elaborating tasks that such committees were entrusted with performing.[110] There is a clear link here to the justification offered by the Commission in the case of the OMC – that there is a basic mismatch between the detailed, deliberative or iterative nature of comitology, and indeed the OMC itself, and the broad focus and expertise of the Union legislature.

Parliament, however, continued to reject such reasons. They are worth serious analysis. The first justification for parliamentary exclusion was often that the issues raised under such committees ought to remain relatively depoliticised. This would fit with a conception of the EU famously offered by Majone – namely that the EU, as a 'regulatory state', has been given power in certain areas precisely to isolate them from short-term political manipulation.[111] Subjecting topics such as risk regulation, or financial services, to the oversight of an elected parliament would turn this reasoning on its head. Better instead that decisions over the regulation of scientific risk, or indeed over the indicators needed to measure social deprivation, be left to administrative

[110] For a classic account of this battle, see K. S. C Bradley, 'The European Parliament and Comitology: On the Road to Nowhere?' (1997) 3 *European Law Journal* 3.

[111] G. Majone, 'The Rise of the Regulatory State in Europe' (1994) 17 *West European Politics* 3; Majone, *Dilemmas of European Integration: The Ambiguities and Pitfalls of Integration by Stealth* (Oxford University Press, 2005) at 23–41.

committees, rather than subject to the whims of elected officials (who often have only their own short-term political interests in mind).

A second justification concerns the idea that Committees deal with technical and scientific information; which requires 'specialist' rather than general knowledge.[112] If this is so, not only would parliamentary representatives be lost in a sea of technical discussion (thus making their input meaningless), but they could also potentially prejudice discussions based not on political affiliation but a pragmatic problem-solving mentality (one where an ethic of sound scientific reasoning prevails).[113] In both of these cases, parliamentary oversight in the name of safeguarding the popular interest could expose delicate regulatory decisions to a political and short-termist logic to which they are quite unsuited. Both arguments were instrumentalised by the Council to justify Parliament's exclusion.

Both, however, were also rejected. As the EP made clear, it was impossible to square the creation of a co-decision procedure with an implementing structure which could lead to its decisions being effectively overturned.[114] Even worse, it was not even clear how many such Committees there were, or how their decisions were made. We see a repeat again of the dual political and legal objections given in the OMC case – on the one hand, the development of comitology seemed to run counter to the new institutional reality of the Parliament as a co-legislator; on the other, it reinforced the idea that the Union was both an opaque and a technocratic political structure.

As Parliament's objections became more vehement (not just rhetorically, but through threats to cut off the Commission's funding), so the Council and Commission responded.[115] The Parliament first gained some influence over the Committees by virtue of the 1999 comitology

[112] R. Dehousse, 'Comitology: Who Watches the Watchmen?' (2003) 10 *Journal of European Public Policy* 5 at 804.

[113] On the presence of deliberative or problem-solving, rather than strategic mentalities in such committees, see C. Joerges and J. Neyer, 'From Inter-Governmental Bargaining to Deliberative Political Processes: The Constitutionalisation of Comitology' (1997) 3 *European Law Journal* 3.

[114] It is notable that, since the inception of the contemporary co-decision procedure at Nice, *all* instances in which the EP has vetoed legislation agreed by the Council have occurred as a consequence of disagreements over the choice of implementing committee (and thus level of parliamentary oversight). See, on this, D. Corona, *Inter-state Bargaining in the Co-decision Procedure: State Interests and Political Dynamics in EC Decision-making*, PhD thesis (European University Institute, 2009).

[115] In practice, the Parliament forced the Council's hand through escalating financial, legal and political penalties. For a summary, see Bradley, n. 110 above, at 231–250.

decision.[116] The decision established rights of information for the Parliament on the agendas, meetings and voting records of comitology committees.[117] It also allowed the EP to adopt a resolution stating that, in its opinion, a committee's action over-reached its implementing powers. At the same time, the decision hardly matched the promise of its preamble – while the Commission was obliged to respond to such a parliamentary resolution, it did not have to in any way take account of, or follow, it.[118]

As a result of this limitation, comitology's relationship to the Parliament was further reformed in 2006.[119] The 2006 comitology decision goes further than ever before, creating a 'regulatory procedure with scrutiny' in which the supervisory powers of the EP are not voluntary, but binding.[120] Its scope, however, is limited. The Parliament may supervise the Commission's exercise of implementing powers only where the Commission is implementing acts agreed under the co-decision procedure, and where the implementing powers concern the addition or deletion of 'essential elements' of the basic legislative act. Where these conditions apply, Parliament may oppose the adoption of secondary legislation where it 'exceeds the implementing powers contained in the basic instrument' or where it is deemed contrary to principles of proportionality or subsidiarity, or the act's 'main aim and content'.[121]

These proposals illustrate an important compromise. As part of the measures, Parliament is given three months to notify its opposition. At the same time, under Article 5(a), the time limits may be cut significantly (with the Court and Parliament able to verify the veracity of the Commission's reasons *ex post*) where 'there are imperative grounds of urgency' to adopt a measure, i.e. where rapid changes in regulatory needs demand a quick decision.[122] This illustrates an important willingness to find a balance between the needs of new governance and traditional concerns over democratic input (one that is certainly

[116] Council Decision 468/1999/EC of 28 June 1999 'Laying Down the Procedures for the Exercise of Implementing Powers Conferred on the Commission'.

[117] *Ibid.*, Preamble, Point 10.

[118] On the limitations of the 1999 Decision, and the debate leading up to its recent revision, see K. S. C. Bradley, 'Halfway House: The 2006 Comitology Reforms and the European Parliament' (2008) 31 *West European Politics* 4.

[119] Council Decision 512/2006/EC of 17 July 2006 'Amending Decision 1999/468/EC' [2006] O.J. L. 200.

[120] *Ibid.*, Art. 5a. [121] *Ibid.*, Art. 5a, s. 4(e). [122] *Ibid.*, Art. 5a, ss. 5–6.

instructive for the OMC case). While Parliament is sensitive to concerns that processes like comitology could be 'juridified' or deprived of their basic logic, it is equally keen not to allow its claims of rapid change and revision to dilute requirements of democratic input.

The debate over the 'parliamentarisation' of comitology provides important lessons for the OMC. Certainly, the method's proponents have relied on similar justifications as those offered by the Commission to justify Parliament's continued exclusion. As Jonathan Zeitlin has argued in the OMC case, Parliament cannot be a 'panacea' for the OMC's ills – instead it is likely to stand in the way of a central insight of the new governance project – that if we are to achieve accountability in new governance, we must do so 'without sovereignty', or without the assurances of a unified popular legislator that the catch-all involvement of the European Parliament offers.[123]

> National Parliaments (and the European Parliament itself) could valuably participate in framing and debating OMC objectives and procedures, monitoring progress towards agreed goals, and reviewing the process in light of the goals achieved. But this would involve a transformation of the conventional conception of Parliaments' role in democratic polities as authoritative principals, delegating detailed implementation of legislation to administrative agents, whose behaviour they seek to control.[124]

The only proper role for Parliament, by this experimental view, is one where democratic legislatures are able to fit the logic of new governance itself – to keep up with the constant and technical elaboration of rules in different national and functional contexts that the OMC embodies. Certainly this is not a role that we could ascribe to the modern EP (or to many parliaments in the domestic context).

It is questionable, however, whether either of the conditions laid out above really apply to the OMC case. As has long been observed, comitology committees, while they deal with issues that are often overtly technical, also invoke sensitive cultural and normative issues.[125] An important example concerns the BSE cases which were discussed in section 4.2. While the issue of permitting or barring certain types of

[123] C. Sabel and W. Simon, 'Epilogue: Accountability Without Sovereignty' in G. de Búrca and J. Scott (eds.), *Law and New Governance in the EU and US* (Oxford: Hart, 2006).

[124] J. Zeitlin, 'The Open Method of Coordination in Action: Theoretical Promise, Empirical Realities, Reform Strategy' in J. Zeitlin and P. Pochet (eds.), *The Open Method of Co-ordination in Action: The European Employment and Social Inclusion Strategies* (Bern: Peter Lang, 2005) at 488.

[125] See Joerges and Neyer, n. 113 above.

animal feed seems a question that would bore most, and therefore should be informed primarily by scientific risk assessment alone, the threshold of acceptable risk is a *political* question. Definitions of what constitutes acceptable and unacceptable levels are likely to vary between different national political cultures (and even within any one society).

With the OMC operating not in areas of scientific risk assessment – where one can appeal to a certain level of technical objectivity – but in social and employment policy, the Majone objection seems even more difficult to sustain (indeed, in the present economic climate, even the notion that *financial* markets should remain 'depoliticised' seems oddly quaint). How can one maintain in all seriousness that decisions over what constitutes an acceptable poverty line are best 'depoliticised', or insulated from electoral input? Instead, such questions are precisely the stuff of which electoral politics is made. If the boundaries of the national welfare state are now merely 'regulatory decisions', what areas are now left open for democratic input? It is clear that the decisions taken by the Committees and executives of the OMC – while they are informed by technical opinion – cannot be justified with reference to criteria of 'efficiency' or 'sound policy' alone. Instead, they require some level of political deliberation (of the kind legislative assemblies provide on a daily basis) if they are to be deemed legitimate.

It is for similar reasons that the second objection to parliamentary exclusion does not hold. Indeed Parliament does not have special 'expertise' on social issues (although the European Parliament, as well as most national assemblies, carries a Social Affairs Committee with overlapping expertise to the ad hoc national representatives who make up bodies like the SPC). One wonders, however, whether 'specialist' expertise is really what processes like the OMC SPSI require, or at the very least, why a 'technical' discourse over indicators cannot be overlain by the generalist discourse, and appeal to a common public interest, that a body like the European Parliament offers.[126]

[126] A commensurable argument is given by Myrto Tsakatika – 'insofar as the governing agent taken as a whole is accountable to the representatives of the demos for all policy areas and the linkages between them, all matters with a public dimension, including omissions and even planning for the future are included. The consequence of such comprehensiveness is that it requires trade-offs between values to be negotiated publicly, allowing citizens to make up their minds about which among these trade-offs are acceptable. They can and do hold the government accountable for the acceptability of the trade-offs rather than for the minutiae of policies.' M. Tsakatika, 'A Parliamentary Dimension for EU Soft Governance' (2007) 29 *Journal of European Integration* 5 at 557.

This concern is heightened when we consider the policy debates in which the current OMC is immersed. The issues surrounding the relationship between the productivist view of social policy inspired by the Lisbon strategy and the emphasis on social cohesion of the method's 'social voices' suggest forcefully that the functional orientation of the OMC cannot be determined by recourse to 'science' or any other neutral or procedural discourse, but invoke a debate over the ends and place of European social policy itself. The OMC – just as it may have the capacity to encourage political debate – could also lead to what has been described in this thesis as 'colonisation': the slow diffusion of an economic discourse neither universally accepted by the European public, nor subject to broad political deliberation.

The best way to guard against this diffusion may be not to invoke the social rights of the Charter, nor to improve the OMC's level of formal bindingness, but instead to expose it to general scrutiny – for the recommendations, objectives and indicators of the OMC to be subject to the kinds of political discussion (from both opponents and *defenders* of the present course of the Lisbon strategy) that can be offered in a general legislative assembly. Any legitimate reform of the OMC must therefore involve supplying it with a more robust parliamentary presence; one able both to better scrutinise the actions of executives under its procedures, and to provide limited, but necessary, channels of political input into a discourse that too often *hides* politics.

How could this presence be secured? Again, the comitology example provides some guiding answers. As we have seen, the 2006 comitology decision, while containing its own flaws, attempts to strike a balance between experimental demands and democratic oversight. It does not establish a permanent parliamentary presence in each implementing Committee, but at the same time, allows the Parliament to 'flag' and respond to issues where it sees either a gross abuse of institutional power, or a decision that invokes sensitive political questions. Where an issue of political contention arises, Parliament is provided with the opportunity to enter into a dialogue with the other institutions about whether the implementing measures are consistent with both their procedures *and* their underlying justifications. Furthermore, Parliament, and not just the Court *ex post*, is allowed to investigate instances where principles such as subsidiarity and proportionality are breached (particularly significant in the OMC case, given its frequent exclusion of local participants). In all of these instances, Parliament is not acting as a legislative overlord, but instead as an institution charged with both defending the common European interest, and providing channels of public accountability.

A credible suggestion for the parliamentarisation of the OMC would involve the application of this compromise to the OMC case. This would involve a number of changes – first the 'co-decision' of the overarching objectives and annual guidelines of each OMC process, including the country-specific recommendations offered under the EES;[127] secondly, scrutiny by the Parliament's social affairs committee of Joint Reports drafted by the Commission on the national strategy plans drafted by national ministries, and on the 'social situation' across the member states; and lastly, parliamentary oversight of the method's most important committees, including the indicators and main groups of the SPC and EPC, as well as the CAP Committee responsible for providing Progress funding. These measures would be underlain with an obligation on the part of these bodies to provide details of their procedures, minutes and memberships to the Parliament's secretariat.

While these measures, in combination, could marginally 'burden' or 'slow down' the OMC's operation, they could allow the OMC to operate not 'in the shadow of the law', but in 'the shadow of politics'; and the rough and tumble of open argumentation, public justification, and the exchange of opinions over the very meaning and future of a 'Social Europe' that this would entail. In the opinion of this author at least, the legitimacy advantages of such a move – both in terms of popular input, and direct accountability and transparency – would more than outweigh any costs considered in terms of the 'dynamism' of the OMC's reporting cycle (which far from being brought to a grinding halt, would benefit from the input of new political voices).

The more difficult question may be over how to secure greater parliamentary involvement at national or regional levels. Certainly traditions of parliamentary scrutiny of EU action vary considerably in different member states. Countries where parliaments provide strong EU mandates to their central governments may see the need for more oversight of the method than states in which foreign policy is largely deemed the prerogative of the federal government alone. Furthermore, the European institutions certainly do not have the legal competence to begin interfering in national parliamentary traditions; a set of

127 In support of this suggestion in particular, see Hatzopoulos, n. 45 above, at 340–341; M. Büchs, 'How Legitimate is the Open Method of Coordination?' 46 *Journal of Common Market Studies* 4 at 781–782.

procedural rules generally out of range even for *national* executives. The power to 'parliamentarise' the OMC's national elements is thus not held at the EU level; but instead depends on the variegated willingness of national parliaments to take up its cause.

The OMC may at the very least, however, carry some incentives to encourage such moves. First of all, the example of the European Parliament itself in taking a greater role in OMC procedures is likely to have a significant bearing on how national parliaments see the OMC – as something more than an executive procedure. Secondly, just as the involvement of local actors, and social NGOs has been dependent on the provision of funding through the OMC's various Community Action Programmes, the significant investment of time and resources national parliamentary scrutiny of OMC reporting would involve would justify the opening up of CAP funding to parliamentary committees.

This involvement may primarily depend, however, on domestic incentives. While on the one hand, the agreement of OMC objectives and guidelines by the Council alone seems to give the national government a strong hand in OMC negotiations, the process of comparative benchmarking central to the method in all policy fields also provides some tools for parliamentary scrutiny.[128] In many states, opposition parties have limited scope to attack the national government on the grounds that EU-level positions should be based on consensus, or that internal disagreement would undermine 'the national position' in EU-level negotiations.

As a counterweight to this, processes of comparative benchmarking potentially allow the opposition to expose examples of government failure, or targets that have been committed to but not reached. This opportunity could be furthered by acting on recent Commission proposals to establish country-specific goals and targets within each national action plan from 2008; a move also demanded by the Lisbon 2020 reforms.[129] As Duina and Raunio explain, 'governments in truth cannot as easily dismiss such criticism as biased, uninformed or irrelevant: the experience of other countries cannot be easily ignored'.[130] In

[128] F. Duina and T. Raunio, 'The Open Method of Coordination and National Parliaments: Further Marginalization or New Opportunities?' (2007) 14 *Journal of European Public Policy* 4.

[129] Commission Communication, n. 42 above, at 5; Commission Communication, 'Working together for Jobs and Growth: A New Start for the Lisbon Strategy' COM (2005) 24 final at 5.

[130] See Duina and Raunio, n. 128 above, at 496.

this way, while reforms to the OMC at the EU level cannot lead to a direct or coerced parliamentarisation of its procedures, a mixture of internal and external incentives could encourage national parliaments to take both the democratic resources, and the outcomes, of the OMC at the national level seriously.

As a final consideration, parliamentary involvement could be strengthened by cooperative relationships *between* parliaments. Arising from concerns about parliamentary exclusion from the direction of the Lisbon strategy, the European Parliament established, in 2004, a 'G-33' group, designed both to bring together different parliamentary committees at the EU level, and to coordinate priorities and procedures between representatives of national and regional parliaments. The mandate of this group was extended in 2006.[131]

If one of the reasons why the OMC disadvantages parliaments is that it places power in the hands of a close network of executive officials, European and national parliaments could use the Lisbon strategy, and its implementation through the OMC, to strengthen *their own* networks, ensuring that the lack of coordination between parliamentary groups does not become a gap that actors within the European Council, or EU-level committees, can exploit. On top of greater participation rights at national and European levels, a more democratic OMC may require a collective assertion of power on behalf of Europe's main legislative branches.

The common outcome of a process of strengthening parliamentary involvement in the OMC would not be to supply the method with a single 'legislator'. That legislator would of course continue to be a divided one; both national and regional authorities in implementing EU objectives, and actors at the EU level directing the future course of the Lisbon strategy. The parliamentarisation of the OMC cannot and will not succeed if its goal is seen as placing new governance processes under the control of a mythical European 'popular sovereign'; one that, in present form, exists not even in the minds of the most rabid Euro-enthusiasts.

Its outcome instead would be providing the process with a form of political accountability that transcends mutual self-interest. Parliaments can provide a forum in which both the substantive

[131] On the activities and remit of the group, see the Parliament Factsheet at www.europarl.europa.eu/parliament/expert/displayFtu.do?id=74&ftuId=FTU_4.1.html&language=en.

direction and political procedures of the OMC are discussed, and where abuses of power, and cosy cooperative relationships, are exposed, or at least put under a significant burden of explanation. The 'dynamic' and 'procedural' nature of the OMC does not obviate parliamentary scrutiny, but instead creates further reasons as to why it is so critical.

8. An ombudsman for new governance: life beyond legality

It would seem a significant shift to move now from the substantive deliberations of the European Parliament to the administrative remedies provided by the European Ombudsman. The Ombudsman – created in 1995 – has been deemed quietly successful by a number of academic commentators, but it is by no means 'sexy' or well-known.[132] It deals mainly with administrative remedies, with a number of complaints relating to matters of minimal public relevance such as the hiring and dismissal of Commission employees (and even employees at the European University Institute!). This function – as a body of administrative review – thus seems to make it a peculiar part of any argument oriented towards 'politicising' new governance; it belongs instead surely to the administrative remedies discussed in section 5.

At the same time, the Ombudsman is both a legal and a political institution. While its primary source of complaints is private individuals, it is far from a judicial body. It both reports to the European Parliament, and treats its complaints not only as individual disputes, but as opportunities to critically review the practice of the European institutions, entering into a proactive dialogue with them over how legal values such as transparency, accountability and political access can be forwarded. This dialogic and political role of the European Ombudsman, as I will argue in this section, may represent its main (under-recognised) contribution to the new governance debate.

Understanding the role and function of the European Ombudsman (EO), as well as in relation to new governance and the OMC, requires firstly, however, some engagement with the role of Ombudsmen in the nation state.[133] The current EO, Nikifores Diamondouros, talks about

[132] See e.g. Chalmers *et al*, n. 80 above, at 344; P. Craig, n. 44 above, at 855.

[133] For more on the national traditions which underlie the statutes governing the EO, see P. Magnette, 'Between Parliamentary Control and the Rule of Law: The Political Role of the Ombudsman in the European Union' (2003) 10 *Journal of European Public Policy* 5 at 678–681.

distinct waves of Ombudsmen in the EU.[134] In the first wave – associated with the Nordic states of the nineteenth century – the Ombudsman carried out functions that we now link to courts: limiting monarchical authority, and acting as a tool for parliament to oversee the activities of the executive. This use – what Habermas described as the first two 'thrusts' of juridification – has also inspired part of the function of the current Ombudsman for the EU. The EO plays a classical adjudicatory role in being entrusted, under Article 228 of the TFEU, with investigating and remedying 'instances of maladministration in the activities of the Union institutions'.

As the twentieth century advanced, however, so the nature of the Ombudsman changed. In its second wave, the Ombudsman took a 'material' turn. Associated with the rise of the welfare state in the late twentieth century, institutions like the Danish Ombudsman, were created as a result of the explosion of public administration that accompanied the welfare state's development. Crucially, this growth in administrative capacity was seen as overwhelming the use of law to carry out its traditional 'adjudicatory' functions in the new welfarist realm. Legal remedies failed for two reasons (reasons that apply forcefully also to the EU case).

> Firstly, access to the Courts is limited both by practical considerations, such as the length and cost of proceedings, and by legal hurdles, such as rules about who may bring proceedings, or about the kinds of acts that may be challenged. Secondly, the criteria of judicial review applied by the Courts were not considered adequate to remedy all of the problems that deserved a remedy.[135]

Restrictive rules on judicial standing, and the specialised or detailed nature of the state's regulatory functions ensured that the 'second wave' of Ombudsmen, far from aping courts, modelled themselves as institutions able to respond to law's very failure, or the perception that legal intervention could 'juridify' or render impossible the kinds of detailed regulatory interventions that welfarist policies required.

The EO's use to the new governance debate reflects this second element to its character. As the treaties make clear, the Ombudsman is to avoid investigating complaints 'where the alleged facts are or have been

[134] N. Diamondouros, 'Legality and Good Administration: Is there a Difference?', Paper Presentation, 6th Seminar of the National Ombudsman of European Union Member States, Strasbourg, October 2007.

[135] *Ibid.*, at 2.

the subject of legal proceedings'.[136] Rather than add an additional layer of judicial protection, the Ombudsman is designed to perform a quite different function when compared to traditional legal remedies. Precisely these differences make the use of the Ombudsman in the new governance case attractive.

The first important difference concerns the actors who may petition the EO. In contrast to the set of corporate or privileged applicants most likely to meet standing rules before the European Court of Justice, the majority of the Ombudsman's cases are received from ordinary European citizens. In 2009, for example, only 16 per cent of applications received by the EO were from corporations or associations, with the vast majority (84 per cent) made up of individual complainants.[137]

Secondly, and perhaps more significantly, the types of remedies that are available to the EO differ significantly from ordinary EU remedies. In the case of traditional legal tools, the main course of action available to the Court for breaches of the Treaty, or maladministration, is to declare the measure or decision void under Article 264 TFEU. There is a clear sense that the law must separate winners and losers – those who acted within their legal entitlements and those who breached them (with one often having to compensate the other). It is clear that in a new governance context – where national governments are encouraged to be creative and proactive in adapting European rules in a domestic context – such a dichotomy is limited in its usefulness.

While the remedies available to the EO are 'softer', they are also potentially better suited to a new governance context, in which cooperative rather than adversarial remedies are called for. As a recent Ombudsman report explains, while many cases are often closed with a finding of 'no maladministration', 'even if the Ombudsman does not find maladministration, he may identify an opportunity for the Institution or body to improve the quality of its administration in the future'.[138] Where such a cooperative solution *cannot* be found, the EO is able to draw upon an escalating series of punitive remedies. First of all, it may make a critical remark about a particular practice, drawing public attention to disparities between institutional codes of conduct and malfeasance in particular cases. Secondly, it may write a draft

[136] Art. 228 (1) TFEU.

[137] *The European Ombudsman: Annual Report 2009* (Luxembourg: Office for Official Publications of the EU, 2009) at 40.

[138] *The European Ombudsman: Annual Report 2007* (Luxembourg: Office for Official Publications of the EU, 2007) at 19.

recommendation inviting the institution or body concerned to comment on a perceived instance of maladministration.

The criticisms offered are not designed merely to censure, but to open up a dialogue about how violations of individual rights, or good administrative practice can be remedied, or how indeed they might be justified. Where adequate explanations are not forthcoming, the outcome is a *political* rather than judicial solution. The principal institution to which the EO reports – as well as its final instance remedy where an institution has failed to meet its recommendations for change – is the European Parliament. Indeed, the Parliament has shown itself, as we will see in later examples, to be quite willing to use these recommendations as a starting point for either institutional censure, or new political proposals.[139]

More significantly, however, the nature of the EO's remedies tells us something about how it sees its institutional role. It is telling that the end point of the process is not simply an outcome designed to redress the claim of a particular individual. Instead, the Ombudsman seeks a political solution; one that is both acceptable to all the parties to the dispute, and that, if necessary, can lead to new initiatives via Europe's Parliament, an institution charged with defending and upholding the broader public interest in good and responsive administration in the Union as a whole.

The current Ombudsman distinguishes his role from the passive series of remedies found in ordinary EU law in precisely these terms – the EO is obliged to take a proactive and dialogical stance both towards citizen involvement in the EU, and towards the Union's political institutions. As he argues:

> Individuals are no longer content to be passive subjects or merely 'les administrés', who wait patiently for the public administration to deliver the correct outcome. They are citizens, who understand both that they have rights, and that public administration involves finding a balance among conflicting interests and among competing principles. To win public trust and acceptance, the public administration needs not only to be respectful and courteous towards citizens, but also to demonstrate that it is accountable and responsive. Among other things, that means being ready to explain and to justify its conduct through genuine and

[139] See the EO's 'Draft Recommendation to the Commission in Complaint 3208/2006/GG' at www.ombudsman.europa.eu/cases/draftrecommendation.faces/en/540/html.bookmark.

> meaningful conduct with citizens, both about matters that affect them personally, and about how the public interest is identified and pursued.

As he goes on to add:

> I doubt that an excessive focus on legality, even a broad view of legality, is sufficient to sustain a culture of service in this sense. There also needs to be a 'life beyond legality.[140]

This 'life beyond legality' concerns the use of the Ombudsman to fulfil functions, and act in areas, that the Court cannot. First he notes that officials often see legal enforcement – in keeping with the pragmatist claims of the third chapter – as associated with blame and punishment. While the apportionment of blame may be necessary in some cases – a precondition for full public accountability – there are question marks over whether this is always consistent with 'good' or 'responsive' administration. As Diamondouros puts it, 'a culture of service is not a culture of blame. If we tell civil servants that good administration is a legal obligation and that poor service is illegal, we may re-enforce a defensive culture'. This 'juridifying' tendency may speak in favour of the more attenuated social role the EO offers.

Secondly, he notes that courts and the EO carry a different operative logic. Courts understandably carry an 'adjudicatory' function. This function is part also of the Ombudsman's task. Taking inspiration from the Charter of Fundamental rights, most of the EO's complaints are brought in the name of a particular individual, and seek to remedy their complaint through a realisable remedy.

At the same time, the Ombudsman also operates in a more complicated arena. He is not merely advancing claims on behalf of the individual, but also aiming towards more accountable and responsive administrative procedures in a broader sense. The outcome of his office is not just to declare one side a winner, and the other to blame, but to encourage both parties to adjust their practices so that similar disputes do not arise in the future (and can leave the process with mutually beneficial outcomes). To this end, the Ombudsman does not just passively respond or react to the individuals before him, but also enjoys his own right of initiative where obvious instances of maladministration present themselves. The iterative logic of 'new governance' itself – that the application and use of rules is not predetermined, but dependent on

[140] Diamondouros, n. 134 above, at 4.

their context, and a spirit of improvement and renewal within them – is evident in the EO approach.

This very 'hybridity' in the very nature of the EO – its presence as an institution sitting between 'adjudicatory' and 'dispute resolution' functions – may represent one of the most important contributions it can offer to methods like the OMC. The Ombudsman is in a position to investigate institutional exclusions, and abuses of power, in OMC procedures, not in order to coerce particular outcomes – a deployment sure to provoke anxiety among the member states – but to encourage, and explore options, for its institutions to be more inclusive and responsive. This is an exercise conducted not behind the back of, but in full cooperation with, the European Parliament, potentially providing a sorely needed mechanism for parliamentary oversight of a procedure which has, as the last section argued, sidelined Parliament all too easily in the past.

The second important contribution the EO could offer concerns its relationship to the national level. At first, one might suspect that this could be an obstacle. Under the terms of the Treaty, the Ombudsman is not permitted to raise complaints relating to the implementation of Union law by national institutions. Given that many examples of possible 'maladministration' under OMC-like methods could occur not just in EU bodies like the SPC, but with national authorities in their reporting processes, this is a significant limitation. It potentially creates a 'gap' in the EO's remit into which a number of activities concerning 'multi-level' forms of governance could fall.

The Ombudsman, however, recognised this limitation early. From its first ever report to the European Parliament, in 1995, it noted that the majority of failed applications concerned complaints related to national authorities.[141] In response, the Ombudsman adopted, in 1997, a statement designed to create a European network of Ombudsmen, linking various Ombudsman offices around Europe. Since then, this network has been strengthened, with the EO developing practices of direct referral to national bodies where a complaint falls outside the EO's institutional mandate.

This represents a type of interactive cooperation that is currently lacking in the case of both the OMC, and the Union's own judicature.

[141] It is notable that this remains the most significant heading for inadmissibility – some 72 per cent of inadmissible cases were dismissed for this reason in 2009, i.e. because they were inadmissible or outside the EO's mandate. See n. 137 above, at 40.

Whereas, in the case of the courts, the combination of restrictive standing rules and a limited preliminary reference procedure has often denied individuals an effective remedy, the development of the EO as a cooperative and multi-level institution presents an opportunity to adapt EU administrative law itself to governance processes that cannot be fully mapped onto either national *or* European levels.

We can illustrate some of these benefits through a final example. In the last decade, the Ombudsman has been particularly active in promoting an access to documents agenda; an agenda which has prompted a deep engagement with the other EU institutions. In particular, the EU has attempted to pursue one of the core purposes of the 2001 Regulation on document access, which was to encourage a more proactive approach to freedom of information. Reflecting on the problem of 'elitist citizenship', i.e. that most requests for documents are made by corporate or other privileged actors, the Regulation urged the Commission, under its Article 11, to create a public and online register of all of its documents. As a result, document access would not require a protracted information request, but would be automatic for any interested citizen.

There have, however, been numerous problems with the register. The principal problem is a basic refusal by the Commission to comply. According to Statewatch – a UK freedom of information NGO – the vast majority of documents on the register prior to 2006 were adopted legislative texts and reports, with most preparatory and internal documents omitted. As a result, the register has failed to provide citizens with more documents than would be accessible anyway through Eur-lex (the online register of Community laws), or the websites of the Commission DGs.

A second problem, relates to comitology. Many of the most significant documents that could represent an 'added value' for the register concern implementing Committees yet, following the 1999 comitology decision, the Commission is obliged only to register those committee documents that it would send to the European Parliament, and is also given significant discretion to refuse to add documents when 'sensitive' issues, or information important to national actors, is at stake.[142] Both of these elements have combined to limit the register's usefulness in allowing private actors access to information vital to scrutinising Commission activities, either in the field of 'new governance' or beyond.

[142] On the comitology register, see http://ec.europa.eu/transparency/regcomitology/index.cfm.

In this example, the Ombudsman has played a vital role. He has effectively mediated between the individual and political institutions. Taking up a complaint by Statewatch in 2006, the EO set about investigating the effectiveness and scope of the Register.[143] In keeping with normal EO procedure, the Commission was asked to respond to Statewatch's complaint. The Commission argued that Article 11 did not oblige the institutions to list all their documents, but only to 'incrementally' expand access. This expansion however was to be mainly focused on the Commission's *legislative* activity. It was also limited, so the Commission argued, by the absence of a single common register, and data-entry service, for all Commission DGs.

While the EO, in its decision, recognised the Commission's incremental approach, it argued that not enough had been done. The Ombudsman noted that the Council and Parliament, in spite of their considerable complexity, *had* managed to create a single register. Why couldn't the Commission do the same? The EO also rejected the idea that the register was intended only for 'legislative' activity.[144] Such documents are also contained on other registers, whereas the intention of the general register was a political and *pre*-legislative one too – to allow individuals to better understand and involve themselves in the law-making process.

The outcome of the EO's decision was firstly a draft recommendation to expand access, and secondly (after a failure by the Commission to agree to its terms) a critical comment, deeming that 'the Commission has chosen instead to propose a narrow definition of what a document is.[145] In my view, this will lead to fewer rather than more EU documents being accessible to the public'. Statewatch was vindicated in its insistence that the passive approach of the Commission to the register constituted 'maladministration'.

At the same time, the mere resolution of the dispute was not an end to the matter. Responding to the EO's comment, the Parliament, in January 2009, adopted a resolution urging the Commission to follow the EO's recommendations.[146] The Parliament argued that the

[143] Draft Recommendation to the European Commission in complaint 3208/2006/GG. See www.ombudsman.europa.eu/recommen/en/063208.htm.

[144] *Ibid.*, at [20].

[145] Reaffirming its initial criticism. See EO Press Release 2/2009: www.statewatch.org/news/2009/jan/eu-sw-ombudsman-complaint-com-register.pdf.

[146] Resolution of the European Parliament 'On Public Access to European Parliament, Council and Commission Documents (Implementation of Regulation 1049/2001)', 2007/2154(INI).

Commission's reasoning was unjustified both according to the wording of Regulation 1049/2001, and given the commitments to transparency contained in both the Charter and Article 1 of the Treaty. The EP, however couched its response to the Ombudsman in broader terms. It argued that the Commission's reasoning called for a wider reappraisal of the Regulation, suggesting a need both to consider the harmonisation of different procedures relating to document access across the EC institutions, and to better incorporate comitology, and a register of comitology documents, within the overall legislative scheme. The final outcome of the EO's decision was not simply the redress of an individual complaint, but a wider inter-institutional reappraisal of document rules, including for new governance processes (with a proposed amendment to the 2001 Regulation now under discussion).[147]

Through this example, we can conclude the wider benefits the birth of the Ombudsman may give new governance procedures more generally. The protection of due process and access rights through bodies like the EO need not lead to a 'juridification' or 'petrification' of its procedures. Instead, it may prompt, and provide opportunities for, wider political appraisal (both 'within' governance processes, and towards general legislative bodies).

9. Societal constitutionalism and social impact assessment: encouraging functional reflexivity

Both the 'legal/administrative' and 'political' potential reforms of the OMC discussed above generally consider constitutionalism in what was described in Chapter 1 as 'vertical' terms, i.e. in terms of considering the boundaries of the political relationship between the individual and the state. Transported to the EU level, a further intermediary is added – a vertical *EU* constitutionalism delineates boundaries between national and European action, as well as between the EU institutions themselves. 'Constitutionalising' new governance in this sense means ensuring that it is consistent with, or respectful of, the necessary autonomy of different governing levels in the EU order (including the rights of the individual him- or herself).

[147] See the Commission's present proposal 'For a Regulation of the European Parliament and Council Regarding Public Access to European Parliament, Council and Commission Documents', COM (2008) 229 final.

At the same time, there are a number of elements that the vertical view of constitutionalism misses out. In particular, it fails to address a set of boundaries that were described in the first chapter as 'functional', i.e. as concerning the separate, and relatively autonomous, fields of policy in which EU law is engaged.[148] In so much as the treaties were originally designed not only to delineate national from European action, but also to separate out different functional spheres – the national welfare state on the one hand, and a transnational European market on the other – the development of the OMC not only potentially challenges the balance of power between the EU and its member states, but also invokes a new series of interdependencies between economic and social policy. Any 'constitutionalisation' strategy for the OMC, which ignored these interdependencies, would run the risk of ignoring some of the principal pathologies of the method to date.

These boundaries have created a set of crucial criticisms of OMC procedures, namely that they potentially violate the autonomy of some of these fields. To take the fate of the 'streamlined' OMC SPSI as one example, while on the one hand, Lisbon's demand for the social inclusion process to 'feed in and feed out' to other Lisbon goals seems a vital part of any truly 'multi-dimensional' process, on the other, the responses of the last chapter indicate a near universal fear among the OMC's 'social voices' that they are being drowned out by a 'growth and competitiveness' narrative (one external to the traditional goal of social policy in protecting individuals from market demands).[149] While the political strategies outlined above, in seeking to publicise the future of the Lisbon strategy, and scrutinise it under the auspices of the EP, have some answers to this problem, a purely vertical form of constitutionalism seems largely to miss rather than address such conflicts.

A comprehensive answer may require a further expansion of our constitutional concepts. Gunther Teubner, addressing functional differentiation at a global level, has argued that the increasing complexity of modern society requires a form of 'societal constitutionalism'; one designed not only to mediate conflicts between the political sphere and the individual, but also the interaction of functional discourses.[150]

[148] See Chapter 1, section 2.2. [149] See Chapter 4, section 5.3.

[150] G. Teubner, 'Societal Constitutionalism: Alternative to State-Centred Constitutional Theory' in C. Joerges, I. J. Sand and G. Teubner (eds.), *Transnational Governance and Constitutionalism* (Oxford: Hart, 2004); see also (including on the wider origins of this concept) P. Kjaer, *Between Governing and Governance: On the Emergence, Function and Form of Europe's Post-national Constellation* (Oxford: Hart, 2010).

Deriving such a societal constitutionalism from Luhmann's conception of the constitution as an instance of 'structural coupling' between functional sub-systems, such a constitutional discourse carries a dual aim.[151] On the one hand, it is oriented towards allowing discourses that depend on each other to interact or 'couple' on a structural basis; on the other, it must ensure that this meeting respects the autonomy of each system (that problems of 'de-differentation', or the blurring of the systemic boundaries upon which the diversity of society depends, can be avoided).[152] To take the example of the classical divide between law and politics, law requires political input to safeguard its legitimacy, yet at the same time, *too much* political integration presents the danger of 'total politics' or of a political usurpation of the independence of legal decision-making. A 'societal constitutionalism' universalises this principle to incorporate the relationship between other functional spheres – between economy and polity; science and religion, and so on. Such a concept may be useful to consider the challenges of the present OMC.

In the OMC context, such a constitutionalism would aim towards addressing the perilous balance between 'reflexivity' and 'colonisation' addressed in the first chapter. The OMC also faces a perilous integration between functional discourses – this time, social and economic. While, on the one hand, any attempt to separate the social OMCs from the single market project, or the financial basis of the welfare state, is fraught; on the other, this 'integration' makes deregulation, or the implicit 'unlearning' of welfare commitments, a threat. In the OMC context, 'constitutionalism' does not just mean the provision of procedural rights, the creation of parliamentary oversight, or any other traditional remedy, but also ensuring that conflicts and relations between the social and economic aspects of the Lisbon strategy, and its different constituent coordination processes, can be managed.

Already, the OMC carries a number of rules (albeit informal ones) designed to partly advance this task. One is the requirement for 'feeding in and out' itself; another is the encouragement, within the overarching objectives of the EES and OMC SPSI, of horizontal coordination or 'joined-up' government between different federal departments when drawing

[151] For an overview of the idea of the Constitution as a structural coupling of law and politics, see M. Dawson, 'Re-capturing the Legal in World Constitutionalism: Comparing Constitutions Through Systems Theory', Paper Presentation, 23rd World Congress of the Philosophy of Law (Cracow), July 2006.

[152] N. Luhmann, 'Operational Closure and Structural Coupling: The Differentiation of the Legal System' (1992) 13 *Cardozo Law Review* 5.

up national action plans. The questionnaire respondents canvassed in the last chapter suggested a number of further proposals in this regard – for example, to ensure the sharing of minutes and agendas between different sectoral committees, like the SPC, EPC and EMCO.[153] All of these measures are proposed with a particular intention in mind – to ensure that opportunities for useful interchange between sectoral coordination processes can be optimised without one ignoring, or placing undue burdens, upon the other.

The most significant such proposal, however, for a form of societal constitutionalism may have emerged in the last few years of the OMC's life. As part of its 'renewed Social Agenda' for 2008–10, the Commission has argued forcefully for a form of 'social mainstreaming' designed to advance social policy objectives not only in areas of soft coordination, but across all areas of European policy:

> As underlined in the Commission's Communication on a holistic, cross-cutting Renewed Social Agenda, it is generally recognised that *social policy considerations must also be mainstreamed throughout other EU policies* (e.g. competition, internal market, economic policy, health, immigration, trade, agriculture etc.). The Commission will pursue its own efforts to produce robust impact assessments on each new policy initiative, and in this context pay particular attention to *social impacts*.[154]

The jewel in the crown of this proposal is the idea of 'social impact assessment', namely that Commission proposals should be measured not only on the grounds of their environmental outcomes (a long-standing practice), but also in terms of their impacts on inequality, social cohesion and the integration of the excluded into the labour market. This essentially extends practices already found in other fields, such as fundamental rights, and gender discrimination policy, to the measurement of social inclusion. In facing new legislative proposals, and in drafting guidelines and recommendations in soft coordination processes, Commission actors would be obliged under this approach to ask a series of foundational questions.

Some of the most important are outlined in the Commission's most recent 2009 Guidelines on Impact Assessment.[155] Whereas one of the principal criticisms of the Lisbon strategy contained in the last chapter

[153] Chapter 4, section 5.1.
[154] Communication on 'A Renewed Commitment to Social Europe', n. 42 above, at 6.
[155] European Commission, 'Impact Assessment Guidelines', SEC (2009) 92.

was that the 'policy-framing' actors of economic coordination processes tended merely to assume the benevolent social side effects of market-coordinating measures, impact assessment is designed to ensure that more concrete impacts are measured and analysed, in order that potential trade-offs between different policy choices can be identified. These questions include 'whether the option will lead directly or indirectly to a rise in inequality' and whether it will 'affect the recognition or implementation of social rights via social protection measures'.[156] These are questions that, the available evidence suggests, have not been successfully 'mainstreamed' across the OMC in all of its policy domains (or in many cases, even asked at all, either of governments or the EU institutions themselves). To do so would be an important first step in strengthening the method's reflexive capacity.

Not only is 'social mainstreaming' a policy proposal, but also one that has been formally incorporated by the Lisbon Treaty, which inserts into the Union's legal framework horizontal social objectives. Article 9 of the TFEU states:

> In defining and implementing its policies and activities, the Union shall take into account requirements linked to the promotion of a high level of employment, the guarantee of adequate social protection, the fight against social exclusion, and a high level of education, training and protection of human health.

Potentially, this is a significant shift. Rather than assume, as the original Treaty did, that more socially cohesive societies would simply follow from the development of the internal market (the old Article 117), or that social policies could be pursued in isolation under 'soft law' methods, the article would commit the EU to the filtration of the objectives of the OMC SPSI across all EU domains (including those where 'harder' legislative competences prevailed).

What are the concrete advantages and disadvantages of such an approach? Its disadvantage is that the impact of impact assessment in other domains, particularly its original 'home' of gender and anti-discrimination policy is the source of much contestation.[157] Some feminist writers have claimed, for example, that the main purpose of

[156] *Ibid.*, at 34.

[157] For two contrasting accounts, see M. A. Pollack and E. Hafner-Burton, 'Mainstreaming Gender in the European Union' (2000) 7 *Journal of European Public Policy* 3; J. Shaw, 'The European Union and Gender Mainstreaming: Constitutionally Embedded or Comprehensively Marginalised?' (2002) 10 *Feminist Legal Studies* 3.

'mainstreaming' is a fragmentation and distribution of the policy goal across multiple areas such that the principal goal itself (i.e. policies and legislation aiming to advance gender equality) is ignored; with positive legislative action sidelined.[158] Impact assessment (IA) tends to measure the 'negative' outcomes of policies in *other* domains, but it is unlikely to act as an inspiration for policy proposals in and of themselves. The problem then could be that the advent of social 'mainstreaming' leads to another dilution of the visibility and credibility of EU social policy; an excuse to put necessary legislative or coordinative reforms on hold.

There are, however, distinct advantages. First of all, as we have discussed, IA has a distinct informational advantage; one that can improve political accountability in the process.[159] Whereas the present OMC is based on a number of shaky assumptions, i.e. that there is a naturally occurring reciprocity between growth and competitiveness policies and the social rights underlying the OMC SPSI, IA allows these assumptions to be placed under an explanatory burden, thus creating a dialogue between defenders of such an approach and critics. Even if such a dialogue does not lead to a change in the indicators or guidelines of the processes themselves, at the very least, it will allow those measures to be based on a broader information base than before, with the voices of 'external' interests considered.

The most significant advantage, however, may be political. Under the OMC as it stands, the primary goal is to achieve effective outcomes that match the political preferences and socio-economic needs of a particular 'sector' of the European polity. This has a tendency, however, to minimise or make invisible considerations elsewhere, leading to policies which unnecessarily limit or conflict with each other. The obligation to make decisions 'in context', including through considerations of social rights, potentially encourages a more holistic approach to decision-making, in which a reflexive awareness of other policy fields is vital.

To the extent that impact assessment encourages a cross-sectoral approach to important decisions (in the OMC, over the range of indicators and the framing of joint reports) it facilitates political judgement over the necessary *trade-offs* between different policy priorities. This

[158] See e.g. M. Stratigaki, 'Gender Mainstreaming v Positive Action: An Ongoing Conflict in EU Gender Equality Policy' (2005) 12 *European Journal of Women's Studies*.

[159] See G. Rowe, 'Tools for the Control of Political and Administrative Agents: Impact Assessment and Administrative Governance in the European Union' in H. Hoffman and A. Turk (eds.), *EU Administrative Governance* (Cheltenham: Edward Elgar, 2006).

message is a strong part of the Commission's early approach to IA, as embodied in its 2002 Communication.

> The new Impact Assessment method integrates all sectoral assessments concerning direct and indirect impacts of a proposed measure into one global instrument, hence moving away from the existing situation of a number of partial and sectoral assessments. It provides a common set of basic questions, minimum set of analytical standards, and common reporting framework. However, its new method will be sufficiently flexible to accommodate the differences between Commission policies and to take into account the specific circumstances of individual policy areas.[160]

If one of the problems of the OMC is its 'micro-political' preference for technical indicators and sector-by-sector procedures, IA provides a certain type of universalising frame for policy. It allows trade-offs, both between different policy choices, and competing visions of EU regulation and its goals, to be identified.

Social impact assessment, on its own, does not provide for a full 'societal constitutionalisation' of the OMC. The outcomes of social IA will remain at the discretion of the Commission and the intergovernmental actors that make up committees like the SPC. It could thus still fall foul of the bare unwillingness to engage that has befallen the notion of 'feeding in and feeding out'. Furthermore, with little basis, at such an early stage in its development, to conduct an empirical assessment of the actual effects of 'social impact assessment' on either the method itself or wider European social policies, we can only be modest in our optimism about its development.

We ought to be optimistic nonetheless. Firstly, unlike 'feeding in and out', social mainstreaming carries a Treaty basis through the horizontal social objectives set out in the new Article 9. It would also be supported by long-established Commission practices in other fields (e.g. environmental and gender policy), rather than simply 'appended' to the OMC SPSI in the manner of the 'feeding in and out' proposal.

Finally, and most importantly, however, it should be seen as a first recognition of the functional interdependencies that processes like the OMC SPSI have thrown up. While the relationship between the Lisbon agenda and the goals of a 'Social Europe' have too often been subsumed within each other, or explained away by reference to a 'virtuous circle' between social and economic policy (and other convenient myths),

[160] Commission Communication 'On Impact Assessment', COM (2002) 0276 final at 2.

social impact assessment offers a serious analysis of what the impacts, relationships and outcomes of an attempt to coordinate fiscal, social and employment policy through European indicators really are. This analytical and reflexive move is an important first step in promoting a larger 'societal constitutionalism' of new governance procedures.

10. Conclusion

Recent years have seen a shift in how many analyse the OMC. We have moved in many cases from a descriptive to a diagnostic or remedial phase. While the theories and contributions outlined in the second chapter attempted to say what governance 'was', or what was 'new' about it, the accounts discussed and analysed here attempt to go further, outlining a reform strategy for the future. As the last chapter pointed out, this is certainly called for. The more optimistic accounts of the OMC, as a shining light for a 'Social Europe', or pathway to an experimental and deliberative ethos more suitable for legitimating post-national forms of law, have come up against the reality of an OMC procedure that has often significantly narrowed both opportunities for political participation, and the policy choices available to national governments in pursuit of social 'reform'.[161]

It is for this reason that a number of reform strategies for the OMC appear infeasible. Foremost among these is Jonathan Zeitlin's suggestion for a 'reflexive' reform strategy for the OMC – one that would apply 'the very logic of new governance to itself'.[162] The difficulty with this is that the very 'logic' of the OMC is part of its problem. This logic is that participation and deliberation are values that will come by themselves, external to the legal and institutional mechanisms necessary for their realisation. It is a logic that claims that political accountability can be safeguarded merely by making law-applying agents accountable to each other. And it is a logic which encourages a 'reflexive relation' between social and economic discourses without telling us how to avoid that reflexivity becoming a colonisation or intrusion of one discourse upon another. Its result has been an OMC process that – while carrying an important role in placing social policy on the European agenda – has too often hidden or narrowed the very questions over Europe's social future it was meant to advance. The paradoxes and

[161] For a summary of these problems, see the conclusions of Chapter 4, section 7.
[162] J. Zeitlin, n. 124 above.

inconsistencies of proceduralist and experimental theories – outlined in the third chapter – continue to haunt the OMC. Our answer in terms of reform cannot be 'more of the same, but better'; it must involve a break with new governance's recent past.

How though to think of a new beginning? 'Constitutionalisation' is certainly an important guiding frame through which to advance the task. Through a constitutional frame, legal analysis has inverted the stylised distinction between law and constitutionalism offered in the early literature of the new governance project. Rather than see law as destroying the very innovations which new governance methods have borne, the project of constitutionalisation suggests that law can act as a set of legal and procedural conditions or constraints *through which* a more legitimate, and process-regarding, form of policy coordination in the EU can take place. By exploring how a number of recent trends in the EU order, such as the development of social rights, and the ever-growing body of administrative rules designed to tame an otherwise arbitrary European administrative space, could help advance a law-mediated form of rule under OMC-like procedures, this chapter has attempted to 'place meat' on the bones of this thesis. Divorcing processes like the OMC from the due process rights, and procedural guarantees that existing forms of European law offer, is a move that even more 'experimental' proponents of new governance have begun to mourn; it is not one that this book would like to repeat.[163]

This chapter has argued, however, that ordinary EU law alone cannot carry the task of 'constitutionalisation'. The attempt to surround OMC procedures with legal boundaries faces a number of difficulties of its own. On the one hand, the uncertain and uneven development of instruments like the Charter of Fundamental Rights hardly suggests their use as a counterweight to deregulatory drift under new governance procedures. On the other, the Court's restrictive rules of standing, and view of participation within new governance processes themselves, creates a paradox within EU administrative law – the very actors most in need of administrative remedies, e.g. those cut out of the

[163] See, as evidence, for example, the preference, described in Chapter 2, for 'hybridity' type theories that seek to combine law and new governance in a single normative system, or the reliance of people like Sabel and Zeitlin in their recent essays on the idea of a 'governance architecture' that subsumes European directives within its ambit. C. Sabel and J. Zeitlin, 'Learning from Difference: The New Architecture of Experimentalist Governance in the EU' (2008) 14 *European Law Journal* 3.

decision-making loop, are often the least likely to have access to them. While we may aspire towards a 'catalytic' court, able to expand the quality and legitimacy of processes like the OMC, the institutions we *have* show neither the temperament nor the willingness to seriously take up the task.

'Constitutionalising' new governance, however, is a project with more than one potential meaning. The meaning on which much analysis rests is the view of the Constitution as a guarantor of basic rights of due process; a view that fails to capture all of what new governance is really seeking from law. The problems of the contemporary OMC cannot be reduced to a set of individual exclusions, or threats to basic rights; instead they concern the way that new governance processes are socially and politically articulated. Despite being seen as a way of recapturing the integration process *from law*, promoting decentralised political dialogue in the process, the OMC has too often descended into a 'micro-politics', able to insulate its activities from general political input and scrutiny. At the same time, its claims to create a more 'Social Europe' continue to flounder on the encasement of processes like the OMC SPSI within the Lisbon strategy. A court-centred strategy for reform seems unlikely to address either of these problems.

The chapter's final political solutions focus on expanding opportunities for political and social contestation of elements of OMC-like methods that have been seen as insider's secrets. The indicators, recommendations, committee structures, and strategic reports of the OMC, by this view, should no longer be subjected to a purely technocratic logic, or rely on 'horizontal' forms of political scrutiny alone; instead they should be subjected to the forms of external influence and review that existing political institutions within the EU order offer. While the reintegration of European and national parliaments should be at the forefront of such a strategy, the responsive forms of review and due process offered by the European Ombudsman, and the requirement to measure the social impacts of prospective reforms are also important additional elements. Together, they can provide means of politicising modes of action that can no longer be insulated or masked through the logic of a more 'dynamic' form of rule.

Constitutionalising the OMC is a tricky business. It requires an expansive view of Europe's constitutional project, just as it demands that we see 'law' and 'new governance' not as oppositional projects, but as potentially enabling, existing in spheres that both contribute to and re-define each other. A successful constitutionalism for the OMC would not only result in an opening and broadening of its procedures, but also in a re-evaluation of the very role of law in the project of Europe's social and political integration.

Epilogue: the future of the Open Method of Coordination

What is the future of the OMC?

This book has charted both the development and the practice of the Open Method of Coordination, from its original promise, to its numerous challenges and failings. It has sought to conceptualise its relationship to law, in order to consider not just the policy outcomes of 'new governance', but also the legal and political relationships that it has created. As we have seen, the OMC is part of a significant 'transformation' in the dominant governing instruments of EU law. This challenge has not only altered our view of what 'rule-making' in a post-national setting means, but also provoked extensive anxieties among important domestic and European actors. The 'rise of new governance' has signified the entry of both a new descriptive reality, and a new set of normative concerns, over the future of the EU legal order.

One wonders, however, if this 'rise' is to be accompanied by a fall. What is the future of methods like the OMC, and how might that future be different from the practice of 'new governance' in the present day? While the late 1990s, and early part of this decade, saw an explosion of open coordination onto the European scene, there are numerous reasons to be sceptical about its place in the EU's legal order in the coming decades. These concerns emerge both from external developments, and from the tensions outlined in the substantive parts of this thesis.

The external concern comes from an obvious source – the potential restrictions on soft governance brought by the rulings of the ECJ in *Laval*, *Rüffert* and *Viking*. Even if the OMC is no 'paper tiger', the Court's restrictive reading of rights to collective action in each of these judgments is a legitimate cause for concern. It leaves open the possibility that – even if governments agree to take forward a particular employment or social inclusion agenda – the national legislation they develop could be restrictively interpreted or overturned by the European Courts at a future date. The future 'success' of the OMC depends on the viability of a national social space that is not automatically circumvented each time it is deemed prejudicial to the fulfilment of internal market law. In combination, the failure of 'feeding in and feeding out' identified in Chapter 4, and the spectre of a more activist Court, does not bode well for those optimistic about the OMC's social role.

In this sense, there seem to be emerging limits to the method's functional expansion. While, in the period following the Lisbon European Council, an OMC procedure was seemingly contemplated for each and every field of EU action, the OMC no longer seems to be developing in new areas.[1] Certainly the most optimistic of all academic theses – that open coordination would become *the* general procedure for the establishment of EU norms has given way to the interspersing of different legislative instruments, with directives and regulations still prevalent even in the fields of employment and social protection policy where the OMC is most active. These external developments suggest that the spread of 'new governance' may be significantly circumscribed in the coming years.

Secondly, however, there are also 'internal' concerns. The very problems that we have listed in this book also suggest a limited future for the OMC, so long as the Commission and Council continue to refuse to take their consequences seriously. While the Commission's most recent Communication on the OMC SPSI contains some positive steps – such as its suggestions of 'social mainstreaming' – it may be too little, too late.[2] In particular, the new 'Lisbon 2020' proposals, agreed by the European Council in June, do little to address the exclusion of two major groups discussed in Chapter 4 – parliaments and local authorities.[3]

[1] Two good portents to consider the recent slowdown in proliferation of OMC procedures are immigration and territorial cohesion policy. In both domains, Commission Communications following Lisbon suggested the adoption of an OMC procedure; a project that has seemingly now been abandoned. NB: a counterpoint might be culture where a recent resolution of the European Council has proposed an OMC for cultural policy. See Council Resolution on 'A European Agenda for Culture' 2007 (287) 01.

[2] Commission Communication, 'A Renewed Commitment to Social Europe: Re-enforcing the Open Method of Coordination for Social Inclusion and Social Protection', COM (2008) 418 final.

[3] The most the Commission and the European Council have to offer is that 'all national, regional and local authorities should *implement* the partnership, closely associating parliaments, as well as social partners and representatives of civil society'. Local and parliamentary authorities are again charged with 'implementing the strategy without having much say in forming its substantive content'. 2020 Communication, n. 6 below, at 27.

The European Parliament, as we have seen, has responded to this exclusion through adding to its voice to calls for the OMC's curtailment.[4] Given its increasing power within the EU's wider constitutional architecture, the actors of the OMC would do well to take this threat seriously. In the case of comitology, the continuous exclusion of the Parliament culminated in threats by its plenary (partly acted upon) to refuse the necessary funding to keep committee structures – the composition and structure of which were almost completely unknown to MEPs – running.[5] A similar move – withholding the 'Progress' funds needed to provide the OMC's surrounding infrastructure – could yet lie in store for the OMC SPSI (arguably it could even be seen as a necessary final wake-up call).

Finally on this point, few serious reforms to the architecture of the OMC SPSI seem to have emerged from the recent reforms to the Lisbon strategy.[6] While the new 'Lisbon 2020' strategy establishes some innovations, such as a headline target to remove 20 million people from poverty, as well as a flagship anti-poverty programme, it does little to address some of the many criticisms outlined in this book. While Lisbon has been frequently derided, for example, for carrying a strong 'implementation gap', the new proposals neither make the dominant instruments of the strategy more prescriptive, nor do they insist on greater regional or parliamentary involvement in the way the strategy is monitored (preferring instead to insist on the central role of a hierarchical actor, the European Council 'taking full ownership of the strategy').[7] To this extent, the future of open coordination under Lisbon 2020 seems to be 'more of the same' rather than a break with the poor record of its predecessor.[8]

In spite of these pessimisms, it is remarkable how durable the OMC has been. At the times when it has been most threatened, e.g. in the discussions over the future of the social OMCs conducted in the wake of

[4] European Parliament Resolution 'On the Institutional and Legal Implications of the Use of Soft Law Instruments', 2007/2028 (INI).

[5] See K. S. C Bradley, 'The European Parliament and Comitology: On the Road to Nowhere?' (1997) 3 *European Law Journal* 3 at 241–243.

[6] Commission Communication, 'Europe 2020: A Strategy for Smart, Sustainable and Inclusive Growth' COM (2010) 2020; Conclusions of the European Council, 17 June 2010, EUCO 13/10.

[7] Lisbon 2020 Communication, *ibid.*, at 4.

[8] See e.g. M. Dawson, 'Learning from Past Failures? Governance in the European Union from Lisbon 2000 to Lisbon 2020' (2010) 17 *Maastricht Journal of European & Comparative Law* 2.

the Kok review, open coordination has somehow emerged anew as a central plank of European policy. To this extent, there also remain distinct grounds to be optimistic about the OMC's future.

Ironically, just as the Court's activities have circumscribed the social options of the member states, and could limit the impact of 'soft law' in the process, so they may also carve out new opportunities for its use. Firstly, while the Court's activities have prompted a significant rethink of the role of internal market law in the sphere of collective action and social rights, so they have provoked a looming national backlash. The very architect of the thesis of economic and social 'de-coupling' that was such an influential justification for the OMC's emergence now argues that member states would be justified in openly defying the ECJ's rulings.[9] One wonders – has Europe's legal structure, for so long tacitly accepted by national courts and administrations – finally overstepped its limits? Certainly Fritz Scharpf is not alone in questioning whether the ECJ carries the legitimacy, on its own, to determine the appropriate balance between the freedom of establishment and a cacophony of domestic social rights.[10]

In some ways, however, precisely the *limits* of the Court's legitimacy and abilities create a need for new *political* initiatives.[11] The OMC – for states seeking to temper the perception that internal market law has gone too far – could offer a forum for governments *themselves* to take the driving seat in answering the question of how the economic commitments of the Treaty can be adequately 'balanced' against legitimate social objectives advanced at the national level. Here, the method's very exclusion of the Court provides a potential fillip, guarding against either the possibility that a political settlement between governments will be judicially rescinded, or the danger of a perceived judicial activism. It was – as Chapter 1 has observed – a feeling among EU policy-makers that a court-centred form of market integrations had reached its limits that led to the OMC's initial development.[12] Could the ECJ's *Laval*

[9] 'The Only Solution is to Refuse to Comply with ECJ Rulings: An Interview with Fritz Scharpf' (2008) 14 *Social Europe* 1. See also, F. Scharpf, 'Legitimacy in the Multi-level European Polity' (2009) 1 *European Political Science Review* 2.

[10] See also, R. Herzog (former President of the Federal Republic of Germany) and L. Gerken, 'Stoppt den EuropäischenGerichtshof', *Frankurter Allgemeine Zeitung* (8 September 2008); C. Joerges and F. Rödl, 'Informal Politics, Formalised Law and the Social Deficit of European Integration: Reflections after the Judgements of the ECJ in Viking and Laval' (2009) 15 *European Law Journal* 1.

[11] On this potential use, see M. Dawson, '3 Waves of New Governance in the European Union' (2011) 36 *European Law Review* 2.

[12] See Chapter 1, section 4.

and *Viking* rulings – if seized upon by the Commission in a further 'renewed' Social Agenda – act as a similar catalyst for changes in the present day?

Our second reason for optimism in the method depends less on its obvious political advantages than the dearth of available alternatives. It is notable that Scharpf – in spite of his denunciation of the Court – also rejected a political way out of the dilemma, through the use of a 'progress' clause limiting the applicability of the market freedoms to programmes of social welfare.[13] There remains little appetite among national governments – even in the wake of the present financial crisis – for a strong legislative programme for the Union in the social field.

Telling in this regard is Wim Kok's mid-term Lisbon review. While – as we saw in Chapter 1 – Kok identified a major 'implementation gap' in the agenda, his solution was to reinforce existing coordination instruments, rather than resort to 'hard' forms of legal or financial coercion; a preference repeated in the current 'Lisbon 2020' architecture.[14] The continued barriers of national compliance, and of entrenched resistance among governments to 'harmonised' social standards, means that 'open coordination' is seemingly 'here to stay'. The alternatives – of either an entirely segmented 'national social state', cordoned off from the reach of European law, or a strong legislative agenda, aiming at minimum standards – are not seen by national governments as viable.

While this may suggest that the OMC still has a future, it should not lead us simply to leave things as they are. Even if – at the level of social law-making – there are limited alternatives *to* OMC-like methods, this is not to suggest that there are not alternatives *within the OMC itself*. Far from being an immutable procedure, with a given operative logic, legal and political academia has been – this book has argued – too quick to provide political justifications for participative and institutional exclusions under new governance that cannot be normatively justified. If the OMC does indeed have something to offer by way of a *political* response to the social storm surrounding the Court's recent jurisprudence, it must be capable of advancing a more reflexive and transparent form of politics that it has achieved to date.

13 Scharpf, n. 9 above, at 20.

14 *Facing the Challenge: The Lisbon Strategy for Growth and Employment – Report of the High Level Group on the Lisbon Agenda* (Luxembourg: Office for Official Publications of the EU, 2004) at 39–45.

In doing so, I can simply point to the possibilities offered in the book's final chapter. While the example of the European Ombudsman indicates that the provision of administrative remedies under EU law need not mean a 'juridification' of new governance procedures, the reforms undertaken to the comitology system equally illustrate that parliamentary input into the OMC is possible without excluding its own participative ethic or achievements.[15] Such reforms would be aimed at using general political institutions to supplement procedures too often engaged in a 'micro-politics' of technical indicators and recommendations, and too unwilling to debate the very questions – over the future direction of European social policy – which might allow popular engagement in its reforms.

Seeing 'new governance' and the OMC in light of an ongoing and procedural 'transformation' of European law is an important legal and sociological exercise. It provides important lessons not just for mechanisms of 'new governance', but for the direction and evolution of EU law more broadly. This exercise, however, is truly useful only if it is seen as opening up, rather than obscuring, the critical normative choices that face European policy-makers and lawyers in the next decade – over how to square European integration both with the 'social sovereignty', and the democratic character, of its nation states.

In diagnosing both the failures and the promise of the contemporary OMC – and the academic debate which surrounds it – and in arguing for a republican constitutionalisation of new governance procedures, I hope that this book has gone some way to advancing that task. The future of 'procedural law-making' in Europe remains open – a comforting, rather than frightening, fact.

[15] See Chapter 5, sections 7–8.

Annex 1 Questions for the respondents

QUESTION 1 – THE ADDED VALUE OF THE OMC

To what extent has the OMC helped to achieve progress in the national policy-making process and at the European Level?

- How and to what extent has the OMC influenced or helped to advance the national policy agenda?
- Have recent reforms and policy initiatives benefited from experience in other countries?
- Is a reflection on the experiences of other EU countries normally carried out in the process leading to the adoption of a new policy measure?
- Has the OMC been an efficient and effective method in view of achieving the common objectives that were established for it?
- To what extent has the OMC contributed to develop a common understanding of the challenges to social inclusion and to pension sustainability in the EU? Has it also contributed to a greater convergence of policy responses?

QUESTION 2 – THE COMMON OBJECTIVES

Are the common objectives still in line with policy priorities and do they still address the most important challenges as identified in the most recent Joint Reports?

- Have the objectives addressed *all* priority policy issues or have there been major gaps or blind spots?
- Has too much attention been devoted to a specific issue (in relation to its political importance)? Are there any objectives that might have become obsolete?
- Among the common objectives, across the different policy sectors, has there been overlap?

- Have the common objectives been formulated in a too general or abstract way/just about right/in too detailed or narrow way?

QUESTION 3 – INDICATORS AND TARGETS

Have indicators fulfilled their role in monitoring the progress achieved towards the common objectives? Have targets proved to be both feasible and effective in driving forward more ambitious policy reform?

- Is the quality of available data sufficient (both European and national data), in particular in view of their policy relevance and timeliness? Are the agreed indicators in line with the existing objectives and are they an effective tool for monitoring the progress achieved?
- On the basis of the indicators that have been used in the Joint Inclusion Report and Joint Pensions Report, please indicate in which areas you feel that improvements should be made.
- Are there indicators that are considered to be obsolete or insufficient to achieve their monitoring function?
- What should be the role of national indicators?
- Have national targets been used in an appropriate way, and is there scope for extending their use?
- Indicate in which areas it might be possible and appropriate to develop EU targets.

QUESTION 4 – MOBILISATION OF ALL ACTORS AND COOPERATION AT NATIONAL LEVEL

Has the OMC, on the national level, been implemented effectively and in a way conducive to better coordination between different government departments and levels, and to greater mobilisation of stakeholders?

Please describe and assess in particular the following aspects:

- the process of preparing, drafting and approving NAP/NSR;
- the involvement of national parliaments;
- the coordination within the government (i.e. between the different ministries, etc.) including the links to the preparation of the budget;
- the coordination and consultation between different levels of public administration on national, regional and local levels. Has the consultation of the regional and local levels produced a visible impact?
- the consultation of other relevant actors, such as stakeholders from the civil society or social partners. Has this consultation produced a visible impact?
- the mobilisation of actors on the national level. Has it been effective? Have new structures been created as a consequence of the application

of the OMC, in particular in view of ensuring the participation of all concerned actors?
- the dissemination of national action plans/strategy reports and of joint reports. Is the level of public awareness of the OMC satisfactory?

QUESTION 5 – WORKING METHODS AT EUROPEAN LEVEL

Have the working methods developed at European level to promote mutual learning and discuss results of the open method of coordination been the most appropriate and effectively managed?

Please comment in particular on the following types of activity:

- The contribution of the Community Action Programme to fight social exclusion, through the various actions that it supports (peer reviews, transnational action projects, awareness raising projects, EU networks of NGOs and local/regional authorities, studies, statistical databases).
- The 'national seminars' that were held in view of drafting the NAPs and NSRs.
- The 'peer reviews' that have been held within the Social Protection Committee and the Indicators sub-group, following up the NAPs and NSRs.
- The seminars and conferences organised by the Presidency or the Commission to debate issues of interest for the OMC.

QUESTION 6 – THE OMC AS PART OF THE LISBON AGENDA

Has the OMC on social inclusion and on pensions been appropriately reflected in the implementation of the Lisbon Agenda? Are the different bodies responsible for the implementation of the different strands of the agenda cooperating among themselves?

- How do you assess the consistency and complementarity between the OMC in the social protection/inclusion field and other processes, such as the European Employment Strategy (EES) or the coordination of economic policies in the framework of the Broad Economic Policy Guidelines?
- How do you assess the role of the Social Protection Committee and its cooperation between other committees and bodies working on economic and social on the European level (the Economic Policy Committee (EPC), the EPC's Ageing Working Group (AWG), Employment Committee, etc.)?
- Would you like to see any modifications to the working methods of the Social Protection Committee, for example, in the light of the EU enlargement or of the future scope of work under streamlining?

QUESTION 7 – SUGGESTIONS FOR THE FUTURE DEVELOPMENT OF THE OMC IN A STREAMLINED CONTEXT

What suggestions would you make for the future development of the OMC?

- In the context of this evaluation, have you any comments or suggestions regarding how health and long-term care can be addressed in the future streamlined process?

Annex 2 List of non-governmental respondents

(NB: responses were also received from all participating governments)

Social partner organisations:

European Centre for Enterprises with Public Participation and of Enterprises of General Economic Interest (CEEP)
European Trade Union Confederation (ETUC)
European Association of Craft, Small and Medium-Sized Enterprises (UEAPME)
Union des Industries de la Communauté Européenne (UNICE)

Non-governmental organisations:

The European Older People's Platform (AGE)
ATD Fourth World
Combined European Bureau for Social Development (CEBSD)
European Anti-Poverty Network (EAPN)
European Disability Forum (EDF)
Eurochild
European Federation of National Organisations Working with the Homeless (FEANTSA)
Fédération Européenne des Restraités et Personnes Agées (FERPA)
The Platform of European Social NGOs (European Social Platform)

Organisations representing other policy actors:

Council of European Municipalities and Regions (CEMR)
European Association of Public Sector Pension Institutions (EAPSPI)
Network of Major European Cities (Eurocities)
European Network of Specialised Equality Bodies (EQUINET)

Annex 3 History and development of the OMC SPSI (1997–2010)

July 1997	Adoption of the Treaty of Amsterdam. Article 2 EC is amended to include as a Union objective 'the promotion of a high level of social protection'. Article 137 empowers the Council to adopt non-legislative measures to combat social exclusion. It formally incorporates both the Social Chapter and the Essen Process (now the European Employment Strategy) into the Treaty framework.
March 2000	Commission publishes a Communication 'Building an Inclusive Europe' advocating the extension of the model of the EES to social inclusion. It calls for the creation of common EU-wide objectives to combat poverty.
March 2000	The Lisbon European Council agrees the two primary targets for the EU in the next decade as the modernisation of Europe's social model, and the pursuit of a more dynamic and competitive economy. Its Presidency Conclusions agree a strategy to combat social exclusion through an Open Method of Coordination, based on common objectives, benchmarking and peer review. The Council extend the OMC to other areas including pensions and the regulation of SMEs.
June 2000	Council Decision 436/2000/EC sets up the Social Protection Committee (SPC). Its mandate is to 'promote exchange of information, experience and good

	practice between the Member States and with the Commission', including through the preparation of national reports, and the development of OMC indicators.
December 2000	The Nice European Council agrees common objectives for combating poverty and social exclusion. The objectives argue that 'employment is the best safeguard against social exclusion' but also consider inclusion in terms of access to education, healthcare and housing. The Treaty repeats Amsterdam's formulation of social inclusion as an EU objective, but excludes legislative action aimed at harmonisation of national provisions.
December 2001	Laeken European Council extends the OMC to the field of pensions.
December 2001	The Commission's proposals for a Community Action Programme to combat social exclusion are adopted. The programme is designed – through seminars, expert studies, and pilot programmes – to facilitate and contribute to the implementation of OMC-inclusion objectives in the member states. It is given a budget of €75 million over four years (2002–06).
December 2002	The original Nice objectives are revised by the Employment, Social Policy, Health and Consumer Affairs Council. The new objectives ask governments to set national targets for poverty reduction, and to include indicators for immigrant and ethnic minorities.
May 2003	The Commission publishes a Communication, 'Strengthening the social dimension of the Lisbon strategy: Streamlining open coordination in the field of social protection'. It advocates the synchronisation of the OMC-inclusion into a three-year cycle alongside the employment and economic coordination processes. It also argues for 'streamlining' – common methodologies, objectives and reporting requirements across the three main social protection strands of inclusion, pensions and health and long-term care.

July 2004	The second round of National Action Plans on inclusion is completed including the first reports from the new EU 10.
February 2005	Following the publication of the Kok Report on a revised Lisbon Strategy, the Commission publishes a Communication to the Spring European Council on 'Working Together for Growth and Jobs'. The Communication encourages a 're-focusing' of the Lisbon agenda in the medium-term on growth and jobs, dropping the original social cohesion objectives of the 2000 Lisbon Council.
December 2005	Following some of its recommendations from 2003, the Commission proposes 'A New Framework for the Open Coordination of Social Protection and Inclusion Policies in the European Union', designed to simplify reporting procedures, and bring the three social protection strands (in social inclusion, pensions and health and long-term care) under common objectives. From 2005, the Commission will produce annual Joint Reports on social protection and social inclusion as well as separate 'Joint Inclusion Memorandums' on the now renamed 'National Strategy Reports'.
March 2006	The European Council agrees a new set of common objectives for social protection and inclusion. 'Effective and mutual interaction' between the social OMCs and the Lisbon objectives is introduced as one of three 'overarching objectives'.
October 2006	Council Decision 1672/2006/EC adopts a further Community Action Programme for Employment and Social Solidarity (Progress). It is designed – among other things – to financially and administratively support the implementation of the OMC's in the social fields from 2007–13.
July 2008	The Commission adopts its Communication on 'A Renewed Commitment to Social Europe: Re-enforcing the Open Method of Coordination for Social Protection and Social Inclusion'. The Communication proposes that 'social impact assessment' be extended to all EU

	policies and legislation. It also proposes quantitative state-by-state targets for poverty reduction.
December 2009	The new Lisbon Treaty officially enters into force following ratification in the Czech Republic. The new Treaty makes binding (subject to reservations and opt-outs) a number of social rights contained in the EU Charter of Fundamental Rights. It establishes new social objectives for the Union under Article 3 TEU.
June 2010	The European Council adopts the renewed 'Lisbon 2020' strategy. It replicates previous EU employment and growth targets but establishes a new target of reducing EU-wide poverty by 20 million by 2020. It mandates individual country targets under the 'Integrated Guidelines for Jobs and Growth'.

Annex 4 The new 'streamlined' OMC SPSI (2008–10)

1

March 2008

Setting Objectives

Commission and Council endorse 'overarching objectives' for the 3 strands, split into 3 pillars (social inclusion, pensions and health/long-term care)

2

June 2008

Creating Indicators

SPC adopt common indicators. Guidelines are issued to the Member States on production of their strategy plans

3

September 2008

National Strategy Plans

National Governments produce 'National Reports on Strategies for Social Protection and Social Inclusion'. They consist of 4 parts – Part 1 a common overview, including the government's strategic approach, Parts 2–4 thematic action plans for the 3 pillars

4

Sept. 2008–February 2009 (ongoing)

Peer review

Mutual learning and review is conducted through: i) SPC meetings on national strategy/implementation reports, and ii) peer review in the context of the Community Action Programme (PROGRESS)

5

February 2009

EU Reports

Commission and Council produce a draft Joint Report on Social Protection and Inclusion, covering: i) common EU-wide concerns, and ii) country-specific reports. They are designed to draw on national reports, and assess progress made in implementation

6

September 2009

National Implementation Plans

The (annual) cycle re-starts. National Governments must, drawing on their national plans, produce reports on the implementation of their original strategy reports. They must also take into account objectives under the 'Integrated Guidelines for Jobs and Growth'

Bibliography

A. ARTICLES AND BOOKS

Adronico, A. and Lo Faro, A., 'Defining Problems: The OMC, Fundamental Rights and the Theory of Governance', in O. de Schutter and S. Deakin (eds.), *Social Rights and Market Forces: Is the Open Coordination of Employment and Social Policies the Future of Social Europe?* (Brussels: Bruylant, 2005)

Alter, K., 'Who are the Masters of the Treaty? European Governments and the ECJ' (1998) 52 *International Organisation* 1

Armstrong, K., 'Tackling Social Exclusion through the OMC: Re-shaping the Boundaries of EU Governance' in T. Borzel and R. Cichowski (eds.), *The State of the European Union* (Oxford University Press, 2003)

'Inclusive Governance? Civil Society and the OMC' in S. Smismans (ed.), *Civil Society and Legitimate European Governance* (Cheltenham: Edward Elgar, 2005)

'How Open is the United Kingdom to the OMC Process on Social Inclusion', in J. Zeitlin and P. Pochet (eds.), *The Open Method of Coordination in Action: The European Employment and Social Inclusion Strategies* (Bern: Peter Lang, 2005)

'The Europeanization of Social Exclusion: British Adaptation to EU Co-ordination' (2006) 8 *British Journal of Politics and International Relations* 1

Governing Social Inclusion: Europeanization through Policy Coordination (Oxford University Press, 2010)

Azoulai, L., 'The Court of Justice and the Social Market Economy: the Emergence of an Ideal and the Conditions for its Realization' (2008) 45 *Common Market Law Review* 5

Bailey, D.J., 'Explaining the Under-development of 'Social Europe': a Critical Realization' (2008) 18 *Journal of European Social Policy* 3

Barnard, C., 'EU Citizenship and the Principle of Solidarity' in M. Dougan and E. Spaventa (eds.), *Social Welfare and EU Law* (Oxford: Hart, 2005)

'Solidarity and the Commission's Renewed Social Agenda' in M. Ross and Y. Borgmann-Prebil (eds.), *Promoting Solidarity in the European Union* (Oxford University Press, 2010)

Barnard, C., Deakin, S. and Hobbs, R., 'Reflexive Law, Corporate Social Responsibility and the Evolution of Labour Standards' in S. Deakin and O. de

Schutter (eds.), *Social Rights and Market Forces: Is the Open Coordination of Employment and Social Policies the Future of Social Europe?* (Brussels: Bruylant, 2005)

Bechman, G., 'Reflexive Law: A New Theory Paradigm for Legal Science?' in A. Febbrajo and G. Teubner (eds.), *State, Law and Economy as Autopoietic Systems* (Milan: Giuffre, 1992)

Bercusson, B., 'Social and Labour Rights under the EU Constitution' in de Búrca and de Witte (eds.), *Social Rights in Europe* (Oxford: Oxford University Press, 2005)

'The Trade Union Movement and the European Union: Judgement Day' (2007) 13 *European Law Journal* 3

Bernard, N., 'Legitimising EU Law: Is the Social Dialogue the Way Forward? Some Reflections around the UEAPME case' in J. Shaw (ed.) *Social Law and Policy in an Evolving European Union* (Oxford: Hart, 2000)

'A New Governance Approach to Economic, Social and Cultural Rights in the EU' in T. Hervey and J. Kenner (eds.), *Economic and Social Rights under the Charter of Fundamental Rights of the European Union* (Oxford: Hart, 2003)

Bernhard, S., 'The European Paradigm of Social Exclusion' (2006) 2 *Journal of Contemporary European Research* 1

Black, J., 'Constitutionalising Self-Regulation' (1996) 59 *Modern Law Review* 1

Blankenburg, E., 'The Poverty of Evolutionism: A Critique of Teubner's Case for "Reflexive Law"' (1984) 18 *Law and Society Review* 2

Blichner, L. and Molander, A., 'Mapping Juridification' (2008) 14 *European Law Journal* 1

Börzel, T., Hofmann, T., Panke, D. and Sprungk, C., 'Obstinate and Inefficient: Why Member States do not comply with European Law' (2010) 43 *Comparative Political Studies* 11

Bovens, M. 'Analysing and Assessing Accountability: A Conceptual Framework' (2007) 13 *European Law Journal* 4

Bradley, K. S. C., 'The European Parliament and Comitology: On the Road to Nowhere? (1997) 3 *European Law Journal* 3

'Halfway House: The 2006 Comitology Reforms and the European Parliament' (2008) 31 *West European Politics* 4

Buchkremer, J. and Zirra, S., 'Europeanization of Social Policies: The Influences of OMC/Inclusion on National Institutions in Germany, France and Italy'. Paper Presentation, ESPAnet conference, September 2007

Büchs, M., 'How Legitimate is the Open Method of Coordination' (2008) 46 *Journal of Common Market Studies* 4

Büchs, M. and Friedrich, D., 'Surface Integration: The National Action Plans for Employment and Social Inclusion in Germany' in J. Zeitlin and P. Pochet (eds.), *The Open Method of Coordination in Action: The European Employment and Social Inclusion Strategies* (Bern: Peter Lang, 2005)

Cappelletti, M., Seccombe, M. and Weiler, J., *Integration Through Law: Europe and the American Federal Experience* (Berlin: De Gruyter, 1986)

Chalmers, D. and Lodge, M., 'The Open Method of Coordination and the European Welfare State' (2003) *ESCR Centre for Risk and Regulation Studies Discussion Papers* 11
Chalmers, D., Davies, G. and Monti, G., *European Union Law: Texts and Materials* (Cambridge University Press, 2010)
Christodoulidis, E., *Law and Reflexive Politics* (Alphen aan den Rijn: Kluwer, 1998)
Cohen, J. and Sabel, C., 'Directly-Deliberative Polyarchy' (1997) 3 *European Law Journal* 4
'Sovereignty and Solidarity: EU and US' in J. Zeitlin and D. Trubek (eds.), *Governing Work and Welfare in a New Economy* (Oxford University Press, 2003)
Corkin, J., *A Manifesto for the European Court: Democracy, De-centred Governance and the Process-Perfecting Judicial Shadow* (EUI Thesis, 2006)
Corona, D., *Inter-state Bargaining in the Co-decision Procedure: State Interests and Political Dynamics in EC Decision-making*, PhD thesis (European University Institute, 2009)
Cottrell, P. and Trubek, D., 'The Law of Global Space: Rethinking the Legalization of World Politics' (2010) *Wisconsin Legal Studies Research Paper Series* 1124
Craig, P., *EU Administrative Law* (Oxford University Press, 2006)
Daly, M., 'EU Social Policy After Lisbon' (2006) 44 *Journal of Common Market Studies* 3
Damjanovic, D. and de Witte, B., 'Welfare Integration Through EU Law: The Overall Picture in Light of the Lisbon Treaty' (2008) *EUI Working Papers (Law)* 34
Dawson, M., 'Re-capturing the Legal in World Constitutionalism: Comparing Constitutions through Systems Theory', Paper Presentation, 23rd World Congress of the Philosophy of Law (Cracow), July 2006
'The Ambiguity of Social Europe in the Open Method of Coordination' (2009) 34 *European Law Review* 1
'EU Law Transformed? Evaluating Accountability and Subsidiarity in the "Streamlined" OMC for Social Inclusion and Social Protection' (2009) 13 *European Integration Online Papers* 1
'Soft Law and the Rule of Law in the European Union: Revision or Redundancy?' (2009) *EUI Working Papers (RSCAS)* 24
'Transforming into What? New Governance and the "Managerial Sensibility" in Modern Law' (2010) *Wisconsin Law Review* 2
'Learning from Past Failures? Governance in the European Union from Lisbon 2000 to Lisbon 2020' (2010) 17 *Maastricht Journal of European & Comparative Law* 2
'3 Waves of New Governance in the European Union' (2011) 36 *European Law Review* 2
Deakin, S., 'Two Types of Regulatory Competition: Competitive Federalism Versus Reflexive Harmonisation. A Law and Economics Perspective on *Centros*' (1999) *Cambridge Yearbook of European Legal Studies*
Deakin, S., 'Regulatory Competition in Europe After Laval' (2008) *REFGOV Working Papers* 16

Deakin, S. and de Schutter, O., 'Reflexive Governance and the Dilemmas of Social Regulation' in Deakin and de Schutter (eds.), *Social Rights and Market Forces: Is the Open Coordination of Employment and Social Policies the Future of Social Europe*? (Brussels: Bruylant, 2005)

(eds.), *Social Rights and Market Forces: Is the Open Coordination of Employment and Social Policies the Future of Social Europe*? (Brussels: Brulyant, 2005)

de Búrca, G., 'The Constitutional Challenge of New Governance in the European Union" (2003) 28 *European Law Review* 6

'New Modes of Governance and the Protection of Human Rights', in P. Alston and O. de Schutter (eds.), *Monitoring Fundamental Rights in the EU* (Oxford: Hart, 2005)

'EU Race Discrimination Law: a Hybrid Model?' G. de Búrca and J. Scott, *Law and New Governance in the EU and US* (Oxford: Hart, 2006)

de Búrca, G. and Scott, J., *Law and New Governance in the EU and US* (Oxford: Hart, 2006)

de Búrca, G. and Zeitlin, J., 'Constitutionalising the Open Method of Co-ordination: What Should the Convention Propose?' (2003) *CEPS Policy Brief* 1

Dehousse, R., 'Comitology: Who Watches the Watchmen?' (2003) 10 *Journal of European Public Policy* 5

Dehousse, R. and Weiler, J., 'The Legal Dimension' in W. Wallace (ed.), *The Dynamics of European Integration* (London: Pinter, 1990)

de Schutter, O., 'The Implementation of Fundamental Rights through the Open Method of Coordination' in de Schutter and Deakin (eds.) *Social Rights and Market Forces: Is the Open Coordination of Employment and Social Policies the Future of Social Europe*? (Brussels: Bruylant, 2005)

de Schutter, O. and Deakin, S. (eds.), *Social Rights and Market Forces: Is the Open Coordination of Employment and Social Policies the Future of Social Europe*? (Brussels: Bruylant, 2005)

'Reflexive Governance and the Dilemmas of Social Regulation' in de Schutter and Deakin (eds.) *Social Rights and Market Forces: Is the Open Coordination of Employment and Social Policies the Future of Social Europe*? (Brussels: Bruylant, 2005)

de Witte, B., 'The Trajectory of Fundamental Rights in the European Union' in de Búrca and de Witte (eds.), *Social Rights in Europe* (Oxford: Oxford University Press, 2005)

Diamondouros, N., 'Legality and Good Administration: Is there a Difference?', Paper Presentation, 6th Seminar of the National Ombudsman of European Union Member States, Strasbourg, October 2007

Dorf, M. and Sabel, C., 'A Constitution of Democratic Experimentalism' (1998) 98 *Columbia Law Review* 2

Dougan, M. and Spaventa, E., 'Wish you weren't here . . . New Model of Social Solidarity in the European Union', in Dougan and Spaventa (eds.) *Social Welfare and EU Law* (Oxford: Hart, 2005)

Duina, F. and Raunio, T., 'The Open Method of Coordination and National Parliaments: Further Marginalization or New Opportunities?' (2007) 14 *Journal of European Public Policy* 4

Enber, A., 'Polanyi's Theory of Public Policy: Embeddedness, Commodification and the Institutional Dynamism of the Welfare State', Paper Presentation, RECON Workshop on 'The Social Embeddedness of Trans-national Markets', Bremen, February 2009

Esping-Andersen, G., *The Three Worlds of Welfare Capitalism* (Princeton: Princeton University Press, 1990)

Everson, M., 'Independent Agencies: Hierarchy Beaters?' (1995) 1 *European Law Journal* 2

Everson, M. and Majone, G., 'Institutional Reform: Independent Agencies, Oversight, Coordination and Procedural Control', in O. de Schutter, N. Lebessis and J. Paterson (eds.), *Governance in the European Union*, (Luxembourg: Office for Official Publications of the European Communities, 2001)

Faulkner, G., *EU Social Policy in the 1990s – Towards a Corporatist Policy Community* (London: Routledge, 1998)

Ferrera, M., *The Boundaries of Welfare: European Integration and the New Spatial Politics of Social Protection* (Oxford University Press, 2005)

Ferrera, M., 'National Welfare States and European Integration: in search of a "Virtuous Nesting"' (2009) 47 *Journal of Common Market Studies* 2

Fuller, L., *The Morality of Law* (New Haven: Yale University Press, 1969)

Gerstenberg, O. and Sabel, C., 'Directly-Deliberative Polyarchy: An Institutional Ideal for Europe?' in C. Joerges and R. Dehousse (eds.), *Good Governance in Europe's Integrated Market* (Oxford University Press, 2002)

Greer, S. L., 'Uninvited Europeanization: Neo-Functionalism and the EU in Health Policy' (2006) 13 *Journal of European Public Policy* 1

Greven, M., 'The Informalization of Transnational Governance: A Threat to Democratic Governance' in E. Grande and L. Pauly (eds.), *Complex Sovereignty: Re-constituting Political Authority in the 21st Century* (University of Toronto Press, 2005)

Goetschy, J., 'The European Employment Strategy: Genesis and Development' (1999) 5 *European Journal of Industrial Relations* 2

Habermas, J., 'Law as Medium and Law as Institution' in G. Teubner (ed.), *Dilemmas of Law in the Welfare State* (Berlin: De Gruyter, 1986)

The Theory of Communicative Action (Vol. 2) (Boston: Beacon Press, 1987)

Between Facts and Norms: Contributions to a Discourse Theory of Law and Democracy (Cambridge: MIT Press, 1996)

'Why Europe Needs a Constitution' (2001) 11 *New Left Review*

Harlow, C., *Accountability in the European Union* (Oxford University Press, 2002)

Harlow, C. and Rawlings, R., *Law and Administration* (London: Butterworths, 1997)

'Promoting Accountability in Multi-level Governance: A Network Approach' (2007) 13 *European Law Journal* 4

Hatzopoulos, V., 'Why the Open Method of Coordination is Bad for You: A Letter to the EU' (2007) 13 *European Law Journal* 3

Héritier, A., 'New Modes of Governance in Europe: Policy-Making without Legislating?', in Héritier (ed.), *Common Goods: Reinventing European and International Governance* (Lanham: Rowman and Littlefield, 2002)

Héretier, A. and Rhodes, M., 'Governing in the Shadow of Hierarchy: New Modes of Governance in Regulation' in Héretier and Rhodes (eds.), *New Modes of Governance in Europe: Governing in the Shadow of Hierarchy* (Basingstoke: Palgrave MacMillan, 2010)

(eds.), *New Modes of Governance in Europe: Governing in the Shadow of Hierarchy* (Basingstoke: Palgrave MacMillan, 2010)

Hervey, T., 'Social Solidarity: A Buttress Against Internal Market Law?' in J. Shaw (ed.), *Social Law and Policy in an Evolving European Union* (Oxford: Hart, 2000)

Hervey, T. and McHale, J., 'Health Law and the European Union' (2007) 13 *European Law Journal* 5

Herzog, R. (former President of the Federal Republic of Germany) and Gerken, L., 'Stoppt den EuropäischenGerichtshof', *Frankurter Allgemeine Zeitung* (8 September 2008)

Hobbs, R. and Njoya, W., 'Regulating the European Labour Market: Prospects and Limitations of a Reflexive Governance Approach' (2005) 43 *British Journal of Industrial Relations* 2

Hobsbawm, E., *The Age of Extremes* (New York: Pantheon, 1994)

Hodson, D. and Maher, I., 'The Open Method of Coordination as a New Mode of Governance: the Case of Soft Economic Policy Coordination' (2001) 39 *Journal of Common Market Studies* 4

Hooghe, L. and Marks, G., *Multi-level Governance and European Integration* (Lanham: Rowman and Littlefield, 2001)

Horvath, A., 'Analysing Deliberation as a Legitimating Principle of the OMC: A Conceptual Framework and Analysis', Paper Presentation, Workshop on Democracy, the Rule of Law and Soft Modes of Governance in the EU, Roskilde, November 2006

Jacobsson, K., 'Trying to Reform the "Best Pupils in the Class?" The Open Method of Coordination in Sweden and Denmark' in J. Zeitlin and P. Pochet (eds.), *The Open Method of Coordination in Action: The European Employment and Social Inclusion Strategies* (Bern: Peter Lang, 2005)

Jacobsson, K. and Vifell, A., 'Integration by Deliberation?: On the Role of Committees in the Open Method of Coordination', Paper Presentation, Workshop on 'The Forging of Deliberative Supra-Nationalism in the EU' (Florence) February 2003

Joerges, C., 'Scientific Expertise in Social Regulation and the European Court of Justice: Legal Frameworks for De-nationalized Governance Structures' in C. Joerges, K. H. Ladeur and E. Vos (eds.), *Integrating Scientific Expertise into Regulatory Decision-making: National Traditions and European Innovations* (Berlin: Nomos, 1997)

'The Law's Problem with the Governance of the European Market' in C. Joerges and R. Dehousse (eds.), *Good Governance in Europe's Integrated Market* (Oxford University Press, 2002)

'Deliberative Supra-nationalism: Two Defences' (2002) 8 *European Law Journal* 1

'What is Left of the European Economic Constitution? A Melancholic Eulogy' (2005) 35 *European Law Review*

'Deliberative Political Processes Revisited: What Have We Learnt About the Legitimacy of Supra-National Decision-Making?' (2006) 44 *Journal of Common Market Studies* 4

'Integration Through De-Legislation: An Irritated Heckler' (2007) *European Governance Papers* 3

'Re-conceptualizing the Supremacy of European Law: A Plea for a New Supra-national Conflict of Laws' in B. Kohler-Koch and B. Rittberger (eds.), *Debating the Democratic Legitimacy of the European Union* (Lanham: Rowman and Littlefield, 2007)

'A New Alliance of De-legalisation and Legal Formalism? Reflections on Responses to the Social Deficit of the European Integration Project' (2008) 19 *Law and Critique* 3

Joerges, C., Meny, Y. and Weiler, J. H. H. (eds.), 'Mountain or Molehill: A Critical Appraisal of the Commission White Paper on Governance' (2001) *Jean Monnet Working Papers* 6

Joerges, C. and Neyer, J., 'From Inter-Governmental Bargaining to Deliberative Political Processes: The Constitutionalisation of Comitology' (1997) 3 *European Law Journal* 3

Joerges, C. and Rödl, F., 'Social Market Economy as Europe's Social Model?' (2004) *EUI Working Papers (Law)* 8

'On the Social Deficit of the European Integration Project and its Perpetuation through the ECJ Judgements in Viking and Laval' (2008) *RECON Online Working Papers* 6

'Informal Politics, Formalised Law and the Social Deficit of European Integration: Reflections after the Judgements of the ECJ in Laval and Viking' (2009) 15 *European Law Journal* 1

Kennedy, D., 'Comment on Rudolf Wiethölter' in C. Joerges and D. Trubek, *Critical Legal Thought: An American-German Debate* (Baden Baden: Nomos, 1989)

'Challenging Expert Rule: the Politics of Global Governance' (2005) 27 *Sydney Law Review* 2

'Remarks on New Governance', Paper Presentation to the Workshop on New Governance, Harvard Law School, February 2005

Kenner, J., 'The EC Employment Title and the Third Way: Making Soft Law Work?' (1999) 15 *International Journal of Comparative Labour Law and Industrial Relations* 1

Kilpatrick, C., 'New EU Employment Governance and Constitutionalism', in G. de Búrca and J. Scott (eds.), *Law and New Governance in the EU and US* (Oxford: Hart, 2006)

King, M., 'What's the Use of Luhmann's Theory?' in King and Thornhill (eds.) *Luhmann on Law and Politics: Critical Appraisals and Applications* (Oxford: Hart, 2006)

Kjaer, P., '3 Forms of Governance; 3 Forms of Power' in E. Erikssen, C. Joerges and F. Roedl, *Law, Democracy and Solidarity in a Post-national Union* (London: Routledge, 2008)

Between Governing and Governance: On the Emergence, Function and Form of Europe's Post-national Constellation (Oxford: Hart, 2010)

Koskenniemi, M., 'International Law: Constitutionalism, Managerialism and the Ethos of Legal Education' (2007) 1 *Journal of European Legal Studies* 1

Koskenniemi, M. and Leino, P., 'Fragmentation of International Law? Post-modern Anxieties' (2002) *Leiden Journal of International Law* 15

Kröger, S., *Soft Governance in Hard Politics: European Coordination of Anti-Poverty Policies in Germany and France* (Wiesbaden: VS Verlag, 2008)

Laffan, B. and Shaw, C., 'Classifying and Mapping OMC in Different Policy Areas' (2005) *NEW-GOV Working Paper* 2/D09

de Lange, R., 'General Aspects of the Horizontalization of Law Enforcement in a European Perspective', in Vervaele (ed.), *Compliance and Enforcement of European Community Law* (Alphen aan den Rijn: Kluwer Law, 1999)

Legrand, P., 'Against a European Civil Code' (1997) 60 *Modern Law Review* 1

Lenoble, J., 'OMC and the Theory of Reflexive Governance' in S. Deakin and O. de Schutter (eds.), *Social Rights and Market Forces: Is the Open Coordination of Employment and Social Policies the Future of Social Europe*? (Brussels: Bruylant, 2005)

Lenoble, J. and de Munck, O., 'Transformations in the Art of Governance' in O. De Schutter, N. Lebessis and J. Paterson (eds.), *Governance in the European Union* (Luxembourg: Office for Official Publications of the European Communities, 2001)

Liebfried, S. and Pierson, P., 'Semi-sovereign Welfare States: Social Policy in a Multi-tiered Europe', in Liebfried and Pierson (eds.), *European Social Policy: Between Fragmentation and Integration* (Washington: Brookings Institute, 1995)

Locke, J., *Two Treatises on Government* (Cambridge University Press, 1967)

Lodge, M., 'Comparing Non-Hierarchical Governance in Action: the Open Method of Coordination in Pensions and Information Society (2007) 45 *Journal of Common Market Studies* 2

Luhmann, N., 'Operational Closure and Structural Coupling: The Differentiation of the Legal System' (1992) 13 *Cardozo Law Review* 5

'Some Problems with Reflexive Law' in Teubner and Febbrajo (eds.) *State, Law and Economy as Autopoietic Systems: Regulation and Autonomy in a New Perspective* (Milan: Guiffre, 1992)

'Limits of Steering' (1997) 14 *Theory, Culture and Society* 1

'Operational Closure and Structural Coupling: the Differentiation of the Legal System' (2002) 13 *Cardozo Law Review* 5

Law as a Social System (Oxford University Press, 2004)

Mabbett, D., 'Learning by Numbers? The Use of Indicators in the Coordination of Social Inclusion Policies in Europe' (2007) 14 *Journal of European Public Policy* 1

MacCormick, N., *Questioning Sovereignty* (Oxford University Press, 1999)

Maduro, M., *We the Court: The European Court of Justice and the European Economic Constitution* (Oxford University Press, 1998)

Magnette, P., 'Between Parliamentary Control and the Rule of Law: The Political Role of the Ombudsman in the European Union' (2003) 10 *Journal of European Public Policy* 5

'European Governance and Civic Participation: Beyond Elitist Citizenship?' (2003) 51 *Political Studies* 1

Maher, I., 'Law and the Open Method of Coordination: Towards a New Flexibility in European Policy-making?' (2004) 2 *Zeitschrift für Staats- und Europawissenschaften* 2

Majone, G., 'Independence v Accountability? Non-Majoritarian Institutions and Democratic Government in Europe' (1994) *EUI Working Papers (SPS)* 3

'The Rise of the Regulatory State in Europe' (1994) 17 *West European Politics* 3

Dilemmas of European Integration: The Ambiguities and Pitfalls of Integration by Stealth (Oxford University Press, 2005)

'The Future of the Union: Montesquieu versus Madison; in Majone, *Dilemmas of European Integration: The Ambiguities and Pitfalls of Integration by Stealth* (Oxford University Press, 2005)

Manow, P., 'Model Deutschland as an Inter-denominational Compromise' (2000) *Harvard CES Working Papers* 3

Marion Young, I., 'Difference as a Resource for Democratic Communication', in J. Bohman and W. Rehg (eds.) *Deliberative Democracy: Essays on Reason and Politics* (Cambridge: MIT Press, 1997)

Marlier, E., Atkinson, A. B., Cantillon, B. and Nolan, B., *The EU and Social Inclusion: Facing the Challenges* (Bristol: Policy Press, 2007)

Marshall, T. H., *Social Policy* (London: Hutchinson, 1975)

Martinsen, D., 'Social Security Regulation in the EU: The De-Territorialization of Welfare?' in G. de Búrca (ed.), *EU Law in the Welfare State* (Oxford University Press, 2005)

Mashaw, J. L., 'Structuring a "Dense Complexity": Accountability and the Project of Administrative Law' (2005) *Issues in Legal Scholarship* 4

McCormick, J., *Habermas, Weber and the Transformation of the European State* (Cambridge University Press, 2007)

Michelman, F., 'How Can the People Ever Make the Laws? A Critique of Deliberative Democracy' in J. Bohman and W. Rehg (eds.), *Deliberative Democracy: Essays on Reason and Politics* (Cambridge: MIT Press, 1997)

Morgan, G., *The Idea of a European Super-state: Public Justification and European Integration* (Princeton University Press, 2005)

Möllers, C., 'European Governance: Meaning and Value of a Concept' (2006) 43 *Common Market Law Review* 2

Moravcsik, A., 'The European Constitutional Compromise' (2005) *EUSA Review*

'The European Constitutional Compromise and the Neo-Functionalist Legacy' (2005) 13 *Journal of European Public Policy* 2

Mossialos, E., Permanand, G., Baeten, R. and Hervey, T., *Health System Governance in Europe: the Role of EU Law and Policy* (Cambridge University Press, 2010)

Nance, M. and Trubek, D., 'The Strange Case of the Posted Workers Directive: EU Law as Reflexive Coordination?', Paper Presentation, Workshop on Laval and Viking, Cambridge University, September 2008

Nance, P. and de la Porte, C., 'The OMC – A Deliberative-Democratic Mode of Governance?: The Case of Employment and Pensions' (2004) 11 *Journal of European Public Policy* 4

Nicolaides, P., *Improving Policy Implementation in an Enlarged European Union: The Case of National Regulatory Authorities* (Maastricht: European Institute of Public Administration, 2003)

Noonan, K., Sabel, C. and Simon, W., 'Legal Accountability in the Service-based Welfare State: Lessons from Child Welfare Reform' (2009) 34 *Law and Social Inquiry* 3

Offe, C., 'The European Model of "Social" Capitalism: Can it Survive European Integration?' (2003) 11 *European Journal of Political Philosophy* 4

Paterson, J., *Behind the Mask: Regulating Health and Safety in Britain's Offshore Oil and Gas Industry* (Aldershot: Ashgate, 2000)

'Reflecting on Reflexive Law' in C. Thornhill and M. King, *Luhmann on Law and Politics: Critical Appraisals and Applications* (Oxford: Hart, 2006)

Peerenboom, R., 'The Future of Rule of Law: Challenges and Prospects for the Field' (2009) *Hague Journal on the Rule of Law* 1

Perez, O. and Teubner, G., *Paradoxes and Inconsistencies in the Law* (Oxford: Hart, 2006)

Pierson, P., 'Irresistible Forces, Immovable Objects: Post-industrial Welfare States Confront Permanent Austerity' (1998) 5 *Journal of European Public Policy* 4

Pochet, P., 'The OMC and the Construction of Social Europe' in Zeitlin and Pochet (eds.), *The Open Method of Coordination in Action: The European Employment and Social Inclusion Strategies* (Bern: Peter Lang, 2005)

Polanyi, K., *The Great Transformation* (Boston: Beacon Press, 1956)

Pollack, M. A. and Hafner-Burton, E., 'Mainstreaming Gender in the European Union' (2000) 7 *Journal of European Public Policy* 3

de la Porte, C., 'The Emergence of the OMC in Social Inclusion', Paper Presentation, ESPANET conference, 24 August 2005

de la Porte, C. and Pochet, P., 'Participation in the Open Method of Coordination: The Cases of Employment and Social Exclusion' in J. Zeitlin and P. Pochet (eds.), *The Open Method of Coordination in Action: The European Employment and Social Inclusion Strategies* (Bern: Peter Lang, 2005)

Radaelli, C., 'The Open Method of Coordination: A New Governance Architecture for the European Union?' (2003) *SIEPS Report* 1

Radulova, E., 'Variations on Soft EU Governance: The Open Method(s) of Coordination' in D. De Bievre and C. Neuhold (eds.), *Dynamics and Obstacles of EU Governance* (Cheltenham: Edward Elgar, 2007)

Reich, N., 'Free Movement v Social Rights in an Enlarged Union: The Laval and Viking Cases before the European Court of Justice' (2008) 9 *German Law Journal* 2

Rhodes, M., 'Employment Policy: Between Efficacy and Experimentation' in H. Wallace, W. Wallace and M. Pollack (eds.), *Policy Making in the European Union* (Oxford University Press, 2005)

Rogowski, R., 'Flexicurity and Reflexive Coordination of European Employment and Social Policies' in H. Jorgensen and P. H. Madsen (eds.), *Flexicurity and Beyond* (Copenhagen: DJOF Publishing, 2007)

Rowe, G., 'Tools for the Control of Political and Administrative Agents: Impact Assessment and Administrative Governance in the European Union' in H. Hoffman and A. Turk (eds.) *EU Administrative Governance* (Cheltenham: Edward Elgar, 2006)

Ruggie, J., 'Embedded Liberalism and the Postwar Economic Regimes' in *Constructing the World Polity: Essays in International Institutionalization* (London: Routledge, 1998)

Sabel, C. and Simon, W., 'Epilogue: Accountability without Sovereignty' in G. de Búrca and J. Scott (eds.), *Law and New Governance in the EU and US* (Oxford: Hart, 2006)

Sabel, C. and Zeitlin, J., 'Learning from Difference: The New Architecture of Experimentalist Governance in the EU' (2008) 14 *European Law Journal* 3

Sandel, M., 'The Procedural Republic and the Unencumbered Self' in G. W. Smith (ed.), *Liberalism: Critical Concepts in Political Theory* (London: Routledge, 2002)

Schäfer, A., 'Beyond the Community Method: Why the Open Method of Coordination was Introduced to EU Policy-making' (2004) 8 *European Integration Online Papers* 13

Scharpf, F., 'Multi-level Governing in Europe' (2000) *MPIFG Discussion Papers* 5

'The European Social Model: Coping with the Challenges of Diversity' (2002) 40 *Journal of Common Market Studies* 4

'The Only Solution is to Refuse to Comply with ECJ Rulings: An Interview with Fritz Scharpf' (2008) 14 *Social Europe* 1

'Legitimacy in the Multi-level European Polity' (2009) 1 *European Political Science Review* 2

'The Asymmetry of European Integration or Why the EU Cannot be a "Social Market Economy"' (2009) 9 *Socio-economic Review* 1

Community and Autonomy: Institutions, Policies and Legitimacy in Multi-level Europe (Frankfurt: Campus, 2010)

Schelkle, W., 'EU Fiscal Governance: Hard Law in the Shadow of Soft Law?' (2007) *Columbia Journal of European Law* 13

Scheuerman, W., 'Reflexive Law and the Challenges of Globalization' (2001) 9 *Journal of Political Philosophy* 1

'Democratic Experimentalism or Capitalist Synchronisation: Critical Reflections on Directly-Deliberative Polyarchy' (2004) *Canadian Journal of Law and Jurisprudence* 17

Scott, C., 'Accountability in the Regulatory State' (2000) 27 *Journal of Law and Society* 1
Scott, J. and Holder, J., 'Law and New Environmental Governance in the European Union', in G. de Búrca and J. Scott (eds.), *Law and New Governance in the EU and US* (Oxford: Hart, 2006)
Scott, J. and Sturm, S., 'Courts as Catalysts: Re-thinking the Judicial Role in New Governance' (2007) 13 *Columbia Journal of European Law* 3
Scott, J. and Trubek, D., 'Mind the Gap: Law and New Approaches to Governance in the European Union' (2002) 8 *European Law Journal* 1
Selznick, P. and Nonet, P., *Law and Society in Transition: Towards Responsive Law* (Washington: Octagon, 1978)
Shapiro, M., 'Implementation, Discretion and Rules' in Vervaele (ed.), *Compliance and Enforcement of European Community Law* (Alphen aan den Rijn: Kluwer Law, 1999)
Shaw, J., 'The European Union and Gender Mainstreaming: Constitutionally Embedded or Comprehensively Marginalised?' (2002) 10 *Feminist Legal Studies* 3
Shklar, J., *Legalism: Law, Morals and Political Trials* (Cambridge, MA: Harvard University Press, 1986)
Simon, W., 'Solving Problems vs Claiming Rights: The Pragmatist Challenge to Legal Liberalism' (2004) 46 *William and Mary Law Review* 127
Smismans, S., 'EU Employment Policy: Decentralization or Centralization through the Open Method of Coordination?' (2004) *EUI Working Papers (Law)* 1
'How to be Fundamental with Soft Procedures? The OMC and Fundamental Social Rights' in G. De Búrca and B. de Witte (eds.), *Social Rights in Europe* (Oxford University Press, 2005)
'Reflexive Law in Support of Directly-Deliberative Polyarchy; Reflexive Deliberative Polyarchy as a Normative Frame for the OMC' in S. Deakin and O. de Schutter (eds.), *Social Rights and Market Forces: Is the Open Coordination of Employment and Social Policies the Future of Social Europe*? (Brussels: Bruylant, 2005)
'New Modes of Governance and the Participatory Myth' (2008) 31 *West European Politics* 5
Snyder, F., 'The Effectiveness of European Community Law: Institutions, Processes, Tools and Techniques' (1993) 56 *Modern Law Review* 1
Stewart, R. B., 'The Reformation of American Administrative Law' (1975) 88 *Harvard Law Review* 8
Stratigaki, M., 'Gender Mainstreaming v Positive Action: An Ongoing Conflict in EU Gender Equality Policy' (2005) 12 *European Journal of Women's Studies*
Streeck, W., 'From Market-Making to State Building: Reflections on the Political Economy of European Social Policy' in S. Liebfried and P. Pierson (eds.), *European Social Policy: Between Fragmentation and Integration* (Washington: Brookings Institution, 1995)
'Neo-Voluntarism: A New European Social Policy Regime?' in Gary Marks *et al.* *Governance in the European Union* (Thousand Oaks: Sage, 1996)

Sunstein, C., 'Legal Interference with Private Preferences' (1986) 53 *University of Chicago Law Review*

Teubner, G., 'Substantive and Reflexive Elements in Modern Law' (1983) 17 *Law and Society Review* 2

'Autopoiesis in Law and Society: A Rejoinder to Blankenburg' (1984) 18 *Law and Society Review* 2

'Juridification: Concepts, Aspects, Limits, Solutions' in Teubner (ed.) *Juridification of Social Spheres: A Comparative Analysis in the Areas of Labour, Corporate, Antitrust and Social Welfare Law* (Berlin: De Gruyter, 1987)

(ed.), *Juridification of Social Spheres: A Comparative Analysis in the Areas of Labour, Corporate, Antitrust and Social Welfare Law* (Berlin: De Gruyter, 1987)

Autopoietic Law: A New Approach to Law and Society (Berlin: De Gruyter, 1988)

Law as an Autopoietic System (Oxford: Blackwell, 1993)

'Global Bukowina: Legal Pluralism in the World Society' in Teubner (ed.), *Global Law Without a State* (Aldershot: Ashgate, 1997)

'Societal Constitutionalism: Alternative to State-Centred Constitutional Theory' in C. Joerges, I. J. Sand and G. Teubner (eds.), *Transnational Governance and Constitutionalism* (Oxford: Hart, 2004)

de Tocqueville, A., *Democracy in America* (London: Penguin, 2003)

Trubek, D. and Mosher, J., 'New Governance, Employment Policy and the European Social Model' in J. Zeitlin and D. Trubek (eds.), *Governing Work and Welfare in a New Economy* (Oxford University Press, 2003)

Trubek, D. and Trubek, L., 'Hard and Soft Law in the Construction of Social Europe: The Role of the Open Method of Co-ordination' (2005) 11 *European Law Journal* 3

'New Governance and Legal Regulation: Complementarity, Rivalry and Transformation' (2007) 13 *Columbia Journal of European Law* 3

Trubek, D., Cottrell, P. and Nance, M., 'Soft Law, Hard Law and European Integration: Toward a Theory of Hybridity' in de Búrca and Scott (eds.), *Law and New Governance in the EU and US* (Oxford: Hart, 2006)

Tsakatika, M., 'A Parliamentary Dimension for EU Soft Governance' (2007) 29 *Journal of European Integration* 5

Vervaele, J. A. E. (ed.), *Compliance and Enforcement of European Community Law* (Alphen aan den Rijn: Kluwer Law, 1999)

Visser, J., 'The OMC as Selective Amplifier for National Strategies of Reform. What the Netherlands wants to learn from Europe', in J. Zeitlin and P. Pochet (eds.), *The Open Method of Coordination in Action: The European Employment and Social Inclusion Strategies* (Bern: Peter Lang, 2005)

Vos, E., 'The Rise of Committees' (1997) 3 *European Law Journal* 3

Walker, N., 'Legal Theory and the European Union: A 25th Anniversary Essay' (2005) 25 *Oxford Journal of Legal Studies* 4

'Constitutionalism and New Governance in the European Union: Rethinking the Boundaries', in de Búrca and Scott (eds.), *Law and New Governance in the EU and US* (Oxford: Hart, 2006)

Weiler, J., 'The Transformation of Europe' (1991) *Yale Law Journal* 100

The Constitution of Europe: Do the New Clothes Have an Emperor and Other Essays on European Integration (Cambridge University Press, 1999)
'Epilogue: "Comitology" as Revolution – Infranationalism, Constitutionalism and Democracy' in C. Joerges and E. Vos (eds.), *EU Committees: Social Regulation, Law and Politics* (Oxford: Hart, 1999)
'Federalism and Constitutionalism: Europe's *Sonderweg*' (2000) *Jean Monnet Working Papers* 10
Wiethölter, R., 'Materialization and Proceduralization in Modern Law' in Teubner (ed.), *Dilemmas of Law in the Welfare State* (Berlin: De Gruyter, 1986)
Wilkinson, M., 'Three Conceptions of Law: Towards a Jurisprudence of Democratic Experimentalism' (2010) *Wisconsin Law Review* 2
Willke, H., 'Three Types of Legal Structure: The Conditional, the Purposive and the Relational Program' in G. Teubner (ed.), *Dilemmas of Law in the Welfare State* (Berlin: De Gruyter, 1986)
'Societal Guidance through Law?' in Teubner and Febbrajo (eds.), *State, Law and Economy as Autopoietic Systems* (Milan: Giuffre, 1992)
Zeitlin, J., 'Social Europe and Experimentalist Governance: Towards a New Constitutional Compromise?' in G. de Búrca (ed.), *EU Law and the Welfare State: In Search of Solidarity* (Oxford University Press, 2005)
'The Open Method of Co-ordination in Action: Theoretical Promise, Empirical Realities, Reform Strategy', in J. Zeitlin and P. Pochet (eds.), *The Open Method of Coordination in Action: The European Employment and Social Inclusion Strategies* (Bern: Peter Lang, 2005)
'Strengthening the Social Dimension of the Lisbon Strategy' (2007) *La Follette Working Papers* 22
'The Open Method of Coordination and Reform of National Social and Employment Policies: Influences, Mechanisms, Effects' in J. Zeitlin and M. Heidenreich (eds.), *Changing European Employment and Welfare Regimes: the Influence of the Open Method of Coordination on National Reforms* (London: Routledge, 2009)
Zeitlin, J. and Pochet, P. (eds.), *The Open Method of Coordination in Action: The European Employment and Social Inclusion Strategies* (Bern: Peter Lang, 2005)
Zürn, M., 'On the Conceptualization of Postnational Politics: The Limits of Methodological Nationalism', Paper presented to Workshop on Global Governance, Robert Schuman Centre, Florence, April 2001
Zürn, M. and Joerges, C. (eds.), *Law and Governance in Post-national Europe: Compliance Beyond the Nation-state* (Cambridge University Press, 2005)

B. COMMISSION COMMUNICATIONS AND STAFF DOCUMENTS

Commission Green Paper on European Social Policy: Options for the Union, COM (1993) 551, November 1993
Commission Communication 'Concerning the Implementation of the Protocol on Social Policy', COM (1993) 600 final

Commission Communication 'On the Precautionary Principle', COM (2000) 1 final
Commission Communication 'On Impact Assessment', COM (2002) 0276 final
Commission Communication 'Working Together, Working Better: a New Framework for the Open Coordination of Social Protection and Social Inclusion Policies in the EU', COM (2005) 706 final
Commission Communication 'Working Together for Jobs and Growth: A New Start for the Lisbon Strategy', COM (2005) 24 final
Commission Communication 'On the Social Agenda', COM (2005) 033 final
Commission Staff Document, 'Evaluation of the Open Method of Coordination for Social Protection and Social Inclusion', SEC (2006) 345
Commission Communication, 'On Modernising Social Protection for Greater Social Justice and Economic Cohesion: Taking Forward the Active Inclusion of People Furthest From the Labour Market', COM (2007) 620 final
Commission Communication to the Spring European Council on 'Integrated Guidelines for Jobs and Growth (2008–2010)', COM (2007) 803
Commission Communication on 'A Renewed Social Agenda: Opportunities, Access and Solidarity in 21st Century Europe', COM (2008) 0412 final
Commission Communication, 'A Renewed Commitment to Social Europe: Re-enforcing the Open Method of Coordination for Social Inclusion and Social Protection', COM (2008) 418 final
Commission Proposal 'For a Regulation of the European Parliament and the Council Regarding Public Access to European Parliament, Council and Commission Documents', COM (2008) 229 final
Commission Staff Document, 'On the Application in 2007 of Regulation EC No. 1049/2001 Concerning Access to Community Documents', COM (2008) 630 final
Commission Communication, 'Impact Assessment Guidelines', SEC (2009) 92
Commission Report, 'On the Application in 2008 of Regulation EC No. 1049/2001 Concerning Access to Community Documents', COM (2009) 331 final
Commission Communication, 'Europe 2020: A Strategy for Smart, Sustainable and Inclusive Growth', COM (2010) 2020
Commission Staff Document, 'Lisbon Strategy Evaluation Document', SEC (2010) 114 final

C. RESOLUTIONS OF THE EUROPEAN PARLIAMENT

Resolution of the European Parliament on 'Analysis of the Open Coordination Procedure in the field of Employment and Social Affairs, and Future Prospects', 2002/2223 (INI)
Resolution of the European Parliament 'On Public Access to European Parliament, Council and Commission Documents (Implementation of Regulation 1049/2001)', 2007/2154 (INI)
Resolution of the European Parliament 'On the Institutional and Legal Implications of the Use of Soft Law Instruments' 2007/2028(INI)

D. OTHER EU DOCUMENTATION

Rapport des Chefs de Délégations aux Ministres des Affaires Etrangères (Bruxelles, 1956)
Social Aspects of European Economic Co-operation: Report by a Group of Experts (ILO, 1956)
Eurobarometer No. 40: Public Opinion in the European Union (Office for Official Publications of the European Communities, 1993)
European Social Policy: A White Paper (Office for Official Publications of the European Communities, 1994)
European Governance: A White Paper, COM (2001) 428 final
Indicators in the Field of Poverty and Social Inclusion (Social Protection Committee Indicators sub-group, 2001)
Final Report of Working Group XI on Social Europe, CONV 516/1/03 REV 1 (2003)
Final Report of Working Group VI on Economic Governance, CONV 357/02 (2003)
Mid-year Report from the Indicators Sub-group (Social Protection Committee Indicators sub-group, 2003)
Facing the Challenge: The Lisbon Strategy for Growth and Employment, Report of the High Level Group on the Lisbon Agenda (Office for Official Publications of the European Communities, 2004)
Report on Social Inclusion 2005: An Analysis of the NAPs on Social Inclusion Submitted by the 10 New Member States (Office for Official Publications of the European Communities, 2005)
Common Objectives for the Open Coordination Process in Social Inclusion and Social Protection (European Council, 2006)
Final Synthesis Report of the EU Programme to Promote Member State Cooperation to Combat Social Exclusion and Poverty (Office for Official Publications of the European Communities, 2006)
Portfolio of Over-arching Indicators in the Streamlined Social Inclusion, Pensions and Health Portfolios (Social Protection Committee Indicators sub-group, 2006)
Evaluation of the EU Programme to Promote Member State Co-operation to Combat Social Exclusion and Poverty (Luxembourg: Office for the Official Publications of the European Communities, 2007)
Joint Report on Social Protection and Social Inclusion (Office for the Official Publications of the European Communities, 2007)
Peer Review and Assessment: Operational Guide (Office for Official Publications of the European Communities, 2007)
European Ombudsman: Annual Report 2008 (Office for Official Publications of the European Communities, 2008)
Joint Report on Social Protection and Social Inclusion (Office for the Official Publications of the European Communities, 2008)
Portfolio of Overarching Indicators in Streamlined Social Inclusion, Pensions and Health Portfolios (SPC, 2008)
The European Ombudsman: Annual Report 2009 (Luxembourg: Office for Official Publications of the EU, 2009)

Proposal for a Regulation 'On the Effective Enforcement of Budgetary Surveillance in the Euro Area', COM (2010) 524 final

Proposal for a Regulation 'On Enforcement Measures to Correct Excessive Macro-economic Imbalances in the Euro Area', COM (2010) 525 final

E. NGO REPORTS

Local Authority Involvement: Reports on the National Action Plans for Social Inclusion (European Public Social Platform, 2001–2003)

Report on the Representativeness of European Social Partner Organizations (IST/ Université catholique de Louvain, 2002)

Feeding in and Feeding out: The Extent of Synergies between Growth and Jobs Policies and Social Inclusion Policies Across the EU (Network of Independent Experts, 2007)

Making Lisbon Deliver for People Experiencing Poverty: EAPN Response to 2006 Implementation Reports on the National Reform Programs (EAPN, 2007)

The 2006–2008 National Reports on Strategies for Social Protection and Social Inclusion: What do they Deliver for People in Poverty? (EAPN, 2008)

Index